Ernest Cruikshank

The documentary history of the campaign upon the Niagara frontier

in the year 1812

Ernest Cruikshank

The documentary history of the campaign upon the Niagara frontier in the year 1812

ISBN/EAN: 9783337147754

Printed in Europe, USA, Canada, Australia, Japan

Cover: Foto ©ninafisch / pixelio.de

More available books at **www.hansebooks.com**

THE DOCUMENTARY
HISTORY OF THE CAMPAIGN

— UPON THE —

NIAGARA FRONTIER IN THE YEAR 1812.

COLLECTED AND EDITED FOR THE LUNDY'S LANE HISTORICAL SOCIETY

BY MAJOR E. CRUIKSHANK,

AUTHOR OF THE "STORY OF BUTLER'S RANGERS," &C. &C.

WELLAND:
PRINTED AT THE TRIBUNE.

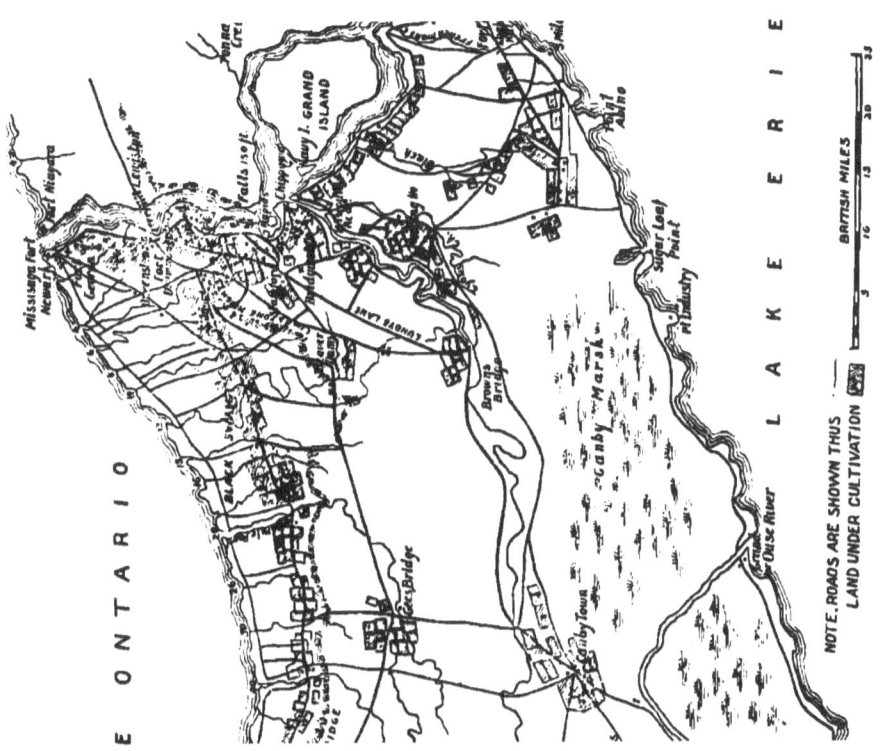

The Militia Law of 1808.

CHAPTER 1.

An Act to explain, amend and reduce to one Act of Parliament the several laws now in being, for the raising and training of the Militia of this Province.

Passed March 16th, 1808.

Whereas, a well regulated militia is of the utmost importance to the defence of this Province, and whereas the laws now in force are in some respects defective, be it therefore enacted by the King's Most Excellent Majesty, by and with the advice and consent of the Legislative Council and Assembly of the Province of Upper Canada, constituted and assembled by virtue of and under the authority of an Act passed in the Parliament of Great Britain entitled, "An Act to repeal certain parts of an Act passed in the fourteenth year of His Majesty's reign entitled an Act for making more effectual provision for the Government of the Province of Quebec, in North America, and to make further provision for the Government of the said Province," and by authority of the same, that from and after the passing of this Act, the governor, lieutenant-governor or person administering the Government of this Province shall and may from time to time constitute and appoint under his hand and seal a sufficent number of colonels, lieutenant-colonels, majors and other officers to train, discipline and command the militia of this Province, according to the rules, orders and directions hereinafter mentioned, and the officers so appointed for the militia shall rank with the officers of such of His Majesty's forces as may for the time being serve within the Province as the youngest of their respective rank, which said officers respectively shall within six months after their several appointments take the oath of allegiance to his present Majesty, his heirs and successors, before the magistrates assembled in quarter sessions within the district to which such officers respectively belong.

II. And be it further enacted by the authority aforesaid, that it shall and may be lawful for the colonel or officer commanding any regiment or battalion of militia, and he is hereby required to specify to each captain of a company of his regiment or battalion the limits from within which the militiamen of such captain's company shall be enrolled.

III. And be it further enacted by the authority aforesaid, that every male inhabitant from sixteen years of age to sixty shall be deemed capable of bearing arms, and shall enroll his name as a militiaman on the first training day on which the said companies shall be drawn out in the division or limit in which his place of abode may be, and shall at such meeting give in his name, age, and place of residence, and if he has thereto but lately removed, he shall make the same known, together with the place from whence he removed, and every such inhabitant who shall not attend and give in his name to the captain or officer commanding the company for such division or limit, so that his name may be enrolled as a militiaman, shall for such neglect forfeit and pay the sum of ten shillings, to be recovered and applied in the manner hereinafter mentioned: Provided, nevertheless, that no inhabitant shall be convicted of the offence herein described unless it is proved at the time of trial that the same inhabitant had been notified either personally or by leaving a verbal notice at his usual place of abode of the time of meeting at least six days previous thereto: Provided always, that no person above the age of fifty years shall be called upon to bear arms, except on the day of annual meeting, or in time of war or emergency.

IV. Provided always, and be it further enacted by the authority aforesaid, that the neglect of any person so to present himself for enrolment and exercise shall not be construed to prevent the captain or officer commanding the company of militia of the limits wherein the place of residence of any such person may be from entering the name of such person, and such captain or officer commanding such company as aforesaid is hereby required to enter the name of every person as shall come to his knowledge upon the enrolment of his company, and when so entered every such person shall be subject to perform all and every the like militia duties, and under the same penalties as if he had personally presented himself for enrolment: provided also, that if any difference shall arise between any captain or officer and any militiaman touching the age of such militiaman, it shall be incumbent on the said militiaman to prove his age.

V. And be it further enacted by the authority aforesaid, that the colonel or officer commanding each regiment or battalion shall, on the fourth day of June in each and every year respectively, or in case it shall happen on a Sunday then on the next day, and oftener if he thinks it necessary, call out the militia of each regiment or battalion to be reviewed or exercised, and in his absence from the county, or in case of his removal or death, the said militia shall be called out by the next senior officer of such regiment or battalion, and every person liable to serve in such militia, whether officer or private, neglecting or refusing to attend (except in case of sickness or having obtained leave of absence) shall forfeit and pay, if an officer, forty shillings, and if a non-commissioned officer or private, ten shillings: but if it shall appear to the colonel or officer commanding such regiment or battalion that it shall be more conducive to the interest of such regiment or battalion that the militia of the same be reviewed at different times and in separate bodies, it shall and may be lawful for the colonel commanding such regiment or battalion to call out a part of the militia at some convenient time and place and the remaining part at some other convenient time and place, as to him shall seem meet, and at every such review the captain or officer commanding each company shall give to the colonel, or in his absence to the next senior officer, fair written rolls of their respective companies, and the colonels or other commanding officers shall transmit returns to the governor, lieutenant-governor or person administering the Government within fourteen days after the fourth day of June in each and every year, under the penalty of five pounds for each captain or officer commanding a company, and for each colonel or officer commanding a regiment or battalion ten pounds, for such neglect or refusal.

VI. And be it further enacted by the authority aforesaid, that it shall and may be lawful for the governor, lieutenant-governor or person administering the Government to appoint a proper person to be adjutant-general of the said militia, who shall do all matters and things appertaining to the said office of adjutant-general.

VII. And be it further enacted by the authority aforesaid, that the captains of militia shall draw out their respective companies not less than twice or more than four times in every year (giving six days notice thereof) at the most convenient time and place in the county or riding, and shall inspect their arms and instruct them in their duties, and every person after such notice as aforesaid, who shall neglect to attend or shall disobey, whether subaltern officer or private, (except in case of sickness or leave of absence,) shall forfeit and pay, every officer the sum of forty shillings, and every non-commissioned officer or private the sum of ten shillings for every such neglect or disobedience.

VIII. And be it further enacted by the authority aforesaid, that in time of war, rebellion or any other pressing exigency, it shall and may be lawful for the governor, lieutenant-governor, or person administering the Government, to call forth any of the different companies of militia, and to march them from their respective counties, ridings, towns, townships or parishes to any part of this Province, there to serve in conjunction with other militia or with His Majesty's forces, and any person refusing to obey such order or command, or absconding from or neglecting to repair to the place he is ordered to, being a commissioned officer, shall forfeit and pay the sum of fifty pounds and be held unfit to serve His Majesty as an officer in any military capacity: and, being a non-commissioned officer or private, shall forfeit and pay the sum of twenty pounds, and in default of payment for such refusal or neglect, such officer, non-commissioned officer or private, shall be committed to the common gaol of the district for not less than six nor more than twelve calendar months, except such person shall satisfy the colonel or officer commanding such regiment or battalion to which he belongs that such refusal or neglect arose from sickness, or that he was absent upon leave. Provided always that no part of the militia called forth in the manner aforesaid shall be obliged to continue in actual service for more than six months at one time, and no militia-man shall be so called out who shall be above the age of fifty years, unless the whole of the militia of any district or battalion to which he may belong shall be called out and embodied. Provided, also, that it shall not be lawful to order the militia or any part thereof to march out of this Province, except for the assistance of the Province of Lower Canada (when the same shall be actually invaded or in a state of insurrection), or except in pursuit of an enemy who may have invaded this Province, and except also for the destruction of any vessel or vessels built or building, or any depot or magazine formed or forming, or for the attack of any enemy who may be embodying or marching for the purpose of invading this Province, or for the attack of any fortification now erected, or which may be hereafter erected, to cover the invasion thereof.

IX. And be it further enacted by the authority aforesaid, that it shall and may be lawful that the governor, lieutenant-governor or person administering the Government to call out detachments of the militia, and to limit and fix the number of men to be called out in such detachments: and in cases of emergency by actual invasion or otherwise, when it may not be practicable to consult the governor, lieutenant-governor or person administering the Government of this Province, it shall be and may be lawful for the senior colonel, or in his absence the lieutenant-colonel, of the several regiments or battalions to limit and appoint the number of men that he shall judge necessary to be called out, and for that purpose to issue his orders to the several commanding officers, and also to direct and authorize any officer, having first obtained a warrant for such purpose from one of His Majesty's Justices of the Peace, to impress such carriages and horses as the service may require, for the use of which the owner or the owners thereof shall be entitled to receive the sum of seven shillings and six pence per day for every cart or carriage with two horses or oxen during such time as the same shall be employed or detained on public service; provided always, that whenever it shall happen that only part of the militia of this province shall be called out for actual service, it shall and may be lawful for any person being of the militia of the county or riding that may be so called out to provide and send an able-bodied man to serve in the said militia in his stead, and such able-bodied man shall be taken and received as a proper substitute for such person living in the county or riding that would otherwise be obliged to serve in the said militia called out as aforesaid.

X. And be it further enacted by the authority aforesaid, that in the several counties and ridings, where the number of men would be sufficient, the militia shall be formed into regiments, consisting of not more than ten nor less than eight companies, which companies shall consist of not more than fifty nor less than twenty private men, and the field officers of such regiment shall be as follows, that is to say: One colonel, one lieutenant-colonel and one major, and where the number of companies shall be under eight and not less than five, such militia shall be formed into a battalion, and the field officers of such battalion shall be one lieutenant-colonel and one major only, and in each regiment or battalion of militia there shall be one captain, one lieutenant and one ensign to each company.

XI. And it be further enacted by the authority aforesaid, that to every regiment of militia there shall be, in addition to the officers already mentioned, one adjutant and one quartermaster, and that every field officer commanding a regiment or battalion shall fix the number of sergeants who shall serve in his regiment or battalion, and the captains of the said companies shall respectively nominate the sergeants thus fixed and make a return of their names to the field officer commanding such regiment or battalion, who is hereby authorized to approve or disapprove of such nomination.

XII. And it be further enacted by the authority aforesaid, that in the several counties and ridings where the militia men are not in number sufficient to form a regiment or battalion according to the interest and meaning of this act, the militia of such counties or riding shall be formed into independent companies, each company to consist of not more than fifty or less than twenty private men, with one captain, one lieutenant and one ensign in each company, and that the governor, lieutenant-governor or person administering the Government may, when he shall think proper, join together any number of independent companies and form a battalion or battalions, or may incorporate them with any other regiment or battalion of militia: provided the number of companies in any such regiment or battalion be not thereby made to exceed the number of companies of which a regiment or battalion of militia is hereinbefore directed to consist.

XIII. And be it further enacted by the authority aforesaid, that every non-commissioned officer or private who shall refuse to obey the lawful orders of his superior officer or officers when employed on militia duty, or shall quarrel with or insult by abusive words or otherwise any officer or non-commissioned officer being in the execution of his duty, shall for every such offence forfeit and pay a sum of money not exceeding five pounds nor less than ten shillings, current money of this province, at the discretion of the justice or justices imposing such fine, and according to the nature of the offence.

XIV. And be it further enacted by the authority aforesaid, that every person who now is enrolled in any regiment, battalion or independent company shall, within six months after the passing of this act, and every person who shall hereafter be enrolled, of any regiment, battalion or independent company of militia shall, within six months after such enrolment, provide himself with a good and sufficient musket, fusil, rifle or gun, with at least six rounds of powder and ball, and shall come provided with the same at each and every time when he shall be called out, either for the purpose of review, exercise or actual service, and if any person so enrolled shall neglect or refuse to provide himself or to come so provided as in the case of review or exercise, he shall for each offence be liable to a penalty of five shillings, and in the case of actual service, to a penalty of forty shillings, to be levied in the manner hereinafter mentioned: Provided always, that when and so often as any militiaman shall make it appear to his captain or officer commanding the company that he has not been able to procure such musket, fusil, rifle or gun, it shall and may be lawful for such captain or officer commanding such company to admit of such excuse and certify the same in writing accordingly, in which case such militiaman shall not be liable to pay the said fine of five shillings in case of review or exercise and forty shillings in case of actual service.

XV. And be it further enacted by the authority aforesaid, that every person who shall sell or barter any part of the arms and equipments which may be delivered to him out of His Majesty's stores, or who shall destroy the same, and every person who shall buy or by barter obtain such arms or equipments, shall severally and respectively forfeit and pay the sum of five pounds for every offence on conviction thereof by the oath of any one creditable witness before two justices of the peace residing within the county where the same has been committed, and in case the person or persons so selling any part of his arms or equipments as aforesaid, or the person or persons obtaining the same in manner aforesaid, being thereof convicted as aforesaid, shall refuse or neglect to pay the said sum of five pounds, it shall and may be lawful for the said justices, by a warrant under their hands and seals, to commit such person or persons to the gaol of the county or district where the offence shall be committed, for any space of time not exceeding two months: Provided always that it shall and may be lawful for the said justices to discharge the person or persons so offending any time before the expiration of the said two months, when the person or persons so convicted as aforesaid shall tender to the said justices the penalty inflicted by this Act.

XVI. And be it further enacted by the authority aforesaid, that at all times when the militia may be called out and embodied for actual service the officers, non-commissioned officers and private men of the several regiments, battalions and independent companies of militia, shall from the time of their being drawn out and embodied as aforesaid, and until they shall return to their respective towns, townships, parishes or places of abode, remain under the command of the governor, lieutenant-governor, or person administering the Government, or other officer having the command of them, and shall be liable to punishment for mutiny and desertion as hereinafter mentioned: that is to say, that every officer, non-commissioned officer or militiaman who shall presume to use traitorous or disrespectful words against His Majesty's royal person, or disrespectful words against any of the royal family, if a commissioned officer shall, upon conviction thereof before a general courtmartial, as hereinafter directed to be established, be cashiered: if a non-commissioned officer or private, he shall suffer such punishment as by the sentence of the said courtmartial shall be awarded.

XVII. And be it further enacted by the authority aforesaid, that any officer, non-commissioned officer or militiaman who shall behave himself with contempt or disrespect towards the governor, lieutenant-governor or the person administering the Government for the time being, or shall speak words tending to their hurt or dishonor, shall be punished according to the nature of his offence by the judgment of a general courtmartial.

XVIII. And be it further enacted by the authority aforesaid, that any officer, non-commissioned officer or militiaman who shall begin, excite, cause or join in any mutiny or sedition in the regiment, detachment, troop or company to which he belongs, or in any other regiment, detachment, troop or company, whether of embodied militia or of His Majesty's regular or provincial forces in any camp or post, or upon any party, detachment or guard, on any pretence whatsoever, shall suffer death or such other punishment as by a general court-martial shall be awarded.

XIX. And be it further enacted by the authority aforesaid, that any officer, non-commissioned officer or militiaman who being present at any mutiny or sedition shall not use his utmost endeavors to suppress the same, or coming to the knowledge of any mutiny or or intended mutiny shall not without delay give information thereof to his commanding officer, shall suffer such punishment as by a general courtmartial shall be awarded.

XX. And be it further enacted by the authority aforesaid, that all officers, non-commissioned officers and militiamen, who shall be convicted of having deserted to the enemy, shall suffer death or such other punishment as shall be awarded by a general courtmartial.

XXI. And be it further enacted by the authority aforesaid, that any non-commissioned officer or militiaman who shall quit or otherwise absent himself from his regiment, detachment, troop or company without a furlough from his commanding officer, or who shall withdraw himself from the regiment, detachment, troop or company then in service, whether of the militia or of His Majesty's regular or provincial forces, shall, upon being convicted thereof, be punished according to the nature of his offence, at the discretion of a courtmartial, and in case any officer of the militia shall knowingly receive and entertain such non-commissioned officer or militiaman, or shall not after his being discovered to be a deserter immediately confine him and give notice to the regiment, detachment, troop or company in which he last served, he, the said officer so offending, shall on being convicted thereof before a general courtmartial be cashiered.

XXII. And be it further enacted by the authority thereof, that if any officer, non-commissioned officer or militiaman shall be convicted of having advised or persuaded any other officer or militiaman to desert His Majesty's service, he shall suffer such punishment as shall be awarded by a general courtmartial.

XXIII. And be it further enacted by the authority aforesaid, that when the militia of this province shall be called out on actual service, in all cases where a general courtmartial shall be required, the governor, lieutenant-governor or person administering the Government, upon complaint and application to him made through the colonel or officer commanding the body of militia to which the party accused may belong, shall issue his order to the said commanding officer to assemble a general courtmartial, which said courtmartial shall consist of a president, who shall be a field officer, and twelve other commissioned officers of militia; provided always, that in all trials by general courtmartial, to be held by virtue of this act, the governor, lieutenant-governor or person administering the Government, shall nominate and appoint the person who shall act as judge advocate, and that every member of the said court-martial before any proceedings be had before that court, shall take the following oath before the said judge advocate, who is hereby authorized to administer the same, viz:

" You, A. B., do swear that you will administer justice to the best of your understanding in the matter now before you, according to the evidence and, the militia laws now in force in this province without partiality, favor or affection: and you further swear that you will not divulge the sentence of the court until it shall be approved by the governor, lieutenant-governor or person administering the Government: neither will you upon any account, at any time whatsoever, disclose or discover the vote or opinion of any particular member of the courtmartial, unless required to give evidence thereof as a witness by a court of justice in due course of law. So help you God.

And so soon as the said oath shall have been administered to the respective members, the president of the court is hereby authorized to administer to the judge advocate or the person officiating as such, an oath in the following words:—

" You, A. B., do swear that you will not upon any account, at any time whatsoever, disclose or discover the vote or opinion of any particular member of the courtmartial, unless required to give evidence thereof as a witness by a court of justice in a due course of law. So help you God."

And the said judge advocate shall, and he is hereby authorized, to administer to every person giving evidence before the said court, the following oath:—

" The evidence that you shall give to this courtmartial upon the trial of A. B., shall be the truth, the whole truth and nothing but the truth, so help you God."

Provided always that the judgment of every such courtmartial shall pass with the concurrence of two-thirds of the members, and shall not be put in execution until the governor, lieutenant-governor or person administering the Government has approved thereof: Provided always, that no officer serving in any of His Majesty's other forces shall sit in any courtmartial upon the trial of any officer or private man serving in the militia.

XXIV. And be it further enacted by the authority aforesaid, that during the time in which the said militia shall be embodied for actual service they and every of them, as well officers as privates, shall be liable and subject to all and every the provisions, regulations, matters and things in this Act contained respecting the said militia, and also in cases to which the provisions of this Act do not extend, to all the rules, regulations, pains and penalties of any Act or Acts of the British Parliament that are or may be in force for the punishment of mutiny and desertion, not contrary to this Act; provided nevertheless, that no sentence of any courtmartial so to be constituted and established under and by virtue of this Act shall extend to the loss of life or limb, unless for desertion, mutiny and sedition, traitorous correspondence, or for traitorously delivering up to the enemy any garrison, fortress, post, or guard, anything herein contained or any statute, law, or usage to the contrary notwithstanding: provided always, that in no case whatsoever shall any non-commissioned officer or private man, for any offence by him committed be subjected to the punishment of being whipped by the sentence of any courtmartial whatsoever.

XXV. And be it further enacted by the authority aforesaid, that in all cases where a militia officer not on actual service shall be guilty of improper conduct or do anything unbecoming his character as such officer, not otherwise provided for in this Act, the governor, lieutenant-governor, or person administering the Government, upon complaint and application made to him through the colonel or other field officer of militia commanding the respective regiment or battalion to which the said officer against whom the complaint is made may belong, or in case the said colonel or other field officer is the party accused, to the next in command, to issue his order to assemble a court of enquiry, which court shall consist of one field officer in rank superior to the officer accused, who shall be president thereof, together with not not less than four other commissioned officers; and such court of enquiry shall examine witnesses and take every necessary step to investigate the matter alleged in the complaint against the said militia officer and report the evidence in that behalf brought before them to the governor, lieutenant-governor, or person administering the Government, for his decision thereon.

XXVI. And be it further enacted by the authority aforesaid, that except in time of actual service, the judges of the court of King's bench, and clergy, the members of the legislative and executive councils and their respective officers, the members of the house of assembly for the time being and the officers thereto belonging, His Majesty's attorney general, solicitor general, the secretary of the Province and all other civil officers who have been or hereafter may be appointed to any civil office in this Province under the great seal of the same, as well as all magistrates, sheriffs, coroners, half-pay officers, militia officers having served by virtue of any militia commission in any part of His Majesty's dominion (who may not have been removed for any offence as an officer of militia, or who may have obtained leave to resign his commission), the surveyor-general and his deputies duly appointed, seafaring men actually employed in the line of their calling, physicians, surgeons, the masters of the public schools, ferrymen and one miller to every grist mill, shall be and are hereby excused from serving in the said militia: Provided always that this Act and the exceptions herein contained shall not prevent, and it is hereby declared that the same shall not be construed to prevent any or every of the above mentioned person or persons from holding commissions as officers in the militia in this Province: Provided always that it shall and may be lawful for the governor, lieutenant-governor or person administering the Government of this Province by warrant under his hand and seal to exempt any of the persons hereinbefore enumerated from being called out on the service aforesaid.

XXVII. And be it further enacted by the authority aforesaid, that the persons called Quakers, Mennonists and Tunkers, who from certain scruples of conscience decline bearing arms, shall not be compelled to serve in the said militia, but every person professing that he is one of the people called Quakers, Mennonists or Tunkers producing a certificate of his being a Quaker, Mennonist or Tunker signed by the clerk of the meeting of such society, or by any three or more of the people called Quakers, Menonnists or Tunkers, shall be excused and exempted from serving in the said militia: provided, nevertheless, that every such person that shall or may be of the people called Quakers, Mennonists or Tunkers, from the age of sixteen to sixty, shall, on or before the first day of December in each and every year, give in his name and place of residence to the treasurer of the district where he or they shall reside, and pay to such treasurer to and for the public uses of such district in time of peace the sum of twenty shillings, and in time of actual invasion or insurrection, or when any part of the militia of that district shall be called out on actual service, the sum of five pounds, and in default of such payment, it shall and may be lawful on information or complaint on oath made by the said treasurer before any justice of the peace of such district, for such justice to issue his warrant under his hand and seal to levy the same by distress and sale of the offender's goods and chattels, returning so much of the said distress as shall exceed the sum of twenty shillings per annum in time of peace and five pounds per annum in time of actual invasion or insurrection, or when any part of the militia of that district shall be called out on actual service, deducting therefrom the charges and all other incidental expenses of such distress and sale, as well as the expenses of summoning such offender before such justice as aforesaid, shall be by him within the space of two calendar months paid into the hands of the colonel, or in his absence, the next senior officer of the regiment, battalion or independent company of the division where the offence has been committed, to be applied for the like purposes as the fines, forfeitures and penalties imposed by this act, and for want of such distress the justice before whom such person shall have been summoned, shall commit him to the common gaol of the district until he shall pay and satisfy such sum, together with the reasonable charges incident to such conviction; provided, nevertheless, that no person or persons so committed shall in any case be detained in custody longer than the space of one calendar month: provided also, and it is hereby enacted, that each and every of the persons usually called Quakers, Mennonists and Tunkers that have attained the age of fifty years shall not be liable to the payment of such sum of twenty shillings for being exempted from serving in the said militia in time of peace, but that in time of war or other emergency they shall be liable to serve or to the payment of five pounds for being exempted for every year until they shall have attained the age of sixty years.

XXVIII. And be it further enacted by the authority aforesaid, that in time of war when and so often as occasion may require, it shall and may be lawful for the governor, lieutenant-governor or person administering the Government of this Province to employ the militia of this Province either upon land or upon the lakes, rivers, and communications thereof in such parties or detachments as may by him be deemed expedient.

XXIX. And whereas, by a certain clause in this Act it is provided that it shall and may be lawful for the persons therein mentioned on certain occasions to call out detachments of the militia, be it therefore enacted by the authority aforesaid, that the persons to serve on detachment shall be regularly taken from time to time, as they shall be required, from a roster or list to regulate the turn of duty, to be first formed by ballot of each and every person in each respective battalion, regiment or independent company, and that after the same has been formed, when any person shall be enrolled as a militiaman in any battalion, regiment or independent company, the name of such man shall be inserted and follow the last person in the said roster, the initial of whose surname corresponds with the initial of the surname of the man so to be inserted, and when any detachment shall be called out for service the adjutant or officer commanding each regiment, battalion or independent company shall give notice to the persons of their turn of duty.

XXX. And be it further enacted by the authority aforesaid, that when any detachments are formed and called out for public service, it shall and may be lawful for the governor, lieutenant-governor or person administering the Government of this Province to divide the same into smaller detachments or parties and appoint them to serve on board vessels, boats, or batteaux upon any of the lakes, rivers or communications by water of this Province with great guns or artillery, as well as with small arms, as occasion may require, and shall and may appoint them to be stationary in any of the creeks or harbors of the said lakes, or in any of the rivers of the province, and also to train and exercise the same to the use of great guns and artillery as well by land as by water.

XXXI. And whereas it may be convenient to form one or more troops of cavalry, be it therefore enacted by the authority aforesaid, that it shall and may be lawful for the governor, lieutenant-governor or person administering the Government of this Province to form and embody such troop or troops and to employ the same on such duties as the necessity of the service may require.

XXXII. And be it further enacted by the authority aforesaid, that all detachments to be called out and employed as aforesaid, shall, and may, if need require, be detained on such service for and during the space of six months at one time and no longer: provided, that every such detachment be relieved by the arrival of a fresh detachment, sufficient for the indispensable occasions of the service at such period, for which purpose, it shall and may be lawful for the proper officer one week at least before the expiration of the said period of service to call together the remaining parts of the regiment, battalion or independent company or so many as may be necessary according to their several terms, to be regulated by the roster as aforesaid, to relieve such detachment.

XXXIII. Provided always, and be it further enacted by the authority aforesaid, that if such detachment cannot be replaced by an equal number of men of the remaining part of such regiment, battalion or independent company, respectively, then and in such case every detachment to be relieved as aforesaid shall ballot or draw lots for such a number of men as may be wanting to make the succeeding detachment equal to the detachment to be relieved, and the parties whose names shall be drawn shall be liable to serve with the said detachment, but in the case of a partial relief they shall be the first to be relieved, either wholly or by ballot, according to the number to be relieved.

XXXIV. And be it further enacted by the authority aforesaid, that when any person shall have been convicted of any offence against this Act and shall refuse to pay the fine, forfeiture or penalty imposed on such offender, it shall and may be lawful to and for the justice or justices before whom such person shall have been convicted to commit such offender to the common gaol of the district until he shall pay and satisfy such fine, forfeiture or penalty, together with the reasonable charges attending such conviction: Provided, nevertheless, that no person or persons so committed shall in any case be detained in custody longer than the space of one calendar month, except in such cases as are otherwise provided for by this Act.

XXXV. And be it further enacted by the authority aforesaid, that no persons who have been discharged from His Majesty's service as non-commissioned officers shall be obliged to serve in any station in the militia in this Province inferior to that which they held in His Majesty's service, unless, having been non-commissioned officers in the said militia, they may have been reduced according to law.

XXXVI. And be it further enacted by the authority aforesaid, that no person enrolled in the militia shall absent or withdraw himself from any place of review or exercise without having first obtained leave of his commanding officer so to do, under the penalty of forty shillings if a commissioned officer, and ten shillings if a non-commissioned officer or private.

XXXVII. And be it further enacted by the authority aforesaid, that if any sergeant of militia, when thereunto requested by his superior and proper officer, shall neglect or refuse to warn the militiamen of the company which he belongs to appear at the place of enrolment or exercise, he shall for every such neglect or refusal pay the sum of forty shillings.

XXXVIII. And be it further enacted by the authority aforesaid, that every sergeant in the militia duly appointed shall be exempt from serving as constable for and during such time as he shall hold such appointment as sergeant.

XXXIX. And be it further enacted by the authority aforesaid, that if any person be wounded or shall be disabled when employed on actual service, upon an invasion, insurrection or rebellion, he shall be taken care of and attended during the time of such disability agreeably to his rank.

XL. And be it further enacted by the authority aforesaid, that when any person shall be summoned before two of His Majesty's justices of the peace as aforesaid for having neglected or refused to do such things as by this Act are required of him to be performed, and shall, upon the oath of one credible witness before such justices be duly convicted of such offence, such person shall pay the charges and expenses of and incident to such conviction, and that all fines, penalties and forfeitures by this Act imposed, on default of payment, shall be levied by distress and sale of the goods and chattels of the offender by warrant under the hands and seals of the justices before whom the said offender shall be convicted, rendering the overplus (if any) to the said person whose goods and chattels shall have been so distrained and sold, after deducting therefrom the charges of such distress and sale, and within two months after such conviction and recovery, the sums so recovered shall be transmitted by the justices before whom such information shall have been laid to the colonel, or in his absence, to the next senior officer of the regiment, battalion or independent company, and the said colonels and other officers respectively shall, and they are hereby required, out of the several sums of money which they shall receive for fines, forfeitures or penalties, or otherwise by virtue of this Act, to provide for their regiments in their respective counties or ridings, drums, fifes, colors, banners, regimental books, and for the discharge of other incidental expenses, and in case any any overplus of such monies shall remain in the hands of any such colonel or other officer after providing such articles as aforesaid, such surplus shall be disposed of in premiums to the persons who shall make the best shot at a target or mark upon days of training, and in such proportions as at a meeting the colonels or officers commanding regiments, battalions or independent companies, shall order and direct, and each colonel, or in his absence, the next senior officer of the regiment, battalion or independent company, shall render a certified account thereof in detail, to be transmitted to the governor, lieutenant-governor or person administering the Government, as soon after the thirty-first day of December annually as practicable.

XLI. And be it further enacted by the authority aforesaid, that no order of conviction made by any justice or justices of the peace by virtue of this Act shall be removed by certiorari out of the county, riding, division, or place wherein such order or conviction shall have been made, into any court whatsoever, and that no writ of certiorari shall supersede execution on other proceedings upon any such order or conviction so made in pursuance of this Act, but that execution and other proceedings shall be had and made thereupon, any such writ or writs or allowance thereof notwithstanding: provided always, that the fines, forfeitures or penalties to be levied by virtue of such order or conviction shall not exceed the sum of twenty pounds.

XLII. And be it further enacted by the authority aforesaid, that if any action shall be brought against any person or persons for anything done in pursuance of this Act, such action or suit shall be commenced within six months after the fact committed and not afterwards, and shall be laid in the county, riding or place where the cause of complaint did arise, and not elsewhere, and the defendant or defendants in every such action or suit may plead the general issue and give this Act and the special matter in evidence at any trial to be had thereupon, and if the jury shall find for the defendant or defendants in any such action or suit, and if the plaintiff or plaintiffs shall be non-suited or discontinue his, her or their action or suit, after the defendant or defendants shall have appeared, or if, upon demurrer, judgment shall be given against the plaintiff or plaintiffs, the defendant or defendants shall have treble costs and have the like remedy for the same as any defendant hath in other cases to recover costs by law.

XLIII. And be it further enacted by the authority aforesaid, that all former Acts relating to the raising of the militia within this Province shall from and after the passing of this Act be and are hereby repealed: Provided, nevertheless, that nothing in this Act contained shall in anywise extend or be construed to extend to annul or make void any militia appointment which may have taken place in pursuance of the former Acts relating to the militia forces, or to prevent the completing of any proceedings commenced in pursuance thereof, until new commissions are issued under and by virtue of this Act.

REPORT OF LIEUT.-COLONEL BRUYERES, R. E.

QUEBEC, 24th August, 1811.

Report of the State of the Fortified Military Posts in Both the Canadas.

* * * * * * * * * * *

FORT GEORGE.—Situated on the west bank of the River Niagara, about one mile from Lake Ontario, is an irregular field work, consisting of six small bastions, faced with framed timber and plank. These bastions are connected with a line of picketing, twelve feet in height. The whole of this work is very much out of repair: its situation and construction very defective, and cannot be considered capable of much defence. The troops are lodged in blockhouses within the fort, which contain quarters for about 220 men, exclusive of a spacious building for the officers. The magazine is a stone building, arched, but not bomb-proof.

FORT CHIPPAWA.—Situated on the right bank of the River Chippawa, about 16 miles from Fort George. It is the termination of the carrying place, nine miles from the west landing, and one and one-half miles above the Falls. This post can only be considered a transport post for depositing and forwarding stores to the upper lakes. It consists merely of a large blockhouse, containing quarters for one officer and thirty-six men, and storeroom sufficient for the stores deposited there. It is enclosed with a line of picketing very much decayed, and cannot be considered capable of any defence.

FORT ERIE.—Situated at the entrance to Lake Erie, eighteen miles above Fort Chippawa. The old fort on the borders of the lake is in ruins and totally abandoned. The construction of a new fort, projected by Lieut.-General Mann, on the rising ground above the site of the old fort, to be built of masonry, was begun in the spring of 1805, in conformity with a report approved by Lord Hobart, Secretary of State, in a letter to General Hunter. This work was continued until the latter end of the year 1807, when it was put a stop to by order of General Sir James Craig on his arrival at Quebec. At the time of closing, the two piles of barracks, together with the masonry of two bastions fronting the lake, were finished, the ditch excavated and part of the masonry founded of two bastions towards the land. The interior of the barracks, only partly completed, to accommodate troops quartered at the post. The remainder unfinished and has received some injury from remaining so long neglected. Fort Erie cannot be considered a strong military position, but as it is necessary always to have some troops stationed at this post, to carry on transport and communication with Amherstburg and St. Joseph's, the necessary security and accommodation might be probably obtained by completing this post.

(Canadian Archives, Freer Papers, 1811.)

Major-General George Glasgow, R. A., to Sir George Prevost.

REPORT OF THE STATE OF THE MAGAZINES, STOREHOUSES, PLATFORMS, CARRIAGES, ORDNANCE AND STORES, IN CHARGE OF THE FIELD TRAIN DEPARTMENT IN CANADA UNDER THE SUPERINTENDENCE OF THE COMMANDING OFFICERS OF ARTILLERY.

QUEBEC, 18th Sept., 1811.

* * * * * * * * * *

Neither horses nor drivers having been attached to the field train in Canada, the officers and men of the artillery are but little acquainted with the present system of field exercise, and the present strength of the detachment of artillery is by no means in proportion to the services required of so extensive a command.

* * * * * * * * * * *

At Kingston there is a light 6-pounder, a sergeant and two gunners: the magazine unfinished and unprotected.

At York there are two light 6-pounders: neither magazine nor storehouse, one sergeant and one gunner.

At Fort George there are for garrison use six 12-pounders, three 9-pounders and one mortar, all of iron; of brass, one 12-pounder, five light 6-pounders, four 3-pounders and a 5½ inch howitzer with cars, five cast iron mortars with carriages, harness, etc. The magazine is not bombproof: the storehouses are under the barracks, in wooden buildings. A captain, three non-commissioned officers and twenty-one gunners stationed here.

* * * * * * * * * * *

In the present situation of the posts of Upper Canada there is not one situation that can be considered safe as a depot. The works are faced and lined with wood, the bastions connected by palisades. The buildings are of wood, liable at all times to accident by fire, and within the power of an enemy to be burnt whenever he chose to undertake it.

A depot at a distance from the frontier is much wanted, where the powder, ammunition, field pieces, small arms and naval stores not immediately wanted might be kept in more safety, and where an establishment might be formed for making and repairing carriages, and other purposes essential to the service.

York seems to present a situation well adapted for such a purpose.

(Canadian Archives, Freer Papers, 1811.)

Major-General Isaac Brock to Sir George Prevost.

YORK, Upper Canada, Dec. 2d, 1811.

SIR,—The information contained in the message of the President to Congress relative to the existing differences between England and the United States will justify, I presumed to think, the adoption of such precautionary measures as may be necessary to meet all future exigencies. Under this impression, I beg leave to submit to Your Excellency such observations as occur to me to enable you to form a correct judgment of the actual state of this Province.

The military force which heretofore occupied the frontier posts being so inadequate to their defence, a general opinion obtained that no opposition in the event of hostilities was intended. The late increase of ammunition and every species of stores, the substitution of a strong regiment and the appointment of a military person to administer the Government, have tended to infuse other sentiments among the most reflecting part of the community, and I feel happy in being able to assure Your Excellency that during my visit last week to Niagara I received the most satisfactory professions of a determination on the part of the principal inhabitants to exert every means in their power in defence of their property and support of the Government. They look with confidence to Your Excellency for such additional aid as may be necessary in conjunction with the militia to repel any hostile attempt against this Province. I shall beg leave to refer Your Excellency to the communications of Lieutenant-Governor Gore with Sir James Craig (as per margin) for a correct view of the temper and composition of the militia and Indians, and altho' perfectly aware of the number of improper characters who have obtained extensive possessions and whose principles diffuse a spirit of insubordination very adverse to all military institutions, yet I feel confident a large majority will prove faithful. It is, however, certain that the best policy to be pursued, should future circumstances call for active preparations, will be to act with the utmost liberality and as if no mistrust existed. For, unless the inhabitants give an active and

*1st Dec., 1807.
5th Jan., 1808.
20th Feb., 1809, the latter enclosing an extract from correspondence with Lt.-Col. Grant, 41st Regt., dated Amherstburg, 5th Jan., 1808.*

efficient aid, it will be utterly impossible for the very limited number of the military who are likely to be employed to preserve the Province.

The first point to which I am anxious to call Your Excellency's attention is the District of Amherstburg. I consider it the most important, and if supplied with the means of commencing active operations must deter the Americans from any offensive attempt from Niagara westward.

That Government will be compelled to secure their western frontier from the inroads of the Indians, and this cannot be effected without a very considerable force. But before we can expect an active co-operation on the part of the Indians, the reduction of Detroit and Michilimackinac must convince that people (who consider themselves to have been sacrificed to our policy in 1794) that we are earnestly engaged in the war. The Indians, I am given to understand, are eager for an opportunity to avenge the numerous injuries of which they complain. A few tribes at the instigation of a Shawanese of no note, have already (altho' explicitly told not to look for assistance from us) commenced the contest. The stand which they continue to make on the Wabash against about two thousand regulars and militia is a strong proof of the strong force which a general combination of the Indians will render necessary to protect so widely extended a frontier. The garrisons of Detroit and Michilimackinac do not, I believe, exceed seventy rank and file each, but the former can be easily reinforced by the militia in the neighborhood, which tho' not numerous would be sufficient for its defence unless assailed by a force much superior to any we can now command. The Americans would draw their principal force either for defence or attack from the Ohio, an enterprising, hardy race and uncommonly expert on horseback with the rifle. This species of force is formidable to the Indians, altho' according to reports which have reached me by different channels (but none officially) they have lately repelled an attack of some magnitude. Unless a diversion such as I have suggested be made, an overwhelming force will probably be directed against this part of the province. The measure will, however, be attended with a heavy expense, especially in the article of provisions, for not only the Indians who take the field, but also their families, must be maintained. The numerical force of the militia in the vicinity of Amherstburg exceeds by a trifle seven hundred rank and file. Consequently very little assistance can be derived from that source in any offensive operation. Should, therefore, the aspect of affairs hereafter give stronger indications of a rupture, I propose augmenting the garrison of Amherstburg with two hundred rank and file from Fort George and York. Such a measure I consider essentially necessary, were it only calculated to rouse the energy of both militia and Indians, who are now impressed with a firm belief that in the event of a war they are to be left to their fate. Great pains have been taken to instil this idea into the minds of the Indians, and no stronger argument could be employed than the weak state of the garrison. The army now assembled on the Wabash, with the ostensible view of opposing the Shawanese Indians, is a strong additional motive in my mind in support of the measure, for I have no doubt but the instant their service in the field terminates a large portion of the regulars will be detached to strengthen the garrison at Detroit. I have prepared Colonel Procter for such an event, and after weighing the inconvenience to which the service would be exposed if the district were placed under a militia colonel, (an event obvious, unless superseded by a regular officer of equal rank,) I have directed Lieut.-Col. St. George to be in readiness to repair to Amherstburg and assume the command. I entertain a high opinion of this officer, and make no doubt that his intelligence and conciliatory disposition will greatly promote the service. At any rate, I am without a choice, and hope his situation of Inspector of Militia will not be considered a bar to the arrangement. The state of the roads will probably stop this projected movement until the latter end of this month or beginning of next, nor do I intend that the troops should leave their present quarters unless urged by fresh circumstances. I therefore look to receive Your Excellency's commands previous to their departure.

From Amherstburg to Fort Erie, my chief dependence must rest on a naval force for the protection of that extensive coast. But considering the state to which it is reduced, extraordinary exertions and great expense will be required before it can be rendered efficient. At present it only consists of a ship and a small schooner, the latter of a bad construction, old, and in want of many repairs, yet she is the only King's vessel able to navigate Lake Huron, whilst the Americans have a sloop and a fine brig, capable of carrying twelve guns and in perfect readiness for any service. If consequently the garrison of St. Josephs is to be maintained and an attack on Michilimackinac undertaken, it will be expedient to hire or purchase from the merchants as many vessels as may be necessary for the purpose. The Americans can resort to the same means, and the construction and number of their vessels for trade will give them great advantage, besides their small craft or boats in which troops could be easily transported across the waters exceed ours considerably. Indeed, we have very few of that description. I therefore leave it to Your Excellency's superior judgment to determine whether a sufficient number of gunboats for both lakes, so constructed as to draw little water, ought not to be added to our means of defence and offence. It is worthy of remark that the only American national vessel on Lake Ontario, built two years ago and now laying in Sackett's Harbor, has remained without seamen until within the last fortnight, when the officers began to enter men as fast as possible. A lieutenant with a party came to Buffalo (a tolerably large village opposite Fort Erie) and procured several hands, but, not satisfied, a petty officer was sent to our side to inveigle others. The magistrates hearing of this sent to have him arrested, but he with difficulty escaped. The strait between Niagara and Fort Erie is that which in all probability will be chosen for their main body to penetrate with a view to conquest. All other attacks will be subordinate or merely made to divert our attention.

About 3,000 militia could, upon an emergency, be drawn to that line, and nearly five hundred Indians could likewise be collected; therefore, with the regulars, no trifling force could hope for success provided a determined resistance was made, but I cannot hide from Your Excellency that unless a strong military force be present to animate the loyal and control the disaffected nothing effectual can be expected. A protracted resistance upon this frontier will be sure to embarrass their plans materially. They will not come prepared to meet it, and their troops or volunteer corps without scarcely any discipline (as far at least as control is in question) will soon tire under disappointment. The difficulty which they will experience in providing provisions will involve them into expenses, under which their Government will soon become impatient. The car-brigade will be particularly useful in obstructing their passage, and I cannot be too urgent in soliciting the means, both as to gunners and drivers, and likewise as to horses, to render the one at Fort George complete for service. A small body of cavalry would be absolutely necessary, and I have already offers from many respectable young men to form themselves into a troop. All they seem to require are swords and pistols, which the stores below may probably be able to furnish. The situation of Kingston is so very important in every military point of view that I cannot be too earnest in drawing Your Excellency's attention to that quarter. The militia from the Bay of Quinte down to Glengarry is the most respectable of any in the province. Among the officers, several are on half-pay, who still retain a sound military spirit. Those from the Bay of Quinte would be properly stationed at Kingston, but all downwards would naturally desire to be employed to resist any predatory excursions, to which their property would be so much exposed from the opposite shore. I have, besides, been always of the opinion that a strong detachment would follow the route of Lord Amherst and attempt to enter the Province by Oswagatchie. The militia on the whole of that communication cannot therefore be more usefully employed than in watching such a movement, and should the enemy direct the whole of his force by St. Johns, the greater part can, with the utmost facility, join the army acting upon that frontier.

The Militia Act, which I have the honor to transmit, provides for such emergency, and Your Excellency will readily observe among many wise and salutary provisions but few means of enforcing them.

No exertions, however, shall be wanting in my civil capacity to place that body upon a respectable footing. Mr. Cartwright, the senior militia colonel at Kingston, possesses the influence to which his firm character and superior abilities so deservedly entitle him; but as I cannot possibly give the necessary attention to so distant an object, and as a regular officer will be indispensable to direct the operations, one of high rank ought, if possible, to be nominated to that command.

So much will remain to be done, and such high expenses to be incurred in the Quarter Master General's department, that I cannot be too earnest with Your Excellency in requesting that an officer equal to the situation may be appointed. A head to the commissariat will likewise be indispensable.

I have trespassed greatly on Your Excellency's time, but I beg to be permitted to entreat Your Excellency to honor me with such advice and counsel as Your Excellency may suggest, and be assured my utmost pride will be to meet your views and merit your approbation.

(Canadian Archives, C. 673, p. 171.)

Major General Brock to Sir George Prevost.

YORK, December 11, 1812.

SIR,—I had the honor yesterday of receiving Your Excellency's letter of the 1st ultimo, stating your intention of establishing depots of small arms, accoutrements, and ammunition at the different posts in Upper Canada.

Since the settlement of the Province several thousand stands have been at different times issued to the militia, and I have given directions for collecting them, but in all probability great deficiencies will be found; indeed, it has been already ascertained that those delivered in 1795 by Lieut.-General Simcoe are wholly lost to the service. To obviate for the future such an extensive waste, I propose fixing upon proper places at each post wherein the arms may be deposited after the militia have exercised, and I have to request Your Excellency's permission to direct the field-train department to attend to their preservation and keep them in a state of repair, in the same manner as those remaining in store. The expense cannot be great, and in all such cases the infant state of the country obliges the militia to have recourse to the military.

I have recently had occasion to report for Your Excellency's information the total want of stores at this post beyond those immediately necessary for the commissariat. I shall, consequently, be much at a loss to find accommodation for the 2,329 French muskets which Your Excellency has directed to be sent here; and as the only magazine is a small wooden shed, not sixty yards from the King's house, which is rendered dangerous from the quantity of powder it already contains, I cannot but feel a repugnance to lodge the additional 13,140 ball cartridges intended for this post in a place so evidently insecure. But as these arrangements cannot conveniently take place until the opening of navigation, there will be sufficient time to contrive the best means to meet Your Excellency's wishes.

(From Tupper's Life of Brock, p. 130.)

Sir George Prevost to Major General Brock.

QUEBEC, December 24, 1811.

SIR,—I have the honor to acknowledge the receipt of your letter of the 2nd instant, which reached me by the courier on Saturday, and I have not failed to give it that consideration which the importance of the several points to which it alludes entitle it.

In addition to the President's message being full of gunpowder, the report made to Congress by its committee on the state of the foreign affairs of the United States conveys sentiments of such decided hostility towards England that I feel justified in recommending such precaution as may place you in a state of preparation for that event, and with this view you must endeavor to trace an outline of co-operation compensating for our deficiency in strength. I agree with you as to the advantages which may result from giving rather than receiving the first blow, but it is not my opinion war will commence by a declaration of it. That act would militate against the policy of both countries; therefore we must expect repeated petty aggressions from our neighbors before we are permitted to retaliate by open hostilities. It is very satisfactory to observe the professions of the inhabitants of Upper Canada in defence of their property and in support of their Government.

I will look into the correspondence you refer to which took

place between Sir James Craig and Lieut.-Governor Gore in 1807, 1808, and 1809, respecting the temper and disposition of your militia and the policy to be observed in your intercourse with the Indians.

Your views in regard to the line of conduct to be observed towards the militia forces, notwithstanding some existing circumstances unfavorable in their composition, are in my estimation wise, and on such conception I have hitherto acted.

There are too many considerations to allow me to hesitate in saying we must employ the Indians, if they can be brought to act with us. The utmost caution should be used in our language to them, and all direct explanation should be delayed if possible until hostilities are more certain, though whenever the subject is adverted to I think it would be advisable always to intimate that as a matter of course we shall, in the event of war, expect the aid of our brothers. Although I am sensible this requires delicacy, still it should be done so as not to be misunderstood.

I shall call the attention of the commissariat to the supply of provisions that may be required in the Upper Province, and I had, previously to the arrival of your letter, given the deputy-quartermaster-general directions for the building of another schooner for Lake Erie.

I am sorry to observe, both by your Militia Act and returns [that] you are embarrassed with officers holding the rank of colonel. It is certainly desirable that no higher rank should exist than that of lieutenant-colonel commandant, else, in many cases, the officers of militia on service might be seniors to the officers of the line in command of regiments. It is, I am apprehensive, scarcely possible to revoke the commissions of colonel which have been issued to the commanding officers of battalions of militia for that of lieutenant-colonel; therefore if commissions cannot without serious dissatisfaction be withdrawn, you are authorized in that case, in order to preserve the command of the inspecting field officer, to direct Lieut.-Colonel St. George to act with the local rank of colonel in Upper Canada, giving at the same time (should circumstances make it necessary that the troops of the line and those of the militia be called to act together) a corresponding local brevet to such lieutenant-colonels serving in regiments of the line immediately under your command as may appear to you necessary to obviate the inconvenience that may be anticipated from their having junior rank to officers in command of militia regiments, but as this latter arrangement is not free from considerable objection you must modify the measure as much as circumstances will permit.

(From Tupper's Life of Brock, p. 153.)

Memorandum to be Submitted to His Excellency, the Gov.-in-Chief, by Desire of Major-General Brock.

To reinforce the 41st by sending up their recruits, and to send the regiment to Amherstburg, together with 50 artillery.

To send ordnance suited to the reduction of Detroit (4 to 6 eight-inch mortars).

To explain the nature of the offensive operations proposed in that quarter.

Militia on the Detroit side, 300 men, mostly Canadians; Kentucky population, 400,000 souls; Amherstburg furnishes 700 militia; Indians in the vicinity, from 2 to 3,000; at the Grand River, 2 to 300.

To send the 49th or some other effective regiment to the Niagara frontier with a proportion of artillery.

To send a regiment to Kingston, together with a detachment of artillery.

To send an officer of rank to Kingston to take charge of that frontier.

It is proposed to select from the militia 2 companies from each regiment as flank companies, which will produce as volunteers about 1,800 men.

It is proposed to raise corps of volunteers, which may produce 1,200 men.

To lay up ships next winter at York and by degrees remove the naval yard.

To provide materials for ten more batteaux at Kingston and at Amherstburg.

To build one gun-boat, as an experiment, at Long Point.

To send plans of the Quebec boats to York. The gun to unship and lie in the hold in bad weather.

To fortify the harbor of Amherstburg. The co-operation of the N. West and S. West companies. To take the post of Michilimackinac and remove St. Josephs to it.

A small work to protect the anchorage of vessels at Long Point, and to have 6 gun-boats at Long Point if the plan succeeds.

The co-operation of the Indians will be attended with great expense in presents, provisions, &c.

To send a person from Kingston to reconnoitre Sackett's Harbor, and to send from Niagara to examine the harbors and country on the south shore of Lake Ontario to see what preparation and if among merchant vessels.

Captain Gilkinson at Prescott.

To enquire if he will take a naval command.

Captain Fish to command the new schooner to be built at York.

To superannuate Commodore Grant and to appoint Lieut. Hall senior officer.

Lieut. Barwis to command the new schooner.

2nd Lieut. Rolette to be appointed first and to command the *Hunter*.

To superannuate Commodore Steele and to appoint Captain Earle senior officer and to command the *Royal George*.

To appoint and to command the *Moira*.

To mount 6 24-pr. carronades on field carriages, to be used as occasion may require.

To send two companies of the Newfoundland Regiment to act as seamen and mariners.

To augment the establishment by sending an addition of 100 seamen to the lakes.

To purchase all the cordage from Capt. Mills at Amherstburg, as this tends greatly to promote the growth of hemp.

To submit the memo. from Lieuts. Dewar and Hall.

(Canadian Archives, C. 728, p. 68.)

General John Armstrong to Hon. Wm. Eustis, Secretary of War.

RED HOOK, January 2nd, 1812.

DEAR EUSTIS,—Yesterday's mail brought your hypothetical note, which I hasten to answer by a few suggestions that if approved may be readily drawn out into as much detail as may be useful.

1st. An abundant supply of what is technically called the *materiel* of war is indispensable. This single term includes arms, equipments, and ammunition in all their varieties, tents, blankets, and clothing, cavalry and draught horses, oxen, wagons, carts, entrenching tools, &c., &c. To make a competent provision of these will require a large expenditure of money, but to this you must submit for two unanswerable reasons—the one, that without them war cannot be made either morally or successfully; the other, that their cost now will be from 50 to 100 *per cent. less* than it will be *after the declaration of war*.

2d. When obtained, these supplies should be placed in magazines, the location of which must be governed by two considerations—the security of the articles deposited in them, and the facility and safety with which these may be brought into use. To each magazine should be attached a laboratory for fixing ammunition, making and mending gun and other carriages, repairing arms, &c.

3d. If you have remote posts liable to attack and difficult to sustain, and having no direct or important bearing on the progress or issue of the war, hasten to dismantle them and withdraw the garrisons.

4th.—Resting, as the line of Canadian defence does, in its whole extent on navigable lakes and rivers, no time should be lost in getting a naval ascendency on both for *cæteris paribus* the belligerent who is the first to obtain this advantage will (miracles excepted) win the game. Whether the commercial craft at present employed on these waters can be made useful for the purpose, I do not know, but among the sages now assembled at Washington you cannot fail to find some one who can answer the question.

5th.—Without a knowledge, nearly approximating the truth, of the force you will have to contend with, of the disposition made of this, and of the character, physical and artificial, of the posts occupied by it, you will be compelled to make war *conjecturally* and of course on data furnishing no just conclusions with regard to either the number or composition of your own army, or of the kind and extent of operations which ought to be assigned to it. That a state of peace like the present will be more favorable than one of war for acquiring this preliminary information cannot be doubted, and if it be true, as I have been told, that the British posts are victualled by American contractors, these agents (who by their vocation must have free access to them) may probably form the safest and surest medium through which to obtain it. But whatever be the means employed for accomplishing this object, a moment should not be lost in putting them into exercise.

6th.—The number and composition of your army (as already suggested) should be decided by the service given it to perform and the kind and degree of resistance your enemy may be able to oppose to it. Though from present appearances it be true that the exigencies of the war in Europe will disable England from sending promptly any important aid strictly military to the Canadas, it does not follow that she will omit to employ such other means as she may possess to supply the deficiency. Of these the most vexatious to us would be a portion of her armed vessels acting separately or in squadron on our long and defenceless line of sea coast, while at the same time hordes of savages are let loose on the women and children of the West. And that in the event of war, Great Britain will not hesitate to employ this policy in both its branches, cannot be doubted by those who have any recollection of what her past conduct towards the United States has been, or who are now capable of perceiving the impunity to herself and the mischief to us with which she may pursue it.

From this general view of the subject, it follows that in composing your army you must be careful to provide corps specially adapted for two purposes—the *protection of your own frontiers*, eastern and western, and the *invasion* of those of your enemy. Of each of these I offer the following outline :—

For the former, divide your coast into military districts—open in each a rendezous for *volunteer association* and *local defence*, with engagements commensurate with the war and pay enrolments such as are now given to the regular army. Of this description of force the maximum may be *twenty battalions*, located as follows :— One at Portsmouth, two at Boston, one at Newport, three at New York, one at Philadelphia, three at Baltimore, three at Norfolk, two at Charleston, one at Savannah and three at New Orleans. Each of these stations to be well supplied with heavy guns for position, furnaces for heating shot, light pieces well horsed for field service, and muskets and bayonets for camp and garrison duty. Corps thus constituted and equipped, well instructed in the use of their arms and respectably commanded, will do much to check, if they do not entirely prevent, predatory excursion, the evil most to be apprehended from the crews of single ships or from those of small squadrons not sustained by infantry.

For western defence employ western men accustomed to the rifle and the forest and not unacquainted with the usages and stratagems of Indian warfare. To their customary arms add a pistol and sabre, and, to ensure celerity, mount them on horse-back. Give them a competent leader and a good position within striking distance of Indian villages or British settlements. Why not at Detroit, where you have a strong fortress and a detachment of artillerists? Recollect, however, that this position, far from being good, would be positively bad unless your naval means have an ascendency on Lake Erie, because Buffalo, Erie, Cleveland, and the two Sanduskys must be its base or source of supply. The maximum of this corps may be six battalions.

Lastly, for a successful invasion of the Canadas (the great operation of the war, because that only by which Great Britain can be brought to a sense of justice,) you must rely on a regular army. Of this description of force you have now the skeletons of ten regiments, which, if completed, will give you ten thousand combatants—a corps that in the present circumstances of England, and aided by militia for purposes of demonstration, will be competent to great achievements. Hasten then to fill up the rank and file of your present establishment, and to existing inducements for enlisting add an increased pay and a liberal bounty at the end of the war.

Should better information with regard to your enemy's strength make an increase of your own expedient, give one or two additional battalions to each of your seven regiments of infantry—a mode of increasing an army much to be preferred to creations altogether new. For, besides being obviously more economical, the direct association of raw recruits with old soldiers has the effect of making the former efficient in half the time it would otherwise take to do so—the example of comrades being a principle of tuition much more active than the instruction of officers.

On this head it is but necessary to add that the whole of your disposable or field force when obtained should be immediately assembled at some point from which, the moment that war shall be authorized, it may begin its operations. Under present views Albany or its neighborhood should be the place of this rendezvous, because, besides other recommendations, it is *here* that all the roads leading from the central portion of the United States to the Canadas *diverge*, a circumstance which, while it keeps up your enemy's doubts as to your real point of attack cannot fail to keep his means of defence in a state of division.

7th.—In sketching the composition of an army, two branches of it, the one having charge of its discipline and its movement, the other of its subsistence, must not be forgotten. For the first (a General Staff) I refer you to Grimoard's publication, which I sent to the War Department from Paris some years ago. If this book be not already translated into English, no time should be lost in naturalizing it for the use of the army.

The second or feeding department is of three kinds—that founded on Cæsar's maxim that "war should sustain war," though fashionable at present, is in fact a system of indiscriminate plunder, forbidden alike, as I hope, by the moral feelings and political views of the United States. The remaining two are sufficiently known under the names of the contract and commissariat systems. To recommend either, as exclusively and under all circumstances the best, would show only great ignorance or great folly. In old and well-peopled districts where corn and cattle are abundant, prices little subject to change, roads safe and unobstructed, and the means of transportation (trains or boats) easily procured, the contract plan is the best—because the most economical, sufficiently punctual in the discharge of its engagements, and, from the settled character of its terms, rarely if ever embarrassing the Government with extra or unexpected charges. In districts of an opposite character, where the population is thin and poor, supplies scarce and high priced, roads few and bad and much exposed to obstruction, the commissariat must be submitted to, though certainly liable to great abuse from the ignorance, indolence, or knavery of the agents employed. The best remedy for the evils of this system will be found in subjecting the agents to military law and in vigorously enforcing its provisions.

8th and lastly.—A project of campaign conformed to military maxims must embrace three things: 1st—*An object of important or decisive character*, the attainment of which will give a successful issue to the campaign, if not to the war. 2nd—*A line of operation* as short and perpendicular to the object as possible; and 3rd—*A well secured base*, on which must be accumulated and ready for transportation all supplies necessary to sustain the operation. Each of these rules has its own special laws, but it is only of the first that I will say more at present than a few words.

In invading a neighboring and independent territory like Canada, having a frontier of immense extent, destitute of means strictly its own for the purposes of defence, separated from the rest of the empire by an ocean, and having to this but one outlet—this *outlet forms your true object or point of attack*, because if gained, everything depending upon it is gained also. Such was the consequence of the capture of Quebec in the war which ended in 1763, and such would again be the capture of that capital had we the means to effect it. Unfortunately, from deficient foresight in the Government, these are wanting. Still, though unable to do what in the abstract would be best, it by no means follows that we should omit to do what may be both practicable and expedient. Such in my opinion would be the *capture of Montreal*—a post which, commanding alike the navigation of the St. Lawrence and the Ottawa, if seized and held would give the same control over all that portion of the Canadas lying westward of itself that Quebec now exercises over the whole territory. Kingston, York, Fort George, Fort Erie and Malden, cut off from their common base must soon and necessarily fall. To reach this object your line of operation may be taken on either side of Lake Champlain, provided you have secured the command of the lake, in which case also Albany, Greenbush, Troy, Whitehall, &c., covered by a dense population or secured by a large river nowhere fordable by infantry, will give you a sufficient base. When begun the movement should be made rapidly and audaciously, and, the better to secure its success, three demonstrations by masses of militia may be employed: one on the Niagara to keep within their walls the garrisons of Fort George and Erie; a second at Sackett's Harbor, to produce a similar effect on whatever force may be found at Kingston, and a third in Vermont, so placed on the eastern side of the Sorel as to menace the British posts on that river.

Though taking for granted, as stated above, that the capture of Montreal would involve that of all posts westward from itself, it will no doubt be proper that the six battalions of mounted gun-men should march on Malden as soon as they shall be apprised that the campaign on Lake Champlain is opened. And here we must stop, what remains of the subject being *tactical* and governed by circumstances as they occur in the camp or the field, must be entirely left to the genius and judgment of your commanding general.

(From Notices of the War of 1812 by John Armstrong, New York, 1840, Vol. I., pp. 234-41.)

Sir George Prevost to Thomas Barclay, His Majesty's Consul-General at New York.

QUEBEC, 4th January, 1812.

SIR,—Considering the spirit of hostility shown to England by the United States no longer likely to be confined to a paper and commercial warfare, and that, therefore, it is of importance I should receive a correct account of the disposition and news of the American Government, I have sent Captain Coore, one of my aids-de-camp, to Mr. Foster for the purpose, who is instructed to communicate with you as he passes through New York.

(From the Correspondence of Thomas Barclay, p. 302.)

Thomas Barclay to Sir George Prevost.

NEW YORK, 22d January, 1812.

SIR,—I agree with you that the period is fast approaching when these States will take active hostile measures against Great Britain, and it is apparent that their first military measures will be directed against His Majesty's Provinces of Lower and Upper Canada. I am satisfied also that attempts will be made to seduce the inhabitants of Upper Canada generally, and the French Canadians in Lower Canada, from their allegiance. You will pardon, therefore, the liberty I take in recommending the utmost attention in admitting persons within cities of these Provinces, as attempts will be made to introduce characters fitted to persuade and delude the ignorant. There is a man who lives on the line (45) between these States and Lower Canada. Colonel Armstrong knows him; his name is Rous. Of him particular care should be taken and of those who have communications with him. He is a sensible, intriguing, cunning man, eminently qualified for such purposes and well acquainted with all the disaffected Canadians. His movements require special care.

(From the Correspondence of Thomas Barclay, p. 304.)

Captain A. Gray, Assistant Deputy Quartermaster-General, to Sir George Prevost.

YORK, 29th January, 1812.

SIR,—I arrived safe at this place on the evening of the 27th and delivered the money I was entrusted with to Mr. Selby. The weather has been extremely unfavorable, having been exceedingly cold or thawing, all the way from Montreal to York. From Montreal to Kingston occupied 6 days, and from Kingston to York 5 days.

On my arrival at Kingston, I inspected the state of the marine and have the honor to communicate the following particulars for Your Excellency's information:

The *Royal George* lays alongside the wharf, dismantled and her rigging laid up in the sail loft, and reported to be all in good order and in readiness to refit at the shortest notice. But it is a singular circumstance that they have as yet found no way of mounting the carronades sent up last summer to arm this and the other vessels on the lakes. This difficulty arises from the construction of the slide upon which the carronade is mounted. This is upon a new principle and is rather complicated, being of a nature not at all self-evident, as appears from the variety of opinions that prevail as to its object and utility. There ought therefore to have been a plan and description of the slide sent along with them. Major Fuller says in his justification that he has written to Quebec for information on this subject but received no answer. I shall remove this difficulty on my return to Kingston.

Little is done to the *Moira* further than preparing the materials, as they say they wanted orders from Quebec as to lengthening her. There has not, however, been much time lost, as the weather has been very severe. I found, upon examining the vessel, that it would not be advisable to lengthen her, as, notwithstanding the process of salting, many of the timbers are rotten and must be taken out, and what is at this moment of great importance, she could not be got ready in time if lengthened. One of the chief objects in lengthening her was to increase her battery, but this we can do to a certain extent without, as by new spacing the distance of the ports one gun may be added on each side. I have therefore ordered them to proceed immediately with the repairs, and have her ready to sail the moment the lake is open, which they have promised shall be done.

There is every inducement to build the new schooner at York, as, exclusive of the argument already adduced in favor of establishing the naval yard at this place, there are the following considerations, which are of great importance at this moment: First, they have as much to do at Kingston as they can get through with at present in fitting out the *Moira* and mounting the carronades, etc. It would, therefore, extend our resources in ship building if we could at the same time carry on our work at both places. This would also have the effect of paving the way for the removal of the Marine Depot from Kingston to this place, a change greatly to be desired. The *Toronto*, having been broken up here, furnishes an immediate supply of iron work and a variety of other articles that may be worked up in the new vessel, and, in addition to what may be supplied by this means, there is a considerable department of naval stores appropriated to what is termed the civil service of the Province. This store General Brock will use as the service may require. I have gone round the harbor with the General and have examined as far as the season of the year would admit of, the different places pointed out as favorable for building a vessel, and find there will be no difficulty on that head. The General proposes putting the superintendence of the work into the hands of the person who commanded the *Toronto*, who seems to be every way qualified for the task of building and commanding the new schooner.

The officers serving in this division of the Province are in some instances extremely inefficient, and, in short, totally unfit for the situations they hold, especially the deputy-assistant quartermaster-general, and several naval officers. The former Gen. Brock has it in contemplation to remove to York as soon as Your Excellency has fixed upon a proper person to succeed him. This arrangement will be advantageous to Major Fuller, a circumstance which is not to be regretted, as there is nothing to be urged against him but his incapacity and unfitness for the situation he has been unfortunately placed in. The general has no officer here that he can recommend for the situation. Nor does he know of more than one man in the Lower Province that he thinks fit for it. The gent[lema]n the General mentions is Captain King of the artillery, and from what I have heard of his professional character and ability from other sources, I most readily unite with the General in recommending him as a fit person to succeed Major Fuller. If this measure meets Your Excellency's approbation, the sooner the appointment is made the better, as there is great need of *a man of energy and one who can be trusted at Kingston*.

This subject I shall have the honor of explaining more at large on my return.

Captain Steel, senior naval officer, has sent in his resignation, praying to retire on full pay, which I hope may be granted him, as he has been almost half a century in the service and is now in his seventy-fifth year. The next in rank to Captain Steel is Lieut. Earle, commander of the *Moira*, who is an excellent seaman, and from all I can learn every way fit to succeed Captain Steel.

I speak from my own experience, as well as from the opinion entertained of him by General Brock and others who have sailed with him.

General Brock is likewise anxious to get rid of the old Commodore on Lake Erie. This gentleman has likewise been above 50 years in the service, and is 85 years of age. The next in seniority is Lieut. Hall, who is in every respect a proper person to succeed Captain Grant. I have had the same opportunities of attaining a knowledge of his character and abilities and talents that I had of Lieut. Earle, and consider him in all respects equally deserving promotion.

These arrangements, should they meet Your Excellency's approbation, General Brock conceives will enable him to accomplish every object connected with the department, as far as those individuals are concerned, as he has a favorable opinion of Lieut. Dewar, and thinks he will meet with support equal to his wishes on both lakes.

I have communicated to General Brock an extract from the letter I had the honor to write Your Excellency from Montreal relative to the promotion and the protection of the trade of the N. West and S. West companies. The General most perfectly concurs in the ideas submitted in that letter, and has directed me to communicate to you his anxious wish that the post [at] St. Joseph might be removed to the Falls of St. Mary. In short, the General's general policy and plan of defence agrees so exactly with the ideas I had formed previously to my communicating with him that I can be at no loss in giving Your Excellency every information on that head on my return. It may not therefore be necessary to enter more into objects at present. I propose remaining here till after the House of Assembly has met, which will be about a week from this day.

I am induced to make this stay in order that I may obtain more accurate information on several points connected with our defences, etc., as more of information will then be collected from all parts of the country. I shall also have an opportunity of seeing how they go on. I do not imagine my stay at Kingston need exceed 3 or 4 days, as by building the schooner here the business of the department at the station is considerably diminished.

I have also the hope of meeting Lieut. Dewar before my departure from here, as he has obtained leave to come to York. This will afford me the opportunity of giving him more ample instructions as to the duties of the department than I could by letter. There is likewise some interesting information received respecting Detroit, which he and Col. Elliot, who is also expected, will be enabled to confirm.

It seems the Americans are collecting a vast quantity of ordnance at that post, which, with other indications, pretty clearly manifests their intentions in that quarter.

The grant of land to the Glengarry Regt. is a subject upon which General Brock intends to write you, as he fears this measure will create embarrassment and a precedent which cannot be followed up for want of lands to grant, and if not followed, there will not be a man got for the service in future.

The general has an idea that a corps upon the principles contained in the sketch I brought him might easily be procured for the defence of our frontiers without any expectation of land being held out to them, and upon the whole he thinks it a bad precedent and likely to produce discontent. The Genl. intends writing to Your Excellency. He, however, wishes me to mention the circumstances, which I accordingly do without presuming to give an opinion.

I have directed the Kingston paper to be regularly sent to the castle. Mr. Cartwright, of that place, is a striking character. This gent[lema]n has by every means in his power promoted the prosperity of the country, and has on all occasions stepped forward in support of the Gov[ernmen]t. He intends publishing a series of letters in the Kingston paper. The signature, *Falkland*.

We intend to let fly a drive official at them in the next *York Gazette*, as the Genrl. thinks it may have a good effect on both sides. We have got a detailed account from the Prophet's Camp. He has gained a glorious victory. His loss is 25 men, and his No. (number) actually engaged did not exceed 100.

(Canadian Archives, C. 728, p. 77.)

Major General Brock to Colonel Baynes.

YORK, February 12, 1812.

SIR,—I received yesterday your letter dated the 16th and 23rd ult. My attention was so much occupied with my civil duties during the stay of Captain Gray at York that some military points escaped consideration, and I shall now advert to them. As no mention is made of withdrawing the 41st from this Province, I consider the proposed movement of the 49th as intended to give me an accession of strength, and the apprehension occasioned by Captain Gray's report to the contrary is consequently dispelled. The assurance which I gave in my speech at the opening of the Legislature, of England co-operating in the defence of this Province, has infused the utmost confidence, and I have reason, at this moment, to look for the acquiescence of the two houses to every measure I may think necessary to recommend for the peace and defence of the country. A spirit has manifested itself little expected by those who conceived themselves best qualified to judge of the disposition of the members of the House of the Assembly. The most powerful opponents to Governor Gore's administration take the lead on the present occasion. I, of course, do not think it expedient to damp the ardor displayed by these once doubtful characters. Some opposed Mr. Gore, evidently from personal motives, but never forfeited the right of being numbered among the most loyal. Few, very few, I believe, were actuated by base or unworthy considerations, however mistaken they may have been on various occasions. Their character will very soon be put to a severe test. The measures which I intend to propose are:

1.—A militia supplementary act. Sir George will hear the outlines from Captain Gray.

2.—The suspension of the Habeas Corpus—a copy of the act now enforced in the Lower Province.

3.—An alien law.

4.—The offer of a reward for the better apprehension of deserters.

If I succeed in all this, I shall claim some praise, but I am not without my fears. I shall send you the militia act the moment it passes into a law. The more I consider the new provisions, the more I am satisfied (giving, of course, every proper allowance to the disposition of the people,) they are peculiarly calculated to meet the local situation of the country. I have not a musket more than will suffice to arm the active part of the militia from Kingston westward. I have therefore to request that the number of arms may be sent according to the enclosed requisition to the places therein specified on the communication, between Glengarry and Kingston. Every man capable of bearing a musket along the whole of that line ought to be prepared to act. The members of the Assembly from that part of the country are particularly anxious that some works may be thrown up as a rallying point and place of security for stores, &c., in the vicinity of Johnstown. I shall request Colonel Macdonell to examine on his return the ground which those gentlemen recommend as the best suited for that purpose. Being immediately opposite Oswegatchie, some precaution of the sort is indispensable, were it only to preserve a free communication between the two provinces. I have been made to expect the able assistance of Captain Marlow. Should he be still at Quebec, have the goodness to direct his attention on his way up to that quarter. He had better consult Colonel Fraser and Captain Gilkinson, men of sound judgment and well acquainted with the country. The militia will have, of course, to be employed on the works.

I must still press the necessity of an active, enterprising, intelligent commander being stationed on that important line of communication. I wish Colonel Ellice were here to undertake the arduous task, as it is wholly impossible that I can do so. Every assistance in my civil capacity I shall always be ready to give, and to that point my exertions must necessarily be limited. Niagara and Amherstburg will sufficiently occupy my attention. I deliver my sentiments freely, believing they will not be the less acceptable.

I discussed every point connected with Amherstburg so completely with Captain Gray that I do not find anything very essential was omitted. Colonel Macdonnel will be able probably to give us further insight as to the actual state of affairs there. He was to make every inquiry, and, as far as he was permitted to judge himself of the relative strength of Detroit. Lieut.-Colonel St. George preceded him by some days, but in such a state of mind that forbids my placing any dependence on his exertions. When I first mentioned my intention of sending him to Amherstburg he seemed diffident of his abilities, but pleased at the distinction. However, when he received his final instructions, his conduct in the presence of some officers was so very improper, and otherwise so childish, that I have since written to say that if he continued in the same disposition he was at liberty to return to Niagara: I did not order him directly back, because at this time I consider an officer of rank necessary at Amherstburg, particularly during the absence of Messrs. Elliott and Baby, who are both attending their parliamentary duties. You will imagine, after what I have stated, that it is the influence of his rank that I alone covet, and not his personal aid. He has very fortunately given timely proof that he is in no way ambitious of military command, therefore unfit for so important a command. Should it please His Excellency to place the 41st and 49th at my disposal, I propose sending the former regiment to Amherstburg, as we cannot be too strong in that quarter. I have already explained myself on that point, and Captain Gray is furnished with further arguments in support of the measure.

I have delayed to the last the mention of a project which I consider of the utmost consequence in the event of hostilities. I set out with declaring my full conviction that, unless Detroit and Michilimackinac be both in our possession immediately at the commencement of hostilities, not only the district of Amherstburg, but most probably the whole country as far as Kingston, must be evacuated. How necessary therefore to provide effectually the means of their capture. From Amherstburg it will be impossible to send a force to reduce Michilimackinac; unless we occupy completely both banks no vessel could pass the River St. Clair. What I therefore presume to suggest for His Excellency's consideration is the adoption of a project which Sir James Craig contemplated three years ago. The North-west Company undertook to transport 50 or 60 men up the Ottawa, and I make no doubt would engage again to perform the same service. If therefore a war be likely to occur at the time the canoes start from Montreal, I should recommend 40 or 50 of the 49th light company and a small detachment of artillery embarking at the same time for St. Joseph's. Should hostilities commence, the North-west Company would not object to join their strength in reduction of Michilimackinac, and should peace succeed the present wrangling the 49th detachment could be easily removed to Amherstburg.

(From Tupper's Life of Brock, pp. 147-150.)

Fourth Session of the Fifth Provincial Parliament

Met at York on the third day of February and prorogued on the sixth day of March following in the fifty-second year of the reign of George III.

ISAAC BROCK, ESQUIRE, PRESIDENT,

Anno Domini 1812.

CHAPTER III.

An Act to extend the provisions of an Act passed in the forty-eighth year of His Majesty's reign, entitled "An Act to explain, amend and reduce to one Act of Parliament the several laws now in, being for the raising and training the militia of this Province."

(Expired 1813.)

Fourth Session of Fifth Provincial Parliament.

CHAPTER VI.

An Act for granting to His Majesty a sum of money for the use of the militia of this Province. [Temporary.—£5,000 to be applied in defraying the expense of training and exercising the militia in such manner as the governor, lieutenant-governor or person administering the Government of the Province shall direct.]

Major-General Brock to Noah Freer.

YORK, February 12, 1812.

SIR,—I have directed the Assistant Deputy Commissary-General at Amherstburg to purchase 2,000 bushels of Indian corn.

Corn will be absolutely necessary in the event of war, and should peace follow the existing discussions the Indians will gladly receive it in lieu of other food. It is to be procured, if possible, on the American side, that our own stock may remain undiminished. Several agents have already arrived from the Lower Province and made large purchases of flour; if therefore our contracts are not soon concluded we shall be at the mercy of these gentlemen. I have not considered myself justified in interfering in the business of the commissariat. I have been informed very lately that my account has been charged with £20 for my portion of the expense of a canoe employed in taking Governor Gore and myself to York; perhaps His Excellency may consider this a fair public charge.

(From Tupper's Life of Brock, pp. 151-2.)

(From the Buffalo Gazette, Wednesday, February 19, 1812.)

We are sorry to state that the valuable mills of John Fanning, Esquire, of Chippawa, were destroyed by fire on Sunday evening last.

Governor Tompkins to General Porter.

ALBANY, 29th February, 1812.

DEAR SIR,—The enclosed letter is from Judge Ostrom of Utica, who wishes an appointment in the army. He was formerly a decided Federalist and represented Oneida County in the Assembly for several years. But disappointment in 1810, and disgust with the Federal party since, have caused him to avow himself a Republican for upwards of a year past. He is well qualified for a majority in the army, and I can recommend him cheerfully for that appointment. Senator Bloodgood has given me the preceding account of his politics. He considers him a Republican and well qualified for the army.

I presume you are acquainted with Judge Ostrom, for which reason, and also because I understand it has been referred to the members of this State to select a list of officers which it is to furnish for the new army, I have ventured to trouble you with this business.

By a list, which it is understood is before the Secretary of War, I learn that the names of *Benjamin Walker, William North, Samuel A. Barker, Aquila Giles* and *Solomon Van Rensselaer* are presented for the first grades of command which will be allowed to this State. Our Republicans will illy brook it that the command of an army in a contest with Great Britain should be entrusted to such men.

(MSS. of Hon. P. A. Porter.)

Major-General Brock to Sir George Prevost.

York, U. C., February 25th, 1812.

Sir,—I cannot permit Colonel Macdonell to go hence without giving Your Excellency a short account of our proceedings here. I had every reason to expect the almost unanimous support of the two branches of the Legislature to every measure Government thought necessary to recommend, but after a short trial found myself egregiously mistaken in my calculations.

The many doubtful characters in the militia made me very anxious to introduce the oath of alienation into the bill. There were twenty members present when this highly important measure was lost by the casting voice of the chairman. The great influence which the fear and number of settlers from the United States possess over the decisions of the Lower House is truly alarming, and ought by every practical means to be diminished.

To give encouragement to real subjects to settle in this Province can alone remove the evil. The consideration of the fees ought not to stand in the way of such a politic arrangement.

And should Your Excellency ultimately determine to promise some of the waste lands of the Crown to such Scotch emigrants as enlist in the Glengarry Regiment, I have no hesitation in recommending in the strongest manner the raising of a Canadian corps upon similar offers, to be hereafter disbanded and distributed among their countrymen in the vicinity of Amherstburg. Colonel Macdonell being in full possession of my sentiments on this subject, I beg leave to refer Your Excellency to him for further information.

The bill for the suspension of the Habeas Corpus, I regret to say, was likewise lost, by a very trifling majority. A strong sentiment now prevails that war is not likely to occur with the United States, which I believe tended to influence the votes of the members —I mean of such who, tho' honest, are by their ignorance easily betrayed into error.

The low ebb of their finances appears to stagger the most desperate Democrats in the States, and may possibly delay the commencement of hostilities. But should France and England continue the contest much longer, it appears to me absolutely impossible for the United States to avoid making this election, and the unfriendly disposition they have for some years evinced against England leaves little doubt as to their choice. Your Excellency, I am sensible, will excuse the freedom with which I deliver my sentiments.

Every day hostilities are retarded the greater the difficulties we shall have to encounter. The Americans are at this moment busily engaged in raising six companies of rangers for the express purpose of overawing the Indians, and are besides collecting a regular force at Vincennes, probably with the view of reinforcing Detroit; indeed report states the arrival of a large force at Fort Wayne, intended for the former garrison. Their intrigues among the different tribes are carried on openly and with the utmost activity, and as no expense is spared it may reasonably be supposed that they do not fail of success. Divisions are thus uninterruptedly sowed among our Indian friends and the minds of many estranged from our interests. Such must inevitably be the consequence of our present inert and neutral proceedings in regard to them.

It ill becomes me to determine how long true policy requires that the restrictions now imposed upon the Indian Department ought to continue, but this I will venture to assert that each day the officers are restrained from interfering in the concerns of the Indians, each time they advise peace and withhold the accustomed supply of ammunition, their influence will diminish, till at length they lose it altogether. It will then become a question whether that country can be maintained.

I find that ever since the departure of Priest Burk from Sandwich the £50 per annum paid from the military chest to that gentleman has been withheld, on what account I have not been able to ascertain. The person now in office is highly spoken of, and as several gentlemen of the Catholic persuasion have applied to me to intercede with Your Excellency to renew the allowance, I presume to submit the case to your indulgent consideration.

(Canadian Archives, C. 676, p. 92.)

Major-General Brock to Sir George Prevost.

YORK, March 9, 1812.

SIR,—As the transactions which have occurred in the House of Assembly in regard to the Chief Justice may be represented at Quebec in a manner to excite wrong impressions, I deem it proper to furnish Your Excellency with a summary of the whole business.

The inordinate power assumed by the House of Assembly is truly alarming, and ought to be resisted, otherwise the most tyrannical system will assuredly be pursued by men who suffer themselves to be led by a desperate faction that stop at nothing to gratify their personal resentment.

Mr. Nichol is a gentleman of education, and who in the district in which he resides has done essential good in opposing the democratic measures of a Mr. Willcocks and his vile coadjutors. The palpable injustice committed against his person by dragging him at midnight, without any previous warning, one hundred miles, from his home to the bar of the House, and then committing him to gaol under the most frivolous pretenses, has greatly alarmed the most thinking part of the community. Efforts are to be made by several respectable characters to get into the next Assembly, but such is the spirit which unfortunately prevails that I much fear they will be foiled in their attempt. I was inclined to dismiss the House before the members passed such harsh resolutions against the Chief Justice, but his friends recommended that they should be allowed to proceed without interruption.

(From Tupper's Life of Brock, pp. 156-7.)

Colonel Baynes to Major General Brock.

QUEBEC, March 10, 1812.

SIR,—I regret to find by your late letters to Sir George Prevost that your expectations from your Legislature have not been realized to the extent of your well grounded hopes. Sir George, who is well versed in the fickle and intractable disposition of public assemblies, feels more regret than disappointment. He has a very delicate card to play with his House of Assembly here, who would fain keep up the farce of being highly charmed and delighted with his amiable disposition and affable manners. They have even gone the length of asserting that these traits in his character have afforded them the most entire confidence that in his hands the Alien Act would not be abused. They have, however, taken the precaution of stripping it of its very essence and spirit, while last year they passed it without a division, when Sir James [Craig,] on whose mild and affable disposition they did not pretend to rely, told them that it could only alarm such as were conscious of harboring seditious designs. They have passed an amendment to the militia bill which, though not affording all that was required, is still a material point gained : 2000 men are to be balloted to serve for three months in two successive summers. One of their strongest objections was the apprehension of the Canadians contracting military habits and enlisting into the service.

Sir George has directed me to inform you that he will be ready to render you any assistance in his power to strengthen the Upper Province, but that unless reinforcements arrive from England, (in which case you may depend upon having a due proportion put under your immediate command) his means of doing so are very limited. His Excellency is not sanguine in his expectations of receiving reinforcements this summer; on the contrary, the appearance of hostilities beginning to abate at Washington, and the pledge held out in the Prince Regent's speech, of supporting with energy the contest in Spain and Portugal, are likely to prevent more troops being seen in this quarter unless a more urgent necessity of doing so should appear. I will not comment on American politics, in which we all appear to agree, that the deep-rooted jealousy and hatred of that people must in the end lead to hostilities, and that it behooves us not to lose sight of an event which if not prepared to meet we shall find more difficult to repel. Under this impression, Sir George is disposed to promote the several plans you have recommended to him relating to the general line of conduct you would wish to adopt in defence of the important Province committed to your charge. If no additional force be sent out he will send up the strong detachment of the 41st, composed of uncommonly fine young men and in very good order. The General has it also in view to send you a strong detachment of the Newfoundland regiment, selecting their seamen and marine artificers who will be most useful in the proposed works to be carried on at York, and here I am apprehensive that the means of augmenting your strength must be bounded unless the Glengarry levy can be rapidly formed; and Sir George is sanguine in his expectations of its being speedily placed upon a respectable footing; in that case it could occupy Kingston and that line of communication between the Provinces which you deem so essential to be guarded. This corps will have the very great advantage of starting with a better selected body of officers of any Fencible regiment in Canada. I hope you will feel inclined to bring forward Shaw as one of your captains, as without your countenance I fear he will find it an arduous task to provide for himself and his brother. The uniform of the corps is to be green, like that of the 95th Rifles.

Sir George expressed himself very sensible of the policy of the line of conduct you would wish to pursue respecting the Indians, but as other considerations of the greatest political delicacy are so minutely interwoven with them, and as the American government are already inclined to view every transaction with those people with a jealous and suspicious eye, he would recommend the utmost caution and forbearance, lest a different line of conduct might tend to increase the irritation between the two governments, which it is evidently the wish of Great Britain to allay.

* * * * * * * * * * *

(From Tupper's Life of Brock, p. 159.)

(From the Buffalo Gazette, Wednesday, March 11, 1812.)

What does it mean ? By a law of Upper Canada lately passed the militia of that Province are to turn out and drill six days in every month.

General Order.

Headquarters, April 2d, 1812.

The Commander-in-Chief is required by the President of the United States to order into service for the defence and protection of the frontiers of the State detachments of the militia thereof, to be stationed at Niagara, Oswego and near the mouth of the Black River. Major-General Widrig will, therefore, without delay, detach from his division (excluding the Onondaga brigade) six hundred men, including officers, and will organize them into eight companies, will assign the captains and subalterns, and will have them ready to march at a moment's warning.

He will also report to the Commander-in-Chief one lieutenant colonel and two majors whom he can recommend to be assigned to the command of the detachment. Should any company of artillery or part thereof exceeding thirty men, uniformed and equipped, volunteer their services they will be accepted and organized as part of the above mentioned detachment and will be equipped with field pieces, implements and ammunition by the State. The above mentioned detachment will be stationed near the mouth of the Black River. Major-General Widrig will also require Brigadier-General Ellis to furnish from his brigade, and have in readiness to march to Oswego at a moment's warning, two companies of infantry, or one company of artillery of not less than forty men and one company of infantry of one hundred men, including officers; the latter to have one captain, two lieutenants and one ensign, or if there be two companies of infantry of the ordinary number, then each company to have one captain, one lieutenant and one ensign, to be assigned by General Ellis. The places of rendezvous for the detachments from each brigade are to be fixed by the respective Brigadier-Generals and reported to the respective Major-Generals.

Major-General King will detach from the Madison and Cortlandt brigades of infantry two hundred and fifty men, to be in readiness to march to Oswego whenever orders to that effect may be received, and to organize them into three companies, with one captain, one lieutenant and one ensign to each company. The detachments from Onondaga, Madison and Cortland Counties will, upon their arrival at Oswego, be formed into one corps, to be commanded by a field officer whom the Commander-in-Chief will assign for that purpose.

Major General Hall will forthwith detach from the Seventh division of infantry under his command six hundred men, including officers, and will organize them into eight companies and assign captains and subalterns to command the companies. The detachment from his division will be directed to rendezvous in such parcels and at such places as he shall designate, and will from thence proceed to the post of Niagara. Lieut.-Col. Philetus Swift will take command of the detachment from the Seventh division. The commandant of the Genesee brigade will detach one major, and the commandant of Niagara brigade one other major, who, together with Lieut.-Col. Swift, will compose the field officers of the detachment. The regimental staff will be selected by the commandant of the detachment and be reported to the Major-General.

The officers who are charged with the execution of this general order are instructed to be prompt and vigilant in its execution and to encourage by all lawful means volunteers for the detachment. The Commander-in-Chief cherishes a lively hope that the patriotic and brave spirit which pervades the divisions from which the above detachments are to be taken will immediately fill the required quota with volunteers.

Volunteers under and pursuant to the Act of Congress of the 6th of February, authorizing the President to accept the services of volunteers, will be preferred, and the general and field officers will accept such volunteers accordingly as part of the detachments.

By order of the Commander in Chief.

ANTHONY LAMB, Aid-de-Camp.

(Tompkins Papers, New York State Library.)

Governor Tompkins to Colonel Philetus Swift.

ALBANY, 2d April, 1812.

DR. SIR,—Perhaps you did not expect the evening that you left Albany that I should so soon have occasion to accept the offer of your services. The enclosed papers will make you acquainted with the proceedings which I have been directed by the President to pursue in relation to the detachment of the militia. You may consider yourself in service from the day of the receipt of this letter, and will consult with General Hall and exert yourself to get volunteers or others enrolled and ready to march whenever ordered, which will be the moment the contractors arrive and proceed westward to supply provisions, which will be in a day or two.

You are at liberty when the detachment shall be ordered to rendezvous to call on the keepers of the arsenals at Canandaigua and Batavia for arms and ammunition to supply such of the volunteers and others as may be deficient, and to show the keepers this letter as evidence of your authority so to do. You will receipt to them whatever they may deliver.

Col. Burnet is appointed Brigadier-General, which will satisfy him why he was not assigned to the command of Lt. Col'cy: Major

Reddington is appointed Lt.-Col. in the stead of Col. Stanley, resigned. I will, if possible, send their commissions by the messenger whom I have employed to convey the General Orders and other papers to the respective officers.

P. S.—I should think Major Gansen or Major Sutherland of Genesee would be a good appointment for that county.

I have this moment received a line from the War Department, saying that volunteers under the Act of the 6th of February last, authorizing the President to accept volunteers, would be preferred. If I do not procure a copy of that Act to transmit by this conveyance I will forward it speedily by mail.

I have procured a copy and have had it printed with a caption for volunteering. I am in hopes you and the majors can obtain volunteers sufficient for the detachment, and therefore send you several copies.

(Tompkins Papers, New York State Library.)

Governor Tompkins to Lieut.-Col. George Fleming.

(Undated.)

(2nd April, 1812?)

SIR,—I had recommended to the committee on the defence of the frontiers to provide amongst other things for the appointment of a Commissary of Military Stores for the Western District, with a salary of 750 or 1000 Doll's. They unanimously agreed to that among other things and reported a bill accordingly, which was kept back, perhaps designedly, until I found it my duty to prorogue the Legislature. The bill will undoubtedly pass in May, when it is my intention, if the Council approve it and you consent, to avail the State of your experience and knowledge in military science.

In the meantime I am desirous of availing the State of your usefulness in another way. I have received a requisition from the President to detach and station at Niagara, Oswego and the mouth of Black River portions of the militia. The number to be stationed at Oswego will consist of 400, among whom may be one company of artillery. I am desirous that you should take the command of the last mentioned detachment, and for that purpose have enclosed you an appointment as my aid, with the rank of lieutenant-colonel.

Should this appointment and the consequent command meet your acceptance, you may consider yourself in service from the receipt of this letter, and may visit and make the necessary arrangements with Genl. Ellis of Onondaga Hollow, Genl. Knapp of Cortlandt County, and Genl. Hurd of Cazenovia, from whose brigades the Oswego detachment is to be taken.

Should you accept this command you will please to advise me of your steps and of the places at which communications from the Adjutant Genl., from the contractor for provisions, or from myself, will reach you.

A copy of the President's requisition, of my Genl. Order thereon, and of my letters to Major-Genls. King and Widrig, within whose division the three above mentioned brigades are situated, are enclosed for your information.

My General Orders refer to a commandant of the Oswego detachment to be assigned by me. You may shew the respective generals your commission and this letter as evidence of your being authorized and assigned as such commandant.

P. S.—I am just advised by the Secretary of War that volunteers under the Act passed 6th Feby. last will be preferred. I will send a copy of that Act by the first opportunity, if I do not get it in season to accompany this letter. Those of the detachment who may not be equipped and supplied with muskets, &c., from the Onondaga arsenal, you will give your receipt for what is received there and shew this letter as your authority for requiring them.

The Act and caption for volunteering are enclosed. The inducements contained in the Act, together with the consideration that young men who acquire a little knowledge of tactics will probably be selected to officer the army, will, I hope, produce a sufficient number of volunteers. Their tour of duty will not probably be arduous nor exceed two months.

(Tompkins' Papers, New York State Library.)

Sir George Prevost to Lord Liverpool.

QUEBEC, 3rd April, 1812.

No. 37.

MY LORD,—Before Your Lordship receives this you will have learned Henry's treachery. From Mr. Henry's residence in this country, his religion, his thorough acquaintance with the Canadian character and language, and above all his deep resentment against its government, Bonaparte may give him a favorable reception with a view of keeping his talents in reserve. I think the next measure of hostility Mr. Madison will practice will be to cause a declaration of war to be laid upon the tables of Congress. I have therefore addressed the general officers commanding in the Provinces, recommending the utmost caution and prudence in their intercourse with the United States. I enclose an extract from my letter to Major General Brock, that to Sir John Sherbrooke contains the same except as respects the fort of Detroit.

(Canadian Archives, Q. 117-2, p. 181.)

Extract of a Letter from Sir George Prevost to Major General Brock, dated at Quebec, 31st March, 1812.

I have carefully examined Lieutenant Colonel Macdonnel's report on the American fort at Detroit, written at your desire, from information he had received during a residence of a few days in the vicinity. Whatever temptations may offer to induce you to depart from a system strictly defensive, I must pointedly request that, under the existing circumstances of our relations with the Government of the United States, you will not allow them to lead you into any measure bearing the character of offence, even should a declaration of war be laid on the table of Congress by the President's influence, because I am informed by our Minister at Washington there prevails throughout the United States a great unwillingness to enter upon hostilities, and also because the apparent neglect at Detroit might be but a *bait* to tempt us to an act of aggression, in its effects uniting parties, strengthening the power of the Government of that country, and affording that assistance to the raising of men for the augmentation of the American army without which their ability to raise one additional regiment is now questioned. You are, nevertheless, to persevere in your preparations for defence, and in such arrangements as may, upon a change in affairs, enable you to carry any disposable part of your force against the common enemy.

(Canadian Archives, Q. 117-2. p. 183.)

Major-General Brock to Lieut.-Col. Robert Nichol, Commanding 2d Regiment Norfolk Militia.

YORK, April 8, 1812.

SIR,—The power which is vested in the person administering the Government by the amended Act of the militia, passed the last session of the Provincial Parliament, of forming two flank companies to be taken indiscriminately from the battalions, being limited to the end of the ensuing session, would almost deter me from incurring public expense upon a system which will cease to operate before its utility and efficiency can well be ascertained.

But, being anxious at this important crisis to organize an armed force with a view of meeting future exigencies, and to demonstrate by practical experience the degree of facility with which the militia may be trained for service, I have to request you to adopt immediate measures for forming and completing among such men as voluntarily offer to serve, two companies, not to exceed one captain, two subalterns, two sergeants, one drummer and thirty-five rank and file, each in the regiment under your command.

You will have the goodness to recommend two captains whom you conceive the best qualified to undertake this important duty; the nominating of subalterns is left to your discretion.

Such other regiments as are conveniently situated to receive military instruction shall have an opportunity afforded them of shewing their ardor in the public service, which cannot fail of creating a laudable emulation among the different corps.

Assisted by your zeal, prudence and intelligence, I entertain the pleasing hope of meeting with very considerable success, and of being able to establish the sound policy of rendering permanent to the end of the present war a mode of military instruction little burdensome to individuals and every way calculated to secure a powerful internal defence against hostile aggression.

Printed rules and regulations for your future guidance are herewith forwarded. The most simple and at the same time the most useful movements have been selected for the practice of the militia.

Experience has shown the absolute necessity of adopting every possible precaution to preserve in a proper state the arms issued to the militia, and of guarding against the heavy defalcations which have heretofore occurred.

You will make application to the officer commanding at Fort Erie for the number of arms and accoutrements wanting to complete the men actually engaged to serve in the flank companies, and that officer will be instructed to comply with your requisition upon your transmitting to him duplicate receipts, one of which is to be forwarded to headquarters, that you become responsible for the articles delivered to your order. At the same time the most liberal construction will be given to any representation accounting for such contingencies as are incidental to the service.

(From Life and Correspondence of Major General Sir Isaac Brock by Ferdinand Brock Tupper, London, 1847, p. 163.)

Sir George Prevost to Lord Liverpool.

QUEBEC, 14th April, 1812.

No. 38.

MY LORD,—Considering a naval force properly constructed the most efficient and cheapest mode of defence, I have gradually increased the naval force on the lakes, and I have ordered five companies of the Royal Newfoundland Regiment to proceed to Upper Canada as soon as the season will permit, to be employed afloat, being men accustomed to boats and vessels.

I am convinced that Kingston is a very exposed and unfit situation for our vessels to winter, and I propose the removal of the naval establishment by degrees to York.

(Canadian Archives. Q. 117-2, p. 194.)

Sir George Prevost to Lord Liverpool.

QUEBEC, 20th April, 1812.
No. 40.

MY LORD,—

The recent passing of an Embargo Act in Congress, the orders issued for the march of 1,600 men to reinforce the American positions on Lakes Erie and Ontario and the River St. Lawrence indicate an inevitable disposition for hostilities, which have induced me to accept the services of 500 Canadian youth, to be formed into a corps of light infantry or voltigeurs.

As soon as the organization of the militia is *en train*, I propose visiting Upper Canada to concert with Major-General Brock a general plan of offensive and defensive operations in the event of the democratic spirit of the United States having put the dispute beyond the bounds of accommodation.

(Canadian Archives. Q. 117-2, p. 214.)

Mr. Augustus J. Foster, His Majesty's Minister at Washington, to Lord Castlereagh.

WASHINGTON, April 21st, 1812.
No. 25.

MY LORD,—I have received Your Lordship's despatch No. 1, that I should make diligent inquiries into the actual military establishment of the United States in the different arms, and transmit such plans of the forts, military posts, &c., as I could secure. I expect to be able to forward a complete statement by the May packet.

The militia in the northern, and particularly in the eastern States, are well trained and armed. The General, who has been lately appointed Commander-in-Chief, (Dearborn), is a heavy unwieldy-looking man, who was a major in the American war and was a prisoner in Canada. He has apparently accepted his appointment with great reluctance, having hesitated till within a few days. His military reputation does not stand very high, nor does that of Mr. Thomas Pinckney, the second Major General.

General Dearborn and his Aid-de-Camp, Mr. Melvin, who was

a banker in Paris, and when nominated as a Deputy Commissary was not confirmed in the Senate on account of the badness of his character, have left this city for Albany to superintend the preparations in that quarter, where 1600 militia have been ordered out, 500 to be stationed at Niagara, 500 nearly opposite Kingston, and 600 at Champlain. It was reported that Governor Hull would succeed Mr. Eustis as Secretary of War, but he has been made a brigadier-general and proceeded to his Government, where his first object will be to withdraw to Detroit a remote garrison of 60 men stationed on the southern shore of Lake Michigan [at Chicago] and are said to be in great danger of being dislodged by the Indians. Mr. Lewis is confirmed as Quartermaster-General. He is son-in-law of Mr. Livingstone, formerly Minister to France, and was himself once Governor of New York and possesses considerable popularity in the State.

There is a cannon foundry near here, from which 100 cannon have been lately sent to New York, many of them cast-iron. They have 50 more now on hand. I am told that a quantity of harness for upwards 1,000 horses is making expedition to New York, and that considerable supplies are daily sending to Albany, the contractors having shipped for that place every barrel of beef and pork in the market.

Colonel Porter has obtained for his brother the contract for supplying the troops, which, it is said, will be very profitable to him. Colonel Porter, who was said to be very much against the war measures towards the third month of the session, and was considered as having abandoned Mr. Madison's party for that of Mr. Clinton, is now said to have changed his line of policy once more. He is absent from Congress, and is now reported to be endeavoring to save Mr. Madison's influence in the northern part of the State.

. . . .

(Canadian Archives. Q. 119. p. 265.)

(From the Buffalo Gazette, Tuesday, April 21, 1812.)

A Speck of War.

To the Editors of the Buffalo Gazette:

GENTLEMEN,—To prevent the erroneous impression which exaggerated reports may have in the public mind relative to an unauthorized circumstance which took place yesterday, we enclose the correspondence on the subject, and request you will have the goodness to insert it in your first *Gazette* published after the receipt hereof.

We are, &c.,
THOS. DICKSON,
R. GRANT,
JAMES KERBY.

Messrs. Salisburys, Buffalo.

Messrs. Thomas Dickson, R. Grant, James Kerby, William Robertson:

GENTLEMEN,—The inhabitants of this part of the country have thought advisable to meet together to make some preparation against attacks of Indians or vagabonds that may take place (which we have reason to believe we have sufficient grounds for so doing.) While in the peaceable manner we were doing our business without any intention of insult or menace to any person or persons on your side, some bad disposed man or men discharged three musket shots from the door of John Smith in your village, no doubt with a view to insult our people, one of which balls struck within eighteen inches of a person here.

We think this highly improper at this time, and presume any good man on your side will think with us, and that you will take every measure to prevent the like again, as, if repeated, the fire will certainly be returned, and we know not where it will end.

We remain, &c.,
BENJAMIN BARTON,
RUFUS SPALDING,
JOSHUA FAIRBANKS.

Lewiston, April 17, 1812.

QUEENSTON, 18th April, 1812.

GENTLEMEN,—We have to acknowledge the receipt of your letter of yesterday, and regret that the conduct of an inconsiderate boy at this place in firing across the river should have caused an uneasiness or drawn from you (previous to any communication with us as to our knowledge of the circumstance) the intimation that if repeated "the fire will certainly be returned" from your side.

That disposition which unanimously exists here for the promotion of uninterrupted harmony between the countries has induced the Magistrates in Quarter Sessions to take immediate steps to punish the offender, and in consequence he has been this day bound under recognizance to answer at the next assizes for the offence.

We trust this example will be followed with equal promptitude and a similar disposition on your part should any like instance occur.

We respectfully are,
THOMAS DICKSON,
R. GRANT,
JAMES KERBY.

To Messrs Benjamin Barton, Rufus Spalding, Joshua Fairbanks.
(File in Buffalo Public Library.)

Major General Brock to Sir George Prevost.

YORK, April 22, 1812

SIR,—I had the honor to receive Your Excellency's letter, dated the 24th ultimo, and I entreat you to believe that no act within my control shall afford the Government of the United States a legitimate pretext to add to a clamor which has been so artfully raised against England.

We have received the account of the removal of the embargo, and that the most rigorous measures have already been adopted to prevent the least infringement of it upon the Niagara River. Armed men in colored clothes are continually patrolling along the shore. These troops are stated to have recently arrived, but I have not been able to ascertain whether they belong to the new levy or to the militia. They are reported to amount to about 300. Colonel Procter has doubtless written fully on the subject, but unfortunately the letters by some negligence were left at Niagara. The accounts, which have reached me, are not therefore so satisfactory as could be wished. An idle boy is stated to have wantonly fired with ball at the guard opposite Queenston, and it appears that the Americans were guilty of a similar outrage, by firing during the night into a room in which a woman was sitting. Luckily no mischief followed. Being detained here upon civil business, I have sent Captain Glegg over to see how matters stand and to arrange with civil and military authorities the best means of preventing a recurrence of a practice which may easily lead to serious consequences. I hope to be at Niagara myself the day after to-morrow.

I beg leave to assure Your Excellency that I receive with no small degree of pride the praise bestowed on my endeavors to improve the militia system of this Province, and as the bill underwent some alterations after the departure of Colonel McDonnell, particularly in limiting its operation to the end of the ensuing session, I shall have the honor to forward for Your Excellency's information the law as now enforced. I have by partial and gentle means already commenced to give it operation, and make not the least doubt that a sufficient number will be found ready to volunteer to complete the flank companies, and I here beg leave to parade the flank companies six times in each month, but, as no provision is made for remunerating the men, I presume to submit for Your Excellency's indulgent consideration that the commissaries be instructed to issue rations for the number actually present at exercise. These companies, I expect, will be composed of the best description of inhabitants, who in most cases will have to go a great distance to attend parade, and unless this liberal provision be allowed will be liable to heavy expense or be subject to considerable privations. According to my present arrangements, the number embodied will not exceed 700, and when the companies are completed throughout the provinces they must be calculated at 1,800, and as during harvest and the winter months few or no parades will take place, the total expense attending the measure can be of no material consequence in a pecuniary point of view, and may in a political light be productive at this juncture of considerable benefit.

I have likewise to request that such portion of clothing as Your Excellency can conveniently spare from the King's stores may be forwarded to enable me to clothe such companies as are the most likely to be called upon duty.

I am anxious to hear the real object of the embargo; should it be directed solely against England the probability is that it leads to a war; but should France be included in its operation nothing of the kind need be dreaded.

In the expectation of having the honor of seeing Your Excellency shortly at York, I limit for the present the works of the military artificers at this place in preparing a temporary magazine for the reception of the spare powder at Fort George and Kingston, and the excavation of the ditch for the proposed fortifications of the spot on which the government house stands.

I transmit for Your Excellency's perusal a detailed account of the transactions which led to the unjustifiable censure passed by the House of Assembly upon Chief Justice Scott. It is written by Mr. Nichol himself, and the warmth with which he has expressed his indignation at the wanton exercise of a power yet undefined, as far as regards this Province, is not therefore surprising. I am convinced that whenever the business is brought legally before the judges they will refuse to sanction the enormous power, under the name of privilege, which the House arrogates to itself. The executive will in that case be placed in a very awkward predicament. Mr. Nichol, having commenced civil actions against the speaker and sergeant-at-arms for false imprisonment, will, should he succeed in obtaining damages, bring the question with double force on the tapis. The violence and ignorance which in all probability will mark the proceedings of the House cannot fail of producing a dissolution. I apply forcibly to ministers for instructions, but should they be contrary to the opinion which the judges of the Court of King's Bench have formed of the law, I am led to believe they will not influence the members; therefore one of two alternatives must be resorted to, either the appointment of more docile judges or the decision of the question by a British Act of Parliament. I trust, for the tranquillity and prosperity of the Province, that the latter mode may be preferred. I have thus freely, and perhaps with rather too much haste to be sufficiently explicit, stated the difficulties which in all likelihood I shall have to encounter at the next meeting of the legislature. Should the effect of the embargo appear to be directed solely at Great Britain, I shall avail myself of the confidence placed in me and order the purchase of horses to enable the car brigade to act in case of necessity. This being a service which requires infinite trouble and practice to bring to any degree of perfection, cannot be too soon attended to.

(From Tupper's Life of Brock, pp. 167-170.)

Major General Brock to Mr. Noah Freer, Military Secretary to the Governor General.

YORK, April 23, 1812.

SIR,—I transmit herewith for the information of the Commander of the Forces a letter received from the Earl of Liverpool, authorizing an increase of £200 per annum to the salary of Colonel Claus, Deputy Superintendent of the Indian affairs, to commence from the first of January last.

The inconvenience to which the public service has already been exposed, owing to a scarcity of specie; the likelihood of the evil being increased by the operation of the embargo, and the almost total impossibility in the event of war of getting a sufficient supply to defray the ordinary expenses of Government, have led me to consider the best means of obviating so serious a difficulty. And having consulted with some of the principal merchants as to the practicability of introducing a paper currency with any probability of success, I think myself warranted in stating that such an arrangement would, particularly in the event of war, be generally supported throughout the Province. The old inhabitants understand perfectly the circulation of paper as a substitute for specie, and having been formerly in the habit of receiving the notes of private individuals, they would not hesitate taking the more certain security of Government, especially if convinced that payment could not be made in any other way.

The commissaries ought to be instructed to receive this paper as cash, giving bills in return on Quebec. It is supposed that the circulation of 10 or £15,000 would answer every purpose. No note under 5s. or above £10 should be issued. The accompanying letter from Mr. Selby, the Receiver-General, will fully elucidate the business.

I have to acknowledge the receipt of your letter of the 1st of April. The Commissary-General will, doubtless, have been apprized that his instructions to Mr. McGill arrived in time to supersede those he received from me. Too great dependence ought not to be placed on the surplus of the several species of stores at the different posts. I have reason to think that at Amherstburg nearly the entire excess will be found damaged and unserviceable. Being desirous to ascertain the actual state of the stores at that post, I directed a month ago a regular survey to be taken of every article, and the moment I receive the report it shall be forwarded to head-quarters.

Flour has risen to eight dollars and one-half per barrel. The effect of the embargo is not yet felt. Upwards of 40,000 barrels, the produce of the south of Lake Ontario, will be kept by it from the Montreal market.

(From Tupper's Life of Brock. pp. 170-1.)

(*From the Buffalo Gazette, Tuesday, April 28, 1812.*)

We understand a company of VOLUNTEERS from Batavia have arrived at Lewiston.

On Tuesday the 21st inst. upwards of 170 men VOLUNTEERED their services to form two companies in this village, to act when an emergency should call for.

(File in Buffalo Public Library.)

Sir George Prevost to Major General Brock.

QUEBEC, April 30, 1812.

SIR,—I have just heard from Mr. Foster that the Secretary at War at Washington has transmitted orders to Governor Tompkins of New York, to send 500 of the State Militia to Niagara: 500 to the mouth of the Black River opposite to Kingston, and 600 to Champlain, in consequence of the hostile appearances in Canada. Mr. Foster is of opinion the Government of the United States calculates that something will happen on the part of these men to produce a quarrel with the British troops, which may lead to retaliation on both sides and occasion hostilities to commence, as in this way alone it seems thought an unjust war can be forced on the American people, who are represented as really averse to it. We must therefore use every effort in our power to prevent any collision from taking place between our forces and the American.

I have also received information that the American garrison at Fort Chicago, not exceeding 60 men, has been ordered to Detroit in consequence of apprehensions from the Indians.
(From Tupper's Life of Brock, pp. 172-3.)

Thomas Barclay, H. M. Consul-General at New York, to Sir George Prevost.
(Extract.)

NEW YORK, May 5th, 1812.

You may consider war as inevitable. It will take place in July at the latest. Upper Canada will be the first object. Military stores of all kinds and provisions are daily sending from hence towards the lines: 13,500 militia, the quota of this State, are drawn and ordered to be in readiness at a moment's notice.
(Canadian Archives. Q. 117-2. p. 311.)

(From the Buffalo Gazette, Tuesday, May 5, 1812.)

The troops from Batavia, who lately volunteered their services to defend our frontiers from "nocturnal incursions." stationed at Lewiston, have evacuated that town and returned to their respective homes.
(File in Buffalo Public Library.)

From Colonel Baynes to Major-General Brock.

QUEBEC, May 14, 1812.

SIR,—I have great satisfaction in telling you that I have reported the Glengarry Light Infantry more than complete to the establishment of 400 rank and file, and have received Sir George Prevost's commands to recruit for a higher establishment: indeed the quotas the officers have suggested to fulfill will nearly amount to double that number, and from the very great exertions I have no doubt of succeeding by the end of this year. Two officers have divided Nova Scotia and New Brunswick for their hunting ground, and are permitted to receive Acadians, and Lieutenant Ronald McDonnell of the Canadians proceeds in a few days to Pictou and the Highland Settlements on the coast and gulf. He is an officer that appears eminently qualified for that service, and he is sanguine that the proffer of lands in the Scotch settlements of Upper Canada will induce great numbers to enter. I am assured from various channels that the men I have got are generally young, rather too much so, and of a good description, there being very few Yankees among them.

. . . .

Sir George has announced his intention of recommending Battersby to be Lieutenant-Colonel of the Glengarry corps, and ordered him to take command of the recruits assembled at Three Rivers. Your Major of Brigade (Thomas Evans) will be recommended to succeed to his majority in the King's Regiment.

(From Tupper's Life of Brock, pp. 172-3.)

Major General Brock to Sir George Prevost.

YORK, U. C., May 15th, 1812.

SIR,—I have this day been honored with Your Excellency's confidential communication dated the 30th ulto.

I have long since thought that nothing but the public voice restrained the United States Government from commencing direct hostilities, and it is but reasonable to expect that they will seek every opportunity to inflame the minds of the people against England, in order to bring them the more readily into their measures. It will be my study to guard against any event that can give them any just cause of complaint, but the proximity of the two countries will in all probability produce collisions, which, however accidentally brought about, will be represented as so many acts of aggressions. It would not surprise me if their first attempt to create irritation was the seizing the islands in the channel, to which both countries lay claim. Such was represented to Sir James Craig on a former occasion to be their intention.

In addition to the force specified by Your Excellency, I understand that six companies of the Ohio militia are intended for Detroit. Our interest with the Indians will materially suffer in consequence of these preparations being allowed to proceed with impunity. I have always considered that the reduction of Detroit would be the signal of a cordial co-operation on their part, and if we are not in sufficient force to effect this object no reliance ought to be placed on the Indians.

About forty regulars were last week added to the garrison of Niagara, and by all accounts barracks are to be immediately constructed at Black Rock, almost opposite Fort Erie, for a large force.

I returned three days ago from an excursion to Fort Erie, the Grand River, where the Indians of the Six Nations are settled, and back by the head of the lake. Every gentleman with whom I had an opportunity of conversing assured me that an exceeding good disposition prevailed among the people. The flank companies in the districts in which they have been established were instantly completed with volunteers, and, indeed, an almost unanimous disposition to serve is daily manifested. I shall proceed to extend this system now that I have ascertained the people are so well disposed, but my means are very limited.

I propose detaching one hundred rank and file of the 41st to Amherstburg almost immediately.

(Canadian Archives, C. 676, p. 112.)

Sir George Prevost to the Earl of Liverpool.
(Extract.)

No. 46.

QUEBEC, 18th May, 1812.

MY LORD,—In obedience to the command signified to me in Your Lordship's despatch No. 7, of the 13th February, I now have the honor to report upon the military position of His Majesty's North American Provinces and the means of defending them.

. . . .

Fort George is a temporary field work now repairing to render it tenable, but in its most improved state it cannot make much resistance against an enemy in considerable force. The garrison consists of a captain's command of artillery and about 400 men of the 41st, the whole under Colonel Procter. The militia in the neighborhood does not exceed 2,000 nominal men. At Fort Erie there is a captain's command of the 41st, and at Chippawa a subaltern's. The American posts opposite are Fort Niagara, Fort Schlosser, Black Rock, and Buffalo Creek. In event of hostilities it would be highly advantageous to gain possession of Fort Niagara to secure the navigation of the river.

York has a good harbour, and is best adapted for a depot for military stores when converted into a post of defence, and also for a dock yard. The militia is computed at 1500 men.

Kingston, at the head of boat navigation of the St. Lawrence, is contiguous to a very flourishing settlement on the American frontier, and exposed to a sudden attack, which, if successful, would cut off communication between the Canadas and deprive us of our naval resources. The garrison consists of four companies of the 10th Royal Veteran Battalion, under Major McPherson. The militia are about 1,500. The Americans have posts in the vicinity, not only opposite, but above and below, with good harbours, which are open to the resources of a very populous country. In event of war this post is indispensably necessary for preservation of communication to establish a strong post for regulars and militia to secure the navigation of the St. Lawrence above the rapids to Lake Ontario.

The total number of militia in Upper Canada is calculated at 11,000 men, of which it might not be prudent to arm more than 4,000.

(Canadian Archives, Freer Papers, 1812-13, p. 3.)

(From the Buffalo Gazette, Tuesday, May 19, 1812.)

A company of the 100,000 men, from the town of Hamburg, under the command of Major Whaley, arrived in this village last evening on their march for Lewiston.

Other companies are on their way from the different parts of the Genesee county for the frontier.

Colonel Swift of Ontario County, who is appointed to command on the frontiers, arrived in this village on Sunday last.

Perhaps no recruiting regiment in this country ever met with so great success as that of the Glengarry Sharp Shooters. This regiment has had enlisting orders about five weeks, and it is said they have already enlisted about 500 men. The Newfoundland and Canadian Fencible Regiments are also said to have improved by this uncommon spirit for enlistment, but, altho' their success has been uncommonly good it does not in any shape equal that of the Glengarry Regiment.—*Montreal Courier.*

(File in Buffalo Public Library.)

Major D. Noon, Dy. Q. M. G. of State of New York, to General P. B. Porter, Q. M. General of that State.

OGDENSBURG, 20th May, 1812.

DEAR SIR,—Since I had the honor of addressing you last I have made the necessary arrangements at Sackett's Harbor and at Gravelly Point to accommodate two hundred and seventy men at each place, if required. Captain Wolsy of the U. S. brig *Oneida* was so good as to give up his barracks, which were occupied by his crew during the winter, until the first of November next. This by some improvement will make very comfortable barracks for the present, and give time to build others, if required. I am also happy to inform you that since my arrival at this place I have been able to make a purchase of a range of buildings which was formerly occupied as a ropewalk, having an excellent frame, for the term of three years from the first of July next, at which time the lease from the first purchaser expires, subject to a small ground rent a year.

It is with great difficulty I could get any ground near the village, and the State owns none, from the bad conduct the inhabitants say of the last soldiers quartered here—I would rather say from the great desire the inhabitants have to smuggle without the aid of soldiers. The whole is 700 feet by 15, and the frame already is 230 by 15, which will contain about 300 men very comfortably, as from the manner I intend to make the divisions and berths they will make very good winter quarters. I have nothing more to say at present, but should wish to be informed in what manner I may get money, should the same be wanting, and also your opinion respecting blankets, as I have been very much inquired of respecting them, as some officers told me they had some men who could not get on for want of means to buy. Our enemies on the other side of the river are making all the preparations in their power. There has passed about sixty boats full of recruits for Montreal, and the same number of boats going up with ammunition and arms, &c., in a few days, in my sight. The inhabitants of this place don't feel much alarmed, as they say the Indians opposite to this and below are divided, and, if report say right, friendly to our Government. I expect to be able to get away from here in about four days for Sackett's Harbor and Oswego, where I expect to have the pleasure of hearing from you. Since writing the above there has arrived here about 50 men, and more expected. I am ready for them.

(MSS. of Hon. P. A. Porter.)

Colonel Baynes to Major General Brock.

QUEBEC, May 21, 1812.

SIR,—Sir George has allowed me to make the following extract from a despatch of Mr. Foster's, dated the 28th April, which I do in the Minister's own words: "The American Government affect now to have taken every step incumbent on the executive as preparatory to war, and leave the ultimate decision to Congress, as vested by the constitution in that body, which is fluctuating as the seas. There is a great party in the House of Representatives for war, composed principally of the western and southern States—members who have little to lose and may gain, while the northern and eastern States are vehement against it. The embargo seems to have been resolved upon because at the moment they did not know what else to do. The Cabinet wished only sixty days—the Senate made it ninety. Our Government leaves no room to expect a repeal of the Order-in-Council, yet they wait for the return of the *Hornet*. Something decisive must then be known; perhaps when they become completely convinced of Bonaparte's playing upon them, it will end in declaring against France. The question of adjournment was lost, notwithstanding there was an absolute majority known a few minutes before in its favor, revolutionists jealous of younger men taking a lead. The army cannot, I conceive, soon be filled up —they get few recruits."

You will have heard, long ere you receive this, that the 49th Regiment is ordered home; the 41st are by the same authority to return to Europe, but Sir George will not, under existing circumstances, attempt to relieve the posts in Upper Canada, so that there will be no immediate change in your quarter. Sir George regrets that he has not field officers of the description you require to command at Kingston and Amherstburg. The only prospect of relief in that respect which he has in view is from the arrival of the absent inspecting field officers.

The arrangement you propose respecting the unfortunate delinquents of the 41st Regiment will perfectly meet the approbation of Sir George, who approved of your not forwarding the resignation of the younger members, or, indeed, of any, if they are worthy of consideration.

Kempt has brought his name into notice in the assault of La Picurina, an outwork at Badajoz, where he commanded, being on duty in the trenches. The Glengarry levy goes on swimmingly.

(From Tupper's Life of Brock. pp. 176-7.)

Sir George Prevost to Major-General Brock.

QUEBEC, May 27, 1812.

SIR,—I am much pleased to find by your letter of the 22d ultimo you had taken precautions to prevent any act occurring within your control that should afford the Government of the United States a legitimate pretext to add to the clamor artfully raised by it against England.

The circumstance which happened to the guard stationed opposite to Queenston arrived here much exaggerated. Your account of it silenced the idle reports in circulation.

I agree with you in deploring the limitation until the end of the ensuing session in the operation of the Militia Act for Upper Canada, but as in the event of hostilities it might not be possible to convene the Legislature, then the bill would in all probability continue in force during the war, provided you were not induced to make an exertion for a more perfect law.

Colonel Baynes having informed me he had an opportunity of communicating with you more expeditiously than by post, I desired him to make you acquainted with the peaceful intelligence I had just received from Mr. Foster; but, although it comes with a good deal of reservation, still it warrants me in recommending the most rigid economy in carrying on the King's service and in avoiding all expense that has not become absolutely necessary, as it is with the utmost difficulty money can be raised for the ordinary service.

I am apprehensive that I cannot look forward to the pleasure of seeing you before the end of August, as my presence in the Province is become indispensably necessary during the first operation of the new militia law.

Many thanks for the particulars of the transaction which led to the censure passed by the House of Assembly on Chief Justice Scott.

(From Tupper's Life of Brock, pp. 177-8.)

Sir George Prevost to Lord Liverpool.

QUEBEC, 27th May, 1812.
No. 49.

MY LORD,—

. . . .

I enclose extracts from Major General Brock's report on the state of affairs in Upper Canada. The most positive directions have been given to the selected officers entrusted with commands on the frontiers contiguous to the posts occupied by the American forces, in addition to the orders relating to the precaution and vigilance become indispensably necessary to observe in their intercourse with the people of the United States, perfect civility, and to prevent the occurrence of circumstances calculated to create irritation between the two countries.

(Canadian Archives, Q. 117-2, p. 312.)

(From the Buffalo Gazette, Tuesday, June 2d, 1812.)

Messrs. Granger, Parrish and Jones held on Tuesday last a council with the chiefs of the Six Nations. There was a full meeting of the chiefs, when they were asked what their determination was in the event of war between the United States and Great Britain. They answered, as we understand, that it was a general understanding among them to take no part, but that they were united in sending a deputation to their brethren in Canada in order to agree upon some plan in case of hostilities between the two countries.

(File in Buffalo Public Library.)

Peter Walton & Son to James Cummings & Co. of Chippawa.
(Extract.)
ALBANY, 6th June, 1812.

We are sorry to inform you that the prevailing opinion of the people in this place is that war would be declared by Congress against Great Britain during the course of this week. All the late news from Washington will warrant this opinion. If they should, under the circumstances it will be very unpopular indeed. Our own opinion is that war will be declared. If so it will operate very much against us all.

Sir George Prevost to Lord Liverpool.
QUEBEC, 9th June, 1812.

No. 52.

Last night I received a secret communication from Consul General Barclay at New York, dated 30th May, 1812.
Extract.
His Majesty's Minister at Washington writes me on the 27th instant that notwithstanding the clear proofs of the continuance of the French Decrees, it seems war will be proposed on Monday, and, it is said, will be carried in the House of Representatives.

(Canadian Archives. Q. 117-2. p. 339.)

Extract from a Letter Dated at Prescott, 14th June, 1812.

A British vessel, the *Lord Nelson*, sailed from this on the 2nd inst., loaded with merchandise, for Queenston and Niagara, and when about 50 miles below that port she and another British vessel in company fell in with the United States Brig *Oneida*. One of the vessels tacked to the northward, the other stood in for the south shore and was brought to by firing three guns at her. She was then boarded and a prize master and crew took possession of the *Lord Nelson* and anchored with her next day in Sackett's Harbor, where she now lies unrigged. The reasons given for taking the vessel are that she was found without a register or Customs House clearance on board. The laws of Upper Canada do not require that a merchant vessel should have either register or clearance.

G. P.

In Sir George Prevost's despatch to Lord Liverpool. No. 53. 22nd June, 1812.
(Canadian Archives. Q. 117-2. p. 349.)

Letter from Prescott, Dated 15th June, 1812.

In addition to the capture of the *Lord Nelson*, I have to acquaint you that the *Ontario* (an American vessel) which had loaded at Queenston with 700 barrels of flour, bound to this place, was on Friday last taken by an American armed boat a little below Carleton Island and carried to Gravelly Point. This vessel had left the United States ports previous to the embargo laws, and had made several voyages within the Province since the opening of navigation. I can hear of no reason why the above named vessel was detained, with a British cargo on board, but that the boarding officer suspected her.

G. P.

Enclosed in Sir George Prevost's despatch to Lord Liverpool, No. 53. 22d June, 1812. (Canadian Archives, Q. 117-2, p. 351.)

Hon. Wm. Eustis, Secretary of War, to Augustus Porter.

WAR DEPARTMENT, June 15th, 1812.

SIR,—Two companies of militia are on their march for Sandusky, and General Hull will receive reinforcements at Detroit. You will, therefore, in addition to the usual deposits and the requisition particularly designated in my letter of May 21st, immediately provide and deposit fourteen thousand rations at Sandusky, and three hundred and sixty-six thousand rations at Detroit. Your letter of May 27 and bond are received.

(From MSS. of Hon. P. A. Porter.)

From the Buffalo Gazette, Tuesday, June 16, 1812.

Colonel Swift has returned from Albany and resumed command of the volunteers on Niagara River. The volunteers have all arrived on the frontier, to the number of 600.

ANOTHER "SPECK."

One of the sentinels at the Rock some time last week having liberty to discharge his musket, levelled his piece across the river and fired the same, intending, as he said, to see how prettily the ball would skip on the water, when the ball, disdaining to be tied down to a milk and water course, overleaped the bounds of reason and the boundary of the United States and deposited its cold self into a rail on a fence near the bank of the river and also near the house of a gentleman, &c. We are assured that the affair will be noticed and may possibly lead to a correspondence.

From the Buffalo Gazette, Tuesday, June 23, 1812.

To the Editor of the Buffalo Gazette:

SIR,—Whilst strict attention has been observed by the inhabitants on the Canada shore opposite Black Rock not to molest or offend any person residing at the Rock or its vicinity, we had reason to expect that a reciprocal attention would have been shown to us, but we are extremely sorry that our expectation has been disappointed, and that our peace has been disturbed and our inhabitants annoyed by some thoughtless or evil disposed person having recently fired several musket balls from the American shore. The whistling of these bullets has been distinctly heard and ascertained by the examination of several reputable persons. One ball came near to the blacksmith shop, one near to Henry Trout's tavern, and one a little lower down the river.

While we regret the cause that has occasioned this statement, we feel confident that it requires only to be made known to the authorities, who assuredly will prevent such licentious behavior in future, and therefore request that you will give it a place in your impartial paper, and oblige

Your humble servants,
JOHN WARREN, SR., J. P.
JOHN WARREN, JR., J. P.
B. HARDISON.
HUGH ALEXANDER.

Fort Erie, 17th June, 1812.

General Order.

HEADQUARTERS, ALBANY, June 23d, 1812.

War is declared by the United States against the Kingdom of Great Britain and Ireland and its dependencies. You will therefore be vigilant and attentive to the safety of the frontier of Onondaga. You are by this letter authorized to order out Major Moseley's battalion of riflemen, (two companies), Captain Mulholland's company of artillery, or any other part of the volunteer or detached troops of your brigade, to reinforce the Oswego detachment upon the requisition of the commandant of that post. Should Col. Fleming accept the office of Commissary, to which he is appointed, Lt.-Col. Erastus Cleveland of Madison County will succeed him in that command.

By order of the Commander-in-Chief.

WILLIAM PAULDING, JR,
Adjutant-General.

To Brig'r General John Ellis.
(Tompkins Papers. New York State Library.)

General Order.

HEADQUARTERS, ALBANY, June 23d, 1812.

You will please to order out immediately and send on in such small detachments as can be accommodated on the road, the troops detached from Ontario, Genesee, and Niagara as part of the 13,500 men. They may be equipped from the arsenal with arms and ammunition; their clothing and blankets must be found by themselves. Camp kettles and other camp equipage will be forwarded immediately. Every officer and every citizen who values the safety of his fellow citizens on the frontier and the dignity and honor of his country will exert himself to the utmost to inspire mutual confidence, to obviate as much as possible the difficulties incident to the assemblage of militia detachments, and by every possible act of kindness to assist and expedite the movements of the brave men who turn out in behalf of their country. Genl. Wadsworth is ordered into service, and will take the command for the present of the detachment already out and of the troops which may be ordered into service on the Niagara frontier.

The declaration of war between the Kingdom of Great Britain and Ireland and its dependencies and the United States, which declaration is enclosed, will call for the services of officers of a higher grade than Brigadier-General in a short time, and you will please hold yourself in readiness accordingly. The troops are, of course, to act offensively whenever an opportunity presents and the commanding officer may deem it to be for the good of the country.

By order of the Commander-in-Chief.

WILLIAM PAULDING, Jun'r,
Adjutant-General.

To Major-General Amos Hall.

(Tompkins Papers, New York State Library.)

General Order.

HEADQUARTERS, ALBANY, June 23d, 1812.

You will exert yourself to forward the military stores which may be wanted from Canandaigua towards the Niagara frontier, and to supply every deficiency as far as may be practicable. If you can procure cannon ball to be cast, let it be done, and let them suit the calibers of sixes, fours, and threes. I have ordered additional troops to the frontier; of course great exertions must be made to have them accommodated in every respect. This duty will fall on your department at present, and I shall expect your usual skill, promptness and patriotism in the performance of them. Camp kettles, a few tents and some knapsacks and a quantity of cannon ball will be sent on to-morrow with orders to proceed with the utmost despatch. Genl. Wadsworth is ordered with the detached troops of Ontario, Genesee, and Niagara to take the command, accommodate them, feed them, cherish them. They will act offensively whenever it may be judged proper.

By order of the Commander-in-Chief.

WILLIAM PAULDING, Jun'r,
Adjutant-General.

To Quartermaster-General Peter B. Porter.

(Tompkins Papers, New York State Library.)

General Order.

HEADQUARTERS, ALBANY, June 23d, 1812.

War is declared between the Kingdom of Great Britain and Ireland and its dependencies and the United States of America and the territories thereof. As the Brigadier assigned to command the most westerly detachment, you are hereby required to assemble the volunteers and detached troops of Ontario, Genesee and Niagara Counties, to cause them to be equipped with arms and ammunition at the Ontario and Batavia arsenals. You are also at liberty to require the use of and transport with the troops the field pieces attached to such companies of artillery within the district above mentioned as shall not volunteer or turn out in defence of the country with patriotic promptitude. Ball for the cannon and the other articles in which the arsenals are deficient will be forwarded without delay.

In the meantime you will be pleased to exert yourself to promote a disposition to maintain the rights and honor of the country, and may proceed to Black Rock with the troops. You may collect or go directly to Lt.-Col. Swift and order the troops to follow. You are at liberty to act offensively as well as defensively, according as in the exercise of a sound discretion may appear most for the safety and interest of the United States and the good people thereof.

By order of the Commander-in-Chief.

WILLIAM PAULDING, Jun'r,
Adjutant-General,

To Brig'r-General William Wadsworth.

(Tompkins Papers, New York State Library.)

Colonel Philetus Swift and Benjamin Barton to Governor Tompkins.

SIR,—Situated as we are on the frontiers and in plain view of the armed force which we expect every day to call our enemy gives us very serious apprehensions of the consequences that may ensue unless timely aid is given to ward off the blow that may fall on this section of the country if war is declared in our present defenceless situation. We consider it our duty to state to you the present prospect of affairs in this quarter in order that Your Excellency may have as much information on the subject as possible, and to enable you to adopt such measures as you may think most advisable for the better defence and security of the frontier. The British on the opposite side are making the most active preparations for defence. New troops are arriving from the Lower Province constantly, and the quantity of military stores, &c., that have arrived within these few weeks are astonishing. Vast quantities of arms and ammunition are passing up the country, no doubt to arm the Indians around the upper lakes, for they have not white men enough to make use of such quantities as are passing. One-third of the militia of the Upper Province are formed into companies called flankers, and are well armed and equipped out of the King's stores and are regularly trained one day in the week by an officer of the standing troops. A volunteer troop of horse has lately been raised and have drawn their sabres and pistols. A company of militia artillery has been raised this spring and exercise two or three days in the week on the plains near Fort George and practice firing, and have become very expert. The noted Isaac Swayzy has, within a few days, received a captain's commission for the flying artillery, of which they have a number of pieces, and we were yesterday informed by a respectable gentleman from that side of the river that he was actually purchasing horses for the purpose of exercising his men. They are repairing Fort George and building a new fort at York. A number of boats are daily employed, manned by their soldiers, plying between Fort George and Queenston, conveying stone, lime, and pickets for necessary repairs, and, to cap the whole, they are making and using every argument and persuasion to induce the Indians to join them, and we are informed that the Mohawks have volunteered their services. In fact, nothing is left undone by their people that is necessary for their defence. It has also been suggested to me by a gentleman of respectability residing there, and which we have every reason to believe to be true, that if war is declared and we remain in the present defenceless situation that an attack will be made on Fort Niagara, and in that case it must fall, as the force they have there is but small and the works in a miserable and decayed situation, and can make but a feeble defence. The object in taking that fortress will be the command of the mouth of the river to prevent any supplies coming to this side by water.

 We have thus endeavored to give Your Excellency some idea of the preparations that are making by the British in Upper

Canada, as well as the people we have to meet if a war takes place. Our great fears are that our Government will consider the taking of that country of so trifling a nature that they will send but a small force and badly supplied. If that should be the case many valuable men will be lost and the invading army shamefully defeated.

We have great confidence that the general Government will adopt such measures as in their opinion will be the best for the welfare and safety of the whole, but from want of proper information may be led into an error. We therefore hope Your Excellency will use your influence with the general Government to have a respectable force on the frontier and well equipped and supplied.

Lewiston, June 24, 1812.

(Tompkins Papers, vol. VII., pp. 234-7, New York State Library.)

Letter to Mr. H. W. Ryland, Secretary to Sir George Prevost.

MONTREAL, 24th June, 1812.

You will be pleased to inform the Governor-General that we have just received by an express which left New York on the 20th inst. and Albany on Sunday last at 6 a. m., the account that war against Great Britain is declared.

No particulars whatever are mentioned, but we cannot doubt of the fact, which we deem it our duty to put His Excellency in possession of without delay and accordingly send this by express.

FORSYTH, RICHARDSON & CO.,
McTAVISH, McGILLIVRAY & CO.

Enclosed in Sir George Prevost's despatch to Lord Liverpool, No. 54, June 25th, 1812.

(Canadian Archives, Q. 118, p. 4.)

Sir George Prevost to Lord Liverpool.

QUEBEC, 25th June, 1812.

No. 54.

MY LORD,—Upon returning from the inspection of a battalion of embodied militia training at some distance from Quebec, the intelligence herewith transmitted was delivered to me, it having arrived two hours before. It comes through so good a channel that I transmit it to Your Lordship by a vessel getting under sail for Cork, altho' I have not received any official communication from Mr. Foster. The writers of the accompanying letter being the principals of the Northwest and Southwest Fur Companies, were so much interested in the question of war that they took extraordinary means to obtain information of the decision of Congress that they might be enabled to preserve much valuable merchandise exposed to the first aggression of the Americans. I hope Your Lordship will send me a supply of money, the want of which I have already so strongly represented.

It is with extreme disappointment that I acquaint Your Lordship that the supply of arms and accoutrements shipped for Canada last autumn has not yet arrived.

(Letter from Forsyth, Richardson & Co. to Mr. Ryland, announcing the declaration of war, enclosed.)
(Canadian Archives, Q. 118, p. 2.)

Colonel Baynes to Major-General Brock.

QUEBEC, June 25th, 1812.

SIR,—Sir George Prevost desires me to inform you that he has this instant received intelligence from Mr. Richardson by an express to the Northwest Company, announcing that the American Government had declared war against Great Britain. This despatch left New York on the 20th instant, and does not furnish any other circumstance of intelligence whatever. His Excellency is induced to give perfect and entire credit to this report, although it has not yet reached him through any official channel. Indeed, the extraordinary despatch which has attended this courier fully explains his not having received the Minister's letters, of which he will not fail to give you the earliest intimation.

Mr. Richardson informs His Excellency that it is the intention of the company to send six large canoes to receive their furs by the Grand River (or Ottawa), and should it be expedient to reinforce the post of St. Joseph, that they will be able to carry six soldiers in each boat. Anxious as Sir George feels to render you every aid in his power and to afford every possible assistance and protection to the Northwest Company, who have on their part assured their co-operation, His Excellency, nevertheless, does not think it advisable under existing circumstances to weaken the 49th Regiment, which occupies so important and critical a station ; nor can he hold out any certain prospect of any further reinforcement until the arrival of the troops he has been led to expect from England, but directs me to assure you of his cordial wish to render you every efficient support in his power.

(From Tupper's Life of Brock, pp. 193-4.)

Division Orders.

BLOOMFIELD, June 26th, 1812.

The detachment of infantry made from the 7th Division, under and by virtue of Division Orders of the 11th of May last, have been organized by the Commander-in-Chief into one brigade, the command whereof is assigned to Brigadier-General William Wadsworth, and is denominated the 7th Brigade. It is composed of three regiments, numbered and commanded as follows:—

18th, Hugh W. Dobbin of Junius, Seneca County.
19th, Henry Bloom of Geneva, Cayuga County.
20th, Peter Allen of Honeoye, Ontario County.

The 18th Regiment will be composed of the detachment from the brigades of Generals McClure, Rea and Hopkins.

The 19th Regiment will be composed of the detachments from Generals Tillotson's and Himrod's brigades.

The 20th Regiment will be composed of the detachments from Generals Wadsworth's and Burnett's brigades.

The officers commanding the 18th Regiment (except one company from General McClure's Brigade) and the 20th Regiment are ordered to concentrate the troops under their respective command in such convenient places as they may think most convenient and proper. The detachments will be furnished from the arsenals at Canandaigua and Batavia with arms, accoutrements and ammunition. Camp kettles and other camp equipage will be furnished and forwarded with all convenient speed. The troops must supply themselves with knapsacks, clothing and blankets.

These regiments, being thus armed and equipped, are ordered to march without delay to the Niagara frontier, under the direction and subject to the orders of Brigadier-General Wadsworth.

To the brigade composed of the above regiments (together with the militia already detached and stationed on the Niagara frontier), the command whereof is assigned Brigadier-General Wadsworth, are assigned for Brigade Staff, Julius Keyes of Clarence, Niagara County, Brigade-Major and Inspector; Henry Wells of Elmira, Tioga County, Brigade-Quartermaster. To the regiments above designated are assigned the following Majors:—

18th Regiment, Major John Morrison of Niagara County. Major James Ganson of Caledonia, Genesee County.

19th Regiment, Major Noah Olmstead of Cayuga County, Major Aranthus Everts of Hector, Seneca County.

20th Regiment, Major George Smith of Livonia, Ontario County; Major Thomas Lee of Benton, Ontario County.

The regimental staff will be selected by the officers assigned to the command of the above regiments respectively.

Every officer commanding a detached regiment will forthwith transmit the Adjutant-General a roster of the names and places of residence of the field and staff officers, an accurate inspection return, and correct copies of the muster rolls of the companies and troops thereof, and will also convey an exact copy of the inspection return to the Commander of the Brigade and send it to the General of the Division, that he may in due season transmit to the Commander-in-Chief an inspection return thereof.

The 19th Regiment and the company from General McClure's brigade are not at present ordered to take the field, but will hold themselves in readiness to march at a moment's notice.

The Major-General, confiding in the patriotism and courage of the brave troops ordered into service, entertains no doubt but their conduct will be such as to ensure the grateful plaudits of their beloved country. As the service into which they are called will be a service of privations and dangers, it is hoped that it will be borne with the fortitude of men and the resolution of freemen, and that the soldiers will carry with them the enduring recollection that as citizens they have assumed the helmet of war for a season the more effectually to secure the blessings of peace, to attain which no sacrifice short of a sacrifice of national honor can be too great.

By order of the Major-General.

GEORGE HOSMER,
Aide-de-Camp.

(From the *Repository* of Canandaigua, June 30th, 1812.)
File in the Wood Library, Canandaigua, N. Y.

District General Order.

NIAGARA, 27th June, 1812.

D. G. O.

Colonel Procter will assume the command of the troops between Niagara and Fort Erie.

The Hon'ble Col. Claus will command the militia stationed between Niagara and Queenston, and Lieut.-Colonel Clark from Queenston to Fort Erie.

The commissariat at their respective posts will issue rations and fuel for the members actually present. The car brigade and those of the Provincial Cavalry are included in the order.

Officers commanding posts or detachments will sign the necessary certificate previous to issuing the rations. The detachment of the 41st, stationed at the Two and Four-Mile Points, will be relieved by an equal number of the First Lincoln Militia to-morrow morning. It is recommended to the militia to bring blankets with them on service.

The troops will be kept in a constant state of readiness for service, and Colonel Procter will direct the necessary guards and patrols, which are to be made down the bank and close to the water's edge.

Lieutenant-Colonel Nichol is appointed Quartermaster-General to the militia forces, with the same pay and allowances as those granted to the Adjutant-General.

MAJOR-GENERAL BROCK.

Issued by order of the Colonel.

JOHN CLARK,
Lieut.-Adjt. 1st Lincoln Militia.

Lieut.-Colonel Robert Nichol to Captain James Cummings.

QUEENSTON, June 27, 1812.

DEAR SIR,—Understanding that there may be some difficulty in getting teams at Chippawa prepared to carry boats, Mr. Phelps' teams are despatched to bring what they can. You will of course pay every attention to their being carefully loaded on the carriage, so that they may not be injured.

You will be pleased to apply to Capt. Bullock to transmit the enclosed letter to Fort Erie without delay.

Colonel Philetus Swift to Governor Tompkins.

HONORED SIR,—This moment, at six o'clock a. m., I received your despatches; although with so much speed, the British had them almost two days before us. I forbear giving you a detail of our circumstances here, as Mr. Barton and myself wrote in full length the last mail, which will be received before this. Our men are in high spirits, and the declaration of war does not dampen the spirits of officers nor soldiers.

Doctor Nathaniel Wilson, who is now surgeon of my detachment, one of our good friends and one whom I can cordially recommend, has a large family to maintain, and his wages is not sufficient support, wishes to be appointed hospital surgeon, if it can be. I wish to retain him in service if possible.

Black Rock, June 27, 1812.

(Tompkins Papers, vol. VII., p. 263, New York State Library.)

General Wm. Wadsworth to Governor Tompkins.

GENESEO, 28th June, 1812.

SIR,—I have received your letter of the 23d instant. I take the command of the troops at Black Rock and its vicinity in obedience to Your Excellency's order with the greatest diffidence, having had no experience of actual service. My knowledge of the military art is limited; indeed, I foresee numberless difficulties and occurrences which will present to which I feel totally inadequate.

I have been ambitious that the regiment and brigade which I have commanded should be distinguished at their reviews, but I confess myself ignorant of even the minor duties of the duty you have assigned me, and I am apprehensive that I may not only expose myself but my Government. Any aid which Your Excellency may think proper to order will be received with thanks. A military secretary intimately acquainted with the details of camp duty would be of great service to me.

Permit me to add that every exertion in my power shall be made to discharge the duties of my office and to merit the approbation of Your Excellency.

(Tompkins Papers, vol. VII., pp. 271-2. New York State Library.)

Major-General Amos Hall to Governor Tompkins.

BLOOMFIELD, June 28, 1812.

SIR,—About an hour since I received a letter by express from General Porter in 18 hours from Buffalo, advising that a small American sloop (called the *Commencement*), owned by Mr. Colt, sailed from that place up the lake about 12 o'clock on that day (Saturday). She had proceeded only about two leagues, when the wind, being light, two large boats, appearing to the spectators on this side to contain about 50 armed men and some ordnance, pursued her from Fort Erie, where the British armed ship is lying, and took her after several fires, the sloop having only four men on board, without arms. The two boats towed her into the harbor at Fort Erie. "The excitement by the event," (the General writes,) "was such that almost every man in Buffalo was anxious to embark in some small boats lying at that place to retake her, and I confess that on the first impression I was disposed to encourage and join them. But our boats being very light, and having nothing but small arms, I considered that it would be a wanton sacrifice of brave and patriotic men to send them out. Besides, the wind springing up, they could not be overtaken before they would reach the fort at Erie." He likewise adds that "I am informed that the British, having earlier information than we had of the declaration of war, have detained Lieut. Gansevoort of the American garrison at Niagara, and a boat's crew that happened to be on the British side on business." He concludes by urging the necessity of the detachment of militia ordered to march from Ontario, Genesee and Niagara Counties being forwarded with all possible speed, stating he would give every facility to their march.

We begin to realize that we are now in an actual state of war, hostilities having actually been commenced by the British on the lakes. Whether they will follow it up vigorously or not is uncertain; that course would be characteristic, and I think we have no reason to expect they will depart from it. I was in Canandaigua this morning, and the opinion there is that they will pursue immediately every advantage to be gained by them.

We feel a general anxiety for our fellow-citizens on the frontiers, it being pretty well ascertained that the British have at least 1,500 regular troops who have seen service that can be brought to act offensively at the shortest notice, if they should think it advisable, together with a considerable body of militia well disciplined and completely armed. With such a force, should they not call to their aid the savage warriors, who are stated to be about 400, they might, notwithstanding the force we have at the post of Niagara, whom I have no doubt would make a brave defence, be able to do much mischief and commit great depredations on the frontiers nearest to the Niagara River. Our whole force, when the second detachment arrives, will probably be about 1,300 effective men.

If the above statements are correct, Your Excellency will judge whether a large force will not be necessary to guard the post and frontier on the Niagara River. In great haste.

N. B.—Four pieces of field artillery and 500 stands of arms, &c., passed Genesee River this morning on the way to Buffalo, taken from the arsenal in Canandaigua by order of the Quartermaster-General. They will possibly arrive at the place of destination on Tuesday.

(Tompkins Papers, vol. VII., pp. 274-7, New York State Library.)

Major-General Amos Hall to Governor Tompkins.

BLOOMFIELD, June 29, 1812.

SIR,—I this morning at 4 o'clock received by express from General Porter (in 12 hours from Black Rock) information that by every appearance on the British shore the troops were preparing to cross the river. The number of the British force is, I believe, about 1,500, as stated in my last letter.

General Porter was very urgent that every assistance should be forwarded that could possibly be put in motion. Major Mullany, commanding officer of the United States regular troops at Canandaigua, was requested to march his men on immediately. I was clearly of opinion that in such an emergency he would be justifiable to comply with the request. I wrote him by express, and at 8 o'clock he informed me that he would march his troops immediately. They will probably pass through Bloomfield this afternoon. The detachment of militia ordered to march will be on the way tomorrow. Everything will be done that the nature of the service and the exigency of the times require to hasten the troops to the Niagara frontier.

We are very much engaged at present in making the necessary arrangements for general defence.

I have ordered a company to be stationed at Sodus and Pulteneyville and one company at the mouth of the Genesee River.

Major Mullany will have about 250 men. But they have no arms, and must be furnished from the arsenal at Canandaigua.

The whole of the arms and accoutrements will be taken from the arsenal at Canandaigua to-day to furnish the last detachment. We shall be in immediate want of a supply, there being few arms and very little ammunition in the country.

I shall not close my letter, but wait till to-morrow morning, expecting to hear something more serious.

30th June, 7 o'clock in the morning.

I this morning received by express from Fort Niagara and Lewiston in less than 12 hours information that 1,500 troops and a large train of artillery were in view nearly opposite the post. Captain Leonard writes that he momently expected the attack to commence, but Mr. Barton thinks they will wait the arrival of their armed vessels.

I have ordered out a part of Captain Pierson's company of dragoons to form a line of communication from Niagara and Buffalo to this county. I shall send by mail, concluding that by express could not gain time to answer the purpose.

N. B.—It is all important that tents, if possible, should be sent on immediately. Camp equipage, I understand, is on the road.

(Tompkins Papers, vol. VII., pp. 281-2. New York State Library.)

Governor Tompkins to Hon. Wm. Eustis, Secretary at War.

ALBANY, 27th June, 1812.

SIR.—Your letter of the 19th inst., announcing the important intelligence of a declaration of war against the United Kingdom of Great Britain and Ireland and its dependencies, was received on Tuesday evening at eleven o'clock. Expresses with the information and with instructions for the commandants of posts on the frontiers were despatched in the course of that night. The express to Sackett's Harbor has returned with the satisfactory intelligence that the officers and men of that detachment are in fine spirits, are tolerably well accommodated, are perfectly united and harmonious, and received the intelligence of war with cheerfulness and determined courage.

In anticipation of orders to that effect, I have directed the frontier posts to be reinforced by detachments of militia of the counties immediately adjoining, and have also ordered into service for the protection of the northern frontier between Lake Champlain and St. Lawrence the militia detached from Washington, Essex, Clinton and Franklin Counties, and have forwarded additional quantities of arms and ammunition and military stores to each point. You were advised by me last winter, and also when the former detachments were ordered out, that the State was not provided with camp equipage, and that we must rely upon the Genl Government for these articles.

It was also my wish that the Genl. Government should have availed itself of my repeated offers to forward and deposit in our frontier arsenals, free of expense, some arms, military stores and camp equipage in preparation for the event which has happened. The United States have now collections of enlisted troops at Plattsburg, Rome, Canandaigua and other frontier rendezvous within 100 rods of our arsenals, and yet these recruits are destitute of arms and ammunition and camp equipage.

Those at Plattsburg are within fifty miles of St. Regis and Cognawago Indians, by whom they might be attacked suddenly and with little hazard; unarmed and unprepared as they are, the regulars could not defend themselves, much less protect the inhabitants.

I do not mention the preceding circumstances by way of complaint, but in the hope and expectation that the statement of them may show you more fully the indispensable necessity of an immediate and earnest attention to the suggestions which follow.

A belief that General Dearborn's headquarters were to be at this place induced me to calculate that by conference and arrangement with him I should be able to procure from the United States at any time those military stores of which we are deficient, but I at the moment of needing his assistance [ascertained] that his headquarters are at Boston. General Gansevoort is very low, and incapable of attending to business of any kind. Col. Simonds has arrived here, but says he was ordered to report himself to Genl. Dearborn, and therefore can take no authority upon himself at present.

The keeper of the stores will not part with cannon, muskets, ammunition or other articles without the order of his superior officer.

Genl. Dearborn has requested me to order out militia for the Champlain frontier, and informs me that the Quartermaster-General will supply camp equipage for them. Upon application to the Quartermaster-General, who is now in Albany, I find there is no camp equipage except a few tents and about sixty camp kettles, which have been in our arsenal at this place for several years. For the delivery of these even I cannot obtain a written order. The Deputy-Quartermaster-General will not give an order for their delivery without written directions from the Quartermaster-General, and the Quartermaster-General does not seem willing to give such written directions, or at least has not done it, although he is perfectly willing I should have the articles. Under such circumstances I shall presume to take possession of them at my own hazard, and shall accordingly forward them to-morrow morning, hoping that my proceedings on the emergency will be approved and confirmed.

The detachments already in service, you will please to recollect, are by your orders separate and independent corps, and the commandants, of course, will be embarrassed as to the course to be pursued by them in case of an attack of a part of the frontier not under their respective commands. Besides, they are in temporary barracks and have no tents or conveniences for removing more than one day's march from their present positions. Having thus stated some of the difficulties I have encountered and am likely to encounter in the protection of an extensive and exposed boundary upon Canada, I beg leave to request the immediate and earnest attention of Government to the following particulars:—

I.—To cause to be forwarded with the utmost possible expedition tents and other camp equipage and knapsacks for the frontier detachments, for without them they can form no offensive operation, and will be very inefficient for defence even. Competent authority ought also to be given to subordinate officers of the proper departments to press on the supply without waiting for the orders to pass through the superior officers of their respective departments should such superior officers be absent at the time.

II.—To send on a General Officer to take command of all the frontier detachments, or authorize me to require Major-Genl. Stephen Van Rensselaer of this city to take the command until further orders, and also to send on some engineers and other proper officers to aid in offensive operations at Niagara, Sackett's Harbor, &c.

III.—To place the cannon, muskets and ammunition, &c., belonging to the United States and now at this place, under the requisition of the Genl. who may proceed to the frontier command, or subject to the orders of some officer who may be stationed here, and to authorize the District Quartermaster in the absence of the Quartermaster-General immediately to comply with the orders of the General commanding on the frontier or of the officer stationed at this place.

Be assured, Sir, that I shall exert every nerve and afford every aid in my power to prosecute the war vigorously, and I hope to an honorable and prosperous termination.

(Tompkins Papers, New York State Library.)

Governor Tompkins to Major-General Dearborn.

ALBANY, June 28th, 1812.

SIR,—Your letter of 23rd instant has been received. I had anticipated your request by ordering the detachments from Washington, Essex, Clinton and Franklin Counties into service, and have fixed the days and places of their rendezvous. Upon application to the Quartermaster-Genl. I find that there are but 139 tents and 60 camp kettles at this place, and even those I take by a kind of stealth. The Deputy-Quartermaster-General declines giving an order for their delivery until he shall have a written order from the Quartermaster-Genl., and the latter is willing I should take them, but will not give the Deputy a written order for that purpose: under such circumstances I shall avail myself of the rule of possession, and by virtue of the eleven points of law send them off to-morrow morning without a written order from any one. You may remember that when you were Secretary of the War Department I invited you to forward and deposit in our frontier arsenals, arms, ammunition and camp equipage, free of expense, to be ready for defence in case of war, and the same invitation to the War Department has been repeated four times since. The United States have now from five to six hundred regular troops at Plattsburg, Rome, Canandaigua, &c., where those arsenals are, and yet those recruits are now and must be for weeks to come, unarmed and in every respect unequipped, although within musket shot of arsenals. The recruits at Plattsburg are within fifty miles of two tribes of Canadian Indians. In case of an attack upon the frontiers that portion of the United States army would be as inefficient and as unable to defend the inhabitants, or themselves even, as so many women.

The militia detachments on the western frontiers received the news of war with cheerfulness and determined courage, and I am happy to find that they are united like brothers, highly improved in discipline, and ready to devote themselves to any service or danger which the good of their country may require.

But they are in barracks, from which they cannot remove a day's march for the want of tents and other equipage, and they are in separate and independent detachments without a general officer to command them or combine their exertions for the accomplishment of any desirable or important object.

The only officer of the United States here who can do anything is the Quartermaster-General, and he has not a tent, campkettle or knapsack in the arsenal (except what I have concluded to send off to-morrow morning as above mentioned) to furnish me.

As to cannon, muskets, ammunition, I can find no one here who will exercise any authority over them or deliver a single article upon my requisition. Neither can I find any officer of the army who feels himself authorized to exercise any authority or do any act which will aid me in the all important object of protecting the inhabitants of our extended frontier, exposed to the cruelties of savages and the depredations of the enemy. If I must rely upon the militia solely for such protection I entreat you to give orders to your officers here to furnish upon my order for the use of the militia detachments all needful weapons and articles, with which the United States are supplied and of which we are destitute.

You may rely upon all the assistance which my talents, influence and authority can furnish in the prosecution of the just and necessary war which has been declared by the constituted authority of our beloved country.

(Tompkins' Papers, New York State Library.)

Governor D. D. Tompkins to De Witt Clinton.

ALBANY, June 29, 1812.

SIR,—I have just received an express from Canandaigua informing me that *Vosburgh* from this city was arrested on his return from Queenston in Canada, where he had been as an express with Foster's dispatches. Those dispatches were dated June 17, at Washington, and arrived in this city on Sunday morning, 21st June, from whence they were forwarded by Vosburgh as express. McTavish, of the house of Caldwell, Fraser & Co. of this city, a Mr. Hart and a certain Solomons were the persons concerned in this city. The Recorder has summoned them before him, and I am just informed that McTavish upon his examination has declared that he received the letters from Samuel Corp of your city and supposed them to be mercantile only. But Vosburgh declares in his affidavit, taken at Canandaigua, that the envelope sent from this city contained information of a declaration of war, and that Mr. Clark of Queenston, to whom he delivered it, so declared before he had opened the enclosed letter of Foster. I give you this information with respect to Mr. Corp that you as mayor of the City of New York may make enquiry into his conduct and participation in aiding and abetting, when he knew war was declared, the minister of the enemy in forwarding information thereof to the British garrisons to enable them to attack our troops unprepared and unadvised of the event, if you should think such enquiry proper and likely to be beneficial.

(Tompkins' Papers, vol. II, pp. 514-5, New York State Library.)

From the Federal Republican of Baltimore, Md., issue of 15th July, 1812.

The news of war reached the British at Fort George by express two days before it was received at our military station. General Brock arrived at Fort George on the 28th June. Several American gentlemen were there on a visit, who were treated very politely by the Governor and sent under protection of Captain Glegg, his aid, to Niagara with a flag. The news of war was very unwelcome on both sides of the river. They have been for six years in habits of friendly intercourse, connected by marriages and various relationships. Both sides were in consternation, the women and children were out on the banks of the river, while their fathers, husbands and sons were busily employed in arming. It was said Captain Glegg had a summons for the surrender of Fort Niagara, but this was contradicted by Captain Leonard, who said the message was simply to inquire whether he had any official notice of the war, and that he answered in the negative.

(File in New York Society Library, New York.)

Militia General Order.

HEADQUARTERS, 28th June, 1812.

M. G. O.

His Honor Major-General Brock has been pleased to make the following promotions and appointments in the First Regiment of Lincoln Militia, viz:—

Captain Wm. Robertson to be Major, vice Muirhead, resigned.

Adjutant John Clark to be Lieut., vice John Secord, appointed to Major Merritt's troop of cavalry.

By order of the General.

J. MACDONELL, P. A. D. C.

Militia General Order.

HEADQUARTERS, NIAGARA, 28th June, 1812.

Militia General Order.

Lieutenant-Colonel Ryerson will order all the arms formerly issued to the late First Regiment of Norfolk Militia to be delivered into his own. Such as are serviceable or can be rendered so he will retain and divide with Major Salmon of the Second Regiment. Such as are unserviceable and cannot be repaired in the London

District will be packed up in boxes and forwarded by the first safe opportunity to Fort Erie, where they will be delivered to the commanding officer at that post.

Lieutenant-Colonel Ryerson will at the same time direct the remains of the ammunition formerly issued to be delivered to him, and will order a board of survey to examine it—he will make a return of whatever is serviceable, specifying the exact quantity of each, also a return of the number of loose balls, powder, and cartridge paper will be forwarded to make the unserviceable cartridges.

Lieutenant-Colonel Ryerson will make a division of the serviceable ammunition with Major Salmon, and will transmit receipts in duplicate for the exact quantity which may be issued to each regiment.

Lieutenant-Colonel Ryerson and Major Salmon will send a boat to Fort Erie with detachments of their respective regiments, commanded by intelligent officers, to receive the arms and ammunition forwarded to that post for them.

These detachments will be supplied with provisions on their arrival at Fort Erie, by application to the commanding officer of that post.

Lieutenant-Colonel Ryerson will give pointed orders to the officers commanding the detachments to be vigilant while employed in this service and to take every precaution against surprize.

Signed by order of His Honor Major-General Brock.

J. MACDONELL, P. A. D. C.

(From the New York Evening Post, Wednesday, 8th July, 1812.)

BUFFALO, June 30, 1812.

On Saturday last, when the schooner *Commencement*, Captain Johnson, was lying off Buffalo Creek waiting a wind, two British armed row boats, fitted out at Fort Erie, put to sea and took the direction of the schooner. Meanwhile Johnson weighed anchor and stood out with a faint breeze, intending if the wind should increase to double Sturgeon Point, but by the time the schooner had beat 6 or 7 miles up the lake the breeze almost fell, and the boats came up with her and captured and towed her into port. The schooner belonged to Mr. Peter H. Colt, merchant at Black Rock, and was loaded with salt. There were forty men on board the boats and only three men and a boy on board the schooner. The crew of the *Commencement* were released on Sunday morning.

Mr. Frederick Miller of this town has been appointed Major-Commandant of the forces at Black Rock. Colonel Swift has taken command at Lewiston. General Porter arrived in town on Saturday, and we understand immediately sent an express to Canandaigua to expedite with all possible despatch the arms and ammunition deposited in the arsenal at that place to Black Rock. Several companies of militia of General Hopkins's brigade have been ordered *en masse* to Black Rock.

The light infantry company of Captain Wells and militia company of Captain Hull are embodied and rendezvous in this village to protect the town.

(File in New York Society Library.)

From the New York Evening Post, Friday, 3rd July, 1812.

Extract of a letter from an intelligent gentleman in Albany to his friend in this city, dated July 1st, 1812:

In the postscript of one of my last letters to you I mentioned that an express had just arrived from the west and that it was rumored Fort Niagara had been taken by the British. This rumor is without the least foundation. The express proved to be the Governor's, giving him information against several persons in this city who, it was alleged, had been aiding the British in forwarding their despatches to Upper Canada, from which it appears they had the declaration of war one day earlier than our garrisons.

The express that carried the news was a cartman of this city, who was apprehended on his return, near Geneva, and is there lodged in jail. The persons said to have been implicated here have been examined and honorably acquitted, as they were concerned in a mere mercantile transaction.

From the Ontario Repository, printed at Canandaigua, June 30, 1812.

We learn that soon after receiving the news of the declaration of war at Canada a British boat captured an American vessel on Lake Erie belonging principally to Mr. Peter H. Colt, who was on board—that an American officer, Lieut. Gansevoort of Fort Niagara, with a sergeant who happened to be over the river at the time the news of war was received, were detained by the British.

An express reached town yesterday morning, which left the lines Sunday evening at 5 o'clock, with information that the British forces were assembling in considerable numbers near the river, and that their movements indicated a preparation to cross to the American shore. In consequence Major Mullany, the commanding officer at this place, immediately prepared his troops, about 200, and marched last evening for the frontier.

(File in the Wood Library, Canandaigua, N. Y.)

From the National Intelligencer of Washington, D. C., 11th July. 1812.

ALBANY, July 1, 1812.

An express arrived here on Monday [June 29] in 36 hours from Canandaigua, announcing to His Excellency the Governor the arrest and imprisonment of Mr. Vosburgh of this city, who was suspected of having carried the despatch of Mr. Foster to the British commandant at Newark. In consequence of the disclosures of Vosburgh several persons of this city have undergone examination before Mr. Recorder Yates. As the object of the express may have been commercial, they have been admitted to bail. Circumstances, however, are dark.

(File in New York Society Library.)

General Amos Hall to General Porter.

BATAVIA, July 1st, 1812, 4 o'clock p. m.

SIR,—I just received your letter by express, requesting to forward on all the arms, &c., &c., that is to be had. About 600 men under the command of Genl. Wadsworth will march from this place to-morrow morning early.

I came to this place to give assistance to the march of the troops.

One regiment will cross Genesee River to-morrow from Ontario County. By Wednesday you will have at the two points of defence a formidable force.

20 of Capt. Pierson's troop are here in fine order and spirits.

It is not possible for me to come on, being totally unprepared. All the arms are coming on, but on men's shoulders, and fine men they are.

(From MSS. of Hon. P. A. Porter.)

General Amos Hall to Governor Tompkins.

BATAVIA, July 1, 6 o'clock p. m.

SIR,—By a letter sent me by express from General Porter, dated at Black Rock July 1, 10 a. m., I learn that he has no doubt an attack is intended, although the exact time cannot be ascertained. He urges me to despatch an express to meet the artillery now on the way from Albany to have them travel day and night. He says "we are miserably deficient—we have men but no arms for them—we want artillery and men who know how to use them." I shall transcribe the following sentences from his letter and leave it to His Excellency to make the comment.

"I hope you will come out and take the command yourself under the present circumstances."

"The feeble force now on this frontier is not sufficient to inspire confidence, and families are moving back."
(Tompkins' Papers, Vol. VII., p. 297, New York State Library.)

From the Aurora of Philadelphia, July 11th, 1812.

GENEVA, N. Y., July 1st, 1812.

In consequence of an express to Major-General Hall, the 18th Regiment, composed of men detached from Brigadier-Generals Rhea's, Hopkins's and McClure's Brigades (one company excepted), commanded by Lieut.-Colonel H. W. Dobbin, and the 20th Regiment, composed of men detached from Brigadier-Generals Wadsworth, and Burnet's Brigades, commanded by Lieut.-Colonel Peter Allen, are ordered to take the field immediately and march to the Niagara frontier. The United States troops, amounting to near 300, stationed at Canandaigua, marched on Monday for Niagara, under command of Major Mullany. Captain Abraham Dox's light infantry company of this village marched this day.
(File in Mercantile Library, Philadelphia.)

John M. O'Connor to General Porter.

BATAVIA, July 1st, 1812.

MY DEAR SIR,—The troops under Major Mullany and the militia under Major-Genl. Hall leave this to-night at 2 o'clock for Lewiston and Niagara *direct*. We bro't on with us 400 stand extra arms which have been distributed to the militia here. Our force alone is 260, exclusive of 50 at Amsterdam and Black Rock (the escort), so that there will be about 800 in all. The militia are flocking in from the eastward, and in a very few days you will be able to muster on the banks of Niagara some thousands. But they are such troops as are not to be opposed to regulars in the open country, and you must remember that our men are but *recruits*. The appearance of this force will certainly prevent an attack on the fort if it arrives in season. Meantime, perhaps, it is *practicable* to make a feint at Black Rock by a great show and bustle and collecting of boats and rafts, which will have the effect of distracting the attention and dividing the forces of the enemy. They will not expect such a feint from militia.

I return, *(I believe)* to Canandaigua to take command of the district. As I don't think there will be any fighting for some time, I prefer going back in consequence of a difference of opinion which has arisen between myself and Major Mullany relative to putting a man under guard, who was mutinous. I confined the fellow (an Irishman) and the major ordered his release, tho' I demanded as a right that he be kept confined till a general court-martial could be assembled. I informed him that the effect of such a course would necessarily prevent my issuing any order till the punishment of the individual, and intimated my intention of appealing to the Colonel or General.

He has so far consulted my feelings on this point as to give me the choice of going back and assuming the district command, which under present appearances I have preferred, especially as our men will return as soon as the eastern militia arrive.

I understand from Capt. McKeon that the artillery will shortly rendezvous at New York and the infantry at Albany.

Commodore Rogers is in pursuit of the Jamaica fleet, and report states his having taken 100 sail. A great many privateers are fitting out in the seaports.

P. S.—I was at Geneva when your express arrived: then I received orders by express to return and instantly rejoined the detachment.

(From MSS. of Hon. P. A. Porter.)

Augustus Porter to General Peter B. Porter.

MANCHESTER, July 2d, 1812.

SIR,—The troops have come in in such numbers that all alarm here has ceased. I think the danger now is that we shall have too great a number. If it were possible to stop the common militia from coming on any more, and let Wadsworth come with his detachment of 1,000 and the regular troops, it would be best. I would, however, let Swift take the responsibility of ordering this. I now think the most important thing to be attended to is the sending to Genl. Hull an express, notifying him that provisions are on the lake but cannot be got up, and advise him to take his own measures to obtain supplies. I think it best to send off the *Contractor*, and for that purpose let her be got ready. I will see Swift to-day, and will be up to-morrow. I shall be under the absolute necessity of purchasing 1 or 200 bbls. of T. B. & Co. pork. Taylor should go after cattle as soon as possible. I send up the bearer after five or six head of cattle, and more, if you have obtained them from the Indians, as you expected I should go up to Black Rock to-day, but am obliged to prepare for troops which Col. Swift will send to-day to this place. I expect a large number will be sent here, as I can accommodate them with a number of empty houses and ropewalk. Do let your deputy send down all the camp kettles you can possibly obtain, the troops here are in want.

P. S.—I have no doubt the enemy have varied their notions of operations and that the attack on Niagara is abandoned, as two companies came up yesterday, one of which has commenced a battery at Queenston and the other gone up the river.

(From MSS. of Hon. P. A. Porter.)

District General Order.

HEADQUARTERS, NIAGARA, July 2nd, 1812.

D. G. O.—

The troops will be formed of four divisions, to be composed of regulars and militia as follows:—

1st or Right Division commanded by Capt. Derenzy, 41st Regt.,
    to consist of a detachment of 41st Regt....................200
A detachment of militia...................................200
                                                                                  400

    2 three-pounders.
2nd Division, Capt. Bullock, detachment 41st Regt...........100
Detachment of militia.....................................200
                                                                                  300

    2 six-pounders.
3rd Division, Capt. Chambers, detachment of 41st Regt........100
Detachment of militia.....................................200
                                                                                  300

    2 three-pounders.
4th or Left Division, detachment 41st Regt..................200
Detachment of militia.....................................300
                                                                                  500

These divisions will be posted in the following manner, viz:—

First or Right Division at Fort Erie.
Second Division—Chippawa.
Third Division—Heights of Queenston.
Fourth or Left Division—Fort George.

The detachment of militia for the first division will be furnished by the 3rd Regiment of Lincoln militia, and will be commanded by ———

The detachment of militia for the second division will be furnished from the 2nd Regiment of Lincoln, and will be commanded by ———

The detachment of militia for the third division will be composed of the flank companies of the 5th and 6th Regiments of Lincoln, and will be commanded by Captain Hatt.

The detachment of militia for the fourth division will be composed of the flank companies of the 1st and 4th Regiments of Lincoln, and will be commanded by Lieut.-Col. Butler.

The first and second divisions will receive their orders from Lieut.-Colonel Clark—the third and fourth from Colonel Claus, to whom the said divisions will respectively report. Reports of all occurrences of consequence will at the same time be made to Major General Brock and to Colonel Procter.

Morning states will be regularly transmitted to Brigade Major Evans by Colonel Claus and Lieut.-Colonel Clark.

Officers commanding militia regiments will direct the officers of their respective corps not embodied to use every exertion to discipline the men under their command, and will have them in constant readiness to march to their respective posts on the shortest notice. They will at the same time give orders for their moving to the point attacked on the first alarm, without waiting for orders to that effect.

Colonel Procter will appoint the stations at the same time of the detachments of Light Dragoons, and will particularly direct that they shall not be detached from their posts except on urgent occasions.

James Muirhead, Esquire, is appointed surgeon to the militia forces and will be stationed at Chippawa, with the pay of ten shillings per diem and the usual allowances.

The officers commanding divisions will be allowed forage for one horse, furnishing the usual certificates.

General Order.

HEADQUARTERS, NIAGARA, 2nd July, 1812.

Report has this instant been made to Major General Brock that the Americans on the opposite side of the river immediately below the Falls, have for these three days past much annoyed his centinels on this side by firing upon them, and in particular by twelve shots fired at them this day about one o'clock p. m. by people who came out of the woods, and who after firing immediately retired.

The Major-General has too high an opinion of the American army to suppose that such conduct could be tolerated even in a state of actual warfare. He therefore hopes that measures will immediately be taken to put a stop to a practice so contrary to the known rules established among civilized nations.

General Order.

HEADQUARTERS, ALBANY, July 2nd, 1812.

I received your letter last evening and beg leave to inform you that last week I sent on about 540 muskets to Canandaigua, making the supply at Canandaigua and Batavia 3,000; and this day an additional quantity of five hundred leaves this for Canandaigua. With the last parcel have gone fixed ammunition, powder, some camp kettles, tents, drums and fifes, knapsacks and cartridge paper; 250 muskets and some ammunition have also been forwarded to Steuben by Mr. Townsend. Cannon ball with some case, grape and canister, for three and six pounders, are also on their way to Canandaigua, with the exception of tents, of which there are none yet here; the preceding supply will be ample, with what Captain Leonard may have at the fort, for the protection of the Niagara frontier.

I hope you will exert yourself for the protection of the frontiers and amongst other things supply some arms and ammunition to the people south of Buffalo, in Chautauqua and Cattaraugus. We shall have our hands full, but I calculate upon the energy and bravery of the officers and soldiers of the western country for the efficient protection of the inhabitants of the frontiers until regular troops shall approach the lines. In all cases where your personal services, by proceeding with detachments to the frontier or otherwise will be useful go, and you shall receive Major-General's pay while out, but not rations.

By order of the Commander-in-Chief,
    WM. PAULDING, Junior, Adjutant-General.
To Major-General Amos Hall.
(Tompkins' Papers, New York State Library.)

Major-General Brock to Sir George Prevost.

FORT GEORGE, July 3d, 1812.

SIR,—I have been anxiously waiting for some days to receive Your Excellency's commands in regard to the measures most proper to be pursued on the present emergency. The accounts received first through a mercantile channel, and soon after repeated from various quarters, of war having been declared by the United States against Great Britain, would have justified in my opinion offensive operations, but the reflection that at Detroit and St. Joseph's the weak state of garrisons would prevent the commanders from attempting any essential service connected in any degree with their future security, and that my only means of annoyance on this communication was limited to the reduction of Fort Niagara, which could be battered at any future period, I relinquished my original intention and attended only to defensive measures. My first object has been the calling out of the flank companies of militia, which has produced a force on this line of about 800 men. They turned out very cheerfully, but already show a spirit of impatience. The King's stores are now at such a low ebb that they can scarcely furnish any article of use or comfort. Blankets, haversacks and kettles are all to be purchased, and the troops in watching the banks of the river stand in the utmost need of tents. Mr. Couche has adopted the most efficient means to pay the militia in paper currency. I cannot positively say the number of militia that will be embodied, but they cannot throughout the Province be 4,000. The Americans are very active on the opposite side, in the erection of redoubts. We are not idle on our part, but unfortunately, having supplied Amherstburg with the guns that post required from Fort George, depending upon getting others from Kingston to supply their place, we find ourselves at this moment rather short of that essential arm. I have, however, every reason to think they are embarked on board the *Earl Moira*, which, according to Major McPherson's report, was to have sailed on the 20th ulto.

The Americans have, I believe, about 1,200 regulars and militia between Fort Niagara and Black Rock, and I consider myself at this moment perfectly safe against attempt they can make. About 100 Indians from the Grand River have attended to my summons; the remainder promise to come also, but I have too much reason to conclude that the Americans have been too successful in their endeavors to sow dissension and disaffection among them. It is a great object to get this fickle race interspersed among the troops. I should be unwilling in the event of a retreat to have three or four hundred of them hanging on my flanks. I shall probably have to sacrifice some money to gain them over. The appointment of some officers with salaries will be absolutely necessary.

The Americans make a daily parade of their force, and easily impose on the people on this side in regard to their numbers. I do not think they exceed 1,200, but they are represented infinitely more numerous. For the last fortnight every precaution has been taken to guard against the least communication, and to this day I am ignorant whether the President sanctioned the war resolutions of the two houses of Congress—that is, whether war be actually declared. The car brigade has been completed for service with horses belonging to gentlemen who spared them free of expense. I have not been honored with a line from Mr. Foster, nor, with all my endeavors, have I been able to obtain information of any consequence.

The *Prince Regent* made her first voyage this morning, and I propose sending her to Kingston to bring such articles as are absolutely necessary, which we know have arrived from Quebec. I trust she will outsail the *Oneida*.

(Canadian Archives, C. 676, p. 115.)

The Quartermaster-General of Militia to Lieutenant-Colonel Clark, Commanding 2nd Lincoln Militia.

HEADQUARTERS, NIAGARA, July 3rd, 1812.

SIR,—I have the honor to acknowledge the receipt of your letter of yesterday's date, in answer to which I am to inform you that none of the articles required by you, excepting nails, are in store here.

The General has, however, ordered camp kettles and haversacks to be made, and as soon as they shall be brought in you shall be supplied with a proportion of each.

You are not to expect tents, and must endeavor to shelter your men in the adjacent houses, barns, &c. The General is constantly employed in devising means to relieve the wants of the militia and to render their situation in every respect as comfortable as his means will admit, and the commissariat have been and are actively engaged in the same pursuit. You must, however, be sensible of the impossibility of complying with all your requisitions.

Muirhead has been appointed to the Medical Department and will reside at Chippawa. He has been amply supplied with everything necessary in that department.

To-morrow is the 4th of July, and should recommend extraordinary vigilance—the enemy may wish to open the campaign by endeavoring to give a little *éclat* to that day.

(Signed.) THE QR. MAS'R-GENL, Militia.

Lieut.-Col. Clark, Comdg. 2nd Lincoln Militia.

Capt. Leonard to Major Adams.

FORT NIAGARA, July 3rd, 1812, 10 o'clock a. m.

DEAR SIR,—I have received yours, with the communication from Col. Porter. I would by all means recommend the detention of every man now present on the river. It would in my opinion have a bad effect on the troops coming on to allow the departure of an individual. Let troops come from the eastward only—organize them as they come on. Keep everything as at present, and we shall soon be able to do something which will make everything secure in this quarter.

(MSS. of Hon. P. A. Porter.)

Major-General Amos Hall to Governor Tompkins.

BLOOMFIELD, July 4th, 1812.

SIR,—The troops now on the road to and at Black Rock will amount to nearly 2,800, three hundred of which are United States troops—this is the number who have been supplied with arms, &c. There was, on examining the arms and accoutrements, a great deficiency in cartridge boxes and flints. It was with difficulty that flints could be procured to furnish two to a firelock, and many of those very indifferent. I do not know the deficiency exactly in cartridge boxes, but I should imagine from the best account I could get that nearly one-third of the firelocks that have been delivered out were delivered without cartridge boxes. The greatest part of the firelocks were prime: some, however, were unfit for actual service—they appeared to be refuse arms.

Nearly 1,000 of the troops now in the field are militia called out on the spur of the occasion from General Rea's and Hopkins' brigades and cannot remain but a short time in the service. They have left their farms, their crops, their all, and will be ruined if they cannot soon return to their homes. The country is new, and most of those soldiers are dependent on their exertions to support their families and meet their engagements. But they are remarkably stout, ablebodied men, and I have no doubt would do their duty as soldiers were they to meet their enemy.

There had been no attack made by the enemy by the last accounts, but one was confidently expected.

The troops have neither tents nor camp equipage of any kind worth mentioning, and what they will do or how they will live is difficult to conjecture. Men taken from comfortable abodes and placed in the open fields with nothing but the heavens to cover them cannot endure for any considerable length of time so great a change. The disorders incident to camps thus formed of citizens will prove more fatal in one season that two campaigns of hard fighting. I hope that no time may be lost in forwarding a suitable number of tents and other camp equipage.

It is not in my power to inform Your Excellency the exact number of the enemy on the frontier at Niagara and Erie.

The number of regulars has been generally computed at 1500. But from some gentlemen with whom I have lately conversed direct from Canada the number is judged to be less, though a reinforcement from Lower Canada is undoubtedly on the way. The number is not ascertained—conjectures are from 1,000 to 1,500.

The whole number of regulars and militia now on the river from Fort George to Fort Erie and at those places, is estimated variously from 1,500 to 5,000.

By the best accounts I can get from gentlemen I have conversed from that quarter as late as Sunday last, 3,000 will be a large calculation. I expect to be more correctly advised in the course of to-morrow, probably by the mail which will pass within two hours.

2 o'clock, p. m. The mail has arrived and brings no new intelligence.

(Tompkins' Papers, vol. VII., pp. 330-2. New York State Library.)

Major Parmenio Adams to General Porter.

Your letter by the Indian, directed to Col. Swift, was received here last evening. I called a number of the officers and principal inhabitants together and had a council with the Tuscaroras, and we all assured them that in our opinion they were perfectly safe, and advised them to return with their families to their village. They appeared to be satisfied with our assurances, and I think will rest easy.

General Wadsworth staid four miles from this last night; will be in here in a few hours. It is not considered advisable to send any of the troops away that has already arrived until more arrive. Two hundred men can be accommodated at Schlosser; Judge Porter sent us word yesterday that that was the case. I think if that number was sent there it would be best. They could act either up or down the river, as occasion would require. The British have completed a battery above Queenston last night and are very busy this morning clearing off the trees.

Enclosed I send you Capt. Leonard's letter. You will see his opinion on the subject of assembling troops.

I refer you to Col. Swift, who will be able to give you every information.

Would it not be advisable for General Porter to come down and see General Wadsworth to consult on operations?

July 3d, 1812.

(MSS. of Hon. P. A. Porter.)

General Order.

ADJUTANT GENERAL'S OFFICE,
NIAGARA, 4 July, 1812.

Major-General Brock has witnessed with the highest satisfaction the orderly and regular conduct of such of the militia as have been called into actual service and their ardent desire to acquire military instruction. He is sensible that they are exposed to great privations, and every effort will be immediately made to supply their most pressing wants, but such are the circumstances of the country that it is absolutely necessary that every inhabitant should have recourse to his own means to furnish himself with blankets and other necessaries.

The Major-General calls the serious attention of every militiaman to the efforts making by the enemy to destroy and lay waste this flourishing country. They must be sensible of the great stake they have to contend for, and will by their conduct convince the enemy that they are not desirous of bowing their necks to a foreign yoke. The Major-General is determined to devote his best energies to the defence of the country, and has no doubt that supported by the zeal, activity and determination of the loyal inhabitants of this Province, he will successfully repel every hostile attack and preserve to them inviolate all that they hold dear.

From the experience of the past the Major-General is convinced that should it be necessary to call forth a further proportion of the militia to aid their fellow-subjects in defence of the Province, they will come forward with equal alacrity to share the danger and the honor.

By command of the Major-General.

ÆNEAS SHAW, Adjt.-Genl. M.

General Return of Troops in Upper Canada.

4th July, 1812.

Royal Artillery—Senior officer, Capt. Holcroft, Fort George—Three officers, two sergeants, one trumpeter, 74 rank and file. Total.. 80

Tenth Royal Veteran Battalion—Major McPherson, Kingston—Sixteen officers, eight sergeants, two drummers, 170 rank and file. Total.. 196

41st Regiment—Colonel Procter, Amherstburg—Thirty-seven officers, 45 sergeants, 20 drummers, 912 rank and file. Total.. 1014

Royal Newfoundland Regiment—Major Heathcote, Kingston—Nineteen officers, 18 sergeants, 14 drummers, 317 rank and file. Total................................... 368

1658

General Return of Troops in Lower Canada.

July 4th, 1812.

	officers	sergeants	drummers	rank and file	Total
Royal Artillery	14	7	7	347	375
Royal Artillery Drivers	—	1	"	30	31
Royal Engineers	3	"	—	—	3
10th Royal Veterans	24	23	7	309	363
1st Battalion, 8th Regiment	39	55	22	946	1062
41st Foot	—	—	—	2	2
49th Foot	22	41	18	664	745
100th Foot	24	31	20	479	554
103rd Foot	25	36	20	700	781
Canadian Fencibles	23	34	21	666	744
Glengarry Light Infantry	31	35	22	435	523
Canadian Voltigeurs	17	17	—	272	306
					5489

D. Noon to General Porter.

OSWEGO, 4th July, 1812.

DEAR SIR,—As soon as news of war being declared arrived at this place I immediately repaired to Sackett's Harbor, and General Brown, who commands that district, ordered me to prepare immediately at Massena, Hamilton, Ogdensburg, Gravelly Point, barracks, &c., to contain about four thousand men. I immediately started to Ogdensburg and the other places and made the necessary arrangements, and no doubt all will be ready in a few days, or as soon as troops can be marched to their respective stations. I have built barracks in the old fort at this place to contain about 700 men, which will probably be as many as will be stationed here.

P. S.—Your brother's vessels are safe at Ogdensburg, and Capt. Wolsy is doing all in his power to collect and arm vessels to carry them up to Sackett's Harbor with the assistance of Genl. Brown.

(MSS. of Hon. P. A. Porter.)

Colonel Baynes to Major-General Brock.

MONTREAL, July 4, 1812.

SIR,—We have a report here of your having commenced operations by levelling the American fort at Niagara. The General is most anxious to hear good and recent intelligence from your quarter. There is no considerable assembly of troops in our neighborhood as yet. The flank companies, embodied under Colonel Young, are on their march, and the 2,000 militia will form a chain of posts from St. John's to La Prairie. The town militia of this and Quebec, to the amount of 3,000 in each city, have volunteered, being embodied and drilled, and will take their proportion of garrison duty to relieve the troops. The proclamation for declaring martial law is prepared and will be speedily issued. All aliens will be required to take the oath of allegiance or immediately to quit the Province. Our cash is at its last issue, and a substitute of paper must per force be resorted to. This has been Sir George's principal object in calling the Legislature together. You have a very arduous and difficult card to play, and have our sincere and confident wishes for your success. Sir George strongly recommends extreme moderation in the use of the Indians, and to keep them in control as much as possible.

(From Tupper's Life of Brock, pp. 196-7.)

Lord Bathurst to Sir George Prevost.

DOWNING STREET, 4th July, 1812.
No. 2.

His Majesty's Government trust that you will be enabled to suspend with perfect safety all extraordinary preparations which you may have been induced to make in consequence of the precarious state of relations between this country and the United States, and as every specific requisition for warlike stores and accoutrements has been completed, with the exception of that for the clothing of the corps proposed to be raised from the Glengarry Emigrants, I have not thought it necessary to direct the preparation of any further supplies.

I conclude that in consequence of the instructions contained in Lord Liverpool's letter of the 30th March, that measures for the formation of that corps have been abandoned

(Canadian Archives, Q. 117-2. p. 185.)

Proclamation.

PROVINCE OF UPPER CANADA.

By Isaac Brock, Esquire, President, administering the Government of Upper Canada, and Major-General commanding His Majesty's forces within our said Province.

To all whom these Presents shall come :—

GREETING,—

Whereas, on the seventeenth day of June last the Congress of the United States of America declared that war then existed between those States and their territories and the United Kingdom of Great Britain and Ireland and the dependencies thereof, and whereas in pursuance of such declaration the subjects of the United

States have actually committed hostilities against the possessions of His Majesty: as President of His Majesty's Executive Council in the affairs of the Province, I do hereby strictly enjoin and require all His Majesty's liege subjects to be obedient to the lawful authorities, to forbear all communication with the enemy or persons residing within the territory of the United States, and to manifest their loyalty by a zealous co-operation with His Majesty's armed force in defence of the Province and repulse of the enemy. And I do further require and command all officers, civil and military, to be vigilant in the discharge of their duty, especially to prevent all communication with the enemy, and to cause all persons suspected of traitorous intercourse to be apprehended and treated according to law.

Given under my hand and seal at arms at York, in the Province of Upper Canada, this sixth day of July, in the year of our Lord one thousand eight hundred and twelve, and in the fifty-second of His Majesty's reign.

ISAAC BROCK, President.

By command of His Honor.
WILLIAM JARVIS, Secretary.

Brigadier-General Wm. Wadsworth to Governor Tompkins.

HEADQUARTERS, LEWISTON, July 6, 1812.

SIR,—Since writing from Genesee and putting part of the detachment ordered out on the march, I came on to this place and have visited Fort Niagara. The fort is very much decayed. There is now at the fort six pieces (six-pounders) mounted. They can be used only in the fort, for want of horses and harness. There are four howitzers and two mortars, neither of them mounted. There are no shells to make use of even were they mounted. Amongst every other difficulty to be surmounted there is no one appears more serious than the want of ammunition.

The store on hand may be considered about 3,600 of powder, and shot in proportion, together with about 16 boxes of musket cartridges and distributed nearly in the following manner:—At Fort Niagara, thirty cwt. powder, and the remaining 600, a part at this place and part at Black Rock: the boxes of cartridges are at the several places of rendezvous. Four field pieces have been ordered in from Ontario: two are at this place and two at Black Rock. To make them useful it will be necessary to have horses for moving them.

The arms that were drawn by Lieut.-Colonel Swift are many of them unfit for service. They will be inspected very soon, when it will be known how many of them are fit for use. The detachment from Ontario County will be here this morning. The detachments from Genesee and Niagara are principally out, and will be organized under Lieut.-Colonel Dobbin.

When the several detachments that are ordered out are inspected there will probably be the following number and organized in the following manner:

Under Lieut.-Colonel Swift		400
" " "	Allen	400
" " "	Dobbin	300
		1100

Absent	336
Sick	20
Dead	4
	360	360
		1460

The detachments when made, to which the above officers were assigned, was as follows:—

Lieut.-Colonel Swift		600
" "	Allen	510
" "	Dobbin	350
		1460

There are in the fort under Captain Leonard 150, and on the 4th inst. were marched in by Major Mullany of the United States army, his corps of about 250, making in the fort 400, together with 1100 detached militia, making in the whole 1500 now for duty on the frontier. There has been considerable sickness in Lieut.-Col. Swift's regiment.

Having duly considered the importance of procuring harness for the field pieces in the fort and having horses to move them as well as to exercise the four pieces in the field, I shall request General Peter B. Porter to procure the harness as soon as necessary and to purchase twenty horses, which will be only the one-half that will be requisite for the use of the ten pieces, that is to say, six from the fort and four now in the field. As for procuring a further number, under the existing circumstances I shall wait your order.

It may hereafter be thought advisable to take the pieces now in the fort to the field; if so a further number of twenty horses more will be required.

The preparations on the opposite side of the river are very considerable. Between Lake Ontario and Fort George there are three breastworks hove up, between Fort George and Queenston there are two, and south of Queenston on the north side of the mountain they have one. With the naked eye it appears strong, built of stone and will probably mount two or three pieces. Those between the lake and Fort George mount seven or eight pieces, part twelve and part six-pounders. Those in Fort George Captain Leonard says are twelve-pounders.

The circumstance of there being but 30 cwt. of powder for the use of the fort is very unpleasant, for in case of an attack from Fort George on our fort Captain Leonard could make but about one hour's defence, for the powder would be wasted and a retreat would then be necessary. This further shows the importance of having horses and harness prepared to move the pieces in the fort to the field, as well as to have them for defence.

Two regiments of militia, one from Genesee, commanded by Lieut.-Colonel Daniel Davis, and one from Niagara County, when notified of the importance of having additional strength on the line, very promptly appeared with haste to the field. Lieut.-Colonel Daniel Davis's regiment appeared fuller than at any former call.

The call of the regiment was undoubtedly justifiable from an appearance on the opposite side of the river. There is yet considerable appearance of their determination to act offensively.

It is a cause of much regret that there are no tents, camp kettles or any description of camp equipage now in this quarter.

The dissatisfaction of the two regiments of militia is not to be surmounted in any other way than to dismiss them to save the disagreeable necessity of their dispersing without permission. They were called out at a moment's notice, and could make no preparation for themselves and they found very little made for them. They were able to draw but little bread, and to draw flour seemed useless, for they had not any utensils to cook it in. Such pails and kettles as were to be had were purchased, but in the distribution there was not one to a company. From such information as I am able to collect from intercepted letters and other ways, I have much reason to believe our enemy have three thousand men now in the field and one thousand more subject to a very short call, exclusive of three hundred Indians, said to be armed complete.

Their strength taken into consideration, when it being the probability that they will make an attack, I cannot consider myself justified in saying that the river will be sufficiently guarded unless there are three thousand men placed between the lake and the mountain and one thousand from the mountain to Buffalo. Taking this number for the standard, it will require 2,500 men to make such a resistance as prudence might dictate and to cease the prevailing opinion in Genesee and Niagara Counties that they are in danger.

I would renew my assurances of a determination to persevere and leave nothing undone that is in my power to do.

(Tompkins' Papers, vol. VII., pp. 343-7, New York State Library.)

From the New York Evening Post, Wednesday, July 15.

CANANDAIGUA, July 7, 1812.

Of the force which the British have on the Niagara, various accounts are given. The number of regular troops is probably not far from 1500—of militia ready for service about 3000. With respect to the Indians which are said to have joined them, their numbers are stated by different reports from 150 to 1000. We have reason to believe it would approach nearer the fact to say there were none.

General Brock, Governor of Upper Canada, commands in person.

Nothing momentous had occurred at the last dates. The vessel of Mr. Colt, mentioned in our last as being captured by the British, had been restored and Lieut. Gansevoort, who was in their power when the news of war being declared was received, has been suffered to return to the American garrison.

The apprehension that a descent would be made by the British with a view to take the American garrison, Fort Niagara, has subsided. Had they contemplated its capture they would have done it before we increased our forces in its neighborhood.

We understand that Fort Niagara is in a decayed state, with only six pieces of cannon and 120 men. We do not know the number of men stationed on the river from Black Rock to the fort, probably there are 300 regulars and 1500 or 2000 militia.

(File in New York Society Library.)

From the Aurora of Philadelphia, July 18th, 1812.

CANANDAIGUA, July 7.—A number of waggons of warlike stores and several companies of drafted and volunteer militia left this town last week for the frontiers, among them Captain A. Dox's infantry, Captain Stanley's riflemen and Captains Bogert's and Hart's militia.

Major General Hall has put in requisition the whole militia of his division to march when wanted.

(File in Mercantile Library, Philadelphia.)

PUBLIC SPEECHES.

Public speeches delivered at the Village of Buffalo on the 6th and 8th days of July by Hon. Erastus Granger, Indian Agent, and Red Jacket, one of the principal chiefs and speakers of the Seneca Nation, respecting the part the Six Nations would take in the present war against Great Britain.

BUFFALO.

Printed and sold by S. H. & H. A. Salisbury; sold also at the Canandaigua and Geneva book stores.

1812.

SPEECHES.

[This Council was convened at the request of the Hon. E. Granger, Esq., Indian Agent. The sachems, chiefs and warriors of the Six Nations of Indians, residing in the United States, were present.]

MONDAY, July 6, 1812.

Red Jacket.

Addressing himself to the Agent, spoke as follows:

BROTHER,—We are glad of having an opportunity once more of meeting you in council. We thank the Great Spirit that has again brought us together. This is a full meeting. All our head men are present. Every village is represented in this council. We are pleased to find Mr. Parrish, our interpreter, is present. He has attended all our councils since the last war, and is well acquainted with all the treaties we have made with the United States.

The voice of war has reached our ears and made our minds gloomy. We now wish you to communicate to us everything which your Government has charged you to tell us concerning this war. We shall listen with attention to what you have to say.

Mr. Granger's Speech.

Brothers of the Six Nations:—

I am happy to behold so many of you assembled together at this time. I observe that the chiefs of the Seneca, Onondaga, Cayuga and Tuscarora Nations, and some of the Delawares are present. The Mohawks who live in Canada are not represented, and the Oneidas, living at a distance, could not attend. Brothers, you will now listen to what I say.

At the close of the Revolutionary war the United States held a treaty with the Six Nations at Fort Stanwix. They restored to you the country of land which they had conquered from you and the British and set you down once more on your old seats. Several treaties have since been made with you, but that which particularly binds us together was made at Canadaigua about sixteen years since.

The chain of friendship then formed has been kept bright until this time.

In this great length of time nothing material has happened to disturb the peace and harmony subsisting between us. Any momentary interruptions of peace which have taken place have been happily settled without injury to either party. Our friendship has remained unbroken.

BROTHERS,—The prosperity and happiness of the Six Nations have always been objects which the United States have had in view.

You have enjoyed with us all the blessings which the country afforded, consistent with your mode and habits of living. We have grown up together on this great island. The United States are strong and powerful: you are few in numbers and weak, but as our friends we consider you and your women and children under our protection.

BROTHERS,—You have heretofore been told that the conduct of Great Britain towards us might eventually lead to war. That event has at length taken place. War now exists between the United States and the British Nation. The injuries we have received from the British have at length forced us into a war.

I will now proceed to state to you the reasons why we have been compelled to take up arms.

For a number of years past the British and French who live on the other side of the great waters have been at war with each other, shedding each other's blood. These nations wished us to take a part in their war. France wished us to fight against Great Britain. Great Britain wanted us to join against France. But the United States did not wish to take any part in their quarrels. Our object was to live in peace and trade with both nations. Notwithstanding our endeavors to maintain friendship with them, both France and Great Britain have broken their treaties with us. They have taken our vessels and property and refused to restore them or make compensation for the losses we have sustained.

But the British have done us the greatest injury. They have taken out of our vessels at least six thousand of our own people, put them on board their ships of war and compelled them to fight their battles. In this situation our friends and connexions are confined, obliged to fight for the British.

BROTHERS,—If you consider the situation in which we are placed, you cannot blame us for going to war. I will ask you a question. Suppose that the Mohawk Nation, who live in Canada, were at war with a nation of Indians at the westward. Both of these nations being your friends, you were determined to take no part in their disputes, but to be at peace with both—to visit them and trade with them as usual. In consequence of this determination, you should send messages with speeches to inform them of the system you had adopted. But the Mohawks, not satisfied in seeing you in prosperity, enjoying the blessings of peace, visiting and trading with them—determine to make you feel the evils of war unless you agree to give up all intercourse with those they are at war with. This you cannot consent to: you want the privilege of selling your furs and skins where you can find the best market. The Mohawks still continue to flatter you—say they are your friends—put on smiling faces and speak good words. But in the meantime, while professing friendship towards you, they fall upon your hunting and trading parties as they travel back and forth—strip them of their property—leave them naked in the world and refuse to make satisfaction. Not only this, but they come near your village and there murder your people—others they take when found from home, bind them fast and compel them to go and fight their battles.

BROTHERS,—Could you for a moment submit to such treatment? Would you not all as one rise from your seats and let the enemy feel your vengeance? If you are warriors, if you are brave men, you certainly would. What I have stated is exactly our case. The British have done us all these injuries and still continue to do us wrong without a cause. The United States have risen from their seats—they have raised their strong arm and will cause it to be felt.

BROTHERS, I feel it my duty at this present time to point out to you the straight path in which you ought to walk. You well recollect the advice given you by the people of the United States at the commencement of the Revolutionary war against Great Britain. You were then requested to stay at home—to sit upon your seats at your own council fires and to take no part in the war.

It would have been happy for you had you followed this good advice. But the presents and fair speeches of the British poisoned your minds. You took up the hatchet against us and became our enemies. At the close of the war with Britain (the event you well know) the United States had it in their power to have cut you off as a people, but they took pity on you and let you return to your former seats.

Your Great Father, the President of the Seventeen Fires, now gives his Red Children the same advice that was given you at the beginning of the last war: that is—*That you take no part in the quarrels of the white people.* He stands in no need of your assistance. His warriors are numerous, like the sand on the shores of the great lakes which cannot be counted. He is able to fight his own battles, and requests you to stay at home, cultivate your fields and take care of your property. If you have any regard for your women and children—if you have any respect for the country in whose soil repose the bones of your fathers—you will listen to his advice and keep bright the chain of friendship between us.

You have been invited to join the British in this war. Reflect for a moment on the consequence of complying with their request. You will lose your property in the United States. We shall soon take possession of Canada. They will have no land to sit you down upon. You will have nothing to expect from our mercy. You will deservedly as a people be cut off from the face of the earth.

The late delegation which you sent to Canada was told that they ought not to put any confidence in the United States—that if you did we should deceive you—that the United States kept no promises made to Indians.

BROTHERS,—I now ask in what have the United States deceived you? Have they not punctually paid your annuities as they became due? Have not the Senecas received annually the interest of their money in the public funds? Has not the State of New York honestly fulfilled her engagements with the Oneidas, Onondagas and Cayugas? Have not the Tuscaroras been assisted in the sale of their property in North Carolina and in obtaining a pleasant seat purchased of the Holland Land Company? I again ask, have not the United States observed good faith towards you? Have they deceived you in any one thing? I answer, they have not.

Knowing as you do that we are your friends, will you act like children and suffer yourselves to be imposed upon at this time by our enemies?

BROTHERS,—It was our wish that the Six Nations should all be agreed as one man, but the Mohawks and some few others living on the British side, have been so foolish as to declare in favor of war. The good advice you lately gave them has not been attended to. They are now at Newark in arms against the United States. I am sorry they have not listened to good counsel. You, however, have done your duty and you are not to blame for their folly. They will soon find they have done wrong and must suffer the consequence.

BROTHERS,—Continue to listen.

You have been frequently told, that in case we went to war, we did not want your assistance. The same thing has this day been repeated. But I find some of your young men are restless and uneasy. They wish to be with our warriors and I am sensible the Chiefs have not power to control them. As I observed before, we want not their aid, but we believe it to be better for them to be our friends than our enemies.

If they will not be contented to stay at home but must see something of a war, perhaps 150 or 200 will be permitted to stand by the side of our warriors and receive the same pay and provisions which our soldiers receive.

If they should be permitted to join our troops they must conform to our regulations. Your mode of carrying on war is different from ours. We never attack and make war upon women and children, nor on those who are peaceably inclined and have nothing to defend themselves with. Such conduct we consider as cowardly and not becoming a warrior.

BROTHERS,—If you have not sufficient time this evening to deliberate on what I have said, I will meet you to-morrow or next day, and receive your answer.

Red Jacket's Answer to Mr. Granger's Speech.

WEDNESDAY, July 8, 1812.

BROTHER,—We are now prepared to give an answer to the speech you delivered to us in council the other day. We are happy to find so many of the *white* people present. We are not accustomed to transact important business in the DARK! We are willing that the *light* should shine upon whatever we do. When we speak we do it with sincerity and in a manner that cannot be misunderstood.

You have been appointed by the United States an agent for the Six Nations. We have been requested to make you acquainted with the sentiments of those nations we represent. None of the Mohawks, Oneidas, or Cayugas, it is well known, are present. The number of treaties that has passed between the Six Nations and the United States appears to be fresh in your memory. We shall only mention to you some things that were agreed upon in the treaty made at Canandaigua.

We were a long time in forming that treaty, but we at length made up our minds and spoke freely. Mr. Pickering, who was then agent for the United States, declared to us that no breach should ever be made in that treaty. We replied to him, " If it should ever be broken, you will be the first to do it. We are weak. You are strong. You are a great people. You can if you are so disposed place yourselves under it and overturn it, or, by getting upon it you can crush it with your weight." Mr. Pickering again declared that this treaty would ever remain firm and unshaken, that it would be as durable as the largest rock to be found in our country.

This treaty was afterwards shown to Gen. Washington. He said that he was satisfied and pleased with what the agent had done. He told us that no treaty could be formed that would be more binding. He then presented us with a chain which he assured us would never rust, but always remain bright. Upon this belt of wampum, (holding up a belt of wampum curiously wrought) he placed a silver seal [upon which an eagle was engraved, representing the United States.] This belt we always have and wish to look upon as sacred.

In the treaty it was agreed that the Six Nations should receive a small annuity, to show the intention of the United States to continue friendly with them. This has been complied with. It was also agreed that if any injury or damage should be done on either side satisfaction should be made to the party injured. We were a long time in conference before we could make up our minds upon one article of the treaty—what punishment should be inflicted for the crime of murder? Mr. Pickering said that it should be *hanging*. We told him that would never do—that if a white man killed an Indian, the Indians would not be permitted to hang the white man —the sacrifice would be considered too great for killing an Indian. We at length agreed that conciliatory measures should be resorted to, such as would give satisfaction to all parties.

In cases of theft as in stealing horses, cattle, &c., it was agreed that restitution should be made. In this article the whites have transgressed twice where the Indians have once. As often as you will mention one instance in which we have wronged you, we will tell you of two in which you have defrauded us!

I have related these articles of the treaty to show you that it still remains clear in our recollection, and we now declare to you, in presence of all here assembled, that we will continue to hold fast the chain which counsels us together. Some who first took hold of it are gone, but others will supply their place.

We regret extremely that any disturbance should have taken place among the white people. Mischief has commenced. We are now told that war has been declared against Great Britain; the reasons for it are unknown to us. The Six Nations are placed in an unpleasant situation. A part of them are in Canada and the remainder in the United States.

Whilst we were endeavoring to persuade those who live in Canada to remain peaceable and quiet, the noise of war suddenly sounded in our ears. We were told that all communication between us and them would be prevented. We have since heard that they have taken up arms. We are very sorry to hear of this. They are our brothers and relations, and we do not wish that their blood should be spilt when there is so little occasion for it. We hope that the passage is not so closely stopped but that a small door may still be open, by which we may again have an opportunity of seeing our brothers and of convincing them to take no part in a war in which they have nothing to gain.

We know the feelings of the greatest portion of them. We therefore believe that if we have another opportunity we can persuade them to have nothing to do with this war. Our minds are fully made up on this subject, and we repeat that it is our wish to see them once more and to give them our advice about the path they ought to travel.

You (Mr. Parrish) are going to the eastward. You will visit the Oneidas and Cayugas. Relate to them faithfully what has taken place in this council; tell them all we have said, and request that a deputation of their chiefs may be sent to attend our council here. We wish that you would return with them.

[He then brought forward the belt which he had before held up in his hand, and requested Mr. Granger and the others present to look at it and observe whether it was not the one that had been presented to the Six Nations by Gen. Washington.

Red Jacket then held up another belt, much larger, of different colors, which appeared to be very ancient. He continued.]

BROTHER,—I will now state to you the meaning of this belt. A long time ago the Six Nations had formed a union. They had no means of writing their treaties on paper and of preserving them in the manner the white people do. We therefore made this belt, which shows that the Six Nations have bound themselves firmly together; that it is their determination to remain united; that they will never do anything contrary to the interests of the whole, but that they will always act towards each other like brothers.

Whenever for the future you see a small number of our people meeting together to consult about any matter of trifling account, we desire that you would pay no attention to it. It may give you uneasiness, when we have no intention to injure you. This happened but a few days ago. It seems that a white man and two or three Indians living on the same creek had a small conversation, which the mischievous talked about until the whole country was in an uproar, and many families left their country and homes in consequence.

The council held some time since at Batavia was unauthorized by us, and we now declare to you that none have a right to hold council anywhere except at this place, around the great council fire of the Six Nations.

We hope that you will not accept of any of our warriors unless they are permitted by our great council to offer themselves to you. And we should be sorry, indeed, if any of the whites should entice our young warriors to take up arms. We mention these things to show you that we wish to guard against everything that may interrupt our good understanding.

BROTHER,—We hope that what has been said will be generally known to the white people. Let every one recollect and give a faithful account of it. We wish them to know that we are peaceably disposed towards the United States, and that we are determined to keep bright the chain of friendship that we formed with them at Canandaigua.

BROTHER,—We have one thing more to which we would wish to call your attention. We present you the papers (handing to the agent a small bundle of papers), which secure to us our annuities from the U. States. We would be glad to know if this war would affect our interests in that quarter. We also desire that you would inform us whether the monies we have deposited in the [late] bank of the United States will be less secure than if this war had not taken place.

Reply of the Agent.

Mr. Granger, after thanking them for their general and punctual attendance, replied as follows:—

BROTHERS,—You have this day brought forward the large white belt given you at Canandaigua. Your speaker has explained the leading particulars of the treaty made at that time. I am much pleased to find your minds so deeply impressed with them. I now repeat to you that the United States will on their part hold fast to the treaty; they wish you to do the same. Should it be broken on your part, the United States will no longer consider themselves bound by it.

BROTHERS,—It appears that you are still desirous of sending to Grand River to endeavor to prevail on your brethren in that quarter to remain at peace. An undertaking of this kind will be of little use. They will only fill your heads with idle talk, and poison your minds against the United States. Perhaps after crossing Niagara River you will not be permitted to go any further. Should you, however, insist upon it, permission will be granted to four or five of your chiefs to go over, with such instructions as you shall think proper to give them.

But should your young men cross over and join our enemies, they must never expect to be allowed to set their feet on our shores again as friends. Rest assured they will be severely punished for it.

With respect to the property you have placed in the hands of the United States you have nothing to fear, it will be fully as secure as if this war had not happened. Your annuities will be paid to you as formerly and your bank stock be as productive as usual.

I now return you my thanks for the good attendance you have given at this council. I feel pleased that you have again come forward and renewed the covenant of friendship, that you have once more declared your steady attachment to the United States.

Your friend, Mr. Parrish, will soon go to the eastward, where he will see such of your brethren as were not present at this council. In a short time he will return and remain here if he should be wanted through the summer.

[In consequence of the permission of the agent several of the chiefs repaired to Lewiston for the purpose of crossing. Application was made to General Brock (who has the command of the troops in the Upper Province) that they might be suffered to land on the Canada shore. After two days General Brock sent them word that two of their chiefs would be permitted to come over and converse for a few minutes with such of the chiefs belonging to Canada as would be authorized to meet them. They accordingly went over, and after a few minutes' conversation with some of the Canadian chiefs, without effecting their object, they were ordered to return.]

Sir George Prevost to Major-General Brock.

MONTREAL, July 7, 1812.

SIR,—It was only on my arrival at Montreal that I received Mr. Foster's notification of the Congress of the United States having declared war against Great Britain. The fact had been previously ascertained through mercantile channels.

I am convinced you have acted wisely in abstaining from offensive operations, which in their effect might have united a people governed by public opinion, and among whom too much division exists at this moment to admit of its influence in promoting vigorous measures against us.

The manner of the flank companies of militia turning out must have been very satisfactory to you. I hope your supplies of ordnance and ordnance stores on their way from Kingston have arrived safe.

I have caused arms, accoutrements and ammunition to be forwarded for the use of the Cornwall, Stormont and Dundas battalions of militia. Camp equipage for 500 men shall be sent to you as soon as possible, together with muskets.

We are on the eve of substituting paper for bullion. I am

aware of the Canadian prejudice against such a circulating medium, but it must give way to the imperious necessity of the times.

It is highly proper you should secure the services of the Indians, but restrain and control them as much as you can. Whatever appointments you deem indispensably necessary you are authorized to make, as well as the sacrifice of some money to gain them over. It is proper we should maintain our ascendency over the Indians and feed with proper food their predilection for us.

Colonel Lethbridge, an inspecting field officer, is under orders for Kingston, and there to wait your commands.

(From Tupper's Life of Brock, pp. 198-9.)

From the Independent Chronicle, of Boston, 20th July, 1812.

ONONDAGA VALLEY, July 8th.

Since the declaration of war everything goes on briskly in these western wilds. There are already 3,000 troops at Niagara from the counties of Genesee, Steuben, Chautauqua and Niagara. Monday last a considerable number of waggons passed through here loaded with arms, ammunition and shovels.

(From file in Lenox Library, New York.)

Colonel Baynes to Major-General Brock.

MONTREAL, July 8, 1812.

SIR,—I was highly gratified yesterday in receiving your letters of the 3rd July, for we have felt extremely anxious about you ever since we have learnt the unexpected declaration of war, which has been so long threatened that no one believed it would ever seriously take place, and even now it is the prevailing opinion that from the opposition testified by the Eastern States offensive measures are not likely to be speedily adopted against this country. Sir George is inclined to let these sentiments take their course, and as little advantage would accrue by more active measures on our part our present plans are all defensive. General De Rottenburg is arrived and the flank companies embodied are on their way. This corps, with the embodied militia, will form a chain from La Prairie to St. Johns, with a light corps advanced in their front. We have reports of the 103rd regiment being in the river and, it is added, recruits for the 100th Regiment.

Sir George has had applications from so many quarters for militia below Kingston that, to ensure a general arrangement and to adopt the best system that circumstances will admit, he has directed Colonel Lethbridge, the Inspecting Field Officer here, to proceed through the line of settlements to see the several colonels and corps of militia so as to fix their quotas, and afterwards to proceed to Kingston and assume the command of that post, if necessary. He will be placed under your orders, but you will perhaps not wish to bring him in contact with the 41st Regiment, as he is senior to Colonel Procter.

Sir George desires me to say that he does not attempt to prescribe specific rules for your guidance. They must be directed by your discretion and the circumstances of the time: the present order of the day with him is forbearance until hostilities are more decidedly marked.

(From Tupper's Life of Brock, pp. 199-200).

District General Orders.

FORT GEORGE, 9th July, 1812.

D. G. Orders.

The following proportion of officers and non-commissioned officers will be entitled to receive pay and allowances:

ESTABLISHMENT.

	Capt.	Sub.	Sergts.
For every company embodied for service, consisting of 30 rank and file	1	2	2
For Do., consisting of 45 men and not exceeding 80	1	2	3
For Do., consisting of 80 men and upwards	1	3	4

For every 250 men one field officer will be allowed, and so in proportion.

The difference of pay between a subaltern and an adjutant will be allowed for every 200 men. A paymaster will be appointed for the District of Niagara, who will muster on the 23d or 24th of every month all the corps stationed between Niagara and Lake Erie. Pay lists are to be certified on oath by the captains of companies, and commanding officers of posts (whether of the line or militia) will examine and certify their belief as to the correctness of the account.

By order of Major-Genl. Brock.

THOS. EVANS, B. M.

MEMORANDUM.

In consequence of the above order the circular letter from His Honor the President to officers commanding regiments, dated 8th April, 1812, is rescinded, and officers commanding regiments are directed to transmit to headquarters an account of the actual expenses that have been incurred under it.

General Wadsworth to Governor D. D. Tompkins.

HEADQUARTERS, LEWISTON, 8th July, 1812.

SIR,—Since my last of the 5th inst., the unremitted exertions of our opponents in heaving up breastworks is daily to be seen. Not having had any communication across the river since the 5th inst., I cannot relate anything in respect to the strength they may gain, but every operation of theirs since the 5th inst. seems to concur in adding to the belief that there are a large body of men near the frontier, at least as many as was calculated in my letter of the 5th inst,—three thousand near the line and one thousand subject to a moment's call. Our shore must be considered unsafe until we have at least four thousand troops on the line, and would recommend five hundred more, with a view of taking possession of Grand Island. A party of soldiers and Indians seem to be making a drift that way, seemingly with an intention to carry on a correspondence in that quarter with this side or take possession of the island themselves, more particularly to carry on with greater ease a correspondence that is already suspected. The great length of the river that must be guarded requires a great number of soldiers.

From every appearance at present I think myself justified in recommending the number above to be placed on the margin of this river.

I desire that you duly consider what 1500 men can do in opposition to our opponents on a river of the length of the Niagara from Lake Ontario to Buffalo, whose margin is principally covered with timber and bushes.

If it is your pleasure I must express to you my anxiety for the immediate support of some or all of the number proposed.

To be attacked would not be more than I have reason to expect for the last twenty-four hours. I believe it is only owing to want of information of our real situation why we have not been attacked before this time.

The accommodation for the troops in this quarter is much to be lamented. Every preparation is making that can be made without axes, hoes, spades, shovels or anything of the kind.

I hope, sir, my zeal for the honor of our arms and for the comfort of the men under my command will be a sufficient excuse for pressing on Your Excellency the importance of forwarding ammunition, and camp equipage is indispensably necessary, and in case of an action our ammunition would all be wasted and we be left in a deplorable condition.

The soldiers that have last arrived on the frontier are very much worn down with the fatigue of their march and the duty since required of them.

In the event of your sending the reinforcement proposed I would recommend the sending the further number of ten pieces of artillery, as they will be the only implements that will have an effect across the river.

Among the ammunition would recommend grape shot, to be made use of in the event of their attempting to cross the river.

(Tompkins Papers, vol., VII., pp. 373-5, New York State Library.)

From the National Intelligencer of Washington, D. C., 25th July, 1812.

Extract of a letter from a gentleman at Fort Niagara to his friend in this city, dated July 8th:

This garrison and all my property at this place have been in the most imminent danger. I expected every moment that it would be destroyed and myself ruined. The British had the means to lay the whole place in ashes, whilst we were entirely destitute of men, cannon, ammunition and everything else. This danger is not now past, but our prospect of security is more clear than it was last week. This frontier has been in a state of alarm and confusion for almost two weeks past. No business has been done except moving goods and property to places of safety.

(From File in the New York Society Library.)

General Peter B. Porter to Governor Tompkins.

BLACK ROCK, July 9, 1812.

SIR,—I have just returned from Niagara and Lewiston, where I spent two or three days with General Wadsworth. The ordinary militia, who repaired to this frontier in great numbers and with promptitude that has done them great credit, are now mostly dismissed and have returned to their homes, their places being supplied by the detached militia, most of whom have arrived and the remainder coming in daily. Our force when organized a day or two hence will consist of the detached or drafted militia, about 1,500; Colonel Swift's regiment of volunteers, about 550; the regular troops at Niagara fort, about 450, and a few men of the ordinary militia, say 100, who are about to volunteer under the act of the sixth of February, making in the whole about 2,500 men. This force, raw as it is, with only a few pieces of light artillery, and not more than one company (Captain Leonard's) who know anything about artillery, is in my opinion barely sufficient for the protection of this river against a greater number of men with a full supply of heavy ordnance and a powerful train of field artillery managed by experienced troops. I shall not be surprised if the British were to make an attack on us even now, as they know our real strength.

They have on the river from Newark to Fort Erie, inclusive, according to the best information we can get, (and most of the people who cross the river concur substantially in the estimate), from 9 to 1,200 regulars, from 2,000 to 2,500 militia, and about 250 or 300 Indian warriors, making in all about 3,600 men. Such, however, is said to be the disaffection among the militia that no reliance can be placed on them for an attack or perhaps for defence. Our standard once planted on their shore, and supported by a respectable force, I have no doubt that most of the inhabitants would seek protection under it.

I cannot avoid repeating to Your Excellency the opinion I have heretofore expressed, that under present circumstances the policy, interest and quiet of this State and the United States require that no time should be lost in preparing for the invasion of Canada at this point as well as other places. For this purpose we want in the first place artillery of different descriptions, and in the next, men who know how to use it. Our force now on the river, amounting to about 2500 men, improved by a rigid discipline for six or eight weeks to come, with the addition of 2500 regular troops, consisting of a due proportion of artillerists, might pass over the river and subdue the peninsula opposite here, which is the heart of Upper Canada. Our army should also at the same time be prepared to pass the St. Lawrence river below Lake Ontario, to prevent them from concentrating the whole of their force at this point. A general of experience and ability would of course be required to conduct the enterprise. We regret that we have neither had men nor other means to justify any attempt to pass the river; 2,500 men well provided with arms and ammunition might at the first moment have accomplished what will now require double the number. Would it not be well to commence building 50 or 60 boats? I have ventured already to build four, which are indispensable for ordinary uses. The village at the Falls is a place peculiarly fitted for this business. There is plenty of good timber, a saw mill, pitch, oakum, &c., and fine quarters for men. A few ship carpenters, who could be engaged here, and the artificers belonging to the troops, would build them in a few days. The boats there would be perfectly safe as respects the enemy, and could be put into the water above or below the falls.

The troops, who have been thus suddenly and unexpectedly thrown upon the frontier, have subjected me to many serious difficulties and embarrassments and to a heavy responsibility. They have depended on me for almost everything, and it was necessary they should be supplied, having brought with them no means of subsistence for themselves. I am sure that I have acted with a due regard for economy. The detached militia (part of the 100,000) were induced to hasten to this place by the solicitations of the people on the frontier. But most of the ordinary militia who came out were, I believe, brought here by the impulse of their own feelings and a sense of common danger. They were dismissed the moment the danger ceased to be imminent.

Situated as I am, it would be very gratifying to receive from Your Excellency some general instruction as to what I am to do. General Wadsworth has just made a requisition on me for the purchase of twenty horses with harness, &c., for the artillery, also for baggage waggons, &c. Having received no instructions from you how to act, I am placed in respect to such demands in a situation of great delicacy.

P. S.—A man just from Canada states that the British have captured one schooner on the upper lakes and two on Lake Ontario. About 100 British soldiers have been busily employed since yesterday morning in throwing up a breastwork directly opposite to me (about a mile distant), in which they have just placed three nine-pounders. I am requested to ask whether a company of volunteers associating under the act of February 6, and designating for themselves men as officers who now hold no commissions, can be accepted and the officers if approved of by you immediately appointed. A company under these circumstances wish to volunteer near this village.

(Tompkins Papers, Vol. VII., pp. 366-70, New York State Library.)

The Secretary of War to Major-General Dearborn.

WAR DEPARTMENT, July 9, 1812.

[Abstract.]

Instructs him after making arrangements for the defence of the seaboard to proceed to Albany and to send all recruits not otherwise disposed of to that place, or some station on Lake Champlain, to be organized for the invasion of Canada.

Militia General Orders.

NIAGARA, 10th July, 1812.

M. G. Orders,—

Major-General Brock having received information that a large portion of the troops assembled on the other side of the river have retired, and being anxious to afford the militia every indulgence compatible with the safety of the Province, orders that one-half of each corps or company now on duty be permitted to return home on furlough.

Officers commanding will give a preference to those whose presence on the farms are most required to bring in their harvest. A proportion of officers will also be permitted to return to their homes, who will as far as possible adopt measures to secure the return of the men to their duty whenever their services are required.

The men will receive rations according to the distance they have to travel, but during their absence they will not be entitled to pay or rations.

The arms of such men as obtain leave of absence will be left in charge of the commanding officer, who will take care that such of them as do require it will be repaired immediately, and that they are deposited in the most secure place.

By order of the Major-General,

J. MACDONELL, P. A. D. C.

Sir George Prevost to Major-General Brock.

MONTREAL, July 10, 1812.

SIR,—Colonel Lethbridge's departure for Kingston affords me an opportunity of replying more fully and confidentially to your letter of the 3rd instant, than I could venture to have done the day before yesterday by an uncertain conveyance. That officer has been desired to transmit to you, together with this despatch, a copy of the instructions given to him for his guidance until the exigencies of the service make it necessary in your estimation to substitute others, or to employ the Colonel in any other situation of command. In them you will find expressed my sentiments respecting the mode of conducting the war on our part, suited to the existing circumstances, and as they change so must we vary our line of conduct, adapting it to our means of preserving entire the King's Provinces.

Our numbers would not justify offensive operations being undertaken unless they were solely calculated to strengthen a defensive attitude. I consider it prudent and politic to avoid any measure which can have a tendency to unite the people of the American States. Whilst disunion prevails among them their attempts on these Provinces will be feeble. It is therefore our duty carefully to avoid committing any act which may even by construction tend to unite the eastern and southern States, unless by its perpetration we are to derive a considerable and important advantage. But the Government of the United States, resting on public opinion for all its measures, is liable to sudden and violent changes. It becomes an essential part of our duty to watch the effect of parties on its measures, and to adapt ours to the impulse given by those possessed of influence over the public mind in America.

Notwithstanding these observations, I have to assure you of my perfect confidence in your measures for the preservation of Upper Canada. All your wants shall be supplied as fast as possible except money, of which I have so little as to be obliged to have recourse to a paper currency.

The Adjutant-General has reported to you the aid we have afforded in arms and ammunition to your militia at Cornwall, Glengarry, Dundas and Stormont.

To prevent an interruption to the communication between the two Provinces, it is fit a system of convoy should be established between Montreal and Kingston, and as Major-General De Rottenburg is to remain here in command of a cordon of troops, consisting of regulars and militia (established in this neighborhood to prevent an irruption for the plunder of Montreal), whilst I attend to parliamentary duties at Quebec on that subject you may communicate direct with the Major-General, as he has my instructions to co-operate with you in preserving this important object.

(From Tupper's Life of Brock, pp. 200-1.)

District General Order.

FORT GEORGE, 11 July, 1812.

D. G. O.

The militia forces in the district will be provisioned in the same manner, both as to quarters and species of provisions, as the regular troops.

There being no branch of the commissariat in the London district from whence supplies may be received, the proportion of troops called out for the defence of that district will be allowed their full pay so as to enable them to supply themselves.

By order,
THOS. EVANS, B. M.

Augustus Porter to General P. B. Porter.

ERIE, July 11th, 1812.

I arrived here at about ten o'clock this morning and shall leave here and proceed west this afternoon. Before you receive this you will have received Mr. Beard's letter, which came by express from Detroit, and also Mr. Woolverton's letter by the same express. These letters will be handed you by Mr. J. Stoo, who was present when I received them, and I then could do no other than send them by him. I find that I have here about 700 bbls. of flour and a considerable quantity of whiskey. I find that only 250 bbls of flour has been sent to Detroit from here and 220 was sent up by the *contractor* from B. Rock, that a little less than 500 have been sent on. I should expect that all that must now be on hand at Detroit, which would last over 30 days. Grandin has a quantity of flour, say 3 or 400 bbls., at Waterford. He is at Pittsburg, but is daily expected here. I find people more inclined to sell flour than when I was here. I think I shall purchase at $6. I find no boats here. I am told there is a scow up the lake, which I hope. to obtain. I have reason to believe that a vessel might go up safe to Miami, but of this I can judge better when I arrive at Cleveland or Huron, and will then write. I fear it will be difficult to get provisions from here up fast enough in boats. I shall go on to Cayahoga with Beard, and shall send him on from there to advise with Gen. Hull as to the propriety of sending up a vessel, boat, &c.

By Beard's letter from Detroit you will observe that he says the *Contractor* and *Amelia* are both taken. This must be a mistake, which has originated from their not arriving. Capt. Chapin, with the *Cayahoga Packet*, is no doubt taken in going from Sandusky to Detroit, with the officers' baggage and two or three officers on board, and is the vessel that we heard of being taken before I left you: the other vessels, I believe, are all safe, or was when the express left Detroit. I wish very much to hear what is going on with you. Do not fail to drop me a line directed to this place by the mail which comes from Buffalo on Wednesday next.

Since I left you I have been very uneasy respecting beef for the troops at Niagara. I hope you will not fail to contract for the delivery of it in the quarter as I proposed to you, even at 3½ dols pr cwt. I am sure is better than I can do otherwise, as if I undertake to kill myself I shall lose many of the hides, which will spoil. Let the contract extend to the 15th of September or 1st of October.

I find Hale has 300 bbls. flour at Canadaway. I talked with him about it. He expected to get 8 dols per bbl. for it at Buffalo. I desired him to inform himself before he took it down. He agreed he would.

(From MSS. of Hon. P. A. Porter.)

Major-General Brock to Sir George Prevost.

FORT GEORGE, July 12, 1812.

SIR,—With the exception of occasional firing from the opposite shore (the unauthorized act of an undisciplined militia) nothing of a hostile nature has occurred on this communication since I last had the honor of addressing Your Excellency.

The enemy is busy constructing batteries at different points on the river, but he does not appear to have yet received cannon to place in them. We are doing all we can on this side to counteract his views, and the arrival of the *Royal George* and the vessels under his convoy bringing various pieces of ordnance will give us in this respect a decided superiority.

The militia which assembled here immediately on the account being received of war being declared by the United States have been improving daily in discipline, but the men evince a degree of impatience under their present restraint that is far from inspiring confidence. So great was their clamor to return and attend to their farms that I found myself in some measure compelled to sanction the departure of a large proportion, and I am not without my apprehensions that the remainder will, in the defiance of the law, which can only impose a fine of £20, leave the service the moment the harvest commences. There can be no doubt that a large portion of the population in this neighborhood are sincere in their professions to defend the country, but it appears likewise evident to me that the greater part are either indifferent to what is passing or so completely American as to rejoice in the prospect of a change of government. Many who now consider our means inadequate would readily take an active part were the regular troops increased. These cool calculators are numerous in all societies.

The alacrity and good temper with which the militia in the first instance marched to the frontiers have tended to infuse in the mind of the enemy a very different sentiment of the disposition of the inhabitants, who, he was led to believe, would, on the first summons, declare themselves an American State. The display for several days of a large force was made, I have every reason to believe in that expectation.

Nearly the whole of the arms at my disposal have been issued. They are barely sufficient to arm the militia immediately required to guard the frontier. Were I furnished with the means of distributing arms among the people in whom confidence can be placed, they would not only overawe the disaffected but prove of essential use in the event of invasion. The militia assembled in a wretched state in regard to clothing: many were without shoes, an article which can scarcely be provided in the country.

After the cannon, which have arrived this morning, are mounted, I shall consider my front perfectly secure. I do not fancy the enemy will hazard a water excursion with a view to turn my flanks. He probably will wait until winter, when the ice will enable him to cross with the utmost facility between Fort Erie and as far as Long Point. My situation will then depend upon the force the enemy may bring to invade the province. Should the troops have to move the want of tents will be severely felt.

A person who left Sandwich yesterday week pretends that the enemy was then in the act of cannonading the place. I have not heard from Lieut.-Colonel St. George since my last letter to Your Excellency.

An officer is so absolutely necessary to command in the Eastern District that I have consented to Major-General Shaw proceeding thither in that capacity. I have full confidence in his judgment, and his conduct in the field is undoubted. He, of course, will assume the command in virtue of his militia rank, and will be liable to be suspended by any lieutenant-colonel Your Excellency may be pleased to appoint.

The expense of defending this province will unquestionably be great; upon a rough calculation and supposing that 4,000 militia be constantly embodied, it cannot be estimated at less than £140,-000 per annum. However great the sum, it will be applied to considerable advantage, provided Your Excellency be enabled to send reinforcements, as without them it is scarcely possible that the government of the United States will be so inactive or supine as to permit the present limited force to remain in possession of the country. Whatever can be done to preserve it or delay its fall, Your Excellency may rest assured will be exerted.

Having been suddenly called away from York I had not time to close my despatch giving Your Excellency an account of my proceedings during my stay at Amherstburg. I now have the honor to forward two documents detailing the steps taken by the Indian Department to prevail on that unfortunate people to accommodate their differences with the American Government.

(From Tupper's Life of Brock, pp. 202-4.)

District General Order.

FORT GEORGE, 12th July, 1812.

D. G. O.

Mr. John Symington is appointed paymaster to the militia forces stationed in the Niagara District, with the pay of 1s. pr diem and allowances as captain, to take place from the 1st inst. Mr. Symington will afford every information to the officers in command of militia corps so as to enable them to make exact returns (paying particular attention to the broken periods) and on which he will take the measures for directly bringing forward his pay lists to the 24th inst.

(Signed.) By order,

THOS. EVANS, B. M.

District General Order.

FORT GEORGE, 12 July, 1812.

D. G. O.

At all times when vessels shall arrive at any of the posts in this command a boat will be immediately despatched by the officer commanding the posts with a proper person on board to ascertain the number and description of the passengers on board, and who will not be permitted to land until leave is first obtained from said commanding officer unless such passengers should be officers in His Majesty's employ.

No. 2.—It having been reported to the Major-General commanding that one or two of the centinels placed on the bank of the Niagara River have fired upon persons on the opposite shore *without orders;* for so doing, he has been pleased to express his disapprobation of such irregular conduct and to direct that officers commanding at the different posts on the communication will take the necessary steps to prevent a repetition of such discreditable practices. By order,

THOS. EVANS, B. Major.

Orders.

One lieutenant, two sergeants and thirty rank and file from the four flank companies of the Lincoln Militia stationed at Niagara will be furnished for engineers' fatigue at Fort George, and to be on the ground to-morrow at 3 o'clock.

Niagara, 14th July, 1812.

General Order.

HEADQUARTERS, ALBANY, July 13, 1812.

Major-General Stephen Van Rensselaer having been requested to repair to the command of the militia heretofore ordered into the the service and to be hereafter ordered into the service of the United States, for the defence of the northern and western frontiers of this State between St. Regis and Pennsylvania, enters upon his command this day. All the militia comprehended in the brigades of detached militia organized in the first detached division by General Orders of the 18th day of June last, together with the corps commanded by Lieutenant-Colonels Swift, Fleming and Bellinger, are hereby declared to be subject to the orders of Major-General Van Rensselaer without waiting for further general orders on that subject, and all officers commanding the militia from which the first detached division was taken are promptly to obey and respect such division orders accordingly.

By order of the Commander-in-Chief,

WM. PAULDING, Jun'r, Adjutant-General.

(Tompkins Papers, New York State Library.)

Augustus Porter to General Porter.

CAYAHOGA, July 13th, 1812.

SIR,—I am thus far on my way; have determined to go to Detroit. I have engaged one boat only to go on with provisions; have such news from Detroit as determines me to go on to that place. Mr. Thompson will give you the news, which is great. The news I sent on relative to British cruisers being on our shore is incorrect. I wish you by all means to send on the *Contractor* to Erie to load for Miami. I think as she comes on she had best touch at different places along the lake, say at Sandusky or Huron, and enquire the news. Do not fail to send her along. I shall go to Detroit. I shall stay there as long as I shall find it necessary, perhaps all summer. Do write to Mr. Coffin; I have no time to do it. Tell him to do as well as he can. He must abandon everything like farming and attend to the troops. You ought to have people enough to assist. Let us if possible supply the troops, if I should lose all my property by it. Do write me every opportunity.

(From MSS. of Hon. P. A. Porter.)

From the New York Gazette.
(Issue of July 24th, 1812.)

BUFFALO, July 14, 1812.

Major-General Brock is at present at Newark superintending the various defences on the river. He is stated to be an able and experienced officer with undoubted courage. He came from Little York soon after hearing the declaration of war, and it was believed with a serious intention of attacking Fort Niagara, but, contrary to what has been reported, he made no demand of a surrender.

Expecting a descent from the American army, the Canadians have for ten days past been removing their families and effects from the river into the interior. At Newark, Queenston, and other villages on the river there are no inhabitants except a few civilians and officers and soldiers. It is even said that an immense quantity of specie, plate, &c., from various parts of the province have been boxed up and destined for Quebec.

The British are understood to have about six or seven hundred regular troops stationed between the lakes from Fort George to

Fort Erie. These men are generally those who have " seen service " in various parts of the world. The militia of the province are ordered out *en masse*. Great discontent prevails in consequence of this requisition, there being no help to gather in the crops: the clamors of the people are but little short of open rebellion. There is no civil authority in Canada—no magistrates will act—the martial code has usurped the civil law. Many young tradesmen in Canada from the States will be ruined. They are required to take up arms or leave the country. They cannot collect their debts nor bring away their property, but many have come away and left their all in jeopardy.

Fort Erie has been strengthened considerably. A redoubt many rods in length was thrown up on Wednesday and Thursday last on the hill below the house of John Warren, Jr., and directly opposite the dwelling house of General Peter B. Porter at Lower Black Rock. There is also a battery on a point below Chippawa mounted with two pieces of heavy artillery, calculated to play upon the storehouses and mills of Schlosser. Below the Falls there is a small stone battery near the bank of the river where the lower ladder formerly stood. On Thursday evening last a rifleman deserted from the other side and crossed the river below the Falls on a pine log. He stated that but a little way up the river from the battery a field piece was stationed in the bushes to fire into Schlosser Village. The woolen factory of John W. Stoughton, consisting of two carding machines and fulling and dressing machines, is very much exposed. On the hill about half a mile from the stone battery are placed two 18-pounders. The ladders on both sides of the river are taken up. On the hill above Queenston there is a small defence on very commanding ground. Below Queenston, nearly opposite the residence of Benjamin Barton, Esq., there is a defence of several rods in extent. Opposite Youngstown there is another redoubt thrown up. Andrew Baker, son of Judge Baker of this village, together with three other persons, citizens of the United States, escaped from Canada at Long Point in a skiff, and safely arrived in this village on Friday night.

It is stated by gentlemen of intelligence at Lewiston that the Government of Canada have in their employment under pay about 250 Indians armed complete; a part of them are mounted.

Brigadier-General William Wadsworth from Genesee commands the troops on our frontiers. His aids are Major Adam Hoops and Major W. H. Spencer. His headquarters are now at Lewiston. It is impossible to state the exact number of troops under his command because the militia ordered on the lines are returning and the companies composing the regiments under his command have not all arrived, but from what we learn there are in regular troops, volunteers, and detached militia, above 4,000 stationed at Black Rock, Lewiston, Youngstown, and Fort Niagara. The troops are in excellent health, in good spirits and well supplied. They appear quite impatient for want of employment. There has been some firing from the sentries on both sides of the river.

It was reported at Fort Niagara last week that the British have sent from Little York every armed ship in pursuit of the brig *Oneida*.

The British armed ship *Queen Charlotte*, lying at Fort Erie, soon after the declaration of war was received left her moorings and proceeded up the lake, and is now understood to be at Fort Malden, the great depot of Indian supplies. His Majesty's sloop of war *Hunter* has gone up the straits of Mackina and passed into Lake Michigan and captured an American merchant vessel, said to be either the *Mary* or *Salina*. We understand an official account of the capture has been received at Fort Erie.

Sir George Prevost to the Earl of Liverpool.

QUEBEC, 15th July, 1812.

(No. 57.)

MY LORD,—I have the honor to acknowledge the receipt of Your Lordship's despatches of the 30th March, 2nd and 20th April, No. 8, 10 and 15, to which I now beg leave to reply and to offer some observations for Your Lordship's consideration.

. . . .

I find by a communication from Major-General Brock, commanding in Upper Canada, that the American general officer commanding the district of Niagara, having received early information from his government of the declaration of war, had projected the surprise of Fort George, but fortunately the reports of the approach of hostilities and the preparations making for them brought Major-General Brock to the fort, where the display of his vigilance and activity induced them to relinquish the attempt.

Major-General Brock has received certain accounts of war having been declared by the United States against Great Britain, and has reported to me that in consequence it was his opinion he should be justified in offensive operations, but upon the reflection that at Detroit and St. Joseph's the weak state of our garrisons would prevent any essential service connected with their future security, and that his only means of annoyance at present was limited to the reduction of Fort Niagara, which could be battered at any future period, he had therefore relinquished his original intention and should attend only to defensive measures.

I have repeatedly recommended to Major-General Brock and to the officers in command of the other districts of British America an adherence to this system, and I have expressed to them my sentiments respecting the mode of conducting the war on our part suited to existing circumstances, and as they change so should we vary our line of conduct adapting it to our means of preserving entire the King's Provinces.

Our numbers would not justify offensive operations being undertaken unless they were solely calculated to strengthen a defensive attitude.

In the present state of politics in the United States, I consider it prudent to avoid every measure which can have the least tendency to unite the people of America. Whilst disunion prevails among them, their attempts on the British American Provinces will be feeble. It is therefore my wish to avoid committing any act which may even by a strained construction tend to unite the Eastern and Southern States, unless from its perpetration we are to derive an immediate, considerable and important advantage.

Major-General Brock has called out the flank companies of militia, which has produced a force on the line of the Niagara River of about 800 men. They turned out very cheerfully, but already shew a spirit of impatience.

The Americans are very active on the opposite side of that communication in the erection of redoubts. In this respect we are not idle. The Americans have 1200 regulars and militia between Fort Niagara and Black Rock, but Major General Brock, who has taken his station at Fort George, considers himself at present perfectly safe against any attempt they can make.

About 100 Indians from the Grand River have attended to his summons. The remainder promise to come also.

A report has been made to me by Major Macpherson, commanding at Kingston on Lake Ontario, that the Americans have taken possession of Carleton Island near that post and have made prisoners of the small party of the 10th Royal Veteran Battalion stationed on it.

We continue to possess a superiority in vessels of war upon Lake Ontario and Lake Erie.

I find myself seriously embarrassed by a scarcity of arms for the militia of Upper Canada and Lower Canada, who have evinced a desire to co-operate with the regular forces exceeding my expectations.

I fear for the safety of the *Crambo* transport, which sailed from Bermuda for Quebec the 21st of April with 6000 stand of arms on board, and has not since been heard of. I fear that she has been lost in a gale, and I have directed Sir John C. Sherbrooke to send to Quebec half of the arms in store at Halifax, which may exceed 1000 stand.

The difficulties long experienced in obtaining specie for the subsistence of the troops are at an end by the declaration of war, which closes the source from which it came. It has become necessary to substitute paper money for it, as it appears none can be sent from England, and I am about to seek the aid of the Provincial Parliament to give it value and currency. My total inability to supply Upper Canada with specie compelled Major-General Brock to seek the assistance of an association of merchants, a measure which has been attended with considerable success, enabling him to pay his militia forces now embodied, amounting to 4000 men.

. . . .

Major-General Brock is the only General Officer in the extensive district of Upper Canada.

(Canadian Archives, Q. 118, p. 39.)

The Secretary of War to Major-General Dearborn.

WAR DEPARTMENT, July 15th, 1812.

(Abstract.)

Instructing him upon his arrival at Albany to direct his attention to the security of the northern frontier. In addition to authority to require militia for defence, and with a view to offensive operations, he is authorized to accept volunteers from New England, New York and Pennsylvania, and to call into service such a number of volunteers as he may deem requisite.

District General Order.

NIAGARA, 16th July, 1812.

D. G. O.

The officers on duty this morning were exceedingly remiss in allowing a boat to pass within four miles of Missassagua Point without reporting it until too late for it to be intercepted. Colonel Claus will adopt the measures to guard against its recurrence in future.

A proper person will be stationed at the top of the light house every morning at half an hour before daylight, to remain throughout the day, who will be particularly instructed to watch what passes on the lake and on the enemy's side of the river. The officer on duty will frequently visit him to assist in making the necessary observations.

The Major-General was surprised this morning to find that the order for the apprehension of all strangers travelling on any part of the communication was not complied with, and that avowed Americans were permitted to parade the streets and examine the works.

Colonel Claus will explain to every officer and militiaman, that it is expected (whether on or off duty) that they will stop all suspicious characters and take them before a magistrate for examination.

Officers commanding posts will not only examine the arms and ammunition in use, but likewise those which the men on furlough have left in store, and see that the whole be in a state fit for service. They will report having done so.

Notice will be taken on the back of the report of any orders having reached them during the day—the date and purport of the orders already received will be inserted on the morning report of next Monday.

By order of the Major-General,

THOS. EVANS, B. Major.

Daniel Ross to James Cummings.

WOODHOUSE, July 16, 1812.

(Extract.)

We have a little rest now, but I can assure you we have been in great confusion for some time past. It is supposed and hoped by a great many here that there will be no war, which I hope may be the case, but am very dubious. . . . .

Col. Talbot came down yesterday. The four flank companies in front was stationed at Turkey Point. He discharged half of them for a week for their respective homes. Some jangling here between the officers, say Major S. and Gordon, Dan. McCall, &c. No time to give any particulars.

From the Federal Republican of Baltimore, Md., 27th July, 1812.

Extract from a letter dated at Buffalo, 14th July, 1812.

Joseph Willcocks, editor of a little paper which lately died at Newark, and which uniformly opposed and calumniated the Government of Upper Canada, has tendered his services to that Government during the present war.

District General Order.

FORT GEORGE, 18th July, 1812.

D. G. O.

The District General Orders of the 12th inst., respecting the arrival of vessels and examination of passengers, &c., will be enforced at this post by Fort Major Campbell, which officer will prevent any vessel of whatsoever description from sailing without his permission for that purpose.

No. 2.

Fort Major Campbell will in future issue the parole and countersign to the several staff officers and others entitled to receive them, who are at present or may be hereafter stationed at Fort George.

Mr. Muirhead, attached to the forces at Chippawa, will immediately remove from thence to Queenston, there to take charge of the sick until further orders.

Mr. Fleming will succeed Mr. Muirhead in the superintendence of the sick at Chippawa.

By order of the Major-General.

THOS. EVANS,
Brigade-Major.

General Wm. Hull to the Six Nations.

SANDWICH, July 18, 1812.

My Brethren of the Six Nations:—

The powerful army under my command is now in possession of Canada. To you who are friendly it will afford safety and protection. All your lands and all your rights of every kind will be guaranteed to you if you will take no part against us. I salute you in friendship, and hope you will now act such a part as will promote your interest, your safety, and happiness. May the Great Spirit guide you in person.

WM. HULL,
Governor of the Territory of Michigan, and
Commander of the Northwestern Army
of the United States.

(From the *New York Gazette*, August 20th, 1812.)

Major-General Brock to Sir George Prevost.

FORT GEORGE, July 20th, 1812.

SIR,—My last to Your Excellency was dated the 12th instant, since which nothing extraordinary has occurred on this communication. The enemy has evidently diminished his force, and appears to have no intention of making an immediate attack.

I have herewith the honor of enclosing the copy of two letters which I have received from Lt.-Col. St. George, together with some interesting documents found on board a schooner which the boats of the *Hunter* captured on her voyage from the Miamis to Detroit.

From the accompanying official correspondence between General Hull and the Secretary at War, it appears that the collected force which has arrived at Detroit amounts to about two thousand.

I have requested Colonel Procter to proceed to Amherstburg and ascertain accurately the state of things in that quarter. I had every inclination to go there myself, but the meeting of the Legislature on the 27th renders it impossible.

I received this moment a despatch dated the 15th instant, from Lt.-Col. St. George, giving an account of the enemy having landed on the 12th, and immediately after occupying the village of Sandwich. It is strange that three days should be allowed to elapse before sending to acquaint me of this important fact. I had no idea until I received Lt.-Colonel St. George's letter a few days ago that General Hull was advancing with such a large force.

The militia, from every account, behaved very ill. The officers appear the most in fault. Colonel Procter will probably reach Amherstburg in the course of to-morrow. I have great dependence on that officer's decision, but fear he will arrive too late to be of much service. The enemy was not likely to delay attacking a force that had allowed him to cross the river in open day without firing a shot.

The position which Lt.-Colonel St. George occupied is very good, and infinitely more formidable than the post itself. Should he, therefore, be compelled to retire I know of no other alternative than embarking in the King's vessels and proceeding to Fort Erie.

Were it possible to animate the militia to a proper sense of their duty something might yet be done, but I almost despair.

Your Excellency will readily perceive the critical situation in which the reduction of Amherstburg is sure to place me. I do not imagine General Hull will be able to detach more than one thousand men, but, even with that trifling force, I much fear he will succeed in getting to my rear. The militia will not act without a strong regular force to set them the example, and as I must now expect to be seriously threatened from the opposite shore, I cannot in prudence make strong detachments, which would not only weaken my line of defence, but in the event of a retreat endanger their safety.

I have never, as Your Excellency has doubtless noticed, been very sanguine in my hopes of assistance from the militia, and I am now given to understand that General Hull's insidious proclamation (herewith enclosed) has already been productive of considerable effect on the minds of the people. In fact a general sentiment prevails that with the present force resistance is unavailing. I shall continue to exert myself to the utmost to overcome every difficulty. Should, however, the communication between Kingston and Montreal be cut off, the fate of the troops in this part of the Province will be decided. I now express my apprehensions on a supposition that the slender means Your Excellency possesses will not admit of diminution, consequently that I cannot look for reinforcements.

The enemy evidently has no intention at present of penetrating into the Province by this strait. He seems much more inclined to work on the flanks; after they are secured, little remains for him to do.

The last official communication from the Lower Province is dated the 25th ulto. The Adjutant-General then announced the receipt of intelligence by a mercantile house, of war being declared by the United States against Great Britain. I need not entreat Your Excellency to honor me with your commands with as little delay as possible. I consider every moment exceedingly precious.

(Canadian Archives, C. 676, p. 203.)

District General Order.

FORT GEORGE, 20th July, 1812.

No honors to be paid to officers by the guards or sentries on the bank of the river or beach during the day.

From the Buffalo Gazette, Tuesday, July 21, 1812.

Since our last there has been no material change in the posture of affairs on the frontier. Two or three additional companies of volunteers have arrived at Lewiston. The health of the troops is, we understand, rather improved since the late showers and change in the weather. The troops have suffered for the want of experienced cooks, and there is no doubt that several might find employment and very liberal wages by applying at Black Rock or Lewiston.

On Friday last General Wadsworth, accompanied by his aid, Major Spencer, came from his quarters at Lewiston to Black Rock. On Saturday he inspected the troops at that place and those stationed in this village, consisting of Captain Wells's company of light infantry and Captain Cyrenius Chapin's company of artillery.

He spoke in terms of commendation of the progressive improvement in military discipline in some, particularly the company of artillery, and in terms of severe reprehension of the neglect of duty or want of attention or information in others, particularly some of the officers at the Rock.

He returned to his quarters at Lewiston on Sunday.

Dr. Asa Coltrin, who went from this village last spring and established himself at St. David's, near Queenston, is appointed a surgeon in the British army, and is now at Fort George, Newark. His pay is 100 dollars per month, besides rations, forage, &c.

On the 2d instant Messrs. Martin Daley, Luke Draper, and W. Phillips (the two former were connected in the grocery business in this village last summer) were seized within 12 miles of Long Point, U. Canada, as spies. They were marched under guard to a court of three justices of the peace, who, after examining them, without assigning any reason, ordered them to headquarters without delay, upon which they were put on board the schr. *Chippawa* and landed at Fort Erie, and were then put in a waggon and transported to Fort George, and there imprisoned in the guard house, and there continued for 8 days, during which time their keeper gave them only one loaf of bread. They daily offered money to their keeper to buy provisions, but it was with great difficulty they could obtain even the remnants of the officers' table, and these remnants only a few times during the 8 days, and when obtained they were charged at the most extravagant price.

On the evening of the 12th inst., some intelligence of a favorable nature to the prisoners coming from Long Point, they were liberated next morning and sent across the river, and arrived in this village on Tuesday.

The *Royal George* arrived off Niagara River on yesterday week, and anchored near the American garrison over night. On Tuesday she took on board 100 men and several pieces of artillery, and proceeded down the lake. The *Hunter* arrived at Fort Erie some time last week and still remains there.

PROCLAMATION.

The unprovoked declaration of war by the United States of America against the United Kingdom of Great Britain and Ireland, and its dependencies, has been followed by the actual invasion of this Province in a remote frontier of the Western District by a detachment of the armed forces of the United States. The officer commanding that detachment has thought proper to invite His Majesty's subjects not only to a quiet and unresisting submission, but insults them with a call to seek voluntarily the protection of his Government. Without condescending to repeat the illiberal epithets bestowed in this appeal of the American commander to the people of Upper Canada on the administration of His Majesty, every inhabitant of this province is desired to seek the refutation of such indecent slander in a review of his own particular circumstances. Where is the Canadian subject who can truly affirm to himself that he has been injured by the Government in his person, his liberty or his property? Where is to be found in any part of the world a growth so rapid in wealth and prosperity as this colony exhibits—settled not thirty years ago by a band of veterans exiled from their former possessions on account of their loyalty. Not a descendant of these brave people is to be found who, under the fostering liberality of their Sovereign, has not acquired a property and means of enjoyment superior to what were possessed by his ancestors. This unequalled prosperity could not have been attained by the utmost liberality of the Government or the persevering industry of the people had not the maritime power of the Mother Country secured to its colonists a safe access to every market where the produce of their labor was in demand.

The unavoidable and immediate consequence of a separation from Great Britain must be the loss of this inestimable advantage. And what is offered you in exchange? To become a territory of the United States, and share with them that exclusion from the ocean which the policy of their present Government enforces. You are not even flattered with a participation of their boasted independence, and it is but too obvious that once excluded from the powerful protection of the United Kingdom you must be re-annexed to the dominion of France, from which the Provinces of Canada were wrested by the arms of Great Britain at a vast expense of blood and treasure, from no other motive than to *relieve* her ungrateful children from the oppression of a cruel neighbor: this restitution to the Empire of France was the stipulated reward for the aid afforded to the revolted colonies, now the United States: the debt is still due, and there can be no doubt the pledge has been renewed as a consideration for commercial advantages, or rather for an expected relaxation in the tyranny of France over the commercial world. Are you prepared, inhabitants of Upper Canada, to become willing subjects, or rather slaves, to the Despot who rules the nations of Europe with a rod of iron? If not, arise in a body, exert your energies, co-operate cordially with the King's regular forces to repel the invader, and do not give cause to your children when groaning under the oppression of a foreign master to reproach you with having too easily parted with the richest inheritance on earth—a participation in the name, character and freedom of Britons.

The same spirit of justice which will make allowance for the unsuccessful efforts of zeal and loyalty, will not fail to punish the defalcation of principle. Every Canadian freeholder is by deliberate choice bound by the most solemn oaths to defend the monarchy, as well as his own property; to shrink from that engagement is a treason not to be forgiven. Let no man suppose that if in this unexpected struggle His Majesty's arms should be compelled to yield to an overwhelming force that the Province will be abandoned. The endeared relation of its first settlers, the intrinsic value of its commerce and the pretensions of its powerful rival to repossess the Canadas are pledges that no peace will be established between the United States and Great Britain of which the restoration of these Provinces does not make the most prominent condition.

Be not dismayed at the unjustifiable threat of the commander of the enemy's forces if an Indian appear in the ranks. The brave bands of natives which inhabit this colony were, like His Majesty's subjects, punished for their zeal and fidelity by the loss of their possessions in the late colonies and rewarded by His Majesty with lands of superior value in this Province. The faith of the British Government has never yet been violated; they feel that the soil they inherit is to them and their posterity protected from the base acts so frequently devised to overreach their simplicity. By what new principle are they to be prevented from defending their property? If their warfare, from being different from that of the white people, is more terrific to the enemy, let him retrace his steps; they seek him not and cannot expect to find women and children in an invading army; but they are men, and have equal rights with all other men to defend themselves and their property when invaded, more especially when they find in the enemy's camps a ferocious and mortal foe using the same kind of warfare which the American Commander affects to reprobate.

This inconsistent and unjustifiable threat of refusing quarter for such a cause as being found in arms with a brother sufferer in defence of invaded rights must be exercised with a certain assurance of retaliation, not only in the limited operations of war in this part of the King's dominions, but in every quarter of the globe, for the national character of Britain is not less distinguished for humanity than strict retributive justice, which will consider the execution of this threat as deliberate murder, for which every subject of the offending power must make expiation.

God save the King.

                      ISAAC BROCK,
                            Maj.-Gen. and President.

Headquarters, Fort George, 22d July, 1812.

By order of His Honor the President.

                      J. B. GLEGG,
                            Capt. A. D. C.

(Canadian Archives, Q. 315, p. 152.)

Militia General Orders.

HEADQUARTERS, NIAGARA, 22d July, 1812.

Militia General Orders.

Major-General Brock, having ascertained that a very considerable number of the enemy have actually invaded this Province, is under the necessity of directing that such men of the different flank companies of the several Regiments of Lincoln Militia as are now absent upon furlough, or otherwise be immediately ordered to join their respective companies, and that these companies be constantly kept upon their full establishment.

The Major-General is further pleased to direct that the whole of these different regiments be ordered to hold themselves in constant readiness for actual service.

By order of the Major-General.

                      J. MACDONELL, P. A. D. C.

Militia General Orders.

HEADQUARTERS, FORT GEORGE, 22d July, 1812.

Militia Genl. Orders.

Major-General Brock has been pleased to direct that an addition of thirty men be made to the strength of Captain Powell's company of Lincoln Artillery, the men for which are to be taken from the battalion companies of Colonels Warren and Clark's regiments of Lincoln Militia.

By order of the Major-General.

                      J. MACDONELL, P. A. D. C.

Militia General Orders.

HEADQUARTERS, FORT GEORGE, 22d July, 1812.

Militia Genl. Orders.

Colonel Talbot will make detachments from the First and Second Norfolk and the Oxford and Middlesex Regiments of

Militia, to consist together of two hundred men, with a proportionate number of officers, the whole to be placed under the command of Major Salmon of the Second Regiment of Norfolk Militia. This detachment will be assembled as soon as possible in as complete a state as circumstances will admit, for service. Major Salmon will proceed with this force to the Moravian Town on the River Thames, where he will await the arrival of Major Chambers, under whose command he will place himself.

By order of the Major-General,

J. MACDONELL, P. A. D. C.

Inspector-General Nicholas Gray to Governor Tompkins.

HEADQUARTERS, LEWISTON, July 22, 1812.

DEAR SIR,—I arrived here on the 18th inst., and was received with every mark of attention and respect, and yesterday visited the garrison, accompanied by General Wadsworth, whose anxiety for the necessary camp equipage, artillery, arms and ammunition is very great. We have some fine companies of infantry here without belts or cartridge boxes, and all without uniform, except a very handsome company of light infantry raised by Captain Dox of Geneva, and to which evidently every attention has been paid. The enemy have thrown up redoubts on the south and north approaches to Queenston, which command our camp, stores, headquarters, &c., &c. They appear to have in each of them an 18-pounder, and the one on the south side has been levelled at the general's quarters ever since I came here; the distance, about nineteen hundred yards. We feel very anxious for the arrival of some artillery equal to this, and it appears to me that the present situation of the army of the British has given the inhabitants of this part of the Canadas entire control of the army. I have recommended to the general to throw up a redoubt under the brow of the hill above Lewiston, which will remove the enemy's redoubt, destroy Queenston, and enfilade the river and small redoubt immediately opposite the camp of Colonel Dobbins. The enemy unfortunately have the commanding ground everywhere, and even at the garrison commanded by Captain Leonard, who, I believe, is an excellent officer. His situation last Sunday was alarming: three of the enemy's armed ships hove within a very few rods of the garrison, and seemed to threaten an immediate bombardment, but after remaining for a few hours they steered to the northward down the lake. He is in a very defenceless state. I have recommended him to throw up a new bastion in the west, so as to command the British fort and the town of Newark, which will contain seven guns of a large calibre (when he gets them,) the stone tower forming one of the angles, and will be protected on the north and north-east by the messhouse and another stone tower on the east. I proposed to throw up a breastwork from the last mentioned tower to the skirt of the wood, a distance of about three hundred yards, sufficiently high to protect a retreat in case such were necessary. General Wadsworth has this morning ordered a military school, both for officers and soldiers, which you know is much wanting. He pays unwearied attention to the troops, and a system is forming which has for its object the organization of the staff and camp duties. Indeed he is most deficient in his most necessary officer, who is absolutely incapable and negligent. I mean his brigade-inspector, who seems to be in a dream from morning till night. I should strongly recommend the removal of this gentleman, and some capable officer put in his place. His name is Keyes. To the incapacity of this officer the want of due organization is owing in a great measure. It appears to me that the object of the enemy from Fort Erie to Fort George, in throwing up the different redoubts, is to cover a retreat. They have four pieces of artillery at Chippawa, I believe six and nine-pounders; opposite Black Rock one 24, and, I believe, a mortar; and they have within these eight days thrown up a strong redoubt immediately opposite the barracks built by General Peter B. Porter. I recommended him to throw up a breastwork with a short barbette for a piece of artillery, so as to protect the barracks and secure the soldiers on parade, on which he is at work since Monday, But the absolute want of all sorts of working tools has prevented the troops taking measures absolutely necessary to their protection. They have been in want of everything, and have great fortitude and zeal to bear their privations so well. The camps are pretty healthy. Out of 402 men the sick returns are 35. Over at Queenston side the high ground commands everything, and it was with difficulty, after a close examination, I could find any place in which to throw up a redoubt which could not be commanded by this hill. The enemy have a kind of encampment on the top of this hill, and their numbers, as far as I can judge, about three hundred. They are calculated to number, from Fort George to Fort Erie, including militia and Indians, about four thousand 500, including the two garrisons. The Indians are armed and employed, we understand, on Grand Island. A citizen of the States came over yesterday morning with two others, and informed the General that a party of Indians had passed over to Grand Island for the purpose of destroying the military stores along the shore from Black Rock. Your two letters I had the honor of delivering to Colonel Swift, and the promotion of Major Miller was well received. He appears to be a good officer.

There is a party of Major Mullany's regiment which was left behind at the garrison at the request, I believe, of Captain Leonard, at the time he was requested by the neighborhood of Canandaigua to march on here. They have been ordered by the major to repair forthwith to Albany, as it was the request of Colonel Schuyler, but he did not make any application or notification to General Wadsworth, under whose command they now are. The General has deemed it absolutely necessary, from the defenceless state of the garrison, to order them to remain until further orders. Fort George is well provided with arms, ammunition, and soldiers, but is of itself not so strong as the American garrison. All the curtains of it are old rotten pickets, and not even a *fosse* to support them. They are enfiladed by batteries badly constructed, and, in my mind, could be taken without great hazard. The militia of Canada, we understand, have been allowed to go home to the harvest, and I know not a more applicable or better chosen time can occur to overwhelm them than just now, if the troops were prepared and in sufficient numbers to ensure victory. General Hall has not arrived here as yet, but is expected to march this day from his home. The tents, &c., &c., have not as yet arrived, but are also expected, as is some artillery.

I should have had the honor of addressing a letter to you sooner than this, but I was not prepared to give you the information you required. From Buffalo to the American garrison we have 1230 militia and 470 regulars, in all 1700 men, in pretty good health and tolerable spirits. They are both, men and officers, anxious to have the orders to cross over, but they see and hear plainly everything going on on the British side. A few evenings ago a centinel at Black Rock, on his post opposite the British redoubt, in the tone of a veteran with a long monotony of sound, cried, "All's well." Our centinel, who perhaps did not like his own situation, as the evening was a little cold and his post rather exposed, cried out immediately after the other, "All's well, too."

I should feel highly honored by having a letter from Your Excellency, and beg to assure you that every assistance in my knowledge and exertion I shall deem my duty to afford here.

P. S.—There are but twenty light horsemen here to do the duty within an extent of 34 miles. They are chiefly employed in expresses and escorts; are quite inefficient for the duty. The quarters are not the best for them, and they are beginning to feel the weight of duty.

(Tompkins' Papers, Vol. VII., pp. 502-6, New York State Library.)

Militia General Orders.

HEADQUARTERS, FORT GEORGE, 23 July, 1812.

M. G. Orders.

Major-General Brock has been pleased to appoint Captain Henry Warren of the 3rd Regiment of Lincoln Militia to be second major of the same regiment, of which he will immediately assume the command and use every exertion to prepare the whole of the men for actual service.

By order the Major-General.

J. MACDONELL. P. A. D. C.

Major-General Van Rensselaer to His Excellency Governor Tompkins.

OGDENSBURG, July 23, 1812, 8 o'clock p. m.

SIR,—On receiving information that Sackett's Harbor was menaced by the enemy, I deemed it expedient that General Brown should repair there, and accordingly he departed from this place early yesterday morning. One reason for my remaining a day or two longer at this post was to await and possibly improve the success which might attend a projected attack upon a ten-gun British schooner which has for several days been lying at the dock at Prescott, opposite to this place. The proposed attack was concerted by my aid-de-camp, Col. Van Rensselaer, and Col. Benedict, who commands at this post. Yesterday was spent in preparations. The boarding boats were ready at 1 o'clock last night, and the attack was to have been made by land and water at 3 in the morning. But when everything was ready in such a manner as to promise complete success, it was discovered with infinite chagrin and mortification that only *sixty-six* men would volunteer for the service. This number being by no means competent, Cols. Van Rensselaer and Benedict, who would certainly have led the men to action with the most cool and determined bravery, were compelled to abandon an enterprise honorable in itself and upon the result of which might have depended the whole command of the lake and river.

This promising object having been blasted, and, as nothing further of consequence appeared to demand my longer stay here, I was on the eve of my departure at five o'clock this afternoon, when a large armed ship was discovered coming down the river. She has anchored close in shore on the opposite side of the river, near to the schooner, and appears to be a fourteen-gun ship. Considerable solicitude prevails in this place. It is generally believed that the vessels in the harbor are the object of the enemy. The owners of the vessels are preparing to scuttle them or remove them as far out of the reach of the enemy as may be. The troops are busy constructing a fort of timber north of Parish's store, on the best ground for the purpose. But, sir, our very great misfortune is that we have only *two six-pounders*. If this harbor is to be protected it is absolutely necessary that I should be immediately furnished with cannon of a competent calibre for the probably approaching emergency. I shall wait your answer by the return of the express and govern myself accordingly.

(From S. Van Rensselaer's Narrative of the Affair of Queenston in the War of 1812, New York, 1836, Appendix. pp. 20-1.)

Lieut.-Colonel Myers to Captain James Cummings.

FORT GEORGE, July 23, 1812.

SIR,—Upon looking from Wilson's at the Falls last evening after leaving you, I find that Lafferty's can be seen most distinctly, therefore it will not be necessary to put up a staff at the point where we were at the head of the rapids, but the Genl. wishes one to be erected on the point at Chippawa, not so much as an intermediate situation as to give the alarm when required to the garrison, &c., there. You will therefore be pleased to have the pole intended for the head of the rapids put up at Chippawa. The best place at Wilson's is on the cleared point near the paling of Wilson's garden, and not far from the head of the path that goes down to the Table Rock; when you go there you will easily see it. You will please to examine the rising ground at Lundy's Lane (the school house) and find out whether a beacon from that place could be seen from any part of the high lands of Pelham. I request you will have some of the bark, &c., for the fires collected at each post, and the iron baskets shall be sent up as soon as possible. The pole for the corner of the wheat field had better not be put up until you can ascertain how soon the grain will be cut, and when it is cut whether or not we can open a communication across it to the camp; if so the dragoon that would come from Wilson's could ride on across to the camp. Let me hear from you on this, as also on the subject of the ground at Lundy's Lane.

Edward Couche, Deputy Commissary-General, to Captain James Cummings.

FORT GEORGE, 25th July, 1812.

SIR,—Major-General Brock having been pleased to approve of my appointing you to act in the Commissariat Department in this Province, I am to direct that you proceed without loss of time to

Oxford and make arrangements for furnishing about 400 men with provisions, who are expected to arrive there in the course of a few days, under the command of Col. Talbot.

There will, I expect, be little difficulty in procuring cattle for this department in the neighborhood of Oxford, and you will use every exertion to find bread or flour also for their use from the inhabitants.

Should, however, this source of supply fail, I have directed fifty barrels of flour to be forwarded from Long Point to Oxford, and forty barrels of flour, twenty barrels of pork and one cask of salt to Port Talbot. You will of course consult with Colonel Talbot on the best means of transporting the last mentioned provisions to Delaware, or to any other part of the country where they may be required, but it is expressly to be understood that these provisions are not to be consumed until the country can no longer provide a sufficient quantity for the use of the troops.

You will for the present give your receipts to the parties for any articles of provisions, &c., you may receive from them, and I will in a short time arrange their being paid for the same at the current rate of the country.

Deputy Assistant Commissary-General Coffin will furnish you with stationery and forms for your provision accounts, and I expect from your zeal and activity that the troops employed on this arduous service will be well supplied with provisions, and that your accounts of the same will be made up with regularity and correctness.

Major-General Brock has been pleased also to approve of my allowing you the pay of ten shillings stg. per day and forage for one horse until further orders.

You will place yourself under the orders of the officer in command of the detachment with which you are to serve and obey all such instructions as he may find it necessary to give, taking care to make me acquainted with the same as early as possible.

You will further report to me on all heads of service, and state in a particular manner the resources of the country, so that I may form a judgment of what provisions it may be requisite to forward from this garrison.

Major-General Brock to Sir George Prevost.

FORT GEORGE, July 26, 1812.

SIR,—Since my despatch to Your Excellency of the 20th instant I have received information of the enemy having made frequent and extensive inroads from Sandwich up the River Thames. I have in consequence been induced to detach Captain

Chambers, with about 50 of the 41st Regiment, to the Moravian Town, where I have directed two hundred militia to join him. From the loud and apparently warm professions of the Indians residing on the Grand River, I made no doubt of finding at all times a large majority ready to take the field and act in conjunction with our troops, but accounts received this morning state that they have determined to remain neutral, and had in consequence refused (with the exception of about 50) to join Chambers's detachment.

I meditated, the moment I could collect a sufficient number of militia, a diversion to the westward in the hope of compelling General Hull to retreat across the river, but this unexpected intelligence has ruined the whole of my plans. The militia which I destined for this service will now be alarmed and unwilling to leave their families to the mercy of 400 Indians, whose conduct affords such wide room for suspicion—and, really, to expect that this fickle race would remain in the midst of war in a state of neutrality is truly absurd. The Indians have probably been led to this change of sentiment by emissaries from General Hull, whose proclamation to the Six Nations is herewith enclosed.

I have not deemed it of sufficient importance to commence active operations on this line by an attack on Fort Niagara. It can be demolished when found necessary in half an hour, and there my means of annoyance would terminate. To enable the militia to organize some degree of discipline without interruption is of greater consequence than such a conquest.

Everything shall be done in my power to overcome the difficulties by which I am surrounded, but without strong reinforcements I fear the country cannot be roused to make exertions equal, without support, to meet the present crisis.

I proceed immediately to York to attend the meeting of the Legislature. I hope to return on Wednesday. The charge of this frontier will in the meantime devolve on Lt.-Colonel Myers, who appears worthy of every confidence.

The actual invasion of the Province has compelled me to recall that portion of the militia whom I permitted to return home and work at harvest. I am prepared to hear of much discontent in consequence. The disaffected will take advantage of it and add fuel to the flame, but it may not be without reason that I may be accused of having already studied, to the injury of the service, their convenience and humor.

I should have derived much consolation in the midst of my present difficulties had I been honored previous to the meeting of the Legislature with Your Excellency's determination in regard to this Province. That it cannot be maintained with its present force is very obvious, and unless the enemy be driven from Sandwich it will be impossible to avert much longer the impending ruin of the country. Numbers have already joined the invading army, commotions are excited, and late occurrences have spread a general gloom.

I have not heard from Lt.-Colonel St. George, nor from any individual at Amherstburg since I last had the honor of addressing Your Excellency, which makes me apprehensive that Colonel Procter has been detained on his journey too long for the good of the service.

The enemy's cavalry amounts to about 50. They are led by one Watson, a surveyor from Montreal, of a desperate character. This fellow has been allowed to parade with about 20 men of the same description as far as Westminster, vowing as they went along the most bitter vengeance against the first characters of the Province. Nothing can show more strongly the state of apathy in that part of the country. I am perhaps too liberal in attributing the conduct of the inhabitants to that cause.

Mr. Couche has represented to the head of his department the total impracticability of carrying on the public service without a remittance in specie, or a government paper substitute. He was once in expectation of making arrangements with some individuals that would have enabled him to proceed, but I much fear the whole project has fallen to the ground. The militia on this communication was so clamorous for their pay that I directed Mr. Couche to make the necessary advances. This has drained him of the little specie in his possession.

My present civil office not only authorizes me to convene general court martial for the trial of offenders belonging to the militia, but likewise the infliction of the sentence of death—whilst in regard to the military my power is limited to the mere assembling of the court. I beg leave to submit to the consideration of Your Excellency whether, in times like the present, I ought not to be invested with equal authority over each service.

I herewith have the honor to transmit two letters, one from Captain Roberts commanding at St. Joseph's, and the second from Mr. Dickson, a gentleman every way capable of forming a correct judgment of the actual state of the Indians. Nothing can be more deplorable than his description. Yet the United States Government accuse Great Britain of instigating that people to war. Is not the true cause to be found in the state of desperation to which they are reduced by the unfriendly and unjust measures of that Government towards them?

(Canadian Archives, C. 676, p. 408.)

The Secretary of War to Major-General Dearborn.

WAR DEPARTMENT, July 26, 1812.

(Abstract.)

A letter dated the 7th inst. has been received, announcing General Hull's arrival at Detroit with 2,000 men of the 4th United States Infantry, recruits of the 1st do. and Ohio volunteers, in good health and fine spirits. A regiment of the new army from Virginia, and recruits from Maryland and Pennsylvania, have been ordered to join him (General Dearborn) with the 5th Infantry, under Colonel Beall, and a detachment of Colonel Burn's dragoons, now concentrating at Trenton. By General Hull's letter of the 10th inst., it appears that supplies by the lake are cut off, and he has made arrangements for supplying his force from Ohio. General Winchester has been ordered to reinforce him from Kentucky with 1,500 men. You should cut off the British supplies by an adequate force at the rapids below Kingston.

YORK, July 28th, 1812.

Yesterday at an early hour His Honor Isaac Brock, Esq., President, administering the Government of Upper Canada and Major-General commanding His Majesty's forces therein, arrived at this place from Fort George, accompanied by a numerous suite, and proceeded to the Government building at 4 p. m., when he opened the present extra session of the Legislature, and delivered the following speech to both houses:

Honorable Gentlemen of the Legislative Council, and Gentlemen of the House of Assembly:—

The urgency of the present crisis is the only consideration which could have induced me to call you together at a time when public (as well as private) duties elsewhere demand your care and attention.

But, gentlemen, when invaded by an enemy whose avowed object is the entire conquest of this Province, the voice of loyalty as well as of interest calls aloud to every person in the sphere in which he is placed to defend his country.

Our militia have heard that voice and obeyed it. They have evinced by the promptitude and loyalty of their conduct that they are worthy of the King whom they serve and the Constitution which they enjoy, and it affords me particular satisfaction that while I address you as legislators I speak to men who in the day of danger will be ready to assist not only with their counsel but with their arms. We look, gentlemen, to our militia, then, as well as to the regular forces, for our protection, but I should be wanting to that important trust committed to my care if I attempted to conceal (what experience, that great instructor of mankind, and especially of legislators, has shewn,) that amendment is necessary in our militia laws to render them efficient.

It is for you to consider what further improvements they may still require.

Honorable Gentlemen of the Legislative Council, and Gentlemen of the House of Assembly:

From the history and experience of our Mother Country, we learn that in times of actual invasion or internal commotion the ordinary course of criminal law has been found inadequate to secure His Majesty's Government from private treachery, as well as from open disaffection, and that at such times its Legislature has found it expedient to enact laws restraining, for a limited period, the liberty of individuals in many cases where it would be dangerous to expose the particulars of the charge, and although the actual invasion of the Province might justify me in the exercise of the full powers reposed in me on such an emergency, yet it will be more agreeable to me to receive the sanction of the two houses.

A few traitors have already joined the enemy, have been suffered to come into the country with impunity, and have been harbored and concealed in the interior, yet the general spirit of loyalty which appears to pervade the inhabitants of this Province is such as to authorize a just expectation that their efforts to mislead and deceive will be unavailing. The disaffected, I am convinced, are few. To protect and defend the loyal inhabitants from their machinations is an object worthy of your most serious deliberations.

We are engaged in an awful and eventful contest. By unanimity and despatch in our councils, and by vigor in our operations, we may teach the enemy this lesson: That a country defended by FREEMEN, enthusiastically devoted to the cause of their King and Constitution, can never be conquered.

Major-General Brock to Sir George Prevost.

YORK, July 28th, 1812.

SIR,—I consider the enclosed letter (this instant received) from the Hon'ble James Baby of sufficient importance to forward by express.

I conceived the Long Point militia the most likely to show the best disposition of any in this part of the country, and this refusal to join Captain Chambers shows the little dependence to be placed in any of them. My situation is getting each day more critical. I still mean to try and send a force to the relief of Amherstburg, but almost despair of succeeding. The population, although I had no great confidence in the majority, is worse than I expected to find it, and the magistrates, &c., &c., appear quite confounded, and decline acting—the consequence is the most improper conduct is tolerated. The officers of militia exert no authority. Everything shows as if a certainty existed of a change taking place soon. But I still hope the arrival of reinforcements may yet avert such a dire calamity. Many in that case would become active in our cause who are now dormant.

I have the honor herewith to transmit a copy of my speech to the two houses, delivered yesterday. A more decent house has not been elected since the formation of the Province, but I perceived at once that I shall get no good of them. They, like the magistrates and others in office, evidently mean to remain passive. The repeal of the *Habeas Corpus* will not pass, and if I have recourse to the law martial I am told the whole armed force will disperse. Never was an officer placed in a more awkward predicament. The militia cannot possibly be governed by the present law—all admit that fact, yet the fear of giving offence will prevent anything effectual from being effected. I entreat the advice of Your Excellency. Some letters received from individuals represent the conduct of the 41st above all praise. I cannot get a line from Colonel St. George. Colonel Procter was provokingly delayed on his journey. I entreat Your Excellency to excuse the haste with which I presume to address you.

(Canadian Archives, C. 676, p. 217.)

Colonel Baynes to Colonel Lethbridge, Inspecting Field Officer of Militia at Kingston.

HEADQUARTERS, QUEBEC, 28th July, 1812.

. . . .

Sir George would recommend the division from Kingston downwards being "left to you, which will enable General Brock to avail himself of General Shaw's services in the upper part of the country, where officers of rank and experience are much wanted."

(From MSS. in possession of Lieut.-Colonel George A. Shaw.)

From the Buffalo Gazette, Tuesday, 28th July, 1812.

GENERAL HALL AND SUITE ARRIVED.

On Friday evening last General Hall arrived in this village, accompanied by Major William Howe Cuyler and George Hosmer, Esq., as aids-de-camp, and a body guard consisting of a detachment of fifteen men of the East Bloomfield Light Horse, commanded by Sergeant Boughton.

General Hall is now General-in-Chief on our frontier.

On Saturday the General, escorted by a number of the first characters of this village, moved to Black Rock, and after paying his respects to Colonel Swift and other officers, and reviewing and inspecting the troops, he returned to Buffalo.

On Sunday morning the General left this village for Lewiston.

The British have erected another breastwork in a circular form on the hill near Capt. Hardison's, opposite Black Rock. A number of soldiers are stationed behind it.

When General Hall and his suite and escort appeared at the Rock on Saturday it produced considerable bustle on the Canada shore. Expresses were sent off in various directions, troops were marched from Fort Erie to the breastworks, and four pieces of artillery were placed in front of Douglas's, opposite Lower Black Rock.

We learn that a number of soldiers at Black Rock remain sickly. that every attention is paid to them, and that none are dangerously ill.

At Lewiston we learn that the troops are generally healthy.

It is with pleasure we learn that strict and regular discipline prevails in the camp at Black Rock, and that the soldiers are orderly and the non-commissioned officers prompt and attentive in the discharge of their respective duties.

It is reported that a parcel of Indians have left Canada and landed on Grand Island (about 12 miles long and 10 broad, lying in the Niagara River, between Black Rock and Schlosser) for the purpose of making an attack on our frontiers. Two companies of volunteers are stationed on the river between Black Rock and Lewiston.

The Grand Island belongs to our Indians, and if any Indians are on the island it is very probable they are from this side for the purpose of killing game.

A SPY IN CUSTODY.

On Friday, the 24th inst., it was rumored that a man by the name of Elijah Clark, a subject of His Majesty in Upper Canada, was on this side a few miles up the lake, lurking about apparently as a spy. Judge Barker, Capt. J. Wells, and some others, immediately went in pursuit of the fellow. They found Clark in the evening, and arrested him at the house of Mr. Lay, about twenty miles from this village. He appeared considerably agitated, and declined giving any satisfactory information as to his crossing the lake, or who or how many came with him, but by means of vigilance and good management they succeeded in arresting two others by the names of Aaron Brink and David Lee, who rowed the boat from Canada with Clark. On Saturday they were taken to Black Rock, and underwent an examination before Col. Swift and Major Miller. They were committed to the prison of this county till a court martial should be ordered by Major-General Hall. Brink and Lee have been removed from jail, and are under keepers. Clark is well guarded.

These criminals were all born in the United States, and till within a few years since have resided in this village. Clark is a merchant in Canada, a young man, a noisy politician, and always to be found in the majority in whatever government he resides.

Arrived in this village on Tuesday last, Mr. Asa H. Morse, a saddler from York, Upper Canada. Having the day previous left York for Newark on business, he was at Newark, by an officer in the fort (who understood he was an American) presented with three alternatives: to become a prisoner of war or take the oath of allegiance, or depart the country. He begged a little time to go back and settle up his business. The officer bid him "shut up his head." He *departed*.

The property of Mr. Morse thus jeopardized was worth about 500 dollars, which was his all.

Mr. Morse states that there were no regular troops at York, and but one company of volunteers; that the town was in no posture of defence, and that the ships of war at that place had all been ordered down the lake.

Major-General Brock to Sir George Prevost.

YORK, July 29, 1812.

SIR,—I have the honor to transmit herewith a despatch this instant received from Captain Roberts, announcing the surrender by capitulation on the 17th instant of Fort Michilimackinac.

The conduct of this officer since his appointment to the command of that distant post has been distinguished by much zeal and judgment, and his recent eminent display of those qualities Your Excellency will find has been attended with a most happy effect.

The militia stationed here volunteered this morning their services to any part of the province without the least hesitation. I have selected 100 whom I have directed to proceed without delay to Long Point, where I propose collecting a force for the relief of Amherstburg. This example, I hope, will be followed by as many as may be required. By the militia law, a man refusing to march may be fined £5 or confined three months, and although I have assembled the Legislature for the express purpose of amending the act, I much fear nothing will be done. Your Excellency will scarcely believe that this infatuated House of Assembly have refused by a majority of two to suspend even for a limited time the Habeas Corpus.

The capture of Michilimackinac may produce great changes to the westward. The actual invasion of the Province justifies every act of hostility on the American territory.

It was not till this morning that I was honored with Your Excellency's despatches, dated the 7th and 10th instant. Their contents, I beg to assure Your Excellency, have relieved my mind considerably. I doubt whether General Hull had instructions to cross to this side of the river. I rather suspect he was compelled by a want of provisions. I embark immediately in the *Prince Regent* for Fort George. I return here the day after to-morrow, and shall probably dissolve the Legislature.

(From Tupper's Life of Brock, pp. 225-6. Canadian Archives, C. 676, p. 236.)

Major-General Brock to Colonel Baynes.

YORK, July 29th, 1812.

DEAR COLONEL,—I was not favored with your letters of the 8th and 10th instant until this morning. I had not before received any official communication of war being declared, and I assure you began to fear that I was wholly forgot. My situation is most critical, not from anything the enemy can do, but from the disposition of the people—the population, believe me, is essentially bad —a full belief possesses them all that this Province must inevitably succumb—this prepossession is fatal to every exertion. Legislators, magistrates, militia officers, all have imbibed the idea, and are so sluggish and indifferent in their respective offices that the artful and active scoundrel is allowed to parade the country without interruption and commit all imaginable mischief. They are so alarmed of offending that they rather encourage than repress disorders and other improper acts. I really believe it is with some cause that they dread the vengeance of the democratic party, they are such a set of unrelenting villains. But to business—several of my letters must have miscarried, otherwise you would have long since been aware that I requested to reinstate Lieut. Johnston in the Glengarry Regiment. He may not be very efficient, but then consider the claims of his family. Indeed the proposition came originally from you. Should Johnston be rejected, I am under previous engagements to Lamont, therefore cannot give ear to FitzGibbon's application.

I have necessarily so many detachments along my widely extended frontier that I cannot possibly spare an officer. I have therefore detained Lieut. Kerr of the Glengarry. I am obliged to mix regulars with the militia, otherwise could not get on at all. It is a pity you did not understand his wishes in regard to the recruiting business.

What a change an additional regiment would make in this part of the Province. Most of the people have lost all confidence. I, however, speak loud and look big. Altho' you may not be able to cast a look this far, you must not omit Johnstown and Kingston. Some regulars will be highly necessary. I wish very much something might be done for Mr. Grant Powell. He was regularly brought up in England as a surgeon. I intended to have proposed to Sir George to appoint him permanent surgeon to the Marine Department, but I scarcely think that the situation would now answer. His abilities, I should think, might be usefully employed now that so many troops are called out.

Messrs. Dickson, Pothier and Crawford behaved nobly at the capture of Michilimackinac. This event may give a total change to the war in the west. Captain Roberts is spoken of in the highest terms.

(Canadian Archives, C. 676, p. 239.)

Sir George Prevost to Lord Liverpool.

QUEBEC, 30th July, 1812.

(No. 60.)

MY LORD,—The exhausted state of the military chest, and the impossibility of supplementing it except from England, exposes His Majesty's service to serious difficulties, which will not be altogether removed by the Army Bill Law. I will have to contend in enforcing it against the deep-rooted prejudices of the Canadians against paper money. I enclose a representation from the Commissary General of the embarrassments in his department from the difficulties experienced in obtaining the smallest supply of money.

. . . .
. . . .

(Canadian Archives. Q. 118, p. 82.)

Commissary-General William H. Robinson to Sir George Prevost.

QUEBEC, 30th July, 1812.

SIR,—I have this evening received a letter from Deputy-Commissary-General Couche, which occasions me the greatest alarm. He informs me that Major-General Brock has ordered out 4,000 militia, and he begs to be informed in what manner they are to be paid. The expense attending this measure will be about £1,500, a sum which it will be impracticable to find in that country, nor have I the means of affording effectual assistance, and if the militia are not regularly paid great evil will ensue, indeed Mr. Couche represents that symptoms of discontent have already appeared. Besides this, various payments are already at a stand. The prospect of a paper medium being established will be a relief, but without the concurrence of the Legislature of Upper Canada it cannot be counted for a certain assistance, yet I submit the expediency of trying the experiment by sending a packet of our notes to General Brock.

Mr. Couche, in his letter of the 3rd inst., speaks of a currency on a limited scale under the auspices merely of the merchants, upon which he is now silent, therefore I conclude it has not produced the effect we had expected. I beg to suggest that His Majesty's Government be asked to send out specie before navigation closes.

(Canadian Archives. Q. 118, p. 84.)

Sir George Prevost to Major-General Brock.

QUEBEC, July 31, 1812.

SIR,—I have received your letter of the 20th instant, accompanied by a copy of two letters from Lieut.-Colonel St. George, who is in command at Amherstburg, and some interesting documents found on board a schooner which had been taken by the boats of the *Hunter*.

In consequence of your having desired Colonel Procter to proceed to Amherstburg and of your presence being necessary at the seat of government, I have taken upon myself to place Major-

General Sheaffe upon the staff, to enable me to send him to assist you in the arduous task you have to perform, in the able execution of which I have great confidence. He has been accordingly directed to proceed without delay to Upper Canada, there to place himself under your command.

I believe you are authorized by the commission under which you administer the Government of Upper Canada to declare martial law in the event of invasion or insurrection: it is therefore for you to consider whether you can obtain anything equivalent to that power from your legislature. I have not succeeded in obtaining a modification of it in Lower Canada, and must therefore upon the occurrence of either of these calamities declare the law martial unqualified, and of course shut the doors of the courts of the civil law.

The report transmitted by Captain Dixon of the Royal Engineers to Lieut.-Colonel Bruyeres of the state of defence in which he had placed Fort Amherstburg, together with the description of the troops allotted for its defence, give me a foreboding that the result of General Hull's attempt upon that fort will terminate honorably to our arms.

If Lieut.-Colonel St. George be possessed of the talents and resources required to form a soldier, he is fortunate in the opportunity of displaying them. Should General Hull be compelled to relinquish his operations against Amherstburg it will be proper his future movements should be most carefully observed, as his late march exhibits a more than ordinary character of enterprise.

Your supposition of my slender means is but too correct: notwithstanding you may rely upon every exertion being made to preserve uninterrupted the communication between Kingston and Montreal, and that I will also give all possible support to your endeavors to overcome every difficulty.

The possession of Malden, which I consider means Amherstburg, appears a favorite object with the Government of the United States: I sincerely hope you will disappoint them.

Should the intelligence which arrived yesterday by the way of Newfoundland prove correct, a remarkable coincidence will exist in the revocation of our orders in Council as regards America and the declaration of war by Congress against England, both having taken place on the same day in London and at Washington, the 17th June.

(From Tupper's Life of Brock, pp. 227-8.)

Major-General Dearborn to Major-General VanRensselaer.

HEADQUARTERS, GREENBUSH, July 29th, 1812.

SIR,—Your situation, I presume, will enable you to ascertain what force the enemy can bring into action against offensive operations on our part at Kingston and its vicinity, and what forces, in addition to those under your command, would be necessary to render offensive operations in that quarter sure of success. Any information you can give me on this and all other points in relation to your command, and on the general state of things with you and in Upper Canada, is requested, and it is highly desirable that you afford me the earliest information from time to time of any occurrences in your vicinity sufficiently important to be communicated. You will readily perceive the expediency of employing suitable characters for obtaining and communicating to you correct information in relation to the enemy's force, and the disposition of the militia and inhabitants generally in the Province.

Proper encouragement should be given to such persons as you may confide in for their services in this employment, and I shall hold myself accountable for any necessary expenditure attendant on it. I have not had an opportunity of conferring with Governor Tompkins, but as he is shortly expected home I shall soon have the pleasure of a conference in relation to your command and the situation of the frontier generally. Not being informed of the extent of your command, I have written to the commanding officers at Niagara and Plattsburg, from the presumption that there might be three distinct commands, but if I am mistaken I trust no material inconvenience will result from it. Be assured, sir, that your appointment to your present command, your ready acceptance of it, and promptitude in repairing to the frontier, affords high satisfaction to our good citizens, and is peculiarly gratifying to your very humble servant.

(From S. VanRensselaer's Narrative, Appendix. p. 22.)

The Secretary of War to Major-General Dearborn.

WAR DEPARTMENT, July 29, 1812.

(Abstract.)

Enclosing a copy of a letter to Mr. Erastus Granger, authorizing him to organize the warriors of the Six Nations conditionally and report the corps to the commandant at Niagara. They should not be allowed to act except under authority of the commanding general.

Calvin Austin to Augustus Porter.

WARREN, May 5, 1814.

DEAR SIR,—In the month of Aug't, 1812, on my way to Detroit, and on my arrival at Miami, I found about 170 Indians in the settlement. I made an inquiry why they were there. It was stated by Amos Spafford, Esq'r, (then resident,) that they had left the mouth of the river from their planting ground on account of their being threatened by the hostile Indians, and were in a suffering condition for want of provisions. We then gathered them and had a talk, and I recommended that 50 rations per day should be issued by the agent, Capt. Daniel Reece. He supplied to the amount of 400 rations, and then was stopped by me, as I found that several of their young men had left that place and gone to Brownstown. I returned from the River Raisin and advised the Indians to proceed a few miles up the river and they would be secure, &c., &c.

N. B.—These Indians were of the Tawaway tribe.

(From MSS. of Hon. P. A. Porter.)

Colonel Baynes to Major-General Brock.

QUEBEC, August 1, 1812.

SIR,—Sir George yesterday received your letter of the 20th with its several enclosures, which are, I assure you, highly interesting to all, and doubly so to those who feel warmly and sincerely attached to you, and few, I believe, possess more friends and well-wishers than yourself. 100 effectives of the Newfoundland and fifty picked men of the Veterans left this in boats on Thursday, and as it has blown a gale of east wind ever since, have, I trust, made great progress. They were intended to reinforce the garrison of Kingston and to relieve the company of the 49th that escorted stores to that place. Sir George regrets extremely his inability to render you a more efficient aid, but under existing circumstances he does not feel himself warranted to do more. I regret to find your militia at Sandwich so lukewarm, to call it by no harsher name, but I fear little can be expected from those recently settled or of American extraction, and with our Canadians we have found a very reluctant compliance. I trust we may still look for considerable reinforcements from home this year. We are led to expect the 1st battalion of the Royals from the West Indies immediately, destined, indeed, to relieve the 41st. I hope we shall not be disappointed, as our militia will feel bold if well backed, and I am sure Sir George will rejoice in receiving the means of rendering you further assistance. It appears to be credited that the Orders-in-Council were rescinded in as far as regarded America on the 17th June, the day the war vote was carried. This will strengthen the oppositionists in the States, and the timid will feel alarmed, not without reason, when they read the glorious and judicious exploit of Captain Hotham in the Northumberland, 74, in destroying, under circumstances of great difficulty and peril, two French 44-gun frigates and a sloop, which received a superior degree of protection from batteries on the shore than can be afforded to Commodore Rodgers in any harbor of the States.

The Americans are forming depots in the neighborhood of the Montreal frontier and building bateaux on the lake, but they have not brought forward any considerable show of strength. On this appearance of weakness we cannot rely, as it would answer no good end making a parade before they intended to attack. If they be serious in their views on this Province, the attempt will probably be backed by predatory excursions on various points. A corps of militia is kept on the Point Levi side.

Our Legislature meet this day to terminate the session. Our great object has been accomplished in the House, adding the provincial security to the Army Note Bill. The province pays the interest accruing upon the notes and the expense of the establishment, and they are constituted a legal tender. Without this step we were completely at a stand, for we could not obtain money to pay the last month's subsistence to the troops. Great benefit is expected to accrue from the operation of the bill. The clergy have engaged to promote the circulation of the notes, all of which above twenty-five dollars bear interest, and all under are payable on demand.

Adieu, my dear general, may every success and good fortune attend you in the arduous task before you. We cannot command success, but I am sure you will not fail to merit it.

(From Tupper's Life of Brock, pp. 228-31.)

District General Order.

HEADQUARTERS, FORT GEORGE, 1st August, 1812.

D. G. Orders.

Paymasters to the militia will be appointed at York, Fort George, Amherstburg and Kingston, who will regularly muster the militia on the 24th of each month, or as soon after as possible.

The officers in charge of the commissariat at Fort George, Amherstburg, Kingston and York will issue to the paymaster the amount of the monthly estimates of the militia, which are to be certified by the commanding officer of the post, whether of the line or militia.

The paylists will be certified on oath by the captain or officer in command of companies, and the officer commanding the militia will examine and certify their belief as to the correctness of the account.

By command of the Major-Genl.

THOS. EVANS,
Major of Brigade.

Lieut.-Colonel Bruyeres, Royal Engineers, to Major-General Brock.

QUEBEC, August 1, 1812.

SIR,—I take the favorable advantage of this being delivered to you by General Sheaffe to assure you of the sincere interest I feel in the very arduous and important position you are now placed in, to protect and defend a chain of posts and a country that has been so long neglected. This difficult task, placed in any other hands, I should consider very discouraging, but I acknowledge that I look with a certain degree of confidence to your abilities and perseverance in surmounting every difficulty that must unavoidably occur in a service of this nature. I most fervently and earnestly hope that every possible success may attend all your proceedings. I trust that you will always meet with zeal and activity in the officers of my department to perform every part of the duty allotted to their charge. It is very difficult at this distance to suggest any ideas that might be useful, as every operation in which you are engaged must depend so entirely upon local circumstances and the conduct which the enemy may pursue towards attaining the object he has in view. I am glad to find that the near arrival of the Royals, expected at Quebec to-morrow, will give you the reinforcement of the 49th Regiment, which, with the detachments of the Newfoundland and Veterans and gun-boat No. 7, will add something to your present strength.

(From Tupper's Life of Brock, pp. 230-1.)

The Secretary of War to Major-General Dearborn.

WAR DEPARTMENT, August 1, 1812.

(Abstract.)

He encloses a copy of a letter from General Hull, dated 19th July. You will make a diversion in favor of him at Niagara and Kingston as soon as practicable.

Sir George Prevost to Major-General Brock.

QUEBEC, August 2, 1812.

SIR,—Last evening an officer of the 98th Regiment arrived here express from Halifax, the bearer of despatches to me, dated on the 22d ultimo, from Mr. Foster, who was then in Nova Scotia.

I lose no time in making you acquainted with the substance of this gentleman's communication. He informs me that he has just received despatches from England, referring to a declaration of ministers in parliament relative to a proposed repeal of the Orders-in-Council provided the American Government would return to relations of amity with us, the contents of which may induce the American Government to agree to a suspension of hostilities as a preliminary to negotiations for peace: that he proposed sending His Majesty's hired armed ketch *Gleaner* to New York with letters to Mr. Baker, whom he had left at Washington in a demi-official capacity, with directions to communicate with the American minister and to write to me the result of his interview. Should the President of the United States think proper to signify that hostile operations should cease on the American side, Mr. Foster suggests the expediency of my being prepared to make a similar signification on our part.

As I propose sending Colonel Baynes immediately into the United States with a proposal for a cessation of hostile operations, I enclose for your information the copy of my letter to General Dearborn or the Commander-in-Chief of the American forces.

Mr. Foster also submits the propriety of our abstaining from an invasion of the United States territory, as only in such an event could the American Government be empowered to order the militia out of the States. I am led to believe from this that General Hull in possessing himself of Sandwich has exceeded his instructions, particularly as Mr. Foster informs me that Mr. Monroe had told him Fort Malden (Amherstburg) would not be attacked, but that General Hull had stated to a friend of his some time ago that he would attempt it.

A report has been made to me that a frigate and six transports, with the Royal Scots (1st battalion) on board from the West Indies, are just below Bic. In consequence of this reinforcement, I have ordered the company of the 49th Regiment sent to Kingston to remain there, and in addition to the Royal Newfoundland Regiment and a detachment of an officer and 50 Veterans most fit for service, now on their route to that station, I shall order Major Ormsby with three companies of the 49th Regiment to proceed from Montreal to the same post to be disposed of as you may find it necessary.

Lieut.-General Sir J. C. Sherbrooke has informed me that one of the transports with part of the Royals on board has been captured by the United States frigate, the *Essex*; that she has been ransomed, and the officers and troops allowed to proceed upon condition that they are not to serve against the United States until regularly exchanged. The vessels and troops had arrived at Halifax and will shortly be sent hither.

(From Tupper's Life of Brock, pp. 231-2.)

Major-General Dearborn to Major-General VanRensselaer, or the Commanding Officer at Fort Niagara.

HEADQUARTERS, GREENBUSH, Aug. 3d, 1812.

SIR,—You will please take measures for keeping up a correspondence with General Hull and ascertain his movements by express or otherwise, and as he has crossed over to Upper Canada and taken possession of Fort Malden, it will be expedient to make every exertion in your power to co-operate with him. If your force will not admit of any strong offensive operations, it is highly desirable that such diversions should be made in his favor as will prevent the enemy from detaching any force from the vicinity of Niagara to oppose the movements of General Hull. I trust you will soon be called to act in a more decisive manner.

(From S. VanRensselaer's Narrative. Appendix, p. 22.)

District General Orders.

YORK, 3rd August, 1812.

D. General Orders.

1. Lieutenant-Colonel Myers will assume, during the absence of Colonel Procter, the command of the District of Niagara.

2. Major General Shaw, having offered his services in any manner in which they may be useful, Major-General Brock is pleased to appoint him to command between Chippawa and the Sugar Loaf, as Colonel of Militia, with the pay and allowance of Lieutenant-Colonel.

3. It is to be understood that no officer in the militia when embodied will receive a higher rate of pay than Lieutenant-Colonel, and that officers of every rank are subject to the same deductions as the line, including the income tax.

By command of the Major-General.

J. B. GLEGG, A. D. C.

Proceedings of a Council held at York Respecting the Western Frontier.

AT A COUNCIL HELD AT GOVERNMENT HOUSE, YORK, UPPER CANADA,

MONDAY, August 3d, 1812.

Present,—
Major-General Brock.
Honble The Chief Justice.
" James Baby.
" Alexander Grant.
" John McGill.
" Mr. Justice Powell.
" Prideaux Selby.

His Honor the President represented to the Board that the hopes he had entertained from the call of the Legislature were likely to be disappointed.

That the Lower House of Assembly, instead of prompt exertions to strengthen his hands for the government of the militia, providing for security from internal treason by partial suspension of the Habeas Corpus Act, authorizing a partial exercise of Martial Law concurrently with the ordinary course of justice, and placing at his disposal for the defence of the Province the funds not actually applied upon past appropriations, had consumed eight days in carrying a single measure of party—the repeal of the School Bill, and passing an act for the public disclosure of treasonable practices before the Magistrates should have power to commit without bail. That under such circumstances little could be expected from a prolonged session of the Legislature.

That the enemy had invaded and taken post in the Western District: was multiplying daily his preparation to invade in others; that the militia, in a perfect state of insubordination, had withdrawn from the ranks in actual service; had refused to march, when legally commanded, to reinforce a detachment of the regular force for the relief of Amherstburg; had insulted their officers, and some not immediately embodied had manifested in many instances a treasonable spirit of neutrality or disaffection.

That the Indians on the Grand River, tampered with by the disaffected whites, had withdrawn from their volunteer services and declared for a neutrality which in respect of them was equally inadmissible as with the King's other subjects.

That in the Western and London Districts several persons had negotiated with the enemy's commander, hailing his arrival and pledging support. That the regular force consisted of one regiment, the 41st, nine hundred strong, and part of the Royal Newfoundland Regiment, two hundred, with a detachment of Royal Artillery and several armed vessels. That the extent of coast exposed and the great distance of the prominent points had obliged him to divide that force to support and countenance the militia. That the conduct of the western militia had exposed to imminent danger the regular force at Amherstburg, and, however inconvenient, he had made a large detachment of the 41st and militia from the Home and Niagara Districts, with the few Indians not corrupted, to reinforce that garrison if time would admit.

That, on the other hand, the Commandant at St. Joseph had, with the garrison and Indians, taken the Island of Michilimackinac, the garrison of which capitulated without firing a shot.

That in all probability part of that force might descend to Detroit, and in such case a co-operation with the garrison at Fort Amherstburg, reinforced by the detachment now on its march to Long Point, might compel the invaders to retire or surrender, but that no good result from any military expedition could be expected unless more powerful restraint could be imposed on the militia than the actual law admits, and that he had power to restrain the general population from treasonable adherence with the enemy or neutrality by summary proceeding and punishment, nor could the colony be considered safe from the Indians in its very bosom whilst liable to be tampered with by disaffected persons, exposed only to the slow progress of conviction by criminal law.

That with this view of the situation of the Colony, he submitted for the consideration of the Council how far it might be expedient to prorogue the General House of Assembly and proclaim martial law under the powers of the King's Commission, in case of invasion.

The Council adjourned for deliberation.

TUESDAY, 4th August.

The Council met from adjournment of yesterday.
Present,—
The same members.

The Council having deliberated upon His Honor's representation is unanimously of the opinion that under the circumstances of the Colony, it is expedient upon the prorogation of the General Assembly to proclaim and exercise Martial Law, according to the powers of His Majesty's Commission to the Governor-General.

(Canadian Archives, Q., 118, p. 187.)

Major General Brock to Sir George Prevost.

YORK, August 4, 1812.

SIR,—I have the honor to enclose a statement made by me yesterday to His Majesty's Executive Council, which will fully apprize Your Excellency of my situation. The Council adjourned for deliberation, and I have no doubt will recommend the prorogation of the Assembly and proclamation declaring martial law; but doubts occurred in contemplation of such an event, which I take the liberty to submit to Your Excellency and request the aid of your experience and superior judgment.

1. In the event of declaring martial law, can I, without the sign manual, approve and carry into effect the sentence of a general courtmartial?

2. Can I put upon a general courtmartial after martial law is proclaimed any person not a commissioned officer in His Majesty's regular forces? In other words, can officers of the militia set in conjunction with those of the line?

(From Tupper's Life of Brock, pp. 232-3.)

The Secretary of War to Major-General Dearborn.

WAR DEPARTMENT, August 4, 1812.

(Abstract.)

Informing him that the light artillery and Simond's regiment have been ordered to proceed to Albany.

From the Buffalo Gazette, Tuesday, 4th August, 1812.

The account of Hull's occupying Sandwich was known at Newark four or five days before it arrived here, the distance from Detroit to Newark being much less than the route on our side of the lake. It is presumed that troops were immediately sent to Malden, as for ten or twelve days past there have been several movements of British troops on the Niagara River. On Saturday last we are informed that one company of regulars and five flank companies (militia) were sent up to the head of Lake Ontario in boats, from thence (distance about 30 miles) to Detroit River, and to sail down the same to Malden. The flags of truce which so frequently passed and re-passed at Black Rock and other places on the Niagara River during the two first weeks of the war have, we believe, been entirely discontinued. No event of importance has transpired on our frontier since our last. The health of the troops is not materially changed. There has been one death at the Rock last week, and one now lies dangerously ill.

Yesterday a British armed vessel (supposed to be the one lately built at Long Point) came down and anchored at Fort Erie—a merchant vessel came in company, name not known, probably a prize to the arrived ship.

Tuesday morning, 8 o'clock. The brig *Hunter*, ship of war, and sch'r *Nancy*, have left Fort Erie and gone up the lake, probably loaded with military stores for Malden.

INDIAN LOGIC.—The rumor of the British and Indians taking possession of Grand Island (situated in Niagara River and owned by the Senecas) having reached the Senecas, they assembled for the purpose of counselling with their agent, Mr. Granger, on the subject. The famous Red Jacket, after having stated the information they had received, addressed the agent in the following manner:—

BROTHER,—You have told us that we had nothing to do with the war between you and the British, but we find the war has come to our own doors. Our property is taken possession of by the British and their Indian friends. It is necessary for us now to take up the business, defend our property, and drive the enemy from it. If we sit still upon our seats and take no measures of redress the British (according to the customs of you white people) will hold it by conquest, and should you conquer the Canadas, you will claim it upon the same principle, as conquered from the British. We therefore request permission to go with our warriors and drive off those bad people and take possession of our lands.

District General Orders.

YORK, 5th August, 1812.

D. G. Orders.

The business of the commissariat at this post having decreased, Major-General Brock has appointed Mr. William Stanton to act as paymaster to the militia for the York District until further orders. Mr. Stanton is to receive no pay for performing this duty other than what he derived from his situation in the Commissariat Department.

By order of the Major-General.

J. B. GLEGG,
Captn., A. D. C.

From the New York Evening Post, Thursday, 13th August, 1812.

ALBANY, August 10.

We are sorry to learn that most of the young men of the St. Regis tribe of Indians have left their settlement to join the British forces, and that Colonel Louis and several of the aged chiefs friendly to the United States have from fear of their safety also fled from their settlement and taken refuge within the County of Franklin, where they are now supported at the expense of the United States.

(File in the New York Society Library.)

Major-General VanRensselaer to Governor Tompkins.

BUFFALO, 11th August, 1812, 6 p. m.

SIR,—I have to advise Your Excellency that I arrived here last evening, and various considerations induced me to adopt measures for obtaining satisfactory information respecting the situation of General Hull. Accordingly I this morning sent my aide-de-camp to Black Rock, having heard that Judge Porter, brother of the Quartermaster-General, had lately returned from Detroit. Colonel Van Rensselaer has returned, having had a conference with the Quartermaster-General and Judge Porter. The result of the information obtained is substantially this: That Judge Porter left Detroit on the 29th ult.: Gen. Hull was entrenching himself opposite Detroit, and Fort Malden was not taken, as has been reported. Genl. Hull's force was eight hundred. At Brownstown, below Detroit, are fifteen hundred hostile Indians. The Quartermaster-General has lately sent several boats with provisions for General Hull, but unfortunately one boat was taken by the enemy, and unfavorable apprehensions are entertained for the other boats.

It is here generally believed that detachments of troops have been sent from Fort George to relieve Fort Malden: the number remaining behind I have not been able to ascertain, but shall endeavor to make this an object of early enquiry. It is said that the enemy abound on the opposite shore with ordnance and every munition of war. We are here, as indeed at all our posts, lamentably deficient in ordnance. The situation of Ogdensburg, and the necessity of supplying it with heavy ordnance, I have before stated to Your Excellency in my letter by express from that place. Every consideration connected with the success of any operation in this quarter urges me to solicit the earliest possible supply of heavy ordnance and some skilful engineers and artillerists. Without such aid and supplies I can hardly conceive how it will be possible for us to achieve anything of importance or even to defend our posts in case of an attack from the enemy.

I have spent a part of this day with Red Jacket, Cornplanter and a number of other Indians of influence. They very kindly consider me as the messenger of peace and friendship, especially delegated by Your Excellency. Their professions are unreservedly friendly and I believe sincere.

I have this day received a letter from Major-General Dearborn, in which he speaks of Fort Malden being taken. I have given him such information as I possess on that subject.

I shall to-morrow proceed to Black Rock and Lewiston and make further communications of every incident of importance.

(Tompkins' Papers, vol. VIII., pp. 58-61. New York State Library.)

Sir George Prevost to Major General Brock.

MONTREAL, August 12, 1812.

SIR,—Your letter of the 4th instant, enclosing the proceedings of the Executive Council of the 3d, Captain Glegg's letter of the 5th instant, transmitting copies of letters from Colonel Procter to you of the 26th and 30th July, with the correspondence between Brigadier-General Hull and Lieut.-Colonel St. George, and the intercepted correspondence of the former, together with your letter to Colonel Baynes of the 4th instant, were all delivered to me on my arrival at this place yesterday. The information they contain is highly interesting, and I lose no time in despatching to you Brigade-Major Shekleton as the bearer of this letter and for the purpose of receiving whatever communication you may have to make in return. Being fully aware of the necessity of affording you such reinforcements as the exigencies of the service in other parts of the two Provinces would permit, I had previous to the receipt of your letter made arrangements for that purpose.

Major Ormsby, with three companies of the 49th Regiment, protecting a considerable supply of ordnance and ordnance stores, left Lachine on the 6th instant for Kingston and Fort George, taking with him £2,500 for the payment of the regular and militia forces. Major Heathcote, with one company of the 49th Regiment, about 110 men of the Newfoundland Regiment and 50 picked Veterans, are to leave Lachine on the 13th instant. With this detachment an additional supply of ordnance stores and camp equipage for 500 men will be forwarded for Upper Canada, and, as soon as a sufficiency of bateaux can again be collected at Lachine, Colonel Vincent is under orders to proceed to Kingston with the remainder of the 49th Regiment and a subaltern of the Royal Artillery and ten gunners with two 3-pounders.

When these reinforcements reach you, they will, I trust, enable you successfully to resist the internal (as well as external) enemies opposed to you and materially aid the able measures you have adopted for the defence of Upper Canada. With regard to the queries you have submitted to me on the subject of martial law, I have to observe that it has not fallen within my experience to see martial law proclaimed except in those places where it has been declared under the authority of a provincial legislature, which of course regulated the mode in which it was to be executed. As the martial law you propose declaring is founded on the King's commission and upon the extreme case of invasion alluded to in it, I am inclined to think that whatever power is necessary for carrying the measure into effect must have been intended to have been given you by the commission, and consequently that the power of assembling courts martial and of carrying their sentences into execution is included in the authority for declaring martial law. The officers of militia becoming themselves subject to martial law when it is declared, I conceive they may sit upon courts martial with officers of His Majesty's regular forces, but upon both these points I desire not to be understood as speaking decisively—extreme cases must be met by measures which, on ordinary occasions, would not perhaps be justified. Your situation is such as to warrant your resorting to any step which in your judgment the public safety may require. I should therefore think that after taking the best opinions that you can obtain from the first law characters you have about you, respecting the doubts you entertain on this subject, you need not hesitate to determine upon that line of conduct which you shall think will best promote the good of the service, trusting, if you do err, to the absolute necessity of the measure you may adopt as your justification for them to His Majesty's Government.

Your letters of the 26th, 28th, and 29th July, with the several enclosures and papers accompanying them, were received by me shortly previous to my leaving Quebec, the last containing Captain Roberts' official account of the capture of Fort Michilimackinac. Great credit is certainly due to that officer for the zeal and promptitude with which he has performed that service—at the same time, I must confess, my mind has been very much relieved by finding that the capture took place at a period subsequent to Brigadier-General Hull's invasion of the Province, as had it been prior to it, it would not only have been in violation of Captain Roberts's orders, but have afforded a just ground for the subsequent conduct of the enemy, which I now plainly perceive no forbearance on your part could have prevented. The capture of this place will, I hope, enable the Indian tribes in that quarter to co-operate with you in your present movements against the enemy, by threatening his flanks, a diversion which would greatly alarm him and probably have the effect of compelling him to retreat across the river.

I send you enclosed a copy of the official repeal of the orders in council, which I received last night (by express) from Quebec. Although I much doubt whether this step on the part of our Government will have any effect upon that of the United States, the circulation of a paper evincing their conciliatory disposition may tend to increase and strengthen the divisions which subsist among the people upon the subject of the war. I therefore recommend you to have a number of copies struck off and distributed.

Colonel Baynes is still absent upon his mission to the enemy's camp. Your letter to him of the 29th ultimo was received at the same time with those I have last acknowledged. Colonel Lethbridge I have directed to return to Montreal.

The issue of army bills has taken place at Quebec, and I hope to be able shortly to send you a supply of them.

(From Tupper's Life of Brock, pp. 233-6.)

Major-General Dearborn to Major-General Amos Hall, or Commanding Officer on the Niagara Frontier.

HEADQUARTERS, GREENBUSH, Aug. 8, 1812.

SIR,—Having received from Sir George Prevost, Governor and Commander-in-Chief of the forces in Canada by Col. Baynes, his Adjutant-General, despatches from England to our Government of a conciliatory nature, and a proposition on the part of Sir George Prevost, for a mutual cessation of hostilities on the frontiers, I have so far complied with the proposition as to agree to direct the respective commanding officers on the side of the United States to confine their respective operations to defensive measures until they receive further orders. Similar orders are given to the British commanders. You will therefore confine the operations of the troops under your command to defensive measures until they receive further orders. It being explicitly understood that if General Hull should continue to act offensively and any movement of the enemy's troops in your vicinity should take place with a view to offensive operations, it will be considered as an infraction of the agreement, and you will govern yourself accordingly.

(From S. VanRensselaer's Narrative: Appendix, p. 24.)

The Secretary of War to Major-General Dearborn.

WAR DEPARTMENT, Aug. 8, 1812.

(Abstract.)

Should the recruits and volunteers be inadequate for immediate operations he is instructed to call out as many militia as he may need. The repeated attacks of the enemy in the vicinity of Sackett's Harbor require prompt and energetic movements in the vicinity of the lakes.

(From the Buffalo Gazette, Tuesday, 11th August, 1812.)

On Friday and Saturday of last week *eleven native born* citizens of the United States deserted from the British ranks, seized boats, and, crossing Lake Erie, landed eight of them at Canadaway, in Chautauqua County, and the other three at the mouth of Buffalo Creek. They were examined and suffered to depart. Their countenances bespoke the joy and satisfaction they felt on having thus so happily made their escape. They inform us that the British are withdrawing almost all their forces from the Niagara lines to meet General Hull at Fort Malden. If this be true we are led to believe:

There is a tide in the affairs of *war*, which taken at the *ebb* leads on to fortune.

Last Wednesday, before a general court martial, held at the court house in this village, Colonel Philetus Swift, President, commenced the trial of *Elijah Clark*. The charge brought against him was that of being a British spy. The trial continued until Saturday about noon. The decision is not yet known, and probably will not be for several days.

At an Indian Council, held at Cattaraugus on the 29th July, the Indian chiefs requested that no more whiskey should be sold to the Indians.

District General Orders.

HEADQUARTERS, BANKS OF LAKE ERIE,
15 MILES S. W. OF PORT TALBOT,
August 11th, 1812, 6 o'clock p. m.

D. *General Orders.*

The troops will hold themselves in readiness and will embark in the boats at twelve o'clock this night precisely.

It is Major-General Brock's positive orders that none of the boats go ahead of that in which is the Headquarters, where a light will be carried during the night.

The officers commanding the different boats will immediately inspect the arms and ammunition of the men and see that they are constantly kept in a state for immediate service, as the troops are now to pass through a part of the country which is known to have been visited by the enemy's patroles.

A captain with a subaltern and thirty men will mount as piquet upon the landing of the boats, and a sentry will be furnished from each boat, who must be regularly relieved, to take charge of the boat and baggage, &c.

A patrole from the piquet will be sent out on landing to the distance of a mile from the encampment.

By order of the Major-General,

J. B. GLEGG, Capt'n, A. D. C.
J. MACDONELL, P. A. D. C.

Samuel S. Connor, A. D. C. to Major-General Dearborn, to the Commanding Officer at Niagara.

(Undated.)

SIR,—You will please to communicate the enclosed communication, which is from the British Adjutant-General, to the British commanding officer opposite Niagara and Detroit, that he may immediately communicate it to Col. Procter.

(From S. VanRensselaer's Narrative: Appendix, p. 25.)

District General Orders.

HEADQUARTERS, POINT AUX PINS,
LAKE ERIE, August 12th, 1812.

D. General Orders.

It is Major-General Brock's intention, should the wind continue fair, to proceed during the night. Officers commanding boats will therefore pay attention to the order of sailing as directed yesterday. The greatest care and attention will be requisite to prevent the boats from scattering or falling behind.

A great part of the bank of the lake where the boats will this day pass is much more dangerous and difficult of access than any we have passed. The boats will therefore not land excepting in the most extreme necessity, and the greatest care must be taken to choose the best places for landing.

The troops being now in the neighborhood of the enemy, every precaution must be taken to guard against surprise.

By order of the Major-General.

J. B. GLEGG,
Capt'n, A. D. C.

Colonel Baynes to Major-General Brock.

MONTREAL, August 13, 1812.

SIR,—I wrote to you from Albany on the 8th instant, but as my letter was submitted to the inspection of General Dearborn I, of course, confined myself to the sole subject of the armistice entered into with that officer. . . . . A clause admitting reinforcements to pass with stores was readily agreed to on my part. General Dearborn told me that a considerable reinforcement (with stores) was on its way to Niagara, and that he could not delay or alter its destination. I informed him that we were also forwarding reinforcements and stores, and that it would be advisable to agree that all movements of that nature on either side should be suffered to proceed unmolestedly by troops under instructions to preserve defensive measures. I am apprehensive that General Dearborn may not explicitly explain all these points, and I have therefore cautioned all the officers to whom I have communicated them to act with the utmost caution, and to be prepared for all events that may arise. I feel extremely prepossessed in favor of General Dearborn, whose manners appear to evince great candor and sincerity. He assured me that no event of his life would afford him so much happiness as resigning his command in consequence of our honorable adjustment of differences. He told me that General Hull was placed under his orders merely for form's sake, but that he acted by particular instructions from the War Department, and would not consider himself bound to obey any order that was not in conformity with them.

Under all these circumstances, which I have represented to Sir George, I have strongly urged his sending you further reinforcements, which I am sure can be spared. We are at present checked for want of conveyance, but I trust that after the troops now on their route are despatched that Sir George will be induced to send you further aid and that of the best description. I think it of the highest importance, particularly if we are likely to arrange matters with the States, that the balance of military events should be unequivocally in our favor. I found a very general prejudice prevailing with Jonathan of his own resources and means of invading these provinces, and of our weakness and inability to resist, both exaggerated in a most absurd and extravagant degree. A little practical correction of this error would be attended with the best effects.

The 1st battalion of the Royals are upwards of 1,100 strong, but sickly, having suffered from their long residence in the West Indies, and they are in consequence marked for the Quebec garrison.

(From Tupper's Life of Brock, pp. 298-300.)

General Amos Hall to Governor Tompkins.

MANCHESTER, August 13, 1812.

SIR,—In conformity with your directions in your letter of the 8th of July, I repaired without delay to the Niagara frontier. On my arrival I found that considerable apprehension was entertained of an invasion, but before I could form an opinion as to the fact, I found that it would be necessary for me to take a general view of the lines. I spent about a week in the examination and in making such disposition of the troops as appeared to me best calculated to protect and guard the frontier. I, however, found it difficult with the force we had on the lines to distribute the men so as to form a chain of centinels and patrols from lake to lake, and have men left off guard duty sufficient to erect such batteries as have by the advice of Genl. Gray been erected, and to perform other necessary fatigue duty.

One battery has been built on the brow of the hill above Lewiston, which will completely command two batteries erected by the enemy on the opposite side of the river, one being a little below the house of Benjamin Barton, the other about one-third of the way up the hill above Queenston. We have another battery of considerable length erected on the rise of ground opposite lower Black Rock, in front of the barracks. That, however, I consider a protecting rather than commanding work. Another small work has been nearly completed, and has been erected under cover of a thin wood, about half a mile up the river from the barracks. This is thought by General Gray (who is our chief engineer) to be a very commanding piece of ground. It is a small battery, calculated to mount one heavy piece of artillery.

The situation of the batteries erected by the enemy on the opposite side of the river are very correctly described in the eastern papers, and particularly in the papers printed in Canandaigua, which you have undoubtedly seen. No new batteries have been erected on the opposite shore within eight or ten days past.

Our batteries are now nearly ready to receive several pieces of ordnance, and some should be heavy. But the misfortune is we have nothing of the kind. We have only four pieces of field artillery, except what are in the garrison: two four and two six-pounders. Those pieces of heavy artillery mentioned in your letter of the 8th of July have not arrived.

We have had thoughts of supplying ourselves with ordnance from the batteries on the Canada shore. But being well assured that many of the inhabitants are favorable to receiving our troops and would give us aid if we should come in sufficient force to give them protection, and knowing their situation to be such that they would be obliged to take arms if any trifling invasion should be made, it has been thought most advisable to make no attempt until an efficient force might cross, such as to give general protection.

The Quartermaster-General has commenced building boats at Manchester (near the falls), and by the assistance of fatigue parties from the lines we are in hopes to have forty boats completed within two or three weeks at the farthest.

I consider it a great misfortune that we are not now provided with boats and a sufficient number of troops to cross the river. It is a favorable moment, and I regret very much indeed that we are not prepared to improve it.

Detachments of the regular troops and of the militia have within the last ten or fifteen days been ordered up Lake Erie by water, and across the country to Fort Malden, to reinforce the British army in that quarter.

I am very anxious for the fate of General Hull's army, which did not (I have been informed) exceed twenty-two hundred when he crossed the river. Had we had a suitable force and been provided with boats, it would have been in our power to have prevented reinforcements from leaving this part of Upper Canada to the relief of Malden. But boats we had none, and not a sufficient number of troops to have warranted an attack.

We are informed, and I believe the information correct, that the whole force at Fort Erie, and the batteries in its vicinity, did not a few days since amount to more than two or three hundred men at most, and at Fort George their strength, we have reason to believe, is nearly in the same proportion. But the enemy, knowing that we had no means of crossing the river, ventured to leave their forts thus thinly garrisoned.

My opinion is that three thousand men, in addition to our present force, would be sufficient to enable us to erect the American standard on the Canadian side, and support it against any force that could be raised, unless General Hull should be defeated and the troops from that quarter, with a large force of Indians that would immediately follow them, should return to oppose us. In that event, flushed as they would be with victory, a much larger would be necessary. Our lines are at present thinly guarded, and guard duty is hard on the men. It would be a great relief should Your Excellency see fit to order on the 19th regiment detached from the counties of Cayuga and Seneca, the command of which has been assigned to Lieutenant-Colonel Bloom. In case of invasion, or should it be thought advisable to make a descent into Upper Canada, many of the militia in the western part of the State would volunteer. There has been several tenders of the services of companies and battalions since I have been on the lines.

The troops now on the lines are stationed as follows:—Lieut.-Colonel Swift's regiment at Black Rock, except one company on command at Buffalo; four companies of Lieut.-Colonel Dobbin's regiment and one company of Lieut.-Colonel Allen's regiment at the camp near old Fort Schlosser; Captain Dox's volunteer company and three companies of Lieut.-Colonel Dobbin's regiment at Lewiston; Lieut.-Colonel Allen's regiment, excepting one company at the Five Mile Meadows, between Lewiston and Fort Niagara. Part of the regular troops are at Youngstown, the remainder in the garrison.

Our whole force cannot be estimated to exceed fourteen hundred effective men. Twelve dragoons are distributed at the different posts on the lines, who answer for expresses and patrols.

An express has been sent to General Hull, advising him of the reinforcement sent on by General Brock from the British lines and vicinity of the Niagara frontier. The express went from Buffalo on the 5th inst. and reached Cuyahoga in two days. But Judge Porter, who arrived last evening from Detroit, is apprehensive that the communication will be cut off before the express will be able to get through, for he states that McKee, with some other Indian leaders, with about 300 Indians, were at a place called Brownstown, nearly opposite Malden, a short time before he with about forty others came into town, but had crossed over to Malden. He expects all communication will be cut off by this party.

Judge Porter brings reports that Michilimackinac has been taken, that it was given up on summons, not a gun fired. There were seventy men in garrison and about one hundred of the enemy; from twelve to twenty only were white men, the remainder Indians.

General Hull, he states, is erecting a fort nearly opposite Detroit, where he will act on the defensive until he receives a reinforcement. I hope it may arrive in season.

It appears by Judge Porter's account that the General had but 850 effective men on his return with him when he was at Sandwich about two weeks since. There probably might have been about two hundred on command. Admitting that calculation to be correct, one thousand would be all his force. This is a small army in an enemy's country, widely different from being in possession of Malden, as stated in our first accounts.

General Van Rensselaer and suite arrived at this place last evening. He will proceed to the garrison to-morrow. After taking a view of the lines he will take command on this station.

In compliance with Your Excellency's orders, I came on to these lines. I now wait your further orders respecting my services.

The troops here are generally healthy, excepting slight turns of the distempers incident to camps on their first formation. There have been but few cases of fever taken place in the camp for the number of men and the season of the year.

N. B.—August 14.—General Van Rensselaer has taken the command on this station. I find by General Orders by him on the 13th July that he is authorized to call out such parts of the detachments as he may think necessary. He appears very anxious to have it in his power to do something for his country; he will order on more troops immediately.

(Tompkins' Papers, vol. VIII., pp. 53-8, New York State Library.)

From the New York Evening Post, Thursday, 27th August, 1812.

BATAVIA, August 13.

Extract of a letter dated at Buffalo, August 13:

This afternoon the British began to build a breastwork nearly opposite Black Rock. They were scattered in every direction by one discharge of a six-pounder from our shore. The ball struck near the laborers. All was confusion for a short time. An officer on horseback was immediately despatched to Fort Erie. To-morrow morning the British will no doubt resume work.

(From file in New York Society Library.)

From the New York Evening Post, Wednesday, 26th August, 1812.

CANANDAIGUA, August 13.

We are told that the gentleman who brought General Hull's proclamation to the Niagara frontiers turns out to be a citizen of Canada, sent over in the night from Fort Erie, where the proclamation had been received several days earlier than on our side. Calculating on our *snail-like* way of transmitting intelligence, the fellow availed himself of General Hull's paper, which served as a good passport, and, appearing in the capacity of an express, found no difficulty in obtaining information which was his *express* view, and after spending several days along the line he re-crossed in a boat rowed by two men from the British fort.

(From file in New York Society Library.)

General Orders.

HEADQUARTERS, NIAGARA, Aug. 13th, 1812.

Major-General VanRensselaer having been appointed to the command of the troops on the northern and western frontiers of this State, announces his arrival. Having assumed this command, the General assures the officers and soldiers that as on their part he will require prompt obedience to orders and strict discipline, so from him they may expect his unremitting exertions to render their situation at all times as eligible as possible, and when their exertions shall be called for against the enemy he trusts with confidence that they will be such as will redound to the honor of the troops and the service of the country.

The troops at Lewiston will be reviewed and inspected at 10 o'clock to-morrow; for that purpose blank returns will be furnished.

An accurate inspection return will be made out by the commanding officers of companies, who are to account for their men, arms, and accoutrements. In their returns they will note the deficiencies of arms or accoutrements, to the end that measures may be adopted to obtain supplies from the proper departments.

By order of Major-General VanRensselaer.

SOL. VANRENSSELAER, Aid-de-Camp.

General Order.

HEADQUARTERS, ALBANY, 13th Aug., 1812.

The Nineteenth detached regiment of militia of this State, commanded by Lt.-Col. Henry Bloom, being part of General William Wadsworth's detached brigade, pursuant to the directions of the President of the United States, is hereby ordered into the service of the United States, and is to repair to Lewiston or Black Rock and receive and obey the orders of the commanding officer in the service of the United States at that frontier. The regiment will rendezvous in battalions or by regiment, as may be directed by Brigadier-Genl. John Tillotson, who is the senior brigadier-general and will act as Commandant of the seventh division of the militia of this State, in the absence of Major-General Hall.

The non-commissioned officers and privates must severally appear at the place of rendezvous armed with a musket or rifle and equipments accordingly, and with a knapsack, blanket, canteen and necessary clothing. Tents and camp equipage will be provided and be ready for the use of the regiment at the times and places of rendezvous.

By order of the Commander-in-Chief.

ANTHONY LAMB, Aid-de-Camp.

(Tompkins' Papers, New York State Library.)

John Lovett to Joseph Alexander.

NIAGARA FALLS, August 14, 1812.

. . . .

I wrote to VanVechten by the last mail the situation of General Hull. I am inclined to think he is not in a very eligible situation. General Dearborn believes Fort Malden is taken, but it is *not* true. Now, in justification of our General, who God knows would serve his country if he could, I made a little sketch of the country, &c., where and how Hull is situated, in my letter to Van Vechten: read that and you will see what condition we are in, but how is that possible in our present condition? We have eleven cannon for all our extensive lines: no works of any consequence except old Fort Niagara, and that, though once a masterpiece, is all going to decay. From Buffalo to Niagara, both inclusive, we have not 1,000 militia. Capt. Leonard of the garrison at Niagara told me this afternoon that our regulars are 360 and no more. Wait another sentence. Although General Van Rensselaer is incessantly pressing the Commander-in-Chief with that indispensable necessity of a competent supply of heavy ordnance, for engineers, artillerists, still a noble company of 106 artillerists at Niagara are in two or three days to take up their line of march for Albany. This Capt. Leonard told me this day. After all you have heard, you will not, you cannot, believe me, but *hear* me and wait until the next mail, when we shall send the Commander-in-Chief our inspection returns for all the posts. Now, as to the enemy—although they have sent off large detachments, General Wadsworth, who commanded at Lewiston, told me today 1,000 from Niagara to reinforce Fort Malden, yet they appear to be alert all along the lines, yet exceedingly civil, and still with ordnance of every description and all the munitions of war they abound.

Every three or four miles on every prominent point or eminence there you see a snug battery thrown up, and the *last* saucy *arguments of Kings* poking their white noses and round black nostrils right upon your face, ready to spit fire, ball, and brimstone in your very teeth if you were offer to turn squatter on John Bull's land. Niagara, on the British side, or as it is sometimes called Newark, I mean at Lake Ontario, looks wicked everywhere. It is a charming, fertile, broad village, but all a camp, fortified at every point. Capt. Leonard was this afternoon in my presence asked seriously for his professional answer as an able, gallant, and experienced officer: " What number of troops would be competent to promise success in an attack upon Fort George, that is, their main work." I heard the answer: "*Not less than* 2,000 well disciplined troops." Those who know Leonard will believe, for they must respect his opinion. No sooner did we approach with our cavalcade than away ran expresses on the opposite shore at full speed. Here again I saw our old friend, the *Earl of Moira*. While we were reconnoitering the works the *Prince Regent* up sails and stood off north. "Now let the reasonable part of the world judge why Gen. VanRensselaer *cannot act.*

(From a Legacy of Historical Gleanings, by Mrs. C. V. R. Bonney. Albany, N. Y., 1875.)

District General Orders.

HEADQUARTERS, FORT AMHERSTBURG,
August 14th, 1812.

[Circular.]

D. *General Orders.*

Major-General Brock announces his arrival to the troops quartered in the Western District, and directs officers in command will immediately transmit returns of their respective corps.

The Major-General congratulates the troops on the evacuation of the country by the enemy. He is persuaded that nothing but the spirit manifested by those who have remained doing duty, and the judicious measures adopted by Colonel Procter, have compelled him to so disgraceful a retreat.

Colonel Elliott and Major McKee and the officers of the Indian Department are entitled to his best thanks for their judicious management of the Indians, and for the example of gallantry which they have uniformly shown before the enemy.

The Major-General cannot avoid expressing his surprise at the numerous desertions which have occurred from the ranks of the militia, to which circumstance the long stay of the enemy on this side of the river must in a great measure be ascribed. He is willing to believe that their conduct proceeded from an anxiety to get in their harvests and not from any predilection for the principles or Government of the United States. He requests officers commanding corps to transmit to him the names of such militiamen as have remained faithful to their oath and duty, that immediate measures may be taken to discharge their arrears of pay.

The enemy being still in the neighborhood, the whole physical force of the country will be employed to drive him to such a distance as will ensure its tranquillity.

Officers commanding militia corps are responsible that every individual bound to embody himself do immediately repair to this station, in default of which he will be treated as a deserter and subjected to all the penalties of the new Militia Act.

Captains Muir, Tallon, and Chambers, 41st Regiment; Captain Glegg, 49th Regiment; Captain Mockler, Newfoundland Regt., and Captain Dixon, Royal Engineers, are appointed to the rank of Major so long as the local service on which they are employed continues.

The troops in the Western District will be formed into three brigades: The first, under Lieut.-Colonel St. George, to consist of detachments of the Royal Newfoundland Regiment, and of the Kent and First and Second Regiments Essex Militia. The Second, under the command of Major Chambers, consisting of fifty men of 41st Regiment, and the whole of the detachments of York, Lincoln, Oxford, and Norfolk Militia. The Third Brigade, under the command of Major Tallon, will consist of the remainder of the 41st Regiment.

Colonel Procter will have charge of the whole line, under the orders of the Major-General.

James Givins, Esquire, late Captain 5th Regiment, is appointed Provincial Aid-de-Camp, with the rank of Major in the Militia.

By order of the Major-General.

J. B. GLEGG, Major, A. D. C.

District General Orders.

HEADQUARTERS, FORT AMHERSTBURG,
August 15th, 1812.

D. General Orders.

The troops will be in readiness to embark at McGee's Point at three o'clock to-morrow morning. Colonel Elliott will proceed during the night to the eastern shore of the River Rouge, and upon his communicating with the Major-General the troops will immediately commence crossing the river and land between River Rouge and Spring Wells.

Colonel Elliott will place the Indians in a position to take the enemy in flank and rear, should he be disposed to oppose the crossing.

Lieutenant-Colonel St. George will march his brigade this evening and canton the men in the houses close to the spot at which the embarkation is to take place.

The officers of the commissariat will make the necessary arrangements to supply the troops employed on the opposite shore with provisions and every article required by the different departments. During the operations of the troops in the field each man will receive one gill of spirits per day. The number for which provision is to be made may be calculated at two thousand.

By order of the Major-General.

J. B. GLEGG, A. D. C.

The Secretary of War to Major-General Dearborn.

WAR DEPARTMENT, August 15, 1812.

(Abstract.)

Acknowledges the receipt of his letter of the 8th, informing him (the Secretary) of the conclusion of the armistice, and enclosing a despatch for Mr. Baker, the British chargé d'affaires. He is instructed by the President that there does not appear to be any justifiable cause to vary from the arrangements that are in operation. Not a moment should be lost in gaining possession of Niagara and Kingston, and co-operating with General Hull in taking Upper Canada. It is expected that a sufficient force is assembled for this, especially at Niagara. The reinforcement for General Hull was to assemble at Newport, Ky., on the 12th, and should reach Detroit about the 1st September, and 500 men will march from Ohio and will probably arrive before. You are authorized to purchase and arm such vessels on Lake Champlain and other waters as may be necessary.

District General Orders.

HEADQUARTERS, DETROIT,
16th Augt., 1812.

D. G. O.

Major-General Brock has every reason to be satisfied with the conduct of the troops he had the honor to lead this morning against the enemy. The state of discipline which they so eminently displayed, and the determination they evinced to undertake the most hazardous enterprise, decided the enemy, infinitely more numerous in men and artillery, to propose a capitulation, the terms of which are herewith inserted for the information of the troops.

The Major-General requests Colonel Procter will accept his best thanks for the assistance he derived from his experience and intelligence.

General Orders.

HEADQUARTERS, LEWISTON, 16th Aug., 1812.

Major-General Hall will please to order the troops in the vicinity of Niagara Falls to repair to Lewiston as soon as may be convenient, reserving a necessary guard at that place until it shall be relieved by a detachment from Lieut.-Col. Swift's regiment. The court martial, whereof Brigadier-General Wadsworth is president, will adjourn to headquarters, and there finish the business before them.

The troops between Lewiston and Fort Niagara will, with their baggage, march to-morrow morning at 10 o'clock to Lewiston, leaving guards at the places heretofore occupied for watching the movements of the enemy. The quartermaster will furnish the necessary transportation.

Lieut.-Col. Swift will furnish small guards of observation from Buffalo to the Falls of Niagara, inclusive. They are to communicate to the General-in-Chief by runners any movements of the enemy with all possible despatch.

By order of Major-General VanRensselaer.

SOL. VANRENSSELAER, Aid-de-Camp.

John Lovett to Joseph Alexander.

SUNDAY, August 16, 1812.
HEADQUARTERS, LEWISTON.

I had but just arrived yesterday when a firing of musketry commenced on both sides the river at this place.

My General says I was the first man on my horse, and that as I started he called to me three or four times to come back, and the reason he very handsomely assigned was that he expected I was going to run away, and that he should never see me again. However, Gen. Wadsworth and Col. VanRensselaer were on their horses and started with me. We run our horses up such horrid rocky precipices as I never saw men ride before. The firing increased, and the moment we darted out of the bushes on to the open land a soldier, catching his breath, ran up to me and sung out: "General, do ride down into that hollow, for the balls fly dreadfully here." It was partly true; they did fly a little, but I did not observe only two that went near enough to make me grin. Col. V. R. says he heard 6 or 8 about near enough. We pursued on a little further and halted on our horses, inquiring of another soldier what began the skirmish. While he was relating his story there came a ball pretty near us, and had I been shot through I could not have helped laughing to see the poor devil run behind a large black oak tree, draw his arms close to his body, catch his breath and grin. You may depend on it there is something perfectly indescribable in the face of a clown who expects at every breath a ball through his back.

Gen. Wadsworth was extremely cautious to keep his breast towards the balls, saying he "had no notion that a Wadsworth should be shot through the back." However, after six or eight minutes the firing ceased on both sides; the guards were small, and I do not believe there were more than 100 muskets discharged on both sides, but those were four to one by the enemy. So we galloped all back again by another route amidst the plaudits of our clever fellows, and no one more gratified with the little prompt zeal shown than our commander. Now, *this exactly nothing* may by some fool be conjured up as to another *Sackett's Harbor battle*. In the afternoon over came a flag from Lieut.-Col. Myers of the 70th Regt., commanding Fort George, with a letter, demanding the reason why his guards had been fired on, and I have just had the honor of answering his letter to say that two men appeared near the American shore under suspicious circumstances: they hailed the opposite shore, and soon a boat appeared, presumed to be for the object of transporting the two men over, and she was therefore fired upon, and the fire returned. Col. VanRensselaer, decorated with all the pomp of war as the best sample we could give Canada, has just been over with the letter and returned. . . . .

. . . .

9 AT NIGHT.—Huzza! Huzza and tantivy! We have been all day making out and despatching orders to Oswego for a rifle battalion, Cayuga for a troop of horse, to Ontario for Bloom's regiment, &c., and now since dark comes a memorandum from Captain Dox at Albany of the road full of troops, flying artillery, infantry, &c., and all the uniformed companies in the State!! An express from the Governor-General of Canada to Gen. Dearborn, proposing an armistice.

. . . . .

MONDAY, Aug. 17th, 3 p. m.

Mr. Dickson, a gentleman of respectability from Queenston opposite this, is this moment over with a flag of truce. We asked him the news on the Canada shore. He says that all the reinforcements from Ohio to General Hull are cut off and destroyed by the Indians from Brownstown. Since writing the above Peter B. Porter tells me that from information he before possessed he has no doubt of the fact stated by Mr. Dickson.

. . . .

On the night of the the 17th, about midnight, I heard a whoop: "Officer of the guard! Officer of the guard!" Out I ran, for to tell the candid truth I have about done with sleep . . . . . . Well, this was an express with letters from Gen. Dearborn, enclosing a sort of three-legged armistice between some sort of an Adjutant-General on behalf of the Governor-General of Canada and the said General Dearborn, also letters to Lt.-Col. Myers, commanding at Fort George. In the morning we sent down to Niagara, seven miles, sent a flag across with the letters, &c. There is nothing but flag after flag, letter after letter—Gen. Brock gone somewhere, Lt.-Col. Myers not at the fort now, and Major-Gen. Sheaffe, formerly of Boston, (brother of Nancy Sheaffe, tell my wife,) is now commanding at Fort George.

. . . .

The weather is unfavorable, alternate rains, and the sun excessively hot. We have to pay great attention to the health of the men. The duty of our troops is really severe—about 160 mount guard constantly, but no grumbling. The General is indefatigable with them; all the while among the men, and is growing every day more and more the favorite of the whole camp. Five minutes ago we returned through the lines. A man had fallen in a fit. The General looked and felt of him, called one of his mess to go directly with him to his marquee, and by him sent the poor soul a tumbler of wine. Encamping in the midst of the soldiers, and being every hour in their view, pleases all. All the boats which Porter has sent to Gen. Hull are undoubtedly cut off. I do not see how Hull can get out, but he may. I hope so. Freemen and brave soldiers are sacrifices too precious to be offered on the altar to atone for folly and rashness.

. . . .

(From Bonney's Historical Gleanings, pp. 207-9.)

Col. Myers to Sir George Prevost.

FORT GEORGE, UPPER CANADA,
August 17th, 1812.

SIR,—The despatches of Major-General Brock, acquainting Your Excellency of his having proceeded from here to Amherstburg on the 1st instant, leaving me in command of this district, will have no doubt reached you. Since his departure I have sent forward to him sixty rank and file of the 41st Regiment and a like number of militia volunteers. The former sailed from Fort Erie on the morning of the 4th instant, and I have had the satisfaction to hear of their timely arrival at their destination.

Major-General Brock left Long Point on the 8th with about 300 men, including forty rank and file of the 41st Regiment, which had for some time been stationed in that district. The winds were favorable, and he must have reached Amherstburg on the 12th. The greater part of this number proceeded in bateaux.

When the Major-General left this he authorized my opening all his official letters, and it may be satisfactory to Your Excellency to know that under the privilege I unsealed your confidential despatch (Aug. 3d,) addressed to him, and covering a copy of one from Your Excellency to General Dearborn. I instantly sent it forward to the Major-General, and will most strictly govern myself by its contents as long as I retain the command of this line, acquainting Major-General Sheaffe (who I learn is on his way here) thereof upon his arrival.

I have the honor to transmit to Your Excellency a letter from Colonel Procter (August 11th), received yesterday, enclosing a copy of an intercepted despatch from Brigadier-General Hull (August 4th), dated at Sandwich, addressed to the American Secretary at War, the contents appearing highly interesting, and lead to the certain hope of the overthrow of the enemy's force in that quarter.

Since the Major-General left this everything has remained quiet here, although I have heard from two creditable sources of information that the enemy have very lately completed forty boats, equal to the transport of thirty men each, at Tonewanta Creek, near the Grand Island, and that he intends in a few days to attack our flanks.

The armed vessels *Earl Moira* and *Prince Regent* are on our left, the schooner *Lady Prevost* on our right. Every possible preparation that our means will admit of is made for the reception of the enemy, and if he does attempt it I entertain no doubt of successfully opposing him.

Many of the militia have not yet returned from an indulgence that was granted them to assist in the harvest. I believe the grain is principally got in by this time, and I have accordingly requested Major-General Shaw, the Adjutant-General of Militia, to call in all the absentees of the flank companies of the five Lincoln Regiments. Just now they amount to little more than 500 present. If they all come forth they will be about 800, and I have directed that a draft from these five regiments of 500 additional should be held in perfect readiness to join the flank companies at a moment's notice, and that the total remainder of that force should be in preparation to move to this line when called on.

I am concerned to have to add that desertion *to their houses* is rather prevalent among them. Everything on my part shall be done to urge them to activity, and I have great hopes that the good news from Amherstburg will very much stimulate them to exertion.

I find that the troops of the enemy opposite us are extremely discontented, and that numbers of them have gone back into the country.

(Canadian Archives, C. 677, p. 48.)

Major-General Brock to Major Thomas Evans.

DETROIT, 17th August, 1812.

DEAR EVANS,—Detroit is ours, and with it the whole Michigan Territory, the American army prisoners of war. The force you so skilfully prepared and forwarded at so much risk met me at Point au Pins in high spirits and most effective state. Your thought of clothing the militia in the 41st cast off clothing proved a most happy one, it having more than doubled our own regular force in the enemy's eye. I am not without anxiety about the Niagara, with your scanty means for its defence, notwithstanding my confidence in your vigilance and admirable address in keeping the enemy so long in ignorance of my absence and movements, &c.

(From Laura Secord and other Poems, by Mrs. S. A. Curzon: Appendix No. 3, pp. 209-10.)

General Timothy J. Hopkins to Governor Tompkins.

SIR,—Agreeable to the directions contained in the 7th section of an act to organize the militia of this State, passed March 29th, 1809, I transmit to Your Excellency information that I received from John McMahon, Lieut.-Colonel commandant of a regiment of militia organized in the County of Chautauqua during the last session of the Honorable Council of Appointment. The information which follows is nearly in Colonel McMahon's own words:

Since the declaration of war the inhabitants of the town of Chautauqua have been much alarmed with the appearance of two English vessels near their harbor, one of which was observed to be an armed vessel. This circumstance, together with the danger apprehended from the Indians in that quarter, particularly those who live on the Alleghany River, have created so much uneasiness among the inhabitants that many had determined to move off. To prevent this, Colonel McMahon thought it advisable to order out one captain and fifty men to guard the landing portage at Chautauqua for the space of two weeks. Colonel McMahon also informs me that he has, at his own expense, provided the company with provisions.

Buffalo, August 17th, 1812.

(Tompkins' Papers, vol. VIII., pp. 82-3. New York State Library.)

From the New York Statesman, 25th August, 1812.

From a correspondent at Lewiston, August 17th, 1812:

Canadians arrive daily. The Niagara River which in peaceable times can only be crossed with safety in boats, flats, &c., can now be passed with apparent safety on logs, rails, slabs, and even by many without any buoy whatever. Lakes Ontario and Erie, formerly considered extremely dangerous to cross with open boats, no longer present any obstacle to those who are so fortunate as to get possession of a boat—the perils of the sea are absorbed by the fear of being taken back by their friends. A boat of 16 or 18 feet in length lately brought over Lake Ontario (where its width is near 60 miles) three young men who report that at York there are very few soldiers, only two pieces of cannon, but considerable quantities of ammunition and other stores after furnishing the savages with large quantities lately, that the country was drained of soldiers and drafted militia, General Brock having ordered all that could be collected for Malden to fight General Hull. Indeed the latter part of this report is confirmed by all who come from any part of Canada. Further, that a Mr. Wilmot, Surveyor General of Upper Canada, who lived near York for many years, has collected a respectable company of men (about 60 in number) attached to the American cause, and proceeded on his march through the wilderness to join General Hull. Wilmot, they say, is much exasperated against the Government of Canada, and his followers not unlike their leader. Other reports of this nature there are in circulation, the truth of which cannot be ascertained.

(From file in New York Society Library.)

General Orders.

HEADQUARTERS, LEWISTON, 18th Aug., 1812.

Major-General Dearborn having communicated that, agreeably to an arrangement made between him and the Governor-General of Canada through his Adjutant-General, all hostilities between the troops on either side should be suspended until further orders, Major General VanRensselaer directs the officers and soldiers under his command strictly to conform to this arrangement, and if any of the troops have the hardihood to fire on the enemy they will be punished accordingly.

Lieut.-Col. Swift will order under arrest Capt. Dogherty of his regiment for absenting himself from his company, and will investigate the cause of firing of a field-piece at Black Rock on the opposite shore, and by whom, and report the facts to the Major General without delay.

By order of Major General VanRensselaer.

SOL. VANRENSSELAER, Aid-de-Camp.

Militia General Orders.

HEADQUARTERS, AMHERSTBURG,
18th Augt., 1812.

Militia General Orders.

The reports which have reached Major General Brock impeach in so serious a degree the character of many officers of the 1st and 2nd Essex and Kent Regiments of militia that His Honor has thought proper to appoint a Court of Enquiry in order to ascertain by a regular process such as have by any act or neglect of duty during the invasion of this district by the enemy forfeited their claim to the character of officers and gentlemen.

His Honor is perfectly satisfied that there are many of the officers of these Regiments to whom no share of blame can justly attach, and who have throughout evinced every degree of zeal for the service, and he is desirous of giving to such as may have been unjustly accused an opportunity by a public investigation of justifying their character from the imputations cast upon them.

Colonel James Baby, President.
" Matthew Elliott, } Members.
" William Caldwell, }

The court will assemble as soon after the arrival of Colonel

Baby as possibly, and will give to the different officers of these Regiments notice of the time and place of meeting.

By order of the Major General.

J. MACDONELL, Lt.-Col., P. A. D. C.

Major General VanRensselaer to Major General Dearborn.

HEADQUARTERS, LEWISTON,
18th August, 1812, 6 o'clock a. m.

SIR,—Your letter of the 8th inst. by some mismanagement passed this place in the mail last evening on to Niagara, and was sent to me by express from Capt. Leonard at a late hour in the night. I have written General Hull, enclosing your letter to him. I have also written General Porter to forward the despatch to General Hull by some very trusty express. I have written the commanding officer at Fort George, enclosing the letters from Adjutant-General Baynes to him and sent my aid-de-camp, Col. VanRensselaer, to Niagara with orders to pass over with a flag and deliver the letters.

(From S. VanRensselaer's Narrative, Appendix, p. 25.)

Major General VanRensselaer to Lieut.-Col. Myers, 70th Regt.

HEADQUARTERS, LEWISTON, 18th Aug., 1812.

SIR,—I have the honor to acknowledge the receipt of your letter of this date by your flag of truce.

When I this morning transmitted to you the two letters from the Adjutant-General of the British army, I authorized Colonel VanRensselaer, my aid-de-camp, to make with you the necessary arrangements agreed on at Albany.

In your absence from Fort George the letters were left without accomplishing the object. But I am now ready to send an officer to Fort Niagara, there to meet one whom you may appoint to make such arrangements for the government of the troops on the lines as may be proper. In the meantime it is explicitly understood that any movements of your troops in this vicinity to act offensively against Gen. Hull will be considered an infraction of the armistice agreed upon between Gen. Dearborn and the British Adjutant-General.

(From S. VanRensselaer's Narrative, Appendix, p. 26.)

Colonel Christopher Myers, 70th Regt., Deputy Quartermaster-General Commanding the Niagara District, to Major-General VanRensselaer.

CHIPPAWA, 18th Aug., 1812.

SIR,—I have the honor to acknowledge the receipt of your letter of this date, transmitting one from the Adjutant-General of the British army, addressed to Major General Brock or officer commanding at Fort George, relative to refraining from all offensive warfare between the troops of His Majesty the King of Great Britain and the army of the United States of America until further orders; and, taking it for granted that similar directions have been received by you from Gen. Dearborn, I shall strictly conform to those which have just reached me upon the subject, and should you deem any further explanation upon the terms of the armistice requisite I will receive such officer as you may be pleased to send to Fort George for the purpose. My duty, however, will not allow of my being there before Thursday, but from which I trust no inconvenience will arise.

(From S. VanRensselaer's Narrative: Appendix. p. 26.)

From the Buffalo Gazette, Tuesday, 18th August, 1812.

More clearing out. Last Sunday evening two native Americans living in Canada embarked in a crazy boat several miles above Fort Erie, and after tossing about all night in tempestuous Lake Erie, expecting, as they say, every moment to go to the bottom, they safely arrived at 4-Mile Point above this village. They state that it is currently reported in Canada that General Hull has taken Malden.

We also learn that Fort Erie is weak, the cannon being removed to the batteries below.

On Thursday last several soldiers at the Black Rock, being somewhat impatient for want of employment, manned a field-piece (6-pounder) and fired a shot at a small battery on the opposite side of the river. The ball struck a few feet from the battery, and made the men and boys scamper like the nation.

The fate of Clark, lately tried in this village as a British spy, is not officially known. It is, however, rumored that he is sentenced to die. Brink and Lee, it is understood, will be detained as prisoners of war.

Major-General Sheaffe to Major-General VanRensselaer.

FORT GEORGE, 19th Aug., 1812.

SIR,—Having arrived at this post to assume the command of His Majesty's troops stationed in the Niagara District, I have the honor to acquaint you that I shall be happy to receive, as speedily as possible, the officer suggested by Lieut.-Col. Myers to be sent over, if it meet with your concurrence, or, should you prefer it, Brigade-Major Evans, the bearer of this, will communicate my sentiments and arrange with you the mode of carrying into effect the order for a cessation of hostilities betwixt the forces of our respective countries stationed along the Niagara Frontier.

(From S. VanRensselaer's Narrative: Appendix, p. 27.)

General Stephen VanRensselaer to Governor Tompkins.

HEADQUARTERS, LEWISTON, 19th Aug., 1812.

SIR,—After having visited Buffalo, Black Rock, and the camps at Niagara Falls and this place, and having by inspection and other means of information satisfied myself of the efficient force and the state of discipline among the troops, the munitions of war at command, the strength, number, and condition of the enemy I should probably have to engage, and all other circumstances connected with my intended operations, I was perfectly satisfied that although some very imperious considerations urged an immediate descent upon Canada, yet that such descent with my present disposable force would be rashness in the extreme. From Buffalo to Niagara my force of militia is less than one thousand, without any ordnance heavier than six-pounders, and few of them; without artillerists to use the few pieces I have, and the troops in a very indifferent state of discipline. Finding myself in this truly unpleasant situation, I saw but one course to pursue, which was to concentrate the troops scattered on the line, perfect their discipline as fast as possible, and order in such further detachments as might ensure success in my proposed operations. Accordingly, on the 15th inst. I isssued my orders to Lieut.-Colonel Fleming at Oswego to detach and march to this place Major Moseley's battalion of riflemen, on the 16th to Major Septimus Evans of Lieut.-Colonel George D. Wickham's regiment of detached cavalry for a troop of horse from his squadron, to Lieut.-Colonel Henry Bloom of the 19th Regiment of the 7th Brigade of detached militia to march his whole command. With this additional force and such other as I had reason to believe was on the march to this neighborhood and as might be called out on short notice from this and Ontario County, I calculated that the plan which I had adopted might be attempted unless the enemy should be strongly reinforced. With the view of the intended operations, I had on the 15th inst. written to the Quartermaster-General to put immediately in readiness all the boats at his command. Such was the arrangement of the troops on this line, and such my orders issued when, on the night of the 17th, I received by express from Captain Leonard at Niagara a letter from Major-General Dearborn informing me of the agreement he had entered into with the Governor-General of Canada, through his Adjutant-General, for an armistice. By this arrangement communicated to me, which I presume has been done by Your Excellency's approbation and consent, I am instructed to confine the troops under my command to defensive measures only, until further orders, and I have issued my general orders accordingly.

The enclosures from the Adjutant-General of the British army in Canada which I received from General Dearborn I sent yesterday morning by my aide-de-camp, Colonel VanRensselaer, with a flag to Lieut.-Col. Myers, commanding at Fort George, at the same time authorizing Colonel VanRensselaer to enter with Colonel Myers into a definite arrangement for the government of the troops on both sides the line. Colonel Myers was absent, but in the afternoon of yesterday I received a flag acknowledging the receipt of the letters which had been transmitted, with his pledge to conform strictly to the terms of the armistice and his proposition that I should on Thursday next send an officer to Fort George to meet one whom he will appoint, for the purpose of settling definitely the temporary arrangement for the government of the troops, to which I have replied by flag that I am now ready to send an officer to meet such one as he may appoint for the above purpose, but to meet at Niagara, as I consider that place, under existing circumstances, the most proper. I have no reason to doubt but that this arrangement will in two or three days be made in good faith. Suffering all the orders which I have received to proceed and take effect, I shall hold my position until I receive Your Excellency's further orders. An express which has been sent to General Hull ought to have returned several days ago, but has not. I am concerned for his safety, and the more so as I learn that there are various reports with the enemy that there has been an action between their troops and General Hull's. The whole seems to render it at least probable that the troops to reinforce General Hull have been attacked. Some reports say that 300 of our wounded have been taken in boats in their attempt to reach Detroit. From all circumstances which have come to my knowledge, I think there is reason to believe that General Hull is very severely pressed.

(Tompkins' Papers, vol. VIII., pp. 79-82, New York State Library.)

Inspector-General Nicholas Gray to Governor Tompkins.

BLACK ROCK, 19th Aug., 1812.

DEAR SIR,—On the 22d of last month I had the honor of addressing a letter to you from Lewiston. Ever since I have been employed as engineer by Generals Hull and Wadsworth, and I have erected three batteries in this neighborhood: the one on the mountain near Lewiston; one at this place, and one opposite Fort Erie, which gives the advantage of situation, and though we have not as yet mounted a gun on it, it has given alarm there, as the enemy has moved his shipping off from before the fort, and the river and entrance of Lake Erie is now quite open. No ship nor boat can with safety lie before their fort once this battery is mounted. The distance is about three-quarters of a mile, and the ground so level on the Canadian side that we can send shot right into the fort. We want but a thirty-two-pounder here to pull down the scarlet jack of Fort Erie. The battery at Lewiston has a powerful command, is intended for two or three large guns, and keeps the inhabitants of Queenston in perfect subjection. Its elevation above the one-gun battery of the enemy is nearly forty-five feet and can sweep it off the surface of the field, distant from it about four hundred yards and from Queenston about six hundred, and elevated above the village about sixty-eight feet, has the command of Niagara River as far as the range of shot; the river lies straight before it up to our garrison. Major-General VanRensselaer, his aide and secretary, arrived here on Thursday morning last and went forward to Lewiston, where he has made his headquarters. There is a rumor of General Hall returning home in consequence of the arrival of Major General VanRensselaer.

I have been highly flattered by receiving the thanks of the Generals on the lines for the exertions I have made in making their situation secure. General VanRensselaer feels secure even under the guns of the enemy at Queenston, and Colonel Swift, who commands here, has no terror, as he has a battery or two of his own. The inhabitants of Buffalo wish for a one-gun battery to protect their town. Some of them have applied to me to erect one for them, but as yet I have received no orders from the commanding officer here. When I shall receive the orders I shall comply. We are all knocked on the head in consequence of this news of the armistice. It will give you, dear sir, great confidence and pleasure to see with what alacrity all were preparing to cross over to Canada when this news arrived. Shall I take the liberty to ask what it means and how soon shall we be authorized to take out the wooden snappers from our muskets? I judge from the weakness of the enemy on the Canadian side that was a regiment to cross they would not be opposed, not a shot fired at them. There is but thirty-two red coats and the like number of militia stationed here. The latter were decreased to seven or eight all last week and the week before. We are much alarmed here about the situation of the brave General Hull, who, it is much feared, may be in want of provision for his enterprising army—'tis hard the only general who has as yet distinguished himself in this war should want provisions when we who are here idling on the lines should have all the loaves and fishes, neither will our commanding officer here give a direct order or consent that vessels laden with provisions be sent from here, but when applied to by the Quartermaster-General on behalf of his brother (who, poor man, has been dangerously ill since his return from Sandwich and still remains in a doubtful situation,) has quoted a part of General Dearborn's letter, which passage is unsatisfactory. However, the vessels are preparing and will be sent off to Sandwich, as surely this armistice, while it lasts, gives a right to navigate the lake to either army, provided they do not infringe our orders. General Porter has sent from here by the order of Major-General VanRensselaer a messenger by land to inform General Hull of this unpopular armistice, but it is feared by the Quartermaster-General that his journey may be retarded or interrupted at Sandusky, in which case he has a letter to the commanding officer at Malden making him an official messenger, and from Sandusky will take his course by water.

I should be glad to know whether this armistice includes the Indians, and would it not be good policy to annihilate these savages who have interrupted the intercourse from here to Detroit? We have frequent accounts of their barbarities. Had we a General Hull here when I arrived, the United States should have been in possession of Upper Canada, and we should have our quarters in Montreal instead of playing ball on the banks of the Niagara River. Between seventy and eighty fine young men passed through here yesterday to Lewiston to join the army. They are from Ontario county.

I wait in hopes of having the honor of a letter from you, and be assured that all my exertions shall be for the public good.

(Tompkins' Papers, Vol. VIII., pp. 73-6, New York State Library.)

General Orders.

HEADQUARTERS, LEWISTON, 19th Aug., 1812.

The Major General directs that the following regulations shall be observed by the troops under his command:

The reveille will be beat at daybreak, when every officer and soldier will appear on parade and the companies be exercised by their respective commanding officers for one hour; and the like time at 4 o'clock in the afternoon, and by battalions on Tuesdays and Fridays of each week at the company and battalion parades. The field officers will attend and superintend the manoeuvers of their corps. The troop will beat at 9 o'clock a. m., and the retreat at 6 o'clock p. m., when the line will be formed for roll call; the music will take their post on the right of regiments and not on the right of companies. On those occasions the dress of the officers and soldiers is to be clean, and their arms and accoutrements bright and in perfect order. The Major General flatters himself that the troops will vie with each other in the cleanliness of their dress, as well as their soldier-like and orderly conduct when on or off duty. The corps which shall distinguish itself for orderly conduct shall be reported by the Major General to the Commander-in-Chief, and every refractory officer or soldier shall be dealt with as the law and the usages of armies point out, for as they are called upon by their country to defend it, and paid for their services, it is expected "*every man will do his duty,*" for on that the lives of the troops, the honor and success of the enterprises in which in all probability they will shortly be engaged, will depend.

The tatoo will be beat at 9 o'clock, when the men will retire to their tents and the sentinels begin to challenge.

Two captain's and two subaltern's guards will be mounted daily: one captain's guard will take post on the front and one in the rear of the camp, and the subaltern's on each flank. The guards will be sufficiently strong to form a chain of sentinels round the camp, and they will be augmented or diminished as occasion may require. The guards will assemble on the grand parade at half-past 9 o'clock, when they will be formed by the major of brigade and marched off precisely at 10 o'clock. A portion of the music of the line will attend and do duty until the guards are marched off to their respective pickets. The adjutants will march the men detached from the respective regiments for this service to the grand parade, and will be responsible for the soldier-like appearance of the men, arms, and accoutrements. Each man of the guard will be furnished with twenty-four rounds of fixed cartridges; their pieces will be loaded after sunset, and when the guards are relieved they will return to the grand parade, from whence they will be marched in a body by the officer of the day to some convenient spot, where their pieces will be discharged at a target of the size of a dollar, at one hundred yards distance. And on all other occasions firing is strictly prohibited, unless it be by the sentinels at night to give the alarm.

The officer of the day will be taken from the regimental field officers, whose duty it shall be to visit the guards and sentinels three times in the course of the day and three times at night, to regulate the guards, to see that they are vigilant and in soldier-like order, for on their alertness the lives of the men and the safety of the army depend.

The officers are strictly enjoined to attend to the cleanliness of their men; they must frequently visit their tents and examine the situation of them. On the faithful performance of this duty depend the lives and health of the troops.

The commanding officers of regiments and corps will cause two vaults or sinks to be dug in the rear of each company, at least one hundred yards in the rear of the rear tents, in a line parallel to the tents, and if any soldier shall be found to leave excrement in any other place within the line of sentinels he shall be punished.

The grounds in front and rear of the tents is to be levelled and cleaned by the respective companies. The Brigade-Major will direct the Adjutants to cause the music, when not on the march, to practise the different calls and marches.

The Courtmartial, whereof Brigadier-General Wadsworth was appointed President, will meet to-morrow morning at ten o'clock for the trial of such prisoners as may be brought before them. General Wadsworth will please to make the necessary arrangements and meet in such place as he may think convenient.

By order of Major General VanRensselaer.

SOL. VANRENSSELAER, Aid-de-Camp.

From Major General Sheaffe to Major General VanRensselaer.

QUEENSTON, 20th Aug., 1812.

SIR,—Brigade-Major Evans is directed to repair again to your headquarters charged with propositions connected with the armistice, which I hope will prove perfectly satisfactory to you.

(From S. VanRensselaer's Narrative; Appendix, p. 27.)

Major General VanRensselaer to Major General Sheaffe.

HEADQUARTERS, LEWISTON, 20th August, 1812.

SIR,—I have the honor to acknowledge the receipt of your letter of this date, covering the articles which you propose for carrying the armistice into effect. I have to regret the articles proposed are so variant from the orders which I have received that I cannot accede to them.

In the letter which I had the honor to transmit to Lieut.-Col. Myers on the 18th instant it was explicitly stated that any movements of the troops in this vicinity, with a view to act offensively against General Hull, would be considered an infraction of the armistice. If an article fully embracing the above is considered inadmissible, any further attempts for an adjustment will be unavailing.

(From S. VanRensselaer's Narrative: Appendix, p. 29.)

The Secretary of War to Major General Dearborn.

WAR DEPARTMENT, August 20th, 1812.

(Abstract.)

The detachment of militia from Kentucky to reinforce General Hull has been increased by the Governor to 1,600, besides 400 regulars. A company of militia ordered out by the Governor of Ohio to secure the road is reported to have halted at the Miami in consequence of Indians in front. There should be early and effective co-operation at Niagara.

Articles of Agreement for an Armistice.

We, the undersigned, in conformity with the instructions of our respective commanders, hereby agree to a cessation of all acts of hostility between the troops and vessels of all descriptions under our command until we shall receive further orders, and the party who shall first receive orders for the renewal of hostilities shall give four days' notice, computing twenty-four hours to each day, before any offensive operation shall take place.

And we further agree that no reinforcements of men or supplies of ammunition shall be sent by either party higher up than Fort Erie, and it is also to be understood that no reinforcements of men and no supplies of ammunition, which now are or hereafter may arrive in our respective districts, shall be forwarded above that post, and further that no troops are to be sent up from any station in either of our districts above Fort Erie without four days previous notice to be given by the party intending to make such movement. Subject, however, to the above restriction, either party shall be at liberty to make such changes and movements of troops, vessels and boats as he may deem proper.

Agreed to this twenty-first day of August, in the year one thousand eight hundred and twelve.

S. VanRensselaer,
Major General Commanding Frontier.
R. H. Sheaffe,
Major General Commanding Fort George
and Dependencies, &c., &c.

Major General VanRensselaer to Major General Dearborn.

HEADQUARTERS, LEWISTON, August 21st, 1812.

SIR,—Enclosed I transmit you a copy of the agreement this day entered into between Major-General Sheaffe, commanding Fort George and dependencies, &c., &c., and myself for the government of the forces on each side the line. You will readily perceive that terms more favorable than those expected in your letter have been obtained. The agreement speaks for itself.

(From S. VanRensselaer's Narrative: Appendix, p. 31.)

NOTE.—In the copy of the agreement transmitted, the last lines from either to proper are italicised.—ED.

Major General Dearborn to Major General VanRensselaer.

HEADQUARTERS, GREENBUSH, August 21, 1812.

SIR,—Your letter of the 12th inst. has been duly received. As it is believed that a detachment has been made from Niagara to reinforce the garrison at Malden, it will be necessary to be as well prepared as possible to take advantage of the reduced forces in your front as soon as there shall be orders to act offensively. Considerable reinforcements from the detached militia and volunteers are ordered to Niagara, Sackett's Harbor, Ogdensburg and Plattsburg. With the detachment of regular troops under Lieut.-Col. Fenwick there is some heavy ordnance, ammunition and intrenching tools, which will be immediately, with additional ordnance and military stores, sent to Niagara, Sackett's Harbor and Ogdensburg. I have also ordered a considerable number of batteaux from Schenectady to Niagara and Sackett's Harbor, and the construction of suitable

scows at the respective places, including Ogdensburg, for the transportation of ordnance. I hope that Col. Porter will proceed in the construction of boats and scows with all possible despatch. It will be highly gratifying to me to receive intelligence from you by every mail, and in case of emergency by express.
From S. VanRensselaer's Narrative: Appendix, p. 34.

Colonel Solomon VanRensselaer to his Wife.

LEWISTON, NIAGARA, Aug. 21, 1812.

MY DEAR HARRIET,—

. . . .

Major Forman and Jacob TenEyck reached this to-day; the latter informed me he had seen you about a fortnight since and that you were all well. It is unnecessary for me to say how happy it made me. I had only one moment to speak to him, but I shall see him when I have finished this, which goes by mail this evening. When they reached camp I was mounted on my horse to go over to the British side to conclude an armistice, in which I have been engaged for three days in conformity to an arrangement made at Albany between Gen. Dearborn and the British Adjutant-General. I have succeeded, to the astonishment and admiration of all, and until we hear from below we are at peace with our neighbors. In my intercourse with the British officers on the subject of the armistice and from other sources, we have been informed, and I have no doubt of the correctness of the information, of an action fought between Gen. Hull and the British at Detroit, in which our troops suffered severely. From all we can learn he has either been taken or compelled to re-cross the river; but in my negotiations with Major Gen. Sheaffe, Colonel Myers and Major Evans, I kept up such a *bold front* that, although General Dearborn's instructions were confined to their not sending reinforcements to act against Hull, I succeeded in getting the use of the waters of the rivers and lakes. This to the army and merchants is of incalculable value for future operations, and this was effected by a proper disposition of our small forces and holding out to them moderate but strong language. The troops before we came here were scattered along the frontiers; we have concentrated them, and are now getting in fine order. They did nothing before; they are pleased in the change, but in making that change I assure you I have my hands full. We have now eleven hundred only above Oswego, instead of Tompkins's *five thousand*, but 1,500 more are on the march.

(From Bonney's Historical Gleanings, pp. 211-2.)

General Orders.

HEADQUARTERS, LEWISTON, August 22d, 1812.

It is painful to the Major General to find that some part of the troops are so regardless of their duty as to disobey the orders issued for preventing scattering firing in and about the camp. This dangerous and disgraceful practice is once more and for the last time prohibited. If any man of the line (the guards and sentinels excepted) shall after this discharge his firearms without orders he will be instantly confined; and the field and company officers are strictly enjoined to enforce this order.

The Major General regrets that he is compelled to remind the officers of his command of the necessity of being in camp at night, for if *they* will be regardless of their duty, what can be expected of their *men* by such an example? They are in future directed to be at night in their tents, unless otherwise ordered, and in perfect readiness at any moment to commence or repel an attack, to which troops in the face of an enemy are at all times liable.

The officers and troops meet with the perfect approbation of the Major General for their alertness in parading at reveille, with the exception of one or two companies, which were not this morning on parade, and the captain of one company not in camp. But let him beware for the future: if caution and remonstrance will avail nothing, more decisive measures shall.

To-morrow being the Sabbath, the guards will not discharge their pieces until Monday after roll-call, and this regulation will be observed until further orders.

By order of Major General VanRensselaer.

SOL. VANRENSSELAER, Aid-de-Camp.

Lieut.-Colonel Myers to Colonel Lethbridge.

FORT GEORGE, August 22d, 1812.

SIR,—I am directed by Major General Sheaffe to acquaint you that in expectation of your having received orders from Quebec to forward to this post a portion of the reinforcements which it is hoped have arrived at Kingston, and in consequence of my private letter to you of the 15th instant, expressive of the anxiety of Major General Brock upon that point, he has been on the lookout for some of the vessels from Kingston appearing here with the troops, particularly as the wind has been favorable for two days.

The circumstance of the fall of Detroit and the hourly expected arrival here of a number of prisoners to be sent downward, added to the want of troops on this line in the event of a renewal of hostilities, induces Major General Sheaffe to direct me to desire that if the three companies of the 49th Regt. and the detachment of the Newfoundland Regt. have arrived at Kingston, you cause the whole of the former to be immediately embarked on board the *Royal George* and *Duke of Gloucester* and despatched without delay to this post, provided you have not received orders to the contrary from His Excellency the Commander of the Forces or Major Genl. Brock.

Camp equipage for 300 men is to accompany the troops to this station, and upon this subject I have forwarded orders to the Deputy Asst. Qr. Mast'r-Genl. at Kingston.

(Canadian Archives: C. 677, p. 53.)

Major General Sheaffe to Sir George Prevost.

FORT GEORGE, 22nd August, 1812.

SIR,—I have the honor of reporting to Your Excellency that on my arrival at this post on the 10th instant, I found that a letter had arrived from Colonel Baynes, addressed to the officer commanding here, to apprise him that an armistice had been agreed on, and that a correspondence on the subject had been opened between Lieut.-Colonel Myers and M. General VanRensselaer. After my arrival several conferences were held between officers appointed for the purpose; a difficulty as to the terms having arisen, founded on a variation between those stated in Colonel Baynes's letter and instructions which General VanRensselaer had received from General Dearborn, and which required a stipulation on our part that no reinforcements, &c., should be sent up to the troops opposed to B. General Hull. This obstacle was removed in an unexpected manner. I went up to Queenston on the 20th inst. accompanied by Lieut.-Colonel Myers and Brigade-Major Evans, and I sent the latter over to Lewiston with my propositions. On his return he informed me that objections were made to some of them, and that Colonel VanRensselaer, A. D. C. to the General, would come over to me to enter into an explanatory discussion. Before his arrival the express came to me with the intelligence of M. General Brock's important success. It was not communicated to him, but some time was employed in discussion before I acceded to the obligation not to send up reinforcements without four days previous notice, thinking it prudent to avoid exciting suspicion by too ready an assent. I have the honor of transmitting the articles agreed on, and it is moreover understood that boats are not to be assembled at any point on either side under cover of the privilege granted therein. I also enclose herewith a copy of a letter which Lieut.-Colonel Myers has written by my direction to Colonel Lethbridge.

Since Lieut.-Colonel Myers's letter of the 17th instant considerable reinforcements are said to have joined the enemy at Black Rock, and a camp capable of holding at least eight hundred men has been formed at Lewiston. On the 18th there were seventy tents in which it was reported there were six hundred men, but Lieut.-Colonel Myers having caused a few blank cartridges to be fired in quick succession to create an alarm and make them turn out, it had the desired effect, and he did not discover more than two hundred men. Since that period, however, the number of tents has been increased to more than a hundred.

The wind has been unfavorable to M. General Brock for several days, or he would probably have arrived here by this time.

(Canadian Archives: C. 677, p. 55.)

Lieut.-Colonel Philetus Swift to Governor Tompkins.

SIR,—I take the liberty to communicate to you my situation, and the situation of my regiment. I have about four hundred and seventy men, four hundred of whom are good and in high spirits; men that I am willing to risk my life for and with, and believe they are with me, but that is not enough for a regiment. Your knowledge of me will lead you to suppose that it would be pleasing to me to have an opportunity to do my country service, and if I may be allowed to enlist under the Act of the sixth of February last two or three hundred men more as good as I now have, I should feel as if we could tell well in the place of danger. My regiment is all under the Act of Congress except Captain Jennings' company, which I should be glad to get rid of. I have put him under arrest for detaining pay from his men, which would have volunteered had he not advised them otherwise. Captain Joseph Wells, who commands a light infantry company in Buffalo, has been in service since the militia was called out in June by order of General Wadsworth. He has now 26 good men enlisted under the Act of Congress, and I believe could fill his company immediately had he orders from Your Excellency to that effect. He is now under my command and wishes to remain so; on those conditions the men have enlisted, that they belong to my regiment. Captain Mahar mentioned to me this evening that his company of riflemen was called out, and that if they was sent into the lines in this part it was his wish to join my regiment, which would be very agreeable to me and to my regiment.

I have good officers. One company, now commanded by Captain McNair, by Captain Rowley when first ordered into service, who General Wadsworth discharged, has no other officer in the company. Captain Matteson's company has no lieutenant in it.

My men are sickly at present, but I hope on the mending hand. There is 21 sick that are confined to bed, 12 more that are in the hospital, the greater part on the recovery. They have good stores and good attendance. The money sent on for clothing did my men but very little good except Captain Elias Hall, who has bought clothing for his men, and Captain Mahar. It was out of my power to get the others to do the like, and if they remain in service I fear they will be destitute of clothing except they have some sent on. We have been full of trouble and hard duty, without danger to keep us alive. A few days since we had our expectations raised in hopes of a chance to cross the river and by that relieve General Hull or stop the troops that were marching against him, but the orders from General Dearborn blasted all our hopes of that.

My regiment is stationed at Black Rock. We have twenty-two miles of the lines to guard, which makes our duty very hard, while the standing troops (490) and two regiments of six months' men guarded seven miles only; but we do not complain. Permit me to request an answer from Your Excellency as far as respects Captain Wells's company, whether they can be accepted or not.

Black Rock, August 23rd. 1812.

P. S.—Major Frederick Miller entered service the 21st of June by General Porter's and my request, and has been a faithful officer and done great service to our troops. Ensign Chasey of my regiment is worthy the lieutenantcy in that company, which is vacant. If he could have an appointment, I think it would be well.

(Tompkins' Papers. Vol. VIII. pp. 87-91, New York State Library.)

Major General Brock to Colonel Procter.

FORT GEORGE, August 25th, 1812.

SIR,—I wrote to you yesterday informing you that a cessation of hostilities had been agreed upon between Sir George Prevost and General Dearborn, and requesting you in consequence to postpone any attempt upon Fort Wayne or any other post of the enemy. I consider the present forbearance may lead to such consequences that I cannot refrain from sending a second express to urge you to restrain the Indians likewise in their predatory excursions. This, however, ought to be done with the greatest caution and on grounds foreign from the present considerations.

Colonel Myers tells me that he forwarded on the 11th instant a despatch received from Sir George Prevost to me, in which His Excellency so clearly stated the principles of moderation upon which he thought it expedient to act, that I fully expect, should you have received the despatch and perused his sentiments, you will forbear from any hostile aggression, in fact act completely on the defensive.

Should everything remain quiet at Detroit, you will proceed hither, bringing to Fort Erie the detachments which Captain Chambers and Lieutenant Bullock took to Amherstburg. All the spare ordnance is to be transported to Fort Erie.

I should also think that Lieutenant Troughton and a few of his men could be spared for some time from the duties at Amherstburg: in that case you will have the goodness to order them to accompany you.

(From Tupper's Life of Brock, p. 300.)

Major General VanRensselaer to Major General Sheaffe.

HEADQUARTERS, LEWISTON, 25th August, 1812.

SIR,—I have learned with regret that last night a subaltern officer with a few soldiers and citizens, contrary to my orders, passed over from the American shore and on Buckhorn Island surprised and brought off a sergeant and five men with a boat. Early this morning I ordered the sergeant and men released and the boat restored to them.

(From S. VanRensselaer's Narrative: Appendix, p. 31.)

Major General Brock to Major General VanRensselaer.

HEADQUARTERS, FORT GEORGE,
25th August, 1812.

SIR,—Major General Sheaffe having communicated to me your letter of this date, addressed to him, I seize upon the first moment to express my thanks for the measures you have adopted to prevent the possibility of any misunderstanding which might have arisen in consequence of the unauthorized act of one of your subaltern officers.

It was not until my arrival at Fort Erie late in the evening of the 23d instant that I learnt that a cessation of hostilities had been agreed upon between General Dearborn and Sir George Prevost, and I in consequence despatched early yesterday morning an express to Amherstburg, ordering a cessation of all offensive operations against the United States, and likewise to exert every influence in restraining the Indians from committing any acts of hostility.

The fortune of war having put me in possession of Detroit and its dependencies, a small garrison has been ordered to occupy the fort, the chief object of which was to afford protection to the inhabitants of the Territory. I have the honor to enclose a copy of a proclamation which I issued upon this occasion.

(From S. VanRensselaer's Narrative: Appendix, p. 31.)

From the Buffalo Gazette, Tuesday, August 25th, 1812.

The troops stationed at Black Rock yet remain sickly. Those at Lewiston we understand are in excellent health. From the other stations on the lines we have no particular information.

Several works of defence have been thrown up at different points on our lines within the last two weeks. One hundred and fifty tents have been lately pitched at Lewiston.

Deserters from the British service and disaffected inhabitants of Canada are almost daily appearing on our lines. They are generally willing to be examined, and with but a few exceptions give satisfactory accounts of themselves.

Major General Dearborn to Major General VanRensselaer.

HEADQUARTERS, GREENBUSH, Aug. 25, 1812.

SIR,—As soon as practicable after the receipt of this, you will please to have the enclosed letter, directed to the commanding officer of the British forces at Fort George, at Niagara, conveyed to him by a flag, and the letter to General Hull you will please to have forwarded to him by express with as great despatch as practicable, and at the expiration of four days after the letter is delivered to the British commanding officer at Fort George you will consider the temporary conditional agreement for suspending operations between the forces under your command and the British forces in your vicinity as no longer binding, *and you will act accordingly, and you will make every exertion in your power for annoying the enemy, as well as to guard against any attack from him.* Considerable reinforcements have been sent on from Montreal to strengthen their positions in Upper Canada; and I trust you will very soon receive such additional force from this State and from Pennsylvania as will enable you to pass into Canada with safety and effect. A large reinforcement is on its march under Brig.-Gen. Dodge for Sackett's Harbor and Ogdensburg, as well as for Plattsburg. I have ordered thirty batteaux to Niagara and an equal number to Sackett's Harbor, and have directed the building of proper scows for the transportation of ordnance. *If the enemy should have detached from Fort George, it may afford you an opportunity to strike a blow.*

P. S.—Sir, it will be advisable to wait until the arrival of Lt.-Col. Fenwick with the cannon and stores shall be rendered certain within four days before you send the enclosed letter to Fort George. I presume he must arrive before this reaches you, but it may be otherwise.

(From S. VanRensselaer's Narrative: Appendix, p. 36.)

General Orders.

HARRISBURG, August 25, 1812.

The President of the United States having, through the Secretary at War and General Dearborn, under date, respectively, of the 13th inst., required a detachment of 2,000 militia to be marched with the least possible delay from the northwestern parts of Pennsylvania to Buffalo, in the State of New York, duty and feeling direct a prompt compliance with the requisition, giving scope for action to the patriotism evinced by that portion of our citizen soldiers who have volunteered their services under general orders of 12th May last in substitution of the draft required of the State. To obey this call in defence of rights sacred to freemen, to avenge the injuries of the nation and defend the cause of suffering humanity the volunteers of Pennsylvania will not hesitate a moment to meet the avowed enemy of those rights, not only within the limits of the United States, but will without those limits, with ardor seek and with the determination of freemen punish the unprovoked invaders of our rights and property.

For obvious reasons the Adjutant-General has been ordered to designate for service such of the volunteers as can with the least possible delay be marched to the scene of action, and is charged with the organization of the detachment of 2,000 men, conformably to the following plan :—The detachment to constitute a brigade, to consist of four regiments, and each regiment to consist of two battalions, to be arranged by the Adjutant-General at the place of rendezvous.

The general rendezvous will be at Meadville, to which place the volunteers composing the detachment will march with the requisite expedition, so that they will be there on the 25th day of September next. By the twenty-sixth section of the general militia law, among other services by them to be performed, it is made the duty of the brigade inspectors to march each with his proper detachment to the place of rendezvous.

These officers are severally required and directed to provide subsistence and other necessary accommodation for the troops on their march, and detailed accounts for settlement and payment to the accountant officers of the commonwealth.

Apprised of the generally prevailing desire that those appointed to command may be the choice of the commanded, the Governor, agreeably to the tenth section of a supplement to the militia law, passed 26th March, 1808, and the twenty-seventh section of the general militia law, authorizes and directs the officers and privates of the detachment on the day succeeding the 25th day of September next, or those who shall have arrived, to elect, agreeably to the rules prescribed by the militia law, one brigadier-general: each regiment to elect a colonel commandant: each battalion, one major; the brigadier-general to appoint his own brigade major: the field officers of each regiment shall appoint their respective regimental staffs. To expedite the expedition in discharge of his duty, the Adjutant-General will attend and deliver to the officers-elect their commissions.

SIMON SNYDER,
Governor of the Commonwealth
of Pennsylvania.

(From Pennsylvania Archives. Second Series. Vol. XII., pp. 585-8.)

N. B. Boileau to Calender Irvine.

HARRISBURG, August 25, 1812.

To Calender Irvine, Superintendent Military Stores:

SIR,—Your letter of the 17th instant has been received by the Governor, who has issued general orders for 2,409 volunteer militia to rendezvous at Meadville on the 25th day of September next. You will therefore please to interest the proper officers to forward to that place a sufficient number of tents, kettles and other camp equipage necessary for the detachment above mentioned, so as to be ready at the time appointed for assembling the troops at Meadville. There will be in the detachment 1 brigadier, 4 colonels, 8 majors, 46 captains.

P. S.—General Reed will be at Meadville to receipt for the articles delivered. To ensure the number of 2,000, the Governor has ordered out the number of 2,409. It might be prudent to supply for the greater number.

(Pennsylvania Archives, Second Series, Vol. XII., pp. 589-90.)

Governor Snyder to the Brigade Inspectors.

SIR,—You will immediately on the receipt of the General Orders communicate them to the captains or commanding officers of the volunteer companies within the bounds of your brigade, and give every aid in your power to have the companies marched as expeditiously as possible to the place of rendezvous (Meadville) mentioned in General Orders. The troops will be supplied with rations, tents and other camp equipage by the United States. Should there be any deficiency of arms in any of the volunteer companies, you will supply them out of any that may be in the bounds of your brigade. If there cannot be a sufficient number found in that way they will be furnished at the place of rendezvous. Every man will take care to supply himself with a blanket and a knapsack. It is confidently expected that the patriotism of the volunteers is too sincere and ardent to permit them to make any objections to crossing the boundary line of the United States; otherwise they will render no service to their country.

By order of the Governor.

(Pennsylvania Archives, Second Series, Vol. XII., p. 591.)

A Return of the Detached Volunteer Corps.

A return of the detached volunteer corps who have been called on to march agreeably to the within General Orders of 25th August, 1812:—

Division.	Brigade Captain.	No. Men.	Total.
7th Division :	2d Brigade—James McDowel	73	
	Jeremiah Snyder	51	
	Michael Harper	32	
	Andrew Oaks	60	
		—	215
9th Division :	1st Brigade—John Donaldson	93	
	John Amand	30	
	Ner Middleswarth	79	
	Jared Irwin	68	
		—	270
	2d Brigade—John Gaston	79	
	Joseph Dean	42	
	Isaac Blue	42	
	George Eley	67	
		—	230

11th Division:	1st Brigade—Joseph Kleckner..........42		
	John McGarry...........59		
		—	101
	2d Brigade—Jacob Vanderfelt.........33		
	Moses Canan..............33		
		—	66
12th Division:	1st Brigade—Jasper Keller.............49		
	Peter Lane................42		
	Jonathan Roads..........47		
	Richard Maguire..........30		
		—	168
	2d Brigade—William Piper.............68		
	Hugh Gibson 71		
		—	139
14th Division:	1st Brigade—William Sample..........62		
	Thomas Miller............67		
	Edward Thomas.........52		
	James Warner............42		
	David Buchanan..........63		
		—	286
	2d Brigade—Henry Vance...............42		
	William Peterson..........52		
		—	94
15th Division:	1st Brigade—James Turbit.............45		
	David Alters..............58		
	James Scott..............45		
	Walter Lithgow...........53		
	Volunteers.................59		
	John Barrackman.........78		
		—	338
	2d Brigade—James Alexander..........53		
	John Lochry..............66		
		—	119
16th Division:	1st Brigade—Thomas Foster...........31		
	Samuel Withrow..........28		
		—	59
	2d Brigade—Robert Dougherty.........47		
	John Stewart.............43		
	Robert Sto 67		
	Abraham Brickle..........44		
	James Thompson..........50		
		—	251

N. B.—John Fint, brigade inspector, Ninth Division and Second

Brigade, has been subsequent to General Orders directed to order a company, commanded by Capt. Robert McGuigan, to march. Number of men in the company unknown.

WILLIAM REED, Adjutant-General.

(Pennsylvania Archives, Second Series, Vol. XII., pp. 592-3.)

Governor Snyder to General W. Reed.
General Orders.

HARRISBURG, August 26, 1812.

To William Reed, Esq., Adjutant-General of Pennsylvania:

SIR,—You are ordered to attend at Meadville, the new rendezvous for 2,000 volunteers of this State, ordered into service on the northwestern frontier of this commonwealth under a requisition of the proper authority. You will accordingly, with the least possible delay, repair to the said rendezvous and take command of the detachment. The citizen soldiers whereof, officers and privates, as they shall from day to day arrive, are commanded strictly to obey and execute all that you shall lawfully order and direct until a brigadier-general and other officers for said detachment shall have been elected and commissioned, agreeably to the general orders of yesterday. The said brigadier-general having taken the command, is ordered and commanded with the least possible delay to march the brigade under his command to Niagara, and on his arrival immediately report himself to the commanding general of the troops at that place.

SIMON SNYDER,
Governor of the Commonwealth
of Pennsylvania.

N. B. BOILEAU, Aid-de-Camp.

(Pennsylvania Archives, Second Series, Vol. XII., p. 594.)

Governor Snyder to Major General Dearborn.

HARRISBURG, 26th August, 1812.

To General Henry Dearborn, commanding the army of the United States, Greenbush, near Albany, in the State of New York:—

SIR,—Your request under authority of the President, of the 13th instant, which I received by express from this place at Selin's Grove on the 21st, that I would order out 2,000 of the northwestern militia of Pennsylvania, is complied with, as you will perceive by a copy of the General Orders under date of yesterday, which I have the honor to enclose. I take the liberty also to enclose a copy of a letter to me on the same subject from the Secretary at War, because of the variance between the two requisitions. You make the request under the Act of February 28th, 1795, under which the militia cannot be longer retained in service than three months. The Act of the 10th April, 1812, authorizes the retention of militia in service six months. The Secretary at War directs that the detachment shall consist of the propositions recognized in the order of April 15. Your letter says: "There will be no use for cavalry nor any artillery, unless supplied with field-pieces and apparatus complete." On this subject I have by letter of this day said to the Secretary at War that under the belief that the object of both was to have detached for the service the most efficient force, the General Orders are for volunteer infantry and riflemen. They are of the militia of Pennsylvania the best equipped and best disciplined, and in my opinion the most efficient for the service. The number of riflemen is 1,380, of infantry 962, giving a surplus equal to any probable deficiency.

(Pennsylvania Archives, Second Series, Vol. XII., p. 595.)

Governor Snyder to William Eustis, Secretary at War.

HARRISBURG, August 26, 1812.

To Hon. William Eustis, Secretary at War, at the City of Washington:

SIR,—Yours under date of the 13th inst. reached me at Selin's Grove, the place of my residence, on the 21st, by express from Harrisburg. On Sunday evening, the 23d, I arrived at this place, and yesterday General Orders were issued, directing 2,000 volunteer militia to march and rendezvous at Meadville, in the northwestern part of this State, a copy of which order I have the honor herewith to enclose. I also enclose a copy of a letter to me from General Dearborn of the same date and on the same subject. I do this because of the variation between your letter and the General's, the former requiring a detachment of militia under the Act of April 10, 1812, in the proportion recognized in the order of April 15th, under which Act the militia may be retained in service six months: the latter makes the requisition under the Act of Congress of March 28, 1795. Under this last Act the militia cannot be longer retained in service than three months. The General further says there would be no use for cavalry nor artillery unless supplied with field-pieces and apparatus complete. Under the belief the object of both was to have detached for the service the most efficient force, the General Orders are for volunteer infantry and riflemen. They are of the militia of Pennsylvania the best equipped, the best disciplined, and in my opinion the most efficient for the service. The number of riflemen is 1,380, of infantry 962, giving a surplus equal to any probable deficiency. The only artillery in a situation to be efficient is at Philadelphia, a point too remote from the scene of action. If, however, the President should deem it necessary to order out a portion of artillery, upon intimation to me it will be promptly attended to.

(Pennsylvania Archives, Second Series, Vol. XII., pp. 596-7.)

Militia General Orders.

HEADQUARTERS, FORT GEORGE,
26th August, 1812.

Militia General Orders.

Major General Brock has ever felt anxious to study the comforts and convenience of the militia, but the conduct of the detachments which lately accompanied him to Detroit has, if possible, increased his anxiety on this subject. The present cessation of hostilities enables him to dispense with the services of a large proportion of them for a short period.

Officers commanding will grant permission to any number of the flank companies now doing duty, not exceeding four-fifths of the whole, to return to their homes, but the men will be particularly directed to hold themselves in readiness to return at a moment's notice.

The Major General is pleased to direct that a general inspection of the regiments in the Home, Niagara and London Districts be immediately made.

Major General Sheaffe will inspect those in the Home District (except Colonel Beasly's regiment,) Major General Shaw the 1st, 2d, 3d, 4th and 5th Lincoln regiments, and Colonel Talbot the different regiments in the London District.

At these inspections every man liable to serve is expected to be present, and such as are absent are to be accounted for under the following heads:—

First—Age and infirmity.

Second—Quakers, Mennonists and Tunkers.

Third—Absentees, distinguishing from what cause.

It is expected that every individual residing within the limits of a regiment shall be accounted for.

A regular roll of each company will be prepared by the respective captains, and countersigned by the officer commanding the regiment.

The greater the improvement made by the militia in acquiring a knowledge of military discipline, the less necessary will it be to call them from their homes. The Major General therefore is pleased to direct that officers commanding will call out the men of their respective regiments or companies for drill once in every week.

Officers commanding corps are directed to call upon the militiamen of their respective regiments, battalions and companies to take and subscribe the oath of allegiance, as directed in the last Militia Act, previous to the day of inspection, and they will furnish the inspecting officer with a list of the names of such persons as may have refused to take and subscribe the same, if any such there be.

By order of the Major General.

J. MACDONELL,
Lt.-Col., P. A. D. C.

From the National Intelligencer, of Washington, D. C., Sept. 3rd, 1812.

Extract of a letter from Colonel S. VanRensselaer, dated August 26th, 6 p. m.:

"I am this moment called upon to receive a flag of truce from the British, accompanied by an officer from General Hull's army, which surrendered on the 16th inst. to the British General Brock."

A Niagara paper (the *Bee*) of the 22nd inst. states that General Hull had 2,500 men and 25 pieces of cannon, which, together with the American vessels on the lake and Detroit, surrendered to General Brock on the 16th inst. without bloodshed on the part of the British.

General Hull is now on board the *Queen Charlotte*.

(From file in the New York Society Library.)

John Lovett to Joseph Alexander.

HEADQUARTERS, LEWISTON, August 26, 1812.

DEAR SIR,—Yesterday I wrote you, Mr. VanVechten, and Colonel Westerlo, but what I wrote I cannot say; it was a day of turmoil, mortification and humiliation through our camp. Such a flood as the consequences of Gen. Hull's surrender poured in upon us that it required considerable nerve to meet everything, and unluckily Col. VanRensselaer had gone to Buffalo to make some arrangements with Swift's Regiment, which is getting down fast with sickness, and might say too great a want of discipline. Yesterday the first we saw was a guard of about 50 men passing with some wagons on the opposite shore: it was the victorious Brock returning to Fort George. He sent over Col. McDonald, his aid-de-camp, and Major Evans, two strapping lads in scarlet, gold and arms, to make a communication to General VanRensselaer. I went to meet them at an inn near the shore to learn their pleasure, but finding it was *general* and *verbal*, it could not be received. They were, however, very modest, very respectful, and altho' I constantly barred any communication, they still kept bowing and saying that "Gen. Brock only wished to acquaint Gen. VanRensselaer" of this and that and that, &c., &c. In this way they convinced me that Brock had not learned anything of the armistice until he arrived in this neighborhood, that but a very small force was left behind, that Brock, learning the armistice, felt a very friendly disposition, &c. I made my best bow and scraped as fast as I could, but a poor *private secretary alone* against *two* such *scarlet clad champions* had, as you may suppose, an indifferent chance. We parted, but I think Gen. VanRensselaer will shortly receive some written communication from Gen. Brock. In the evening a number of Hull's officers on parole visited Gen. V. R. They were very cautious of their words, but I could discern a degree of disaffection towards Hull. Gen. Hull will probably be sent to Quebec. The militia captured, I understand, are sent home, that's all. Indeed I have not either time or patience to examine into this most nameless affair. I feel what you may suppose. I need say no more.

I was ever proud of my country, and as an American could look any man of any nation at least *horizontally* in the face. But yesterday my eyes seemed to have acquired a new attachment to the ground. I sent Van Vechten a paper giving the detail of the surrender, sent by an express to overtake the mail, hope he got it. And now, my friend, what do you think of *our* situation? It is true we are all tied up with the armistice, but either party may throw it off by four days notice. I don't *believe* the enemy will throw it off. Nevertheless, we have to cast about a little. This part of the country now think their whole salvation rests upon our little raw army. *I think*, I know the fact that after Brock had taken Hull, he expressed his determination to return and take Niagara. I think his mind is altered by the armistice, but he *can* take Niagara any hour he pleases. Yes, my friend, we can't defend Niagara *one hour*. And as for our present camp, I now write with one eye on a single gun on yon hill in Queenston, which would rout us all in three minutes, and we have only two *grasshoppers* to return the fire. The Ohio officers, prisoners, also were last evening with us, say that the Indians with Brock are the finest fellows they ever saw; a size larger than they ever saw. They are commanded by the Prophet's brother Tecumsieh. He is hourly expected at Fort George about seven miles from us, about near enough, and it is said the tawny host is to follow. Well! be it so, one thing our friends may be assured of, we are not scared yet. We shall never be Hulled. Our General is thoughtful but firm. We have been reconnoitering this morning, and shall probably this afternoon fix upon a spot to which we shall remove in case the armistice is broken off. We have a piece of ground in view where our little force may make a tolerable stand, and then secure our retreat unless they flank us wider than I believe their force will admit. At any rate we will not be Hulled—they may *pound* us or *grind* us. Be all of you of good cheer as respects *us*, and use the fate of the other army as you *ought*. Now don't let my good wife get fidgety about me in this new predicament. Tell her I am well and can *run* like a boy and *will not be taken*. I confess we are very solicitous to hear from Washington and know what we are to do, and take our measures accordingly. The night before last one of our rash subalterns with a dozen men went upon Buckhorn Island, surprised a sergeant and five men and brought them off. We broke the armistice, but Gen. V. R. restored the men and wrote General Sheaffe, commanding Fort George and dependencies, &c., &c., &c. (Kites fly best with long tails.) 120 of Swift's little Regt. sick. I told you so, but I am well. The devil seems to have got into everybody.

(From Bonney's Historical Gleanings, pp. 218-9.)

General Dearborn to Sir George Prevost.

HEADQUARTERS, GREENBUSH, August 26th, 1812.

SIR,—It is with regret I have to inform Your Excellency that the President of the United States has received no official information from your Government which will warrant a continuance of the provisional measure that was temporarily agreed on between Your Excellency (through the agency of Col. Baynes) and myself. I have therefore to inform Your Excellency that at the expiration of four days from the time that this communication shall have reached the commanding officer at Montreal, and copies to the same effect shall have been received by the respective commanding officers on the frontier, viz., at Niagara and Ogdensburg on the side of the United States, and the British commanding officers in Upper Canada at Niagara and Kingston, I shall consider the arrangement before attended to for a mutual suspension of active hostilities as no longer obligatory on either party; and if a suspension of offensive operations shall have been mutually consented to between General Hull and the commanding officer of the British force at or near Detroit, as proposed, they will respectively be authorized at the expiration of four days subsequent to their receiving copies of the communication to consider themselves released from any agreement thus entered into.

Captain Pinkney, one of my aides-de-camp, is charged with the conveyance of this communication to Your Excellency or the commanding officer at Montreal. I have sent copies of this communication to the respective commanding officers on the side of the United States, on the frontiers, with copies directed to the British commanding officers at Niagara, Kingston and Detroit, and directions to have the copies intended for the British officers respectively conveyed to them without delay.

I cannot on this occasion refrain from expressing to Your Excellency my ardent wish that measures may speedily be adopted for effecting such an honorable and permanent peace between our governments as will establish the most harmonious intercourse between the two nations so deeply interested in the offices of reciprocal friendship.

(From Canadian Archives, C. 677, p. 58.)

Major General VanRensselaer to Major General Dearborn.

HEADQUARTERS, LEWISTON, 26th August, 1812.

SIR,—I have the honor to enclose you a copy of a proclamation which I have this day received from Major General Brock, under cover of his letter of this date to me, a copy of which letter I also transmit to you. My letter to Major General Sheaffe, of which mention is made, was to disavow the imprudent act of a subaltern officer who with a few soldiers and citizens passed over since the armistice to Buckhorn Island and there surprised a sergeant and five men of the enemy and brought them off together with their boat, which men I ordered to be immediately released and their boat restored.

The surrender of General Hull's army excites a great deal of alarm in this vicinity. I shall, however, as far as in my power check and keep it under.

(From S. VanRensselaer's Narrative: Appendix, p. 32.)

General Order.

HEADQUARTERS, Albany, Augt. 27th, 1812.

In pursuance of a requisition made by the authority of the President of the United States, the Sixth Brigade of detached militia of this State commanded by Brigadier-General Daniel Miller of Cortlandt County and composed of the regiments whereof Farrand Stranahan and Thompson Meade are Lieutenant Colonels Commandant, and the Ninth Regiment of the Third detached brigade of infantry, to the command of which Peter J. Vosburgh has been assigned as Lt.-Col. Commandant, are hereby ordered into the service of the United States, and will rendezvous for that purpose by battalions on Tuesday, the 8th day of September next, at the hour of ten in the forenoon, at such places as the respective commandants of the said detached regiments shall assign for that purpose.

The non-commissioned officers and privates must appear completely equipped with their own clothing and a musket or rifle, cartridge box, knapsack, blanket and canteen. Tents, camp kettles and the means of transporting baggage will be ready on the day and at the respective places of rendezvous.

The volunteers and men drafted from the rifle battalions of Rensselaer County, from Captain Waterman's Light Infantry at Hudson, and from the two light infantry companies at Troy, are expected from and will not rendezvous with the detached corps above mentioned, but will remain and march with their said respective companies as may be directed by future General Orders.

The officers, non-commissioned officers or privates who shall refuse a prompt compliance with this order will be dealt with as directed by the Act of Congress, passed the 26th day of February, 1795, of which a copy is annexed.

The Commander-in-Chief flatters himself that no one will be so unmindful of the duty of a citizen soldier as to incur the penalties of the said Act, but that on the contrary a unanimous disposition will prevail to manifest the promptitude and efficacy of a patriotic militia when called into the service of their country.

By order of the Commander-in-Chief.

ROBERT MACOMB,
Lt.-Col. and Aid-de-Camp.

(Tompkins' Papers, New York State Library.)

General Orders.

HEADQUARTERS, LEWISTON, August 28th, 1812.

The army under the command of Brigadier-General Hull has surrendered at Detroit. This is a national disaster, but it is the duty of *soldiers* to turn even disasters to profit. To this end the General calls upon the troops under his command to make every effort in perfecting that discipline on which they must rely for their own safety and for their country's honor in that crisis which may be fast approaching. The General is persuaded that Americans know the inestimable rights which they enjoy, and he confidently trusts that their bravery to defend is in proportion to the knowledge they possess of those rights.

The troops will be exercised at reveille, and from four o'clock in the afternoon, two hours instead of one, as mentioned in General Orders of the 19th instant.

Capt. Dogherty and Lieut. Hewit of Lieut.-Col. Swift's regiment are released from their arrests, and will return to their duty. This renewed instance of clemency of the Major General it is hoped will be properly appreciated by them. It is not his wish to punish, but orders must and shall be obeyed.

The unhealthy state of the troops under the command of Lieut.-Col. Swift at Black Rock renders particular attention to them and the causes of their maladies necessary. For this purpose Doctor Brown will associate with him Doctor Daniel Chipman, and they will proceed without delay to that place and make full inquiry into the situation of the sick, the causes which have produced the diseases and the manner in which they have been treated, of all which they will make report in writing to the Major General, suggesting the best mode in their opinion to restore those who are sick and preserve the health of the well.

These and all other orders are to be read by the adjutants to the troops under the command of the Major General. The commanding officers of regiments and corps will give orders accordingly.

By order of Major General VanRensselaer.

SOL. VANRENSSELAER, Aid-de-Camp.

Major General VanRensselaer to Major General Dearborn.

HEADQUARTERS, LEWISTON, 28th Aug., 1812.

SIR,—By the mail of this day I received your letter of the 21st inst. I had hoped that His Excellency Gov. Tompkins might have detailed to you the condition of the troops under my command on this frontier, and also the ordnance, etc., at my command. The whole number of militia on this frontier is less than eight hundred, more than one hundred on the sick list, many without shoes and otherwise illy prepared for offensive operations. I have only five or six pieces of ordnance, none larger than six-pounders.

After having satisfied myself of the strength and condition of the enemy, I was fully convinced that however imperious the considerations which urged an immediate descent upon Canada that the result must be unfavorable. I therefore adopted the plan of concentrating my forces scattered on this line and calling in such further reinforcements as might enable me to act. But the face of things is now wholly changed by the incomprehensible disaster of General Hull's army. Within forty-eight hours past General Hull and a considerable portion of his regulars have been marched through Queenston in fair view of my camp. The effects produced by this event are such as you will readily imagine. I understand that Gen. Hull and his troops are now embarking at Fort George, probably for Montreal.

I wait with solicitude to learn the result of our Government's deliberation on the armistice, in the meantime adopting such measures as I must pursue if a recommencement of hostilities shall take place.

I shall immediately apprise Gen. Porter of your instruction respecting boats.

(From S. VanRensselaer's Narrative; Appendix. p. 58.)

General Peter B. Porter to Major General VanRensselaer.

MANCHESTER, Aug. 28th, 1812.

SIR,—Mr. Beard, the person whom I employed to go express to Gen. Hull, has returned with your despatches, which I herewith enclose. On his arrival at Cayahoga he met several boats with the militia prisoners of Gen. Hull's army, and finding it useless as well as impracticable to proceed, he returned. Mr. Beard informs that when these boats were first discovered at and beyond Cayahoga they were supposed to contain an army of British and Indians, whose object it was to over-run the country, and expresses with information to that effect were sent in every direction, and that the inhabitants were in a state of the greatest alarm and confusion and quitting their homes.

Before Mr. Beard left Cayahoga, however, about 1,000 militia had collected, and in the course of the day succeeding his departure it was pretty well ascertained that there would be about 3,000 men at that place, tolerably armed and provided with ammunition and desirous of marching to Detroit: that about 2,000 Kentuckians were on their march to reinforce Genl. Hull, and it was hoped they would fall in with a party of Indians under *Tecumseh* who, it was understood from our prisoners, had left Detroit to take Fort Wayne. Mr. Beard on his return took great pains, and he thinks with effect, to allay the fears of the inhabitants and induce them to remain at home. I send a copy of Genl. Hull's capitulation. Major Cuyler has taken the capitulation to copy, and will send it to you.

(From Bonney's Historical Gleanings. pp. 222-3.)

John Lovett to Abraham VanVechten.

HEADQUARTERS, LEWISTON, 28th August, 1812.

DEAR SIR,—

. . . .

Things are bad enough now. I do not speak of our little camp. We are snug, getting in fine order, and with infinite, unceasing industry, preparing for the worst, while we hope for the best. I speak on the *general scale* of all things around us. Hull's surrender is to me incomprehensible. I had expected his destruction would be certain, but it has come in such a way as I did not expect. Three of his officers say he had a force of 2,200. The British all round assert that he has surrendered between 2,500 and 3,000; his provisions were ample for three more weeks; of ordnance and every munition of war he had abundance, yet he surrendered to a force vastly inferior, probably to 600 or 700 British troops and about the same number of Indians. He fired not a gun, and but one was fired at him. Then *why* did Hull surrender, is the question? No one here can answer. From his officers and all I have seen, it appears that there was through the whole army a very great disaffection towards Hull. Cowardice is pretty generally imputed to him. Many allege corruption; his officers seem greatly distressed at the character of the surrender. Now, the consequences of this affair cast such a blot on the American character as the tears of your children and mine and a hundred more generations can never sponge away.

This event has cemented Canada beyond anything you can conceive. It has a serious face also on our Indians on the whole frontier. The affair with Gen. Harrison gave them the scent of blood and you can depend on it, it has been well improved. Tecumsieh, the Prophet's brother, a warrior of almost unbounded influence, now openly holds the language that the Great Spirit intended Ohio River for the boundary between his white and red children, that many of the first warriors have always thought so, but a cloud hung over the eyes of the tribes and they could not see what the Great Spirit meant, that Gen. Brock has now torn away the cloud and the Indians see clearly that all the white people must go back east of the Ohio, and if any one attempts to cross that river "*Indians will cut their toes off.*" Yesterday I beheld such a sight as God knows I never expected to see, and He only knows the sensation it created in my heart. I saw my countrymen, freeborn Americans, robbed of the inheritance which their dying fathers bequeathed them, stripped of the arms which achieved our independence and marched into a strange land by hundreds as black cattle for the market.

Before and behind, on the right and on the left, their proud victors gleamed in arms and their heads erect in the pride of victory. How many of our unfortunate brethren were in this situation, I know not: the road for more than a mile is perfectly in our view. I think the line, including wagons, pleasure carriages, &c., was half a mile long, scattered. The sensations this scene produced in our camp were inexpressible; mortification, indignation, fearful apprehension, suspicion, jealousy, dismay, rage, madness.

It was a sad day with us, but the poor fellows last evening went on board the shipping and, I presume, passed over to York. I saw a gentleman who was present when Gen. Hull alighted from his carriage at Fort George, hale, corpulent, and apparently in high spirits, and hence will he ever return? He goes to Quebec. Such the scenes before us. All eyes seem now turned on General Van Rensselaer for direction and on our little army for defence. I tell you nothing, but the man who is now on the ground could prevent incalculable mischief in this quarter. It is his respectability and character which effects all that is effected, and I am proud to say he is assiduously, vigilantly and ably supported. We have plenty to do from the 4 o'clock morning gun until 9 at night.

. . . .

I saw a gentleman who had this day seen one of Hull's captains, who openly and roundly asserted that Hull was a *coward*, that as soon as the first gun was fired he sat down with his back against a solid protection.

. . . .

(From Bonney's Historical Gleanings, pp. 230-1.)

General Orders.

HEADQUARTERS, LEWISTON, 29th Aug., 1812.

The Major General is gratified with the attention which is paid by the officers to the health of the men. Striking the tents as has been this morning done will in a great measure prevent disease among the troops, and the General recommends that it will be done as often as occasion may require, and that cleanliness be observed in every particular by individuals of the army. It is absolutely necessary to the preservation of health. It is particularly enjoined on those who have charge of the few sick in this camp and the hospital to see that they are well supplied with everything necessary for their accommodation, and that expert and faithful nurses are provided to attend them.

On this occasion the General cannot refrain from expressing his satisfaction at the attention of the officers in general to their duty, and the orderly conduct of the soldiers in obeying orders. Such cheerful and soldier-like behavior is to him a cheerful presage of what he has to expect from them in the hour "which will try men's souls."

To the commanding officer of the 7th Brigade, and to the colonels of the 18th and 20th Regiments, the General tenders his acknowledgements for their strict attention to the discipline of the troops and the preservation of their health.

By order of Major General VanRensselaer.

SOL. VANRENSSELAER,
Aid-de-Camp.

General Peter B. Porter to Governor Tompkins.

BLACK ROCK, Aug. 30, 1812.

SIR,—I know that you must be borne down by the weight of official duty, and, not having received any answers to my former letters, I have for some time past forborne to trouble you.

I have now only to ask once more *in short*, what I have before pressed on Your Excellency *in detail*, in the hope that you will spare five minutes to answer and relieve me from the state of uncertainty in which I am placed.

My request is that if you consider me in service you would authorize me generally to provide such things in the Quartermaster-General's department as in the opinion of the officers commanding are necessary to the support and successful operations of the army, and that you will forward to me the necessary funds to do it, as it is extremely difficult to raise the requisite sums from bills.

The above is all I have to write on the business of my department, and to which I should be gratified by an answer. What follows Your Excellency will read or not, as leisure or inclination may dictate.

Three days ago we witnessed a sight which made my heart sick within me, and the emotions which it excited throughout the whole of our troops along the line who were eye-witnesses are not to be described. The heroes of Tippecanoe, with the garrisons of Detroit and Mackinac, amounting to about five hundred men, were marched like cattle from Fort Erie to Fort George, guarded by General Brock's regular troops with all the parade and pomp of British insolence, and we were incapacitated by the armistice and by our own weakness from giving them the relief which they seemed anxiously to expect, and could only look on and sicken at the sight.

In March last I urged on the President and to the Secretaries of War and the Navy the necessity of having a naval force on the lakes superior to that of the British, which might have been done at an expense of less than one hundred thousand dollars (as I then demonstrated), and ready to act by the first of July. I also urged them, and have not ceased to do it since, the expediency of having land forces ready to act immediately after the declaration of war at different points along the frontier, so as to prevent the concentration of the British forces at any one place. With 4,000 men on this river one month ago in a condition to act, the whole of Upper Canada and the Indian country would now have been in our quiet possession. But unfortunately the counsels of men who knew the country were rejected or disregarded, and what is now the terrible reverse of the picture, which some regard to their advice, frequently and strenuously urged, would have prevented? Detroit and a brave army taken—the Indians let loose upon our frontiers—the inhabitants flying in every direction—Brock, with his army and Indians and thousands of inspirited Canadians and a powerful train of field and garrison ordnance taken from General Hull, arrived on this frontier and ready to act. Indeed, it is now reduced to a certainty that the inhabitants of this river, with their property, are doomed to feel the scourge and desolation of war. The hour that closes the armistice will bring ruin to most of them who live on this frontier. But I should not be appalled by the prospect if I could see some spirit and energy awakened in those who direct the destinies of the nation. For the last two months I could have traversed the wilds of Canada, fought with Indians only and subjected myself to all the inconvenience of the country without suffering half what I have done by the terrible state of inactivity and uncertainty in which we have been placed, and such are the feelings of all the brave men on this river.

We have been daily amused for two months with news of the approach of heavy ordnance, of flying artillery, of regular troops, &c., &c., to this frontier, but none have arrived. They come to Utica and then disappear. They timidly dance backward and forward in the interior of the country, without knowing what to do or being of service anywhere. The Genesee River, Sodus, Oswego, and the brig at Sackett's Harbor, are all alternately to be defended, as a British ship appears to pass from one end of the lake to the other. This miserable and timid system of defence must be abandoned, or the nation is ruined and disgraced. Make a bold push at any one point and you will find your enemy, give them as much business as they can attend to at Niagara and at Ogdensburg, and you will not see them groping among the marshes of Sodus to pillage the miserable huts of the poor inhabitants. But it is needless for me to say more; my views have been long known.

Excuse the incoherence and abruptness of this letter. It is written in a state of mind little short of distraction, occasioned by the events of the West and the situation of my brother, who has been at the point of death for ten days past, but who, thank God, is now recovering. I trust I am addressing myself to friends, and, I know, with the best motives and wishes for them and my country.

I do not feel disposed to condemn a public man on the slight ground of rumor and before he has had an impartial trial, but I have conversed with several gentlemen who were at Detroit at the time of its surrender, and if their representations are to be credited, that event will make one of the foulest blots on the page of American history. Yesterday a number of men were shot at Fort George in view of our troops. They are supposed to be the unfortunate fellows who joined General Hull in Canada and were surrendered at Detroit, and for whose protection provision should have been made in the capitulation at the expense of the life of every man in the garrison.

I have enclosed a copy of this letter so far as it is contained on the first sheet to the Secretary of War, for whom, indeed, it was intended with the exception of the request at the beginning.

The public mind in this quarter is wrought up almost to a state of madness. Jealousy and distrust begin to prevail toward the general officers, occasioned perhaps by the rash and imprudent expressions on politics of some of the persons attached to them, but principally by the surrender of Detroit, which among the common people is almost universally ascribed to treachery.

I have entire confidence in the honor and patriotism as well as the military promptitude and judgment of General VanRensselaer and shall most cheerfully submit to his guidance. But if it is his wish (and I think it is and that he will express it to you) to return, it would inspire great confidence in the troops and the country to have you or General D. Clinton take the command.

We shall probably be attacked when the armistice is off, but I trust in God, not surrendered.

Governor Tompkins:—

I could wish, if you have no objections, that this letter may be seen by Mr. Clinton, between whom and yourself I ardently hope for the sake of my country in its present perilous situation that the greatest cordiality may exist.

(Copy of a Letter to the Secretary of War.)

BLACK ROCK, Aug. 30, 1812.

SIR,—I enclose you a copy of my letter of this date to Governor Tompkins, to which I must beg your serious attention.

For God's sake, my friend, arouse and put forth the energies of the nation, and let us not be beaten by a petty province. War can never be waged by tedious and two-penny calculations of economy in the office at Washington. The poor but patriotic citizens of Ohio and the frontiers of New York are suffering all the miseries of poverty and war. They alone are called out because, perhaps, their march to the frontiers is shorter, and therefore cheaper, while the rich inhabitants of Pennsylvania are lolling in security and ease.

As one of the inhabitants of this frontier, I can submit to the loss of property; I can see with composure (what is now actually presented to my view) my vessels riding under British colors in a British harbor, but I cannot endure the degradation of my country.

(Tompkins' Papers, Vol. VIII., pp. 96-102, New York State Library.)

Sir George Prevost to Major General Brock.

HEADQUARTERS, MONTREAL, Aug. 30, 1812.

SIR,—I received on the 25th, while at St. John's, your despatch by express from Detroit of the 16th instant. I do most sincerely congratulate you upon the complete success which has attended your measures for the preservation of Amherstburg. The surrender of Detroit, the capture of General Hull's army with so large a proportion of ordnance, are circumstances of high importance to our country, and which have evinced your talents as an officer in command and reflect honor upon you and upon Lieut.-Colonel St. George and Colonel Procter.

I propose sending an aid-de-camp to England with your short despatch, together with such details as I am in possession of, respecting Brigadier-General Hull's previous invasion of Upper Canada and of his foiled attempts to invade Amherstburg, but I shall delay his departure from hence until the 1st of September, in hopes of obtaining from you before that time further particulars of the operations which led to General Hull's disgrace.

Well aware of the difficulties you have surmounted for the preservation of your government entire, I shall endeavor to do justice to your merit in my report to His Majesty's Minister upon the success which has crowned your energy and zeal.

A warrant giving you more extensive power over the sentence of such general courts-martial as you may be called on to assemble, was signed by me ten days since, and has, I hope, reached you.

I am in hourly expectation of receiving from General Dearborn intelligence respecting the reception of the proposed suspension of hostilities in consequence of the revocation of the Orders-in-Council which are a plea for war in the American Cabinet, and also whether Mr. Baker has been allowed to assume *pro tempore* the character of a charge d'affaires at Washington, where Mr. Foster left him in a demi-official capacity. I consider the arrangement entered into by General Dearborn with Colonel Baynes requiring the confirmation of the President to establish its sacredness.

The King's Government having most unequivocally expressed to me their desire to preserve peace with the United States, that they might, uninterrupted, pursue with the whole disposable force of the country the great interest committed in Europe, I have endeavored to be instrumental in the accomplishment of their views, but I consider it most fortunate to have been enabled to do so without interfering with operations on the Detroit.

I have sent you men, money and stores of every kind.

P. S.—I have addressed to you a public letter containing my sentiments upon Major General Sheaffe's alterations in original conclusive and binding conditions transmitted to him by the Adjutant-General.

(From Tupper's Life of Brock, pp. 274-5.)

Major General VanRensselaer to Governor Tompkins.

HEADQUARTERS, LEWISTON, August 31, 1812.

SIR,—Presuming that the surrender of General Hull's army has been officially announced to Your Excellency through the proper channel, I shall not enter into any details upon the event so disastrous to our country. Its consequences must be felt everywhere, but they are particularly distressing upon these frontiers, both to the citizens and the little army under my command. Alarm pervades the country and distrust among the troops. They are incessantly pressing for furloughs under every possible pretence. Many are without shoes; all clamorous for pay. Many are sick. Swift's regiment at Black Rock are about one-fourth part down. I have ordered Doctor Brown to associate Doctor Chapin with him, and to examine as to the causes producing the diseases, the mode of treating them, &c., and to report to me the best means of preserving the health of those who remain well. This duty they are now performing.

Captain Jennings has been tried by a courtmartial and found guilty of such charges as forfeited his commission, and I have approved the sentence. The proceedings in form will soon be forwarded to Your Excellency.

While we are thus growing daily weaker, our enemy is growing stronger. They hold a very commanding position on the high ground above Queenston, and they are daily strengthening themselves in it with men and ordnance. Indeed they are fortifying almost every prominent point from Fort Erie to Fort George. At present we rest upon the armistice, but should hostilities be recommenced I must immediately change my position. I receive no reinforcement of men, no ordnance or munitions of war. I must hope that I shall not long be left in this situation.

Two gentlemen, Messrs. Johnson and Bascom, came over in a flag to the garrison at Niagara, and the first I knew of it they were in my camp. Being satisfied that they were American citizens, men of intelligence and some standing in society, I permitted them to pass on with orders to report themselves to Your Excellency.

There is one fact which, though not immediately connected with my department, I cannot refrain from mentioning. The unfortunate soldiers of General Hull's army who marched by my camp on their way to Lower Canada are very destitute of clothing. Every consideration would urge that some attention should be paid to their condition.

(From S. VanRensselaer's Narrative: Appendix, p. 34; Tompkins' Papers, Vol. VIII., pp. 105-7, New York State Library.)

Sir George Prevost to Major General Brock.

HEADQUARTERS, MONTREAL, Aug. 31, 1812.

SIR,—I had scarcely closed the letters I addressed to you yesterday when an aide-de-camp from Major General Dearborn made his appearance and delivered to me the despatch herewith transmitted. It will expose to your view the disposition of the President of the United States on the provisional measure temporarily agreed upon between the American commander-in-chief and myself in consequence of an earnest desire not to widen the breach existing between the two countries, the revocation of the Orders-in-Council having removed the plea used in Congress for a declaration of war against Great Britain.

I am much disappointed that the particulars of the surrender of Detroit have not as yet reached me, particularly as my aide-de-camp, Captain Coore, is to leave Montreal this evening for Quebec, where a ship of war is on the point of sailing for Halifax, from whence I expect the admiral will give him a conveyance for England.

Being unacquainted with the conditions attached to the surrender of Brigadier-General Hull's army, and giving scope to your expressions of prisoners of war, I have made arrangements for increasing their security against any attempt to rescue them, by ordering Captain Gray to proceed with two flank companies to Prescott.

(From Tupper's Life of Brock, p. 276.)

Militia General Orders.

HEADQUARTERS, YORK, 1st Septr., 1812.

Militia General Orders.

Major General Brock has been pleased to direct that such of the militia as have lately returned from Detroit, and who received leave of absence, shall receive pay and rations till the 24th instant, should their furlough so long continue.

By order.

J. MACDONELL,
Lt.-Col. Militia, P. A. D. C.

Major General VanRensselaer to Governor Tompkins.

HEADQUARTERS, LEWISTON, 1st Sept., 1812.

SIR,—In the letter which I had the honor to address to Your Excellency yesterday, I mentioned the general alarm which the surrender of General Hull's army has spread through the frontier. The inhabitants everywhere think themselves in danger. This is particularly the case in the County of Chautauqua, and in consequence of representations made to me by the inhabitants of that county, I had on the 27th ulto. issued an order to Lieut.-Colonel

John McMahon to order into service two full companies of his regiment for the protection of its inhabitants, designating in my order where they should be stationed. This morning again I have been called upon by Captains Baldwin and Mack, gentlemen of respectability from that county, very earnestly soliciting in behalf of the inhabitants still further force for their protection, and I have issued another order to Lieut.-Colonel McMahon to detach one captain, two sergeants and 26 privates more for the service aforesaid, until Your Excellency's pleasure can be known on the subject.

2d September, 4 o'clock p. m.

Colonel Fenwick has not yet arrived at Fort Niagara, and of course I have not delivered the letter of yesterday received by express from Major General Dearborn. Four or five vessels have just arrived at Fort George, it is supposed with reinforcements. Our enemy appear to be on the alert at every point.

This morning Lieut. Branch with about 40 men and two pieces of flying artillery arrived, also Captain Camp with about 25 dragoons.

P. S.—The company of Captain Jennings in Colonel Swift's regiment had become so clamorous for pay and contended so strenuously that their time had expired that I have ordered them to be discharged. I was strengthened in my belief that this would meet your approbation by learning from Brigadier General Brown that you had ordered Colonel Bellinger's regiment to be discharged.

(Tompkins' Papers, vol. VIII., pp. 103-5, New York State Library.)

Major General VanRensselaer to Major General Dearborn.

HEADQUARTERS, LEWISTON,
1st September, 1812.

SIR,—I have just received your letter of the 25th ult. I shall ascertain the movements and situation of Lieut.-Col. Fenwick with the cannon and stores, and as soon as he can be considered safe I shall terminate the armistice in the manner prescribed.

Upon this occasion I conceive it a duty I owe to my country, to the troops under my command, and to my own character, to state that we are not on this frontier in that condition which the approaching crisis will require. My force of militia, rank and file, now fit for duty, is six hundred and ninety-one, as will appear by the enclosed return. These have to guard a line of thirty-six miles. My sick list is more than one hundred. Many of the men are without shoes, and all are clamorous for pay. Besides, it is a fact that cannot be concealed that the surrender of General Hull's army has spread great alarm among the inhabitants on this frontier, and I every day perceive strong symptoms of distrust among the troops. They have seen their countrymen surrendered without a single effort and marched prisoners before their eyes. They cannot comprehend it.

At this hour, I have received no reinforcements of men, no supplies of ordnance, tents, nor ammunition. There are not ten rounds per man on the Niagara frontier, nor have we lead to make cartridges. We are extremely deficient of medicine and hospital stores; of lint and bandage cloth we have none, nor any surgical instruments. Lieut.-Col. Swift's regiment at Black Rock and the troops in garrison at Niagara have no tents to take the field; unless Bloom's regiment and the troops with Lieut.-Col. Fenwick have tents with them they cannot be covered. This is a brief sketch of our condition. Our enemy are every moment on the alert. They hold a very commanding position on the high ground above Queenston, and are daily strengthing it with men and ordnance. Indeed almost every point of any importance from Fort Erie to Fort George is in some state of defence. At each fort on the lakes their shipping is ready to act. The troops which had been detached from this quarter to act against General Hull have returned, and may now be concentrated at this point. Before the termination of the armistice I must change my position, and can only act on the defensive until I shall be reinforced with troops well disciplined and commanded by able officers.

(From S. VanRensselaer's Narrative: Appendix, p. 37.)

Major General Dearborn to Major General VanRensselaer.

HEADQUARTERS, GREENBUSH, 1st Sept., 1812.

SIR,—I received your letter of the 25th ult. this morning, enclosing a communication from Capt. Leonard. The fall of Gen. Hull and the army under his command is as mortifying, as it was unexpected. We must endeavor to redeem our honor by increasing our exertions. In addition to the militia detachments ordered from this State and two thousand ordered from the northwestern part of Pennsylvania to Niagara, three regiments of the new-raised troops of the army have been some days on their march towards your post. I am forwarding additional supplies of muskets and cannon, with forty batteaux, to Niagara. A detachment of troops will accompany the boats from Oswego. It will be necessary to have teams ready to take the stores and boats from a safe landing place, and it may be well to order a detachment to meet the boats at some distance from Niagara on the shore. I hope Lieut.-Col. Fenwick, with the troops and stores under his command, will have arrived in season. *I have no doubt but that you will improve the earliest opportunity for retaliating on the enemy our misfortunes at Detroit.* Gen. Dodge goes to Sackett's Harbor with a fine force. I have detached Gen. Bloomfield with a brigade of regular troops with artillery, &c., to Plattsburg, and other troops, in addition to the militia of this State and Vermont, will accompany or follow him.

I shall endeavor to draw the reinforcements back from Upper Canada to Montreal.

(From S. VanRensselaer's Narrative: Appendix. p. 40.)

Col. S. VanRensselaer to his Wife.

LEWISTON, 1st September, 1812.

DEAR HARRIET,—I wrote you yesterday by mail, in which letter I gave you an account of all that was passing here. This day we received an express from Genl. Dearborn that the armistice was at an end. But at the time he was despatched from Greenbush they knew nothing of the surrender of General Hull and his army, and what effect that information will have on the measures of a weak and despicable General and Government, time only will determine. We shall at all events go on and make all the arrangements in our power to meet the crisis which, in all probability, is approaching. If nothing is done it will not be our fault, but that of Government. By express and by almost every mail the Governor and Genl. Dearborn have been informed of our situation.

(From Bonney's Historical Gleanings, p. 224.)

From the Buffalo Gazette of Tuesday, 1st September, 1812.

[NOTE—Extras had been issued on Thursday, August 27th, and Saturday, August 29th, giving details of the surrender of Detroit.]

On Tuesday evening last 4 or 5 British vessels hove in sight of the village, and lay a few miles off Buffalo Creek during the night. Yesterday morning they came down and anchored off Fort Erie. About noon a flag of truce came into Buffalo Creek and landed Captain Baker, late of General Hull's army.

The armed ships which brought down Hull's *vanguard* have all returned.

On Wednesday last Major Mullany arrived here from the Canandaigua rendezvous with about 140 troops for the frontier.

Arrived yesterday, 40 mounted artillerists with two pieces of flying artillery, on their way to Lewiston. They state two 24-pounders, four 18-pounders, and four 9-pounders were, coming through Lake Ontario for Niagara.

From the United States Gazette, of Philadelphia, Sept. 25th, 1812.

Extract of a letter from a gentleman of Providence, Rhode Island, now on his travels, dated at Buffalo Creek the 2d inst.:

I am here surrounded by Indians, and the British Fort Erie, 3 miles distant. Six tribes of Indians, who are holding a council in this vicinity, it is said, are offended by a report that they will not be admitted into our army, but I presume they will be convinced to the contrary, though the agent is desirous of their remaining neutral. There are now near 3,000 men, mostly militia and volunteers, on our lines, but having to guard 20 miles of the River Niagara they are much scattered, and an attack has been for the two last days expected, which, if speedily made by the British, I cannot see what will hinder them from possessing all the forts here. There are 10 or 12 small pieces of cannon here (although more are expected) to oppose upwards of 100 pieces on the other shore, some of which are of the heaviest calibre. To complete the gloomy prospect here, our garrison is almost destitute of ammunition; besides our soldiers are very jealous of their officers.

(File in Philadelphia Library.)

From Major General Dearborn to Major General VanRensselaer.

HEADQUARTERS, GREENBUSH, Sept. 2d, 1812.

SIR,—I send this by express for the purpose of putting you on your guard against an attack that I have reason to apprehend is intended by the enemy. A considerable force has lately passed into Upper Canada for the obvious purpose of striking not only at Detroit but at other posts. From the number of troops which have left Montreal for Upper Canada, I am not without fear that attempts will speedily be made to reduce you and your forces to the mortifying situation of Gen. Hull and his army. If such an attempt of the enemy should be made previous to the arrival of the principal part of the troops destined to Niagara, it will be necessary for you to be prepared for all events, *and to be prepared to make good a secure retreat, as the last resort.* I hope, however, you will not be reduced to the mortifying alternative of falling back. But from the unfortunate event at Detroit we may expect great exertions on the part of the enemy, and as far as the means in our power will admit, we, I trust, shall be at least equally vigilant and active.

P. S.—The Frigate *Guerriere* has been captured and sunk by the U. S. Frigate *Constitution*, Capt. Hull.

(From S. VanRensselaer's Narrative: Appendix, p. 42.

General Orders.

HEADQUARTERS, LEWISTON,
2d September, 1812.

SIR,—Major General VanRensselaer directs that you land the troops, cannon, and stores under your command at the Four-Mile Creek, and make every military preparation to protect them, and to give him immediate information of your arrival by express.

By order.

SOL. VANRENSSELAER,
Aid-de-Camp.

Lieut.-Col. Fenwick, Light Artillery.

(From S. VanRensselaer's Narrative: Appendix, p. 39.)

Major General Brock to his Brothers.

LAKE ONTARIO, Sept. 3, 1812.

You will have heard of the complete success which attended the efforts I directed against Detroit. I have received so many letters from people whose opinion I value, expressive of their admiration of the exploit, that I begin to attach to it more importance than I was at first inclined. Should the affair be viewed in England in the light it is here, I cannot fail of meeting reward and escaping the horror of being placed high on a shelf, never to be taken down.

Some say that nothing could be more desperate than the measure, but I answer that the state of the Province admitted of nothing but desperate remedies. I got possession of the letters my antagonist addressed to the Secretary at War, and also of the sentiments which hundreds of his army uttered to their friends. Confidence in the General was gone, and evident despondency prevailed throughout. I have succeeded beyond expectation. I crossed the river contrary to the opinion of Cols. Procter, St. George, &c.: it is therefore no wonder that envy should attribute to good fortune what in justice to my own discernment, I must say, proceeded from a cool calculation of the *pours* and *contres*.

It is supposed that the value of the articles captured will amount to 30 or £40,000; in that case my proposition will be something considerable. If it enable me to contribute to your comfort and happiness, I shall esteem it my highest reward. When I returned Heaven thanks for my amazing success, I thought of you all. You appeared to me happy—your late sorrows forgotten, and I felt as if the many benefits which for a series of years I received from you were not unworthily bestowed. Let me know, my dearest brothers, that you are all again united. The want of union was nearly losing this Province without even a struggle, and be assured it operates in the same degree in regard to families.

A cessation of hostilities has taken place along this frontier. Should peace follow, the measure will be well; if hostilities recommence, nothing could be more unfortunate than this pause. I cannot give you freely an account of my situation; it is, however, of late, much improved. The militia have been inspired by the recent success with confidence—the disaffected are silenced. The 49th have come to my aid, besides other troops. I shall see Vincent, I hope, this evening at Kingston. He is appointed to the command of that post—a most important one. I have withdrawn Plenderleath from Niagara to assist him. Plenderleath is sitting opposite me, and desires to be remembered. James Brock is likewise at Kingston. I believe he considers it more his interest to remain with the 49th than to act as my private secretary; indeed the salary is a mere pittance. Poor Leggatt is dead, and has left his family in the most distressing circumstances. His wife died last year.

. . . .

General Sheaffe has lately been sent to me. There never was an individual so miserably off for the necessary assistance. Sir George Prevost has kindly hearkened to my remonstrances, and in some measure supplied the deficiency. The 41st is an uncommonly fine regiment, but, with few exceptions, badly officered. . .

. . . .

KINGSTON, September 4.

I this instant received your letters by Mr. Todd. So honest John Tupper is gone. I could not have loved a son of my own more ardently. Hostilities, I this instant understand, are to be renewed in four days, and, though landed only two hours, I must return immediately to Niagara, whence I shall write fully.

(From Tupper's Life of Brock: pp. 284-6.)

Lieutenant-Colonel John R. Fenwick, Light Artillery, to Major General VanRensselaer.

FOUR-MILE CREEK, September 3, 1812.

SIR,—Agreable to your instructions, I am landing the ordnance and stores at this place. They are of great importance, and I do not think them safe in this position. The powder I must keep on board, as it will sustain injury by being taken out. I pray you, sir, to assist me so soon as possible, and receive the assurance of my consideration and respect.

(From S. VanRensselaer's Narrative: Appendix, p. 40.)

Colonel Solomon VanRensselaer to Lieut.-Col. Fenwick.

HEADQUARTERS, LEWISTON, September 3, 1812.

SIR,—Major General VanRensselaer has ordered the Quartermaster to proceed immediately to Four-Mile Creek and furnish you with the necessary transportation for the cannon and military stores in your charge, and has also detached one captain, one subaltern and forty men to assist you in their removal and protection to this place. The troops and wagons will reach you this evening.

(From S. VanRensselaer's Narrative: Appendix, p. 40.)

General Orders.

HEADQUARTERS, LEWISTON, 4th Sept., 1812.

The Major General announces to the troops that, agreeable to an order received from Major General Dearborn, the armistice entered into between him and the Governor-General of Canada will be terminated at twelve o'clock at noon on the eighth day of September instant.

The troops under his command will, however, understand explicitly that they are not to act offensively without previous orders from him, but to be vigilant in their duty and ready to execute any command they may receive when a proper occasion presents itself.

The troops will strike their tents to-morrow morning at reveille; the tents, tent poles and baggage will be packed up ready to move in one hour from that time. The quartermaster will measure the space necessary for a double row of tents and furnish the necessary transportation.

A fatigue party of a sergeant, corporal and twelve men will attend at the same time at headquarters.

By order of Major General VanRensselaer.

SOL. VANRENSSELAER, Aid-de-Camp.

Major General Brock to Sir George Prevost.

KINGSTON, September 4, 1812.

SIR,—Upon my arrival here an hour ago, Captain Fulton delivered me Your Excellency's despatch, dated the 31st ultimo, enclosing a letter from General Dearborn, in which the President's disapproval of the armistice is announced. I am in consequence induced to return without loss of time to Fort George. Captain Fulton having expressed a wish to accompany me, I have the more readily consented as he will be able to give you full information of our actual state. The enemy was very busy upon Fort Niagara, and appeared inclined to erect additional batteries. I may perhaps think it proper to stop their career.

I enclose several documents lately received from Colonel Procter at Detroit. That officer appears to have conducted himself with much judgment. I likewise transmit a memorial which I have received from some merchants in the Niagara District, but of course I cannot judge of its merits.

I shall be obliged to Your Excellency to direct a remittance of the £5,000, for which I sent a requisition some time ago, on account of the civil expenditure of this Province, either in Government paper or specie, as you may deem most convenient. I doubt not the former meeting a ready currency.

The very flattering manner in which Your Excellency is pleased to view my services, and your kindness in having represented them to His Majesty's ministers in such favorable light, are gratifying to me, and call for my grateful acknowledgements.

(From Tupper's Life of Brock, pp. 301-2.)

Major General VanRensselaer to Major General Brock.

HEADQUARTERS, LEWISTON, Sept. 4th, 1812.

SIR,—By the articles which I had the honor to conclude with Major General Sheaffe on the 21st ult. for the government of the troops of the United States under my command and His Britannic Majesty's forces on this frontier during the temporary armistice, it was among other things stipulated that "*the party who shall first receive orders for the renewal of hostilities shall give four days' notice, computing twenty-four hours to each day, before any offensive operation shall take place.*"

Having now received orders to terminate the armistice, in conformity to the above recited stipulation I have the honor to transmit you this notice, that the armistice will be terminated at twelve o'clock at noon on Tuesday, the eighth day of September inst.

(From S. VanRensselaer's Narrative: Appendix, p. 41.)

The Secretary of War to Major General Dearborn.

WAR DEPARTMENT, Sept. 4, 1812.

(Abstract.)

Captain Chauncey has been directed to take immediate measures to obtain command of Lakes Erie and Ontario.

Major General Sheaffe to Major General VanRensselaer.

FORT GEORGE, 5th Sept., 1812.

SIR,—I have the honor of receiving your communication signifying the intention on the part of the United States of renewing hostilities after four days shall have elapsed from the period at which the notice was given—thus declaring that the armistice shall terminate at twelve o'clock at noon on the eighth day of this September.

(From S. VanRensselaer's Narrative: Appendix, p. 42.)

Colonel S. VanRensselaer to Abraham VanVechten.

LEWISTON, 5th September, 1812.

MY DEAR SIR,—This morning Mr. Swan arrived (in three days from Albany) on express from Gen. Dearborn with information that a large body of British troops had left Montreal for the opposite bank of this river, and cautioning Gen. V. R. to guard against a surprise from them, and if hard pressed to make a safe retreat. His caution against a surprise is unnecessary, and as for a retreat, we *shall not think* of it until we have tried some blustering Democrats, who pretend to be full of fighting and crossing the river, but their opinions as to crossing no attention will be paid to until it is proper. We should come to action, and then they will be brought to a close one. With the force which arrived yesterday under the command of Lt.-Col. Fenwick, we have in the aggregate of regular troops and militia *two thousand two hundred* men detached on a frontier of forty miles, from Fort Niagara to Buffalo, while the British have opposed to us (besides the force Dearborn speaks of), from every information we can get, and from their appearance every day in our view, at least that number of regular troops, with strong batteries at every crossing point to meet [us], and of these there are but very few, owing to the extreme height of the banks.

In short, we are deficient in almost everything. Four 18-pounders, two twelve pounders, eight sixes, and two fours are all the ordnance we have for the defence of this line; two sixes, honey combed, some of them without shot and six without harness. Fort

Niagara not tenable. (You all suppose it impregnable. Not so, it cannot be maintained fifteen minutes.) The stores are now removing with a view to abandon it, and in this place Capt. Leonard buried two 13-inch mortars and six 8½-inch howitzers for the want of shells.

No surgical instruments, lint, bandage or hospital stores, no forage and no quartermaster. Peter B. Porter has been only twice in camp since we have been here, and instead of getting the force ready is attending to his private affairs. He is an abominable scoundrel, and I make no secret in telling his friends so.

(From Bonney's Historical Gleanings, pp. 226-7.)

Major General VanRensselaer to Major General Dearborn.

HEADQUARTERS, LEWISTON,
5th Sept., 1812, 7 p. m.

SIR,—The express has just arrived with your letter of the 2d inst. I thank you for the information which your letter contains and for suggesting precautions against a disaster which would deeply implicate the honor of my country, the fate of the little army under my command, and my own character.

Every exertion which the small force I command can make to avoid either a surprise or defeat will be attempted. So small and scattered has been my little band, and so depressed by the fate of Gen. Hull, that every movement has been heavy. But within forty-eight hours the scene seems to have changed a little for the better. Lieut.-Col. Fenwick has arrived safe with the cannon and stores. To avoid any possible casualty, I ordered them landed at the Four-Mile Creek, a little below Fort Niagara, and from thence they have been brought by land; the boats have returned. A battalion of about seventy riflemen which, on the 16th ult. I had ordered from Oswego, has this day arrived here.

I have determined, with the concurrence of Lieut.-Col. Fenwick's opinion, to throw up a strong battery on this side of Fort Niagara, on the bank of the river, and there place the four eighteen-pounders. With this view, I went this morning on the spot, and we have broke ground. This evening Lieut.-Col. Fenwick and Capt. Leonard are with me. I understand our movement has produced great activity at Fort George. The enemy have immediately commenced some new works. It is my intention to support the battery near Fort Niagara with as strong a camp as I am able and to cut a road back of it for greater safety in case I should be hard pressed.

Agreeably to your instructions, I waited, for the safety of Lieut.-Col. Fenwick, the cannon and stores, before I gave notice necessary to terminate the armistice conformably to the stipulations between Major Gen. Sheaffe and myself. The notice was delivered at Fort George yesterday before noon, and by it the armistice will be terminated at 12 o'clock at noon on the 8th inst. This day Major Gen. Sheaffe has acknowledged the receipt of my notice. My present camp being within reach of the enemy's guns on the high grounds at Queenston, I have determined to quit. I had designated a spot for my new encampment about one mile from the river, on the ridge road, but I may reconsider this subject. It might be expected from my situation that I could, with facility, obtain correct information of the enemy's force and movements in this vicinity, but such is not the fact. Every effort for that purpose is absolutely vain. I can only obtain information too general to calculate upon. It is generally believed that the enemy are concentrating their forces to this neighborhood, but what their numbers are is to me wholly unknown. They appear to be on the alert.

At Fort Niagara we have (concealed) two thirteen and-a-half inch brass mortars and four eight and-a-half inch howitzers. Capt. Leonard has this evening handed me a memorandum of articles that in his opinion, which I respect, are very much wanted for these pieces and some others, as follows:—

400 shells for the mortars.

1,600 canister and grape shot for the howitzers.

16 dozen portfires—harness complete, for the mortars and howitzers; also wanted, harness for the 6 six pounders now at Fort Niagara.

With the information of which you are possessed relative to my force and that of the enemy, I presume you cannot expect that I shall immediately attempt to act offensively. I shall endeavor to watch the motions of the enemy as far as possible, and so dispose my little force as to avoid a surprise or risking too much with raw troops in case the enemy should cross to attack me. The surrender of Gen. Hull's army has put it in the power of the enemy to turn a strong force to act either defensively or offensively against me. My situation requires arduous duty; it may be critical, but I shall meet events in that manner which my judgment shall dictate as most prudent and safe, and to the utmost of my power discharge my duty.

The conduct of Capt. Hull in the *Constitution* was gallant indeed, and has justified the high expectations we have all entertained of our navy and the brave men who command it.

(From S. VanRensselaer's Narrative: Appendix, p. 43.)

Regimental Orders by Lt.-Colonel Chewett, Commanding 3d Regt., York Militia.

YORK, 5 September, 1812.

In consequence of the flank companies of said regiment, now in the Garrison of York, under the command of Major Allan, having been ordered by Major General Sheaffe on the 4th instant to proceed with all possible speed to Fort George, the following officers, non-commissioned officers and privates detached by their respective quotas from the battalion companies of said regiment are hereby directed to compose the following companies and to do duty in the said garrison until further orders:—

  1st—Captain Denison.
      Lt. Endicott.
      Ensign McArthur.
      3 sergeants.
      42 rank and file.
  2nd—Captain Ridout.
      Lt. Kendrick.
      Ens'n Brooks.
      3 sergeants.
      42 rank and file.
  3d—Captain Hamilton.
      Lt. Playter.
      Ens'n Jarvis.
      3 sergeants.
      42 rank and file.

Major General VanRensselaer to Governor Tompkins.

LEWISTON, Sept. 6, 1812.

SIR,—General Gray yesterday apprised me of his intention to visit his family for a few weeks. I avail myself of the opportunity to express to Your Excellency my approbation of his conduct. He has executed my orders with promptitude and ability. The Genl. is desirous of serving the country if he could obtain a commission in the army. As I have no interest at the palace, I refer him to Your Excellency.

(Tompkins' Papers, Vol. VIII., p. 123, New York State Library.)

Brigadier-General Wm. Wadsworth to Governor Tompkins.

CAMP AT LEWISTON, 6th Sept., 1812.

SIR,—General Gray having determined on a visit to his family, sets off to-morrow. I would refer you to him for the state of affairs on this frontier. He at my request has built a battery on the mountain south of this village, which has met my entire approbation, and has expressed a desire of further serving our country if he could obtain a commission, to which I beg leave to refer him to Your Excellency, and would express my satisfaction of his readiness and with the promptitude which he has at all times executed my commands since his arrival on this frontier.

(Tompkins' Papers, Vol. VIII., p. 124, New York State Library.)

John Lovett to Joseph Alexander.

HEADQUARTERS, LEWISTON, 6 Sept., 1812.

DEAR SIR,—

. . . .

Our situation is becoming daily more and more *interesting*, to say the least of it. I do not know that I ought yet to call it *critical*, though I know that some think it so. What may be the views of the enemy we know not: they are flushed with victory and concentrating their forces very fast against us. The armistice will be terminated by our notice at noon on the 8th inst. To sum all up in one, I should say that from present appearances we must either fight or run, or both, in a few days. This camp, which is within half-point blank shot of the enemy, we shall quit to-morrow morning; the order is given to strike tents at reveille. We shall not quit the neighborhood, but seek a safer place. Things look rather squally all around just at present, but it may clear off again. There are some pretty strong reasons to believe that Brock is preparing to *Hull* us. I don't know but he may, but Albany blood runs pretty steady yet. We have removed most of our stores from Fort Niagara, and are throwing up a battery on this side, in which we mean to place four eighteen-pounders.

The enemy are extending their works at Fort George, and I understand as the light increases that our soldiers discover some new works began last night opposite to us here.

My General is well, firm, brave and prudent. Solomon [Van Rensselaer] would fight all the while if he could get chances, and I rather expect he will soon get enough of it. Col. Fenwick with the cannon and stores have arrived safe. We worked John Bull in the little armistice treaty and got more than they expected.

. . . .

(From Bonney's Historical Gleanings, pp. 228-9.)

General Orders.

HEADQUARTERS, LEWISTON, 6th Sept., 1812.

Lieut.-Col. George Fleming, commanding Fort Oswego, having assigned Walter Cotton as surgeon of Major Charles Moseley's battalion of riflemen, the Major General confirms that assignment and orders that Doctor Cotton do duty accordingly in that corps until further orders.

Major General Hall will please to take command of Lieut. Col. Swift's regiment and the detachment of troops ordered out by Brigadier-General Hopkins and make such disposition of this force as the security of the frontiers may require, and will make weekly reports to Major General VanRensselaer.

Lieut.-Col. Bloom will make morning reports of the regiment under his command to Major General VanRensselaer, and will cause Mr. Rolph, the prisoner, to be delivered to Major General Hall at Black Rock.

By order of Major General VanRensselaer.

SOL. VANRENSSELAER, Aid-de-Camp.

Major General Brock to Sir George Prevost.

FORT GEORGE, September 7th, 1812.

SIR,—On my arrival here yesterday morning, I found that intimation had been received by Major General Sheaffe to renew hostilities at noon to-morrow. During the cessation of hostilities, vast supplies have been received by the enemy. His field artillery is numerous, and I have reason to believe his heavy ordnance has been considerably increased. He is now busy erecting batteries in front of Fort George, and everything indicates an intention of commencing active operations. Reinforcements of troops of every description have evidently arrived.

I have written to Amherstburg for such troops as [Colonel Procter] conceived the state of affairs in that quarter enabled him to part with. Colonel Vincent has likewise been written to on the same subject. The prodigious quantity of pork and flour which have been observed landing on the opposite shore from a number of vessels and large boats, which have entered the river during the armistice, are sufficient to supply the wants for a long period of a considerable force.

I expect an attack almost immediately. The enemy will either turn my left flank, which he may easily accomplish during a calm night, or attempt to force his way across under cover of his artillery. We stand greatly in need of officers, men, and heavy ordnance. Captain Holcroft has been indefatigable and has done everything in the power of an individual, but on such an extended line, assistance is necessary.

I look every day for the arrival of five 24-pounders from Detroit, and other artillery and stores which are not required there, besides two thousand muskets.

We have now three hundred Indians on the ground, and two hundred more are expected to-morrow. They appear ashamed of themselves and promise to wipe away the disgrace into which they have fallen by their late conduct. They may serve to intimidate, otherwise I expect no essential service from this degenerate race.

Should Your Excellency be in a situation to send reinforcements to the Upper Country, the whole of the force at present at Kingston might be directed to proceed hither. One thousand additional regulars are necessary. A force of that description ought to be stationed at Pelham to act as exigencies might require. At present, the whole of my force being necessary for the defence of the banks of the river, no part can look for support.

If I can continue to maintain my position six weeks longer, the campaign will have terminated in a manner little expected in the States. But I stand in want of more artillerymen and a thousand regulars. I have thus given Your Excellency a hasty sketch of my situation, and this I can aver, that no exertions shall be wanting to do justice to the important command with which I am entrusted. Captain Fulton leaves this by the first safe conveyance.

. . . .

It is said that Fort Niagara is to be evacuated.

(Canadian Archives: c. 677, p. 64.)

Major General Dearborn to Governor Tompkins.

HEADQUARTERS, GREENBUSH, Sept. 7th, 1812.

(Abstract.)

Suggests that he (Tompkins) should take the field in person with as large a force as he could speedily assemble and march to the northwestern frontier of the State and inspire fresh vigor into the troops in service, while he hopes the movements towards Montreal will draw some troops from Upper Canada, or that an opportunity may be afforded of striking at their outposts between Lake Champlain and that city.

(MSS. in Third Auditor's Office, Washington, D. C.)

Major General VanRensselaer to Major General Dearborn.

HEADQUARTERS, LEWISTON, 8th Sept., 1812.

SIR,—I have this day received your two letters of the 1st instant, and have made the communication you requested to the contractor.

No occurrence of importance has taken place since I wrote you on the 5th by your express. I have yesterday removed my camp to the Ridge Road, as I proposed. The battery near Fort Niagara is fast progressing, also the cutting of the back road mentioned in my last letter. *The enemy appear to be very active*, but whether their preparations are for offensive or defensive operations is impossible for me to determine.

The night before last two men came over from Canada, but the information they give us is of very little consequence; indeed the character of the men would not give much weight to anything they say. They state that Gen. Brock had returned from York to Fort George—that 1,500 militia were ordered for Fort George yesterday—some troops have passed up this day through Queenston. Not knowing what the termination of the armistice might produce, I have taken every precaution in my power to meet any attempt the enemy might make. But it is now five o'clock and I neither see nor hear of any movements. General Wadsworth and Col. VanRensselaer have been the whole day at Niagara. Should they return before the mail closes and have anything of importance to communicate, I shall add it in postscript.

(From S. VanRensselaer's Narrative: Appendix, p. 45.)

John Lovett to Abraham VanVechten.

HEADQUARTERS, LEWISTON, Sept. 8, 1812.

MY DEAR SIR,—Colonel VanRensselaer has been with General Wadsworth the whole day, and I have been on the jump from dawn of day to this 5 p. m. Brock has returned from York to Fort George, and the enemy are certainly very active, but whether they contemplate defensive or offensive measures it is impossible to say. It would seem that in our situation we might with facility obtain information of the enemy's force and movements. Not so. Not a soul will risk his neck from this side among them, and those who come over are such scamps no trust can be put in them. We have moved our camp from the river to the Ridge Road. In short, the enemy, having put Hull out of the way, have it in their power to turn their whole force against us. Our poor fellows are patient, patriotic and exceedingly attached to their General. They swear he can't be bribed, and to tell you the real truth, this confidence is all that saves us from every sort of disgrace. We are calm, self-collected, and determined to act as near right as we can. But God only knows how we shall come out. A great force is coming on, I understand, but no pay, no shoes, no anything.

The General has gone to have a talk with the Tuscarora tribe this afternoon. The armistice terminated at 12 o'clock, and no movement is made. . . . .
. . . .

(From Bonney's Historical Gleanings, p. 229.)

Lieut.-Col. Fenwick to Major General VanRensselaer.

(Received Sept. 8th, 1812.)

SIR,—I am induced to believe from every observation I have vigilantly made that the enemy is prepared and ready for an attack. They are so with shipping and with boats, which to-day brought them a reinforcement of troops and stores. Our patrols are very lax in their duty. The work erecting cannot be finished *in time* without additional strength. When finished it is not secure without being strongly covered in rear, for we have nothing to prevent their landing, and they can in that case carry the work. The regular force should be concentrated and organized. Our stores should be removed. They are not in safety, for if they throw over two hundred men they can carry the fort. This I beg your consideration to, as your strength is six miles off and four hours time. I have no means of express at my command.

(From S. VanRensselaer's Narrative: Appendix, p. 46.)

General Orders.

HEADQUARTERS, LEWISTON, 9th Sept., 1812.

Lieut.-Col. Bloom will march immediately to the neighborhood of Niagara Falls and relieve the guards of the detachment of United States troops under the command of Major Mullany by his regiment. The commanding officer of this detachment, after being relieved by Lieut.-Col. Bloom, will march with the troops under his command without delay and join Lieut.-Col. Fenwick, and is to be subject to his orders.

By order of Major General VanRensselaer.

SOL. VANRENSSELAER, Aid-de-Camp.

From the Buffalo Gazette, Tuesday, 8th September, 1812.

Lieut.-Colonel Bloom, from Cayuga County, arrived on the frontier last week with the 19th Regiment of detached militia, about 500 strong, belonging to Brigadier-General Daniel Miller's brigade.

We understand that the rifle battalion under command of Major Moseley, from Onondaga, is soon expected at Lewiston.

Last week a full company of light horsemen passed through this village, destined to join the army at Lewiston.

We are happy to have it in our power to state that the report of Dr. Asa Coltrin having accepted a surgeon's berth in the British army is without foundation.

Governor Tompkins to Major General VanRensselaer.

ALBANY, September 9th, 1812.

DEAR SIR,—Your various communications have come to hand, the two last while I was in New York. My return from that place was expedited by the news of Hull's discomfiture. Previously to my leaving this place for New York, I had ordered out two regiments in addition to Bloom's to reinforce you, but their march has been retarded by circumstances over which I had no control. They are now directed to move on with the utmost expedition. Until reinforcements arrive, I am sensible of the delicacy of your situation. Your proceedings hitherto in concentrating in one place and disciplining a large body of your troops, changing your encampments, your disposition of the despatch relative to the termination of the armistice, and every other official act has met my entire approbation and will receive that of your fellow citizens generally. I pray God you may be able to maintain your post until reinforcements shall arrive.

(From S. VanRensselaer's Narrative: Appendix. p. 53.)

Governor Tompkins to Major General VanRensselaer.

ALBANY, September 9th, 1812.

SIR,—The Government has at length awakened to its duty with respect to the command of the lakes. The most unbounded authority has been given to Captain Chauncey for that purpose, and he will be with you soon. Forty ship carpenters came up with me in the last steamboat and have gone westward. Marines and seamen will be on as soon as vessels and gunboats are ready.

A large supply of ordnance of every description is now on its way from New York. The orders embrace Erie as well as Ontario. I despatched an express for Captain Chauncey on that subject from New York on Friday evening to Captain Woolsey. The despatches have returned this morning and gone down by express. Should you, my dear General, be able to maintain your position a short time, these arrangements for the lakes and the reinforcements will place you in a situation of defiance. To enable you so to do more effectually the militia of every description in the counties above mentioned are placed at your disposal, and you may instantly call upon all or any portion of them under the Act of 1795 (enclosed), or under the militia law of this State, and I will approve, confirm and maintain your proceedings. The Quartermaster-General of the State is ordered by me into regular service, and is now in every respect subject to your directions. I have remitted him ten thousand dollars by Major Noon.

You have probably felt hurt at the unfrequency of my answers to your communications, but when I inform you that I have no private secretary here, that the Adjutant-General of the State is in declining health, and that none of my staff or aids are in service or with me, though the latter have volunteered their services without pay and have been with me occasionally at their own expense, and when I inform you further that the drudgery of attending to a variety of details in rendezvousing, supply, equipage and paying troops, &c., devolves upon me or must remain unattended to, I trust you will extend great charity to my apparent inattention to your communications.

(From S. VanRensselaer's Narrative: Appendix. p. 53.)

General Orders.

HEADQUARTERS, ALBANY, Sept. 9, 1812.

Several pieces of ordnance, &c., will leave this for Utica on Thursday with a detachment of United States Horse Artillery. They will arrive at Utica about Tuesday next. The ordnance is to go from thence to Sackett's Harbor, but the detachment will proceed to Niagara. General Dearborn has made a requisition for me to have a detachment of Artillery or Horse Artillery ready at Utica to escort the ordnance to Sackett's Harbor. Your company will rendezvous for that purpose on Monday next and proceed to Utica, where they will remain till the cannon shall arrive and then immediately start with them for Sackett's Harbor and press on with the greatest diligence. There will be a travelling forge for heating shot to fire at shipping from the fort at the harbor.

The contractor at Utica will supply rations, and you will consult Capt. Gibson as to the mode of supplying forage and other articles on your journey. Captain Gibson is an experienced officer of the United States Horse Artillery.

The services of your company are required under and pursuant to the Act of Congress passed 28th February, 1795, of which I send you a copy.

Until your arrival at Utica you will have your men supplied with provisions and forage as cheap as possible, after which the contractor at Utica will supply provisions and your own officer will prepare forage. You may take the field-pieces and other articles attached to your company, or such part as you think proper, along with you. Mr. Tracy will hand you one hundred dollars to defray the incidental expenses of rendezvousing, for which you are to account to me with vouchers as soon as possible.

The alarm and anxiety on the frontiers arising from the disasters at Detroit compel me to require the services of the uniformed volunteer companies immediately, and I trust the protection of women and children, who may but for their assistance be the victims of savage barbarity, will stimulate the patriotism and awaken the fraternal feelings of every man and induce a free, eager and unanimous compliance with this requisition.

To Capt. Asa B. Sizer.

P. S.—On your arrival at Sackett's Harbor you will report yourself to Genl. Jacob Brown or General Dodge, whichever may command there, and obey the orders of the one so commanding.

(Tompkins' Papers, New York State Library.)

Major General Dearborn to Major General VanRensselaer.

HEADQUARTERS, GREENBUSH, Sept. 10th, 1812.

SIR,—Your letter of the 7th by the returning express reached us at 8 o'clock last evening. The safe arrival of Lieut.-Col. Fenwick with the troops, cannon and other stores relieved me from some anxiety. *I am satisfied that the abandonment of the old fort is a prudent measure*, and I have the fullest confidence that whatever relates to your actual command will be performed in the manner that the good of the service and the best interest of the country require.

(From S. VanRensselaer's Narrative: Appendix, p. 55.)

Colonel Baynes to Major General Brock.

MONTREAL, September 10, 1812.

SIR,—Sir George writes to you so fully upon the several subjects to which your letters refer that I have little left to communicate to you. Major Heathcote leaves this to-day with all the small description of ordnance stores intended for Amherstburg, but we have detained the 12-pounders and shot: as you have helped yourself so amply at Detroit it is imagined you do not now want them. I enclose a letter from Captain Roberts, who was, I suppose, induced to address himself direct to headquarters by an opportunity of doing so offering itself at the moment. The northwest gentlemen are very urgent in recommending a reinforcement in that quarter, but Sir George has told them that their representations must be addressed to you, who will act as you deem proper.

Your friend, Mr. Isaac Todd, is arrived and looking much better for his trip. He was suffered to pass by Albany and the lake. He tells me that Mr. Macdonnell is confirmed as Attorney-General, and that the governor's salary is increased £1,000 a year. I sincerely trust that it will soon be your own. Sir George has in his official despatches, after paying that tribute of praise so justly your due, stated as his confirmed opinion that the salvation of the Upper Province has in a very great measure arisen from the civil and military authority being combined in able hands. The prisoners with their general arrived here on Sunday night. As they had not halted since they left Kingston and were in a very dirty state, we kept them here on Monday, and they yesterday proceeded to William Henry, on their way to Quebec. The officers are to be on parole in Charlesbourg and the men confined on board two transports in the river. Sir George has permitted most of the officers who have families with them to return on their parole: four of them are proposed to be exchanged for the officers of the Royal Scots taken by the *Essex* frigate. Sir George has also consented to allow General Hull to return upon his parole. He is loud in his complaints against the Government at Washington, and the General thinks that his voice in the universal cry may be attended with beneficial effects, and has allowed him to return and enter the lists. General Hull appears to possess less feeling and sense of shame than any man in his situation could be supposed to do. He seems to be perfectly satisfied with himself, is lavish of censure upon his government, but appears to think that the most scrupulous cannot attach the slightest blame to his own immediate conduct at Detroit. The grounds upon which he rests his defence are not, I fancy, well founded, for he told us that he had not gunpowder at Detroit for the service of one day. Sir George has since shown him the return of the large supply found in the fort; it did not create a blush, but he made no reply. He professes great surprise and admiration at the zeal and military preparation he has everywhere witnessed; that it was entirely unlooked for, and that he has no doubt that his friend, General Dearborn, will share his fate if he has the imprudence to follow his example. Hull seems cunning and unprincipled. How much reliance is to be placed on his professions time will shew.

General Dearborn has certainly left Albany for Skeensborough, at the head of the lake, where great preparations have been making in collecting boats and sending the regulars from Greenbush to the stations in our vicinity. Major Cotton, with about 300 men, half of the King's Regiment, is stationed at Isle Aux Noix, and two gun-boats have been carried into the river, as the enemy's preparations seem to indicate that quarter as their point of attack. Colonel Murray commands at St. John's, and will give them a warm reception. I do not feel a doubt of Jonathan's complete discomfiture and disgrace if he make the attempt. We could, I fancy, bring as many men as he will be able to persuade into the field and of very superior stuff, for our militia have really improved beyond all expectation in discipline and with it in spirit and confidence. This town would turn out 2,000 volunteer militia, a great proportion of whom are clothed and very tolerably drilled. We have destroyed all the roads of communication in our front, leaving open the water route only, and these woody positions will be shortly occupied by the Indians of this neighborhood and a corps of volunteer *voyageur* Canadians. The enemy's preparations, however, may be a feint to cover some plans in agitation against your Province.

(From Tupper's Life of Brock, pp. 304-6.)

Colonel Procter to Major General Brock.

DETROIT, September 10, 1812.

SIR,—I have just received your letter from Kingston of the 4th instant, and shall act accordingly. Enclosed I send a return of the ordnance and ordnance stores sent in the *Queen Charlotte*; no shot were sent, because, as I understand, there is already a quantity of each calibre at Fort George. The remainder of the prisoners of war, excepting some sick and wounded, were also sent on board the *Charlotte* with a guard of two subaltern officers and forty men of the 41st Regiment, whom I cannot afford to part with. I had ordered the deserters on board, but have had the dissatisfaction to find that they have not been sent. Annexed is also a list of provisions and stores captured on the 16th ultimo. I assented in the absence of Lieut.-Colonel Nichol for a short time on the urgency of his private affairs and the probability of the armistice continuing. Major Givins has been of great assistance to me in his department. I regret his going, but I could not detain him longer than there was a probability of my returning soon to Fort George. As you directed, a sergeant of the 41st Regiment has been appointed to act as deputy barrackmaster at this place. I shall be much gratified if it should be confirmed. I found on my arrival here that the boats and the *engagés* of the South West Company had been detained and employed in the service. They have been under the direction of Lieutenant Bender, 41st Regiment, and have been of the greatest use. They have been provisioned, and I suppose are entitled to pay as militia. I am sending a detachment of the 41st Regiment and militia with 3-pounders to aid the Indians against Fort Wayne. It shall be conducted with every prudence and expedition. The *Detroit* will sail in a few days for Fort Erie. Judge Campbell goes in her. I have required 100 more of the militia, making them 400, besides the 30 mounted who are to keep up the communication with the Moravian Town. 150 of the Mackina Indians are arrived. They met the express sixty miles on this side of Mackina. They are just in time for Fort Wayne. The *Hunter* shall sail without delay.

(From Tupper's Life of Brock, pp. 307-8.)

Lieut.-Col. Fenwick to Major General VanRensselaer.

FORT NIAGARA, Sept. 10th, 1812.

SIR,—Fatigued and harassed as the troops have been, I really do not think our situation a safe one. I submit to your judgment whether the troops should not be concentrated; as they are all young and undisciplined, they may be cut up in detail. The defence of this place is precarious, outside of the storehouse. I apprehend nothing but surprise. We should be, then, prepared to act in force and in any given point. The contractor is very inattentive. Our men are extremely dissatisfied. The enemy has erected another battery. I ordered the light artillery down. They called in their fatigue parties and prepared for attack—the Indians moving in every direction. The movement puzzles them, and I am pleased at giving them so much trouble. I hope I shall have the honor of a visit from you to-morrow.

I salute you, General, with consideration and respect.

(From S. VanRensselaer's Narrative: Appendix, p. 47.)

Major General VanRensslaer to Major General Dearborn.

HEADQUARTERS, LEWISTON, 10th Sept., 1812.

SIR,—When I had the honor of receiving your communication of the 1st inst., acquainting me of the dispositions you are making to reinforce me upon this frontier with men, cannon, musketry, stores, &c., my attention was immediately arrested by the proposition of sending them from Oswego to Niagara or, indeed, any part of that distance, by water. It will be recollected that the passage of Lieut.-Col. Fenwick with boats was rendered safe under a clause of the agreement for the observance of the armistice. But upon the receipt of your letter my own opinion was against risking anything hereafter along that shore by water, but I wished further information on the subject before I should advise you. The opinions of others whom I have advised with on this subject, and who are competent judges, fully accord with my own, that it would be very hazardous for the batteaux to attempt coming from Oswego to Niagara in the very face of our active enemy having command of the water. The batteaux might and probably would have some days of head wind, and in such a case it would be next to impossible that they should escape the observation of the enemy, and when once discovered they would undoubtedly be attacked in some place where the landing could be effected with most difficulty. My opinion is further strengthened by some late movements of the enemy. The day after the termination of the armistice the *Royal George* and another armed vessel chased some vessels returning from Niagara to Oswego into the Genesee River and fired a few shot. This has excited an alarm among the inhabitants, and, according to the custom prevailing on the whole frontier, they have sent a deputation to me praying protection. I have ordered them some ammunition; I can do no more. I am so entirely convinced that the cargoes of the batteaux will be in danger on the passage from Oswego to Niagara that I shall send an express to Three River Point to have the batteaux come up to Cayuga Bridge and there land their cargoes, to be transported by land to this place. I shall bestow further consideration on this subject.*

Believing that the best use I can make of the old mess-house at Niagara is to convert it into a battery, I have ordered the roof to be taken off, the walls above the upper floor to be strengthened by embankments of earth on the inner side, and two twelve-pounders and one howitzer mounted in that battery. It is high and may perhaps avail us something. I expect it will be prepared in this manner in a day or two. I was yesterday there and the roof was nearly taken down.

(From S. VanRensselaer's Narrative: Appendix, p. 47.)

Captain J. Whistler to Gen. VanRensselaer.

PRESQUE ISLE, 11th Sept., 1812.

DEAR GENERAL,—

. . . .

. . . . This moment I have seen a letter from Genl. Wadsworth of the State of Ohio to Genl. Keler of this post, in which he mentioned the capture of Fort Dearborn at Chigkaga and nearly all the garrison put to the sword, and the enemy are now erecting a garrison at the rapids of the Miamy, and a large force of Indians are on their way against Fort Wayne and Vincennes in great expectation of success.

The enemy have left four of the 24-pounders at Malden: the other five of the 24-pounders they have shipped to Fort George. This is all the news I have at present to communicate: the latter, I expect, you ought to be made acquainted with. I think from the large body of Indians which have gone against Fort Wayne you have nothing to fear as to Indians. . . . .

(From Bonney's Historical Gleanings, pp. 230-1.)

Colonel S. VanRensselaer to Major General Morgan Lewis.

HEADQUARTERS, Sept. 11, 1812.

MY DEAR SIR,—To you I am fully persuaded I can write with confidence on the state of affairs in this quarter, and if you think the interest of the service will be promoted by a disclosure of my name, you are at liberty to make any use of it you please, what-

---

* Perhaps some precautions may be adopted to get round the batteaux to the Eighteen-Mile Creek, or to some position on the lake shore, from whence they may be drawn overland to this place.

ever inconvenience it may put me to, for I shall state facts and those only.

Since the surrender of General Hull it has been the study of John C. Spencer, Col. Brooks, Qr.-Mr.-General Porter and several others, to cause confusion and distrust among the troops on this frontier to answer party purposes against the commander. They have so far succeeded in the camp and in the country, that in the former it is only whispered, but in the latter it is openly said, that General VanRensselaer is a traitor to his country, and the surrender of his army when it crosses the river is the price of his infamy. Honest and honorable men must regret this depravity in human nature. Those scoundrels know better, and you and I know that a more honest man does not exist, and one who has the interest of the country more at heart. But, with all his amiable qualities, his usefulness here in my opinion is destroyed by this unjust and unwarrantable jealousy. He cannot enforce that subordination which is so necessary to the safety and glory of the troops he commands. If Gen. Armstrong or any other man of the same politics with the government did command here, this difficulty would be removed. There is a field of glory in view for any man of ambition, which Gen. V. R., as well as myself, would regret to forego if necessity did not compel us: it would be well if Gen. Dearborn could with propriety remove him to New York or some other place where his position may be equal to his sacrifices in private life. We are encamped at this place with two regiments of militia to guard the most important pass on the river: Col. Fenwick with the regular troops in and about Fort Niagara. Col. Bloom's lately come on at Niagara Falls, and Col. Swift's at Buffalo.

The whole effective force of militia, including officers, you will find by the within returns amounts to 1,633 fit for duty. We are in want of almost everything. Our Quartermaster, Peter B. Porter, is speculating and attending to mischief and his private affairs. He speaks in very disrespectful terms of Mr. Madison, and tries to impress on the minds of the people the necessity of a change of men. But, notwithstanding these discouraging prospects, we shall do what men under these circumstances can. A strong battery has been thrown up a mile above Fort Niagara and immediately opposite Fort George, in which the four heavy cannon have been placed, and, contrary to the opinion of Col. Fenwick when he first came on, we will attempt to maintain the fort, which will be all important to our future operations. The roof has been taken from a large stone house, and on the third floor two twelve-pounders and a howitzer placed. This battery commands Fort George and four batteries in the vicinity, and if a parapet of earth well rammed on the inside of the two and-a-half feet stone wall was thrown up it might bid defiance to the enemy, but unfortunately Col. Fenwick and Capt. Leonard are too much addicted to liquor to attend to this duty as they should, and if they were removed from this command it would give rise to much greater dissensions. Besides, we have no one as fit for this all important service as Col. Fenwick, if he was at all times himself. Last Tuesday at 12 o'clock the armistice ceased, on which we supposed the enemy would open their batteries of at least fifty pieces on our lines. Gen. VanRensselaer continued here in order to move the troops to any point that might be attacked, while I went to the garrison below. I found on my arrival all in confusion. I immediately ordered a strong detachment to clear a battery in the stone house, while others were dismounting the two twelves and a howitzer and getting them on the platform, to the command of which Capt. Leonard's company was assigned. The two block-houses, in each of which are six-pounders, Capt. McKeon's company was to defend. All this was accomplished by twelve. At that hour our works, as well as the British, were manned, the matches burning, and I expected every moment to see the rafters of the old mess-house knocked about my head, and I was disappointed, and we have ever since been in peace, but preparing with little trouble to make it as strong as any work can be and ready for action. I enclose the last Buffalo paper.

(From Bonney's Historical Gleanings, pp. 231-2.)

Governor Tompkins to Captain Peter Magher.

ALBANY, Sept. 11, 1812.

I was absent from this place when your letter of the 31st ultimo came to hand.

In compliance with your request, I have addressed a letter to Col. Stranahan, desiring him to attach the eight men drafted from the light infantry company under your command to your company whenever the rest of your company shall come up with his regiment.

There is an indispensable necessity for ordering out a number of independent corps under and pursuant to the Act of Congress passed 20th February, 1795, of which a copy is enclosed for your information. You will therefore assemble the rest of your company and join Col. Stranahan's regiment as soon as possible. Should his regiment have left Litchfield before you can join them, you will follow them with as rapid marches as possible. The bearer takes out tents, camp kettles and knapsacks for your company. They must find their own blankets and canteens; also musket, cartridge box, &c. Those who may be deficient in muskets will be supplied at Canandaigua or on their arrival at Niagara. The propriety of reinforcing General VanRensselaer without delay compels me to urge upon you the most vigilant and prompt attention to the execution of this order. The Brigade-Quartermaster Packard will pay the expense of transportation if you should be able to rendezvous and march with the regiment; but if the regiment should have marched before your company can rendezvous, the bearer is directed to return to Cherry Valley and supply you with some cash to defray the contingent expenses of your march on the road.

To Captain Peter Magher.

(Tompkins' Papers, New York State Library.)

N. B. Boileau to Major General Dearborn.

HARRISBURG, September 11, 1812.

SIR,—Yours of the 2d instant has been duly received by the Governor. I have the honor to inform you that yours of the 13th ult. was received by him at Selin's Grove the 21st. He immediately repaired to the seat of government at this place, and on the 25th issued general orders for twenty-four hundred volunteers to rendezvous at Meadville on the 25th day of the present month, and from thence to march with all possible despatch to Buffalo. On the 26th ult. a letter, enclosing general orders, was directed to you at Greenbush and put in the mail at this place. On the 5th instant the Governor issued general orders, agreeably to the request of the Secretary at War, for two thousand two hundred more of the militia of this State to rendezvous at Pittsburg on the 2d of October, and from thence to join the troops assembling in the State. A letter also, enclosing the last mentioned orders, was put in the mail at this place, directed to you at Greenbush. That the Governor's letter of the 26th ult. has not reached you is a matter of surprise and regret. The detachment assembling at Meadville will proceed on to Buffalo, unless otherwise directed by you. You will therefore forward to the commanding officer of that detachment such orders as you may deem expedient. It will be commanded by a Brigadier-General, but as he was to be elected by the volunteers comprising the detachment, I cannot yet give you his name.

The Adjutant-General, William Reed, Esq., will attend, and is gone to Meadville to take command until the detachment is organized. Any instructions enclosed to him will be punctually attended to. You will therefore please to communicate with him as early as possible.

(Pennsylvania Archives, Second Series, Vol. XII., pp. 610-11.)

Sir George Prevost to Earl Bathurst.

(No. 8.)

MONTREAL, 12th Sept., 1812.

MY LORD,—I have been honored with Your Lordship's despatch of the 4th of July. The despatches I have had the honor of addressing to Your Lordship and to Lord Liverpool since the declaration of war by the Congress of the United States against Great Britain will have afforded sufficient evidence to His Majesty's Government that I could not, consistent with my duty to my king and country, suspend the preparations for defence which I had been induced to make in consequence of the precarious state of the relations between Great Britain and America.

The convincing proof which His Royal Highness the Prince Regent has given of his desire to conciliate the government and people of the United States by his declaration of the 23d of June, is not deemed sufficient by the President for the restoration of tranquillity to the Provinces, and Your Lordship will hear with surprise that every exertion is making by that Government for the subjugation of the Canadas that they may, if successful, be enabled in proud and haughty terms to commence their negotiations for a peace.

Notwithstanding the complete and disgraceful failure of the enemy in their attack upon the western frontiers of Upper Canada, which I have already had the honor of detailing to Your Lordship in my former despatches, I learn by a despatch from M. Genl. Brock, dated at Fort George the 7th inst., that they were assembling in great strength in front of our positions on the Niagara frontier, and that he has every reason to believe from the great reinforcements they had recently received in troops, artillery and stores that they meditate an immediate invasion of the Province in that quarter. Although I have been induced to withdraw from Lower Canada a considerable body of troops for the purpose of enabling Genl. Brock to meet the threatened attacks in the Upper Province, he still urges most strongly for fresh reinforcements to oppose the great force which the enemy are preparing to bring against him, but as the preparations and movements they are making towards the borders of this Province in the neighborhood of Montreal are strongly indicative of their intention and desire to penetrate in that direction, I have not been able in the present weak state of the regular force in this Province to spare one man from its defence. The necessity therefore of strengthening me by a further reinforcement of troops, to be employed both in Upper and Lower Canada, must be obvious to Your Lordship, nor will it, I trust, be disregarded, if the greater interests of the country will admit of it. The disposition of the people in both Provinces, I am disposed to believe, is good, and, provided they can be supported, I think they can be depended upon, but I fear not much reliance can be placed upon them in the hour of adversity.

I am sorry to say the stores and accoutrements are not yet arrived, and that the want of clothing for the Glengarry Fencibles is a very serious inconvenience to His Majesty's service. I now humbly hope the precautionary measures I have considered it my indispensable duty to pursue, and which have hitherto enabled me to check the designs of the Government of the United States, will be favorably represented by Your Lordship for His Royal Highness's gracious approbation.

(Canadian Archives. Q. 118, p. 247.)

Major General Brock to Sir George Prevost.

FORT GEORGE, September 13, 1812.

SIR,—The movements of the enemy just before the expiration of the armistice indicated an intention of commencing active operations, but now everything tends to different measures.

The intelligence lately received and upon which I can safely rely, represents the disposition of the troops on the opposite shore as very licentious and anxious for deserting a service in which they are not only badly fed but remain without pay. The government paper is not received in common intercourse, consequently is inapplicable to the payment of the troops.

Great sickness prevails along the whole line. The officers of the 49th Regt., quartered opposite Black Rock, have observed during the last week one and two military funerals of a day. Nothing can confirm the above statement more strongly than the desertion of seven men from the 6th United States Regiment, six of whom, however, perished in the attempt to cross the river, and of two at noon this day, one of whom effected his purpose, but the other, alarmed at the heavy fire of the guard, returned and was instantly seized. They, of course, complain of bad usage, bad and scanty food and a total want of pay. The two companies to which these men belong arrived during the cessation of hostilities from Bushy Park. They were sixty rank and file each, out of which thirty, independently of those lost since yesterday, have deserted. Many are sick, and almost all determined to seize the first opportunity to follow their example. Nothing can be more wretched than the state of discipline existing among the troops. The militia, they pretend, are better fed and otherwise better treated, which occasions great jealousy. As both private accounts and those of deserters agree as to the main facts, there can be no doubts of much dissatisfaction prevailing among the troops. A great deal could be effected against such a body at this moment, but keeping in view Your Excellency's instructions and aware of the policy of permitting such a force to dwindle away by its own inefficient means, I do not contemplate any immediate attack. The enemy has taken down the roof of the large stone house in Fort Niagara, upon which he has placed two brass twelve-pounders. He has likewise constructed a battery precisely in front of our fort. I am daily in expectation of the arrival of the *Queen Charlotte* from Detroit, which will give us such a superiority in artillery as will soon silence anything that he can bring against the fort.

P. S.—The enclosed is the last communication received from Amherstburg.

(Canadian Archives, C. 677.)

Militia General Orders.

HEADQUARTERS, FORT GEORGE,
13th September, 1812.

Militia General Orders.

His Honor Major General Brock has been pleased to appoint Alexander Bryson, gentleman, to be second lieutenant in Captain Powell's company, 1st Lincoln artillery. Commission dated 13th September, 1812.

By order.

J. MACDONALD,
Lt.-Col., Militia, P. A. D. C.

General Orders.

HEADQUARTERS, GREEN BUSH, September 13, 1812.

Brigadier-General Alexander Smyth will proceed to Niagara and take the command of the brigade composed of the fifth, twelfth, thirteenth, fourteenth, and twentieth regiments as they arrive at or near Niagara, and he will be respected and obeyed accordingly. On his arrival at Niagara, or in the vicinity of Major General Van-Rensselaer's headquarters, he will report himself to that officer.

By order of Major General Dearborn.

E. BEEBE, Acting Adjutant-General.

From Sir George Prevost to Major General Brock.

MONTREAL, September 14, 1812.

SIR,—Captain Fulton arrived on the 11th instant with your letter of the 7th. The intelligence you have communicated by it convinces me of the necessity of the evacuation of Fort Detroit, unless the operations of the enemy bear a character less indicative of determined hostile measures against your line in their front than they did when you last reported to me. You will therefore be pleased, subject to the discretion I have given you under the circumstances to which I have alluded, to take immediate steps for evacuating that post together with the territory of Michigan. By this measure you will be enabled to withdraw a greater number of the troops from Amherstburg instead of taking them from Colonel Vincent, whose regular force ought not on any account to be diminished.

I have already afforded you reinforcements to the full extent of my ability. You must not therefore expect a further supply of men from hence until I shall receive from England a considerable increase to the present regular force in this Province; the posture of affairs, particularly on this frontier, requires every soldier who is in the country.

In my last despatch from Lord Bathurst, dated the 4th of July, he tells me, "that His Majesty's Government trusts I will be enabled to suspend, with perfect safety, all extraordinary preparations for defence which I may have been induced to make in consequence of the precarious state of the relations between this country and the United States, and that as every specific requisition for warlike stores and accoutrements which had been received from me had been complied with, with the exception of the clothing of the corps proposed to be raised from the Glengarry Emigrants, he had not thought it necessary to direct the preparation of any further supplies." This will afford you a strong proof of the infatuation of His Majesty's ministers upon the subject of American affairs, and they shew how entirely I have been left to my own resources in the event which has taken place.

Judging from what you have already effected in Upper Canada, I do not doubt but that with your present means of defence you will be able to maintain your position at Fort George, and that the enemy will be again foiled in any further attempts they may make to invade the Province.

I leave to your discretion to decide on the necessity of sending a reinforcement to Michilimackinac.

(From Tupper's Life of Brock, pp. 308-9.)

General Orders.

ADJUTANT-GENERAL'S OFFICE,
HEADQUARTERS, MONTREAL, 14th Sept., 1812.

His Royal Highness the Prince Regent, in the name and on the behalf of His Majesty, has been pleased to make the following promotions and appointments in the army serving in British North America:—

41ST FOOT.

Lieutenant Charles Lane, from the Hereford militia, to be ensign without purchase.—16th June.

Lieutenant James Perrin, from the Limerick County militia, to be ditto.—30th June.

Lieutenant James Field, from the 1st Somerset militia, to be ditto.—23d June.

ROYAL NEWFOUNDLAND FENCIBLES.

Captain Charles Blankowitz, from half-pay of the Royal Staff Corps, to be captain of a company, vice Nairne, who exchanges.—13th June.

STAFF.

Major John Harvey of the 6th Garrison Battn., to be Deputy-Adjt.-General in Canada, with the rank of Lt.-Col. in the army, vice Ellis, appointed to the 6th Dragoons.—30th June.

LEAVE OF ABSENCE.

Lieutenant Sanderson, 41st Regt., from 4th May to 30th June.
Ensign Biddulph, do., 12th to 1st August.

EDWARD BAYNES.

Colonel Solomon VanRensselaer to General Peter B. Porter.

LEWISTON, 10 o'clock a. m., Sept. 14th, 1812.

SIR,—In consequence of your message to me, several interviews were had between our friends. It was at length agreed between them that they should meet at the first house above the Tonawanto bridge, and proceed from thence to Grand Island to select a spot for our meeting. On their arrival at that place on Saturday propositions to postpone the meeting were made on the part of your friend, which could not be acceded to by mine without consulting me. With that view they were to meet this morning at 8 o'clock at the Falls of Niagara. At this place my friend punctually attended, and now reports that neither your friend nor any apology appeared.

This very extraordinary conduct on your part, together with

the fact of your disclosing the affair in violation of the most solemn pledge of secrecy, and which has been most religiously adhered to on my part and that of my friend, to two or three persons besides your friend, and the information I have just received that General VanRensselaer was made acquainted with it and in consequence of which he has kept a watchful eye on all my actions, shows conclusively that you have trifled with me, and that it never was your intention to meet me, and I now declare that if you do not make me a suitable apology I shall at the proper time publish you to the world as a *poltroon*, a *coward* and a *scoundrel*.

I am, &c.,

SOL. VAN RENSSELAER.

P. B. Porter, Esq., Q. M., G. M. S., N. Y.

(From the *United States Gazette* of 30th January, 1813. File in Philadelphia Library.)

Letter to the Editor of the "Repository," of Canandaigua, N. Y.

MR. BEMIS,—The following interesting information was received from Jasper Parrish, Esqr., interpreter to the Six Nations and sub-agent of Indian affairs. It may be relied on as correct, and you will oblige a subscriber by publishing it in your paper:—

There was lately held at Buffalo a general council of Indians, consisting of the Six Nations and the Stockbridge and Delaware tribes. The council was very numerous and attended by a fuller representation of chiefs than any that has been held for many years. The agent for Indian affairs, Mr. Granger, and the sub-agent, Mr. Parrish, were both present. On the 8th inst., the Senecas, the Onondagas near Buffalo, and the Cayugas unanimously offered to take up the hatchet in favor of the United States in the present war. The chiefs who represented the Onondagas, living eastward of this, the Oneidas, the Stockbridge and Delaware Indians, not feeling authorized to pledge their warriors in so important a matter said they would go home and consult them on that subject, but expressed at the same time the most thorough conviction that all their warriors would also tender their services to the United States. The Indians who attended the council said their interests within the United States were too important to be given up without the strongest efforts to defend them, that they had been advising and laboring with the Indians in Canada for six years to induce them to remain at peace without effect, and were extremely urgent that their services should be accepted. Those who volunteered at the council agreed that they would go home so soon as the council fire was extinguished, arm and equip themselves for battle, and return again to Buffalo in ten days, and as there is no doubt but that the other warriors, whose chiefs were not authorized to pledge them, will adopt the same determination with their brethren, there will probably be within a fortnight at Buffalo between three and four hundred Indian warriors.

It has been uniformly the wish of the government that the Indians should take no part in the war. The Secretary-at-War wrote a letter, which was read and explained in this very council instructing the agent to exert himself to persuade the Indians to remain at peace, but the restless spirit of these sons of nature will not permit them to do so. The chiefs, though they are willing to do whatever they can to further the views of the United States, to whom they feel bound by strong ties, are unable to restrain their warriors. Their young men are clamorous to be employed. Under these circumstances the agent has been instructed to accept their services, to embody and organize them. It is believed by all who are acquainted with the Indian character that in this state of things the inhabitants upon the Niagara frontier will find greater safety than they could do in any other while hostile armies remain in their neighborhood. For if the earnest solicitations of the Indians that we should accept their aid had been denied, they would have been cool, perhaps distrustful towards us, and during this state of things should the British arms obtain any advantages over us, it is not improbable they might be induced to take up arms against us.

Sept. 14, 1812.

(From the *Repository* of Canandaigua, 15th September, 1812. File in the Wood Library, Canandaigua, N. Y.)

General Orders.

HEADQUARTERS, LEWISTON, September 15th, 1812.

The Quartermaster-General and the contractor will furnish on the order of Doctor Brown, hospital surgeon, the necessary supplies for the sick in camp and the hospital. To Doctor Brown the surgeons of regiments and corps will apply for supplies necessary for the accommodation of the sick under their care, and they are strictly enjoined to attend faithfully to the sick of the regiments and corps to which they are assigned, whether the sick are in camp or hospital.

The Quartermaster-General will furnish a sufficient quantity of straw for the accommodation of the troops in the camp and barracks. He will also furnish forage for the dragoon and other public horses, and cause the horses of Captain Camp's troops of volunteer cavalry to be appraised, as the law directs, without delay.

Lieut.-Col. Fenwick, the Quartermaster-General and the Commissary of military stores on this frontier, will without delay make returns to Major General VanRensselaer of all the public property of every description under their charge.

By order of Major General VanRensselaer.

SOL. VANRENSSELAER,
Aid-de-Camp.

Major General VanRensselaer to Lieut.-Col. Fenwick.

HEADQUARTERS, LEWISTON, 15th September, 1812.

SIR,—I have this moment received your note of this date. It is a fact too true that many of the arms both here and at the garrison are not fit for use. The armourers are here busily engaged; nevertheless I send you one of them. Please to order the line of sentries extended up the river as far as you deem expedient.

It seems to be impossible to obtain *grain* for our horses. I have this day issued an order to the Quartermaster-General as to forage, and shall make every effort in my power to get a supply. General Brock will undoubtedly make every effort. Let us employ every moment in making the best possible dispositions to receive him should he attempt an attack. As to the salt, the men and teams were left behind for the express purpose of removing it. If the service requires any more men for fatigue, I will send them immediately.

(From S. VanRensselaer's Narrative: Appendix, p. 49.)

Major General VanRensselaer to Governor Tompkins.

HEADQUARTERS, LEWISTON, 15th Sept., 1812.

SIR,—Agreeably to the instructions contained in Your Excellency's letter of the 14th ult., I have endeavored to keep Major General Dearborn fully advised of all my movements and operations since that time, and to my letters transmitted to him I beg leave to refer Your Excellency for particulars. If the little army under my command has not yet achieved anything very brilliant, I endeavor to console myself with the belief that we have not yet suffered any disgrace. My force is yet small, about 1600 militia. Of course the necessary service renders the duty of the troops very severe. They, however, endure it with as much patience as could be expected from men in their situation, many of them destitute of shoes, and indeed such clothing as is necessary for the approaching season, and they are all extremely clamorous for their pay. Some money must be furnished for the troops in a very short time, or the consequence of omitting it will severely affect the service, and at least render every movement heavy.

Since my first arrival at this frontier, I have found myself much embarrassed with the situation of Fort Niagara. To attempt defending it with the ordnance I found here I considered idle, and after the return of General Brock from Detroit I had great reason to believe that he could command a competent force to carry the garrison should he attack it. But apprehending the very serious consequences which must immediately result from abandoning the fort altogether, I took the precaution of removing the most valuable stores and determined to risk events until Colonel Fenwick should arrive, when I might avail myself of his opinion, at least, and of the ordnance he has with him should it be deemed advisable to attempt holding the garrison. By suspending the notice for the termination of the armistice, Lieut.-Colonel Fenwick arrived safe with the cannon and stores under his charge at the Four-Mile Creek. Fort Niagara became one of the first subjects of deliberation, and it was determined to attempt maintaining it. For this purpose it was deemed expedient to remove the roof from the old stone mess-house and convert the upper story into a battery, to be mounted with two twelve-pounders and one howitzer. I also determined to throw up a strong battery on the bank of the river about a mile above the garrison, nearly opposite the main battery on the Canadian shore, and there mount three 18-pounders. As the enemy can rake the river road from this to the garrison even with musketry, I determined to cut a road for communication from my camp to the garrison in the woods, out of the reach of the enemy's fire. These have been the objects of our fatigue for some days past, and are all of them nearly completed. These operations have produced great activity at Fort George. No sooner were our works commenced, than the enemy began opposing batteries. Their force is certainly very respectable and constantly employed. Whether the enemy will attack Fort Niagara or not, is impossible for me to say. There are some very imperious considerations to urge them to it. Newark is a very considerable village. The enemy have there some good barracks and many accommodations for winter quarters, and [whatever] might be the final result of a bombardment, the enemy must inevitably suffer very considerably. My present opinion is that I had better attempt to maintain the garrison than to risk the consequences of abandoning it.

Liable as I am to an attempt from the enemy at any hour, and my troops worn down by fatigue, I have resorted to a measure which perhaps exceeds the letter of my orders, yet considering that not only the tranquillity of this frontier, but possibly the safety of my little army may yet be at stake, and having been advised by Major General Dearborn to adopt every measure of precaution against surprise from a strong force which he had reason to believe the enemy are directing against me, I have ordered a detachment of 500 men from Brigadier-General Hopkins's brigade, and some companies of the detachment have actually marched. I wish to receive Your Excellency's early instructions on this subject, as at present I only consider these troops ordered out during your pleasure.

From a source not to be doubted I learn that the enemy are forwarding very large supplies of arms and military stores to Upper Canada. One hundred loaded boats have lately come up the St. Lawrence, also two regiments are on the way to Upper Canada.

When I last had the pleasure of seeing Major General Hall, he expressed to me his wish to learn Your Excellency's pleasure as to his continuance in service, and I beg leave also to express my desire that he should be satisfied as to his future course.

Having been advised by Major General Dearborn that forty batteaux with cargoes for the use of this army were on their way from Schenectady to Niagara by the way of Oswego, I have advised him of the danger to be apprehended in a voyage from Oswego to Niagara, as I am clearly of opinion, from the best information, that that passage ought not to be attempted by the boats with their cargoes, and fearing that my despatch might not reach General Dearborn in season for him to act, I have by express ordered the commanding officer of the boats to stop at the Three River Point, come up to the Cayuga bridge and land the cargoes and then to go down to Oswego, adopt every precaution, and attempt to get the boats around to the Eighteen-Mile Creek. The Quartermaster has deputed a person to receive the cargoes at Cayuga, and procure the necessary transport to Black Rock.

The alarm which lately took place in the County of Ontario by the enemy's ships chasing some vessels into the mouth of the Genesee River, has induced Judge Atwater to make a communication to me of a very unpleasant nature. After stating the great zeal with which the militia turned out, he says, "but, sir, I lament when I tell you that neither arms nor ammunition are provided for these brave men: no, not one musket to six men that would cheerfully risk their lives in defence of their country." He says, "they are destitute of arms and ammunition: they are neither of them to be purchased in the county."

(Tompkins' Papers, Vol. VIII., pp. 149-153. New York State Library.)

From the Buffalo Gazette, Tuesday, 15th September, 1812.

Yesterday afternoon the *Queen Charlotte* arrived at Fort Erie in seven days from Detroit. A flag of truce soon landed at Buffalo Creek, Major Atwater and Lieutenant John L. Eastman, who gave an account of the fall of Fort Dearborn. (Chicago.)

On Friday evening, the 11th inst., Major General Hall arrived at this place, where, we understand, he will make his headquarters. He is assigned to the command of the troops at Black Rock, the detachment from General Hopkins's brigade and such other troops as may be ordered into service here. We are correctly informed that 2,000 troops from Pennsylvania are expected at this place. They are to rendezvous at Meadville on the 25th, and will probably arrive here by the last of the month.

Lieut.-Colonel Fenwick of the United States Light Artillery arrived at Fort Niagara on the 4th inst., with some pieces of heavy ordnance by water. He was escorted by two companies of riflemen from Oswego, under the command of Captains Kellogg* and Bristol. We understand these companies will remain on this frontier. They make a very martial appearance.

(File in Buffalo Public Library.)

Major Wm. Howe Cuyler to Colonel S. VanRensselaer.

BUFFALO, 16th Sept., 1812.

MY DEAR SIR,—I enclose you a return of the ordnance, &c., at Buffalo, agreeable to Major Gen. VanRensselaer's request, by Lieut. Gansevoort, immediately on the receipt of which I waited on Genl. Porter and requested a return from him of the ordnance at the Rock, equipage, fixed and unfixed ammunition, which he promised to make me last night. Failing to do so, I this morning addressed a note to him and sent my servant, who, finding he had left the Rock for Lewiston, rode on and overtook him and delivered my note. I have not been furnished with a return from him. I beg you to assure Genl. VanRensselaer that, as speedily as possible after I am furnished with an account of what was required, I shall lose no time in making a return to him. Lt. Gansevoort will inform you of some alarms we have had. My General will communicate with yours. We send you three prisoners from the *Queen Charlotte*, who we have reason to expect have come over with improper views. Lt. Gansevoort has charge of them, and will, of course, take them to headquaters. *In all things* depend upon my most prompt and

* Editor of the *Manlius Times*.

cordial co-operation. I am not yet enabled to make a return of the force at the Rock and this place, owing to the irregularity of the returns made to me, which I am endeavoring to correct as speedily as possible. It shall be made as soon as possible.

(From Bonney's Historical Gleanings, p. 232.)

Extract of a Letter from ——— to Major General VanRensselaer.

16th Sept., 1812.

From Tice Horn's, on Lake Erie, nine miles above Fort George (sic), runs a road in a northwestwardly direction, called the Ridge Road. On this road is stationed a corps of flying artillery of sixteen guns of different bores, with a troop of cavalry of 72 privates. Both corps are militia, but perfectly equipped and in excellent order. No pains have been spared to have the best horses. The artillery is in constant exercise and move with great rapidity. Four hundred men are stationed about a mile and a half in the rear of Fort Erie, and 1,000 are held in constant readiness to march from different points as occasion may require. None of these troops appear on the river in the daytime, (such is the positive orders of General Brock,) but detachments are marched down every night and return before daylight. As I understand my information, these troops, with those that appear on the river, are destined for the defense of the shore from Fort Erie down to the point where the river road is intersected by the Ridge Road. Probably similiar arrangements are made all along the line, according to circumstances.

General Brock has paid attention to every particular that can relate to the future resources of the Province under his charge, as well as to its immediate defence. The harvest has been got in tolerably well, and greater preparation is making for sowing grain than was ever made before. The militia duty is modified as much as possible to suit the circumstances of the people, and measures taken to prevent them from feeling the burden of the war. The women work in the fields, encouragement being given for that purpose.

When General Hull's proclamation appeared it had its effect, there being a security for private property contained in it. Most of the inhabitants would willingly have submitted, but when it was found that private property was seized without [compensation?] the public sentiment entirely changed. The success of General Brock established the change of sentiment. He has since made the most of it, has become personally highly popular and, in short, has taken every measure that a judicious officer could take in his circumstances for the securing of this Province. A determination now prevails among the people to defend their country.

(Tompkins' Papers, Vol. VIII., pp. 175-7, New York State Library.)

Captain Samuel T. Dyson, U. S. Regt. of Artillery, to Major General Brock.

FORT GEORGE, 16th Sept., 1812.

Permit me, Sir, to mention to you the situation of the prisoners under my command. They have received no clothing from the government since last October and are almost destitute of every article of the kind. I understand there are six casks of clothing, an invoice of which I have in my possession, and was destined for Detroit for my company, now lying at Fort Niagara. If there could be any arrangement between the two governments so as to get them across it would relieve the suffering prisoners much. I also take the liberty to mention there are several men among them old, infirm and unfit for any kind of military service, and some with large families of children. If they could obtain a parole to go to the States, it would be a great relief to them.

Governor Snyder to the Secretary at War.

HARRISBURG, 16th September, 1812.

SIR,—To make up possible deficiencies, I ordered to rendezvous at Meadville 2,516 volunteers, at Pittsburg 2,214 drafted militia.

The promptitude with which the orders were obeyed induce the belief that the whole, or nearly the whole, number will rendezvous at both places. Permit me, through you, to suggest to the President the propriety of employing the surplus number of both detachments in the defence of Erie. If the President should so determine, I would further suggest that from the volunteer and drafted men of the Sixteenth Division of Pennsylvania militia, composed of the Counties of Erie, Crawford, Warren, Mercer, Venango, Beaver and Butler, might be detached the said surplus for the defence of that important post. For reasons, I beg leave to refer to the representation made by Judge Moore and others, a copy whereof was forwarded to you under date of yesterday. William Reed, Adjutant-General, who commands both detachments until organized for their march, will promptly obey any directions given by the President. Permit me again to ask an early answer, and to assure you of my perfect consideration and esteem.

(Pennsylvania Archives, Second Series, Vol. XII., p. 616.)

Major General VanRensselaer to Major General Dearborn.

HEADQUARTERS, LEWISTON, 17th September, 1812.

SIR.—The situation of my little army is becoming every day more and more interesting, and I believe existing circumstances would warrant me in saying critical. As soon as our operations at and near Fort Niagara indicated a disposition to maintain the garrison, the enemy became exceedingly active. New works were thrown up and old ones modified to meet us at every point. Their works appear now to be all completed, and they are daily receiving very considerable reinforcements of men. Last evening the *Royal George* arrived at Fort George with about two hundred artillerists. About one hundred boats loaded with stores for the British army in Upper Canada have lately passed up the St. Lawrence. Two regiments of troops are also on their way up, and I am induced to believe that those lately arrived at Fort George are detachments from those regiments. The information which you had received on the subject of the enemy's reinforcements and destination was undoubtedly correct. Troops are also coming down from Fort Malden to Fort Erie. Indeed there can be no possible doubt that the enemy are very actively engaged in concentrating their forces to act in this vicinity. When the scene of action will open, I know not: it probably cannot be far distant. Such movements of the enemy have been observed for three or four days past as have induced many to believe that the hour of attack was at hand. On the 13th instant boats were engaged in putting a considerable detachment of troops on board a ship, which at evening got under way from Fort George and stood out into Lake Ontario. It was apprehended that these troops were that night to be landed on the south side of the lake in the rear of our guards. The night before last the enemy moved some boats from the landing at Queenston down the river. This excited alarm and late last night a rumor ran through the camp that the garrison was actually summoned to surrender. I only mention these things to show you what apprehensions prevail. Should the enemy attack, I have every reason to believe we shall be very severely pressed, but so serious will be the consequences of any retrograde movement or a total abandonment of Fort Niagara that upon mature consideration of all circumstances I have determined to hold if possible my present position and dispute every inch of ground. My force bears no proportion to the duties required, besides the discipline of the troops is not such as to warrant perfect reliance, and many of our arms are not fit for action. These are considerations which you, sir, and my fellow citizens, will do me the justice to bear in mind whatever result may happen. For the application of the means entrusted to me, I hope I shall be able to justify myself to my country. My greatest fear is that the troops destined to reinforce me will not join me in season. In every calculation heretofore made upon my reinforcements, both as to time and strength, I have been disappointed. Col. Bloom's regiment, which was reported to me before its arrival for seven hundred, is little more than four hundred.

I am erecting a storehouse and magazine upon the high ground in the rear of my camp, but for the want of teams, tools, and nails, the work proceeds but slowly. We build with logs, and rive our shingles from bolts of oak. It is with extreme difficulty we can procure teams upon any emergency. The horses of the cavalry and flying artillery are badly supplied with hay, and as for *grain* they are almost entirely destitute. I have completed the road through the woods from my camp to the garrison. Amidst all our difficulties, this is the most cheering day for the troops which I have witnessed. Their clamor for pay has been high and incessant. I felt many of its bad consequences and apprehend still, but assurances now received that their pay is near seem to elate them.

By the return of ordnance which I yesterday received from Fort Niagara, I discover that our two mortars are $10\frac{1}{2}$ inch instead of $13\frac{1}{2}$, as Capt. Leonard's memorandum to me states them. The shells will be calculated accordingly. I have enclosed a copy of a letter which I last night received from General Brock, covering an extract of a letter from Capt. Dyson, of the United States Regiment of Artillery, to him, and I this morning sent Col. VanRensselaer to Fort George, when he had an interview with Capt. Dyson, and such arrangements have been made that Capt. Dyson's company will this day receive their clothing from Fort Niagara. The other companies in Quebec, I learn from General Brock's letter, are in great distress for want of clothing.

P. S.—And to cheer up our hearts, we have picked up a birch bark on which is written a notice from the soldiers to the officers, that unless they were paid they would absolutely quit the field in 8 days from that time.

(From Bonney's Historical Gleanings, pp. 233-4.)

Major General Brock to Colonel Procter.

FORT GEORGE, September 17, 1812.

SIR,—I have had before me your several communications to the 11th instant, addressed to myself and to Major General Sheaffe. I approve of your having detached a party to aid in the reduction of Fort Wayne, not only because its destruction will render your position more secure, but also from the probable result of saving the garrison from sharing the fate of that of Chicago; but it must be explicitly understood that you are not to resort to offensive warfare for purposes of conquest. Your operations are to be confined to measures of defence and security. With this view, if you should have credible information of the assembling of bodies of troops to march against you, it may become necessary to destroy the fort at Sandusky and the road which runs through it from Cleveland to the foot of the rapids. The road from the River Raisin to Detroit is perhaps in too bad a state to offer any aid to the approach of an enemy except in the winter, and if a winter campaign should be contemplated against you it is probable that magazines would be formed in Cleveland and its vicinity, of all which you will of course inform yourself. In carrying on our operations in your quarter it is of primary importance that the confidence and good will of the Indians should be preserved, and that whatsoever can tend to produce a contrary effect should be carefully avoided. I therefore most strongly urge and enjoin your acting on those principles on every occasion that may offer, inculcating them in all those under your influence and enforcing them by your example, whether in your conduct towards the Indians or what may regard them, or in your language in speaking to or of them. I am aware that they commit irregularities at times, which may make this a difficult task, but you must endeavor to perform it, attending at the same time to the means already suggested to you for preventing as much as possible a repetition of disorderly conduct.

Colonel Elliott is a respectable gentlemanly man, but he by no means possesses the influence over the Indians which Captain McKee does. I recommend to you to promote as far as in you lies a good understanding with and between them and to observe a conciliating deportment and language towards the latter, that his great influence may be secured and employed in its fullest extent for the benefit of your district and for the general good. In conversation with him you may take an opportunity of intimating that I have not been unmindful of the interests of the Indians in my communications to ministers, and I wish you to learn (as if casually the subject of conversation) what stipulations they would propose for themselves or be willing to accede to in case either of failure or of success.

I understand that salvage has been demanded from individuals on several accounts for property recovered or restored, for patents, &c., &c. I lament that such a course has been adopted, for it was my intention, and it is now my wish, that our conduct in those matters should be governed by the broadest principles of liberality. You will therefore be pleased to have returned to the several individuals the amount which each may have paid as salvage on any account.

With respect to calling out the militia, I am particularly desirous that it should not be resorted to but in cases of urgent necessity, and then only in such numbers as may be indispensably necessary; if without risk or detriment to the public service any or either of those corps can be spared let them be dismissed.

I wish the engineer to proceed immediately in strengthening Fort Amherstburg, his plan for which I shall be glad to see as soon as possible.

Of the ordnance stores of every description, you will reserve such proportions as may be absolutely required for the public service in your district, and cause the remainder to be embarked and sent down to Fort Erie with the least possible delay.

I cannot at present make the change in the distribution of the 41st Regiment which you propose, but whenever circumstances may permit I shall be happy to accede to your wishes.

(From Tupper's Life of Brock, pp. 310-12.)

Major General VanRensselaer to Major General Brock.

HEADQUARTERS, LEWISTON, Sept. 17, 1812.

SIR,—I have the honor to acknowledge the receipt of your letter of yesterday evening, and extract of a letter addressed to you on the 15th instant by Captain Dyson of the United States regiment of artillery, also a packet addressed to the Honorable Albert Gallatin, Secretary of the Treasury of the United States.

Colonel VanRensselaer will have the honor to deliver this communication, and I have entrusted him to solicit your permission for an interview with Captain Dyson for the purpose of ascertaining particularly the condition of the prisoners of war under his charge, to the end that they may be relieved from Fort Niagara if practicable, and if not that I may, without delay, state their condition to the government, that they may receive from the proper department the earliest possible supplies.

The women and children and such other persons as have accompanied the detachment from Detroit and ought to be here received, I will immediately receive at Fort Niagara or such other convenient place as you may order them to be landed at.

In a communication which I some time since had the honor of receiving from Lieut.-Colonel Myers, he assured me that it had been the constant study of the general officer commanding on this line to discountenance by all means in his power the warfare of sentinels, yet the frequent recurrence of this warfare within a few days past would warrant the presumption that a different course has been adopted. I wish to be assured of this fact.

(From Tupper's Life of Brock, pp. 312-3.)

Major General Brock to Major General VanRensselaer.

HEADQUARTERS, FORT GEORGE, Sept. 17, 1812.

SIR,—I have the honor to acknowledge the receipt of your letter of this date. Captain Dyson has obtained my permission to cross on his parole to the United States; he, however, requested to remain till tomorrow to settle with the men of his detachment. He shall in the meantime have an interview with Colonel Van-Rensselaer.

Measures will be immediately taken to land the women and children at Fort Niagara.

It has been with the utmost regret that I have perceived within these few days a very heavy firing from both sides of the river. I am, however, given to understand that on all occasions it commenced on yours, and from the circumstances of the flag of truce which I did myself the honor to send over yesterday having been repeatedly fired upon while in the act of crossing the river, I am inclined to give full credit to the correctness of the information. Without, however, recurring to the past, you may rest assured on my repeating my most positive orders against the continuance of a practice which can only be injurious to individuals without promoting the object which both nations may have in view.

(From Tupper's Life of Brock, p. 313.)

Militia General Orders.

HEADQUARTERS, FORT GEORGE, 17th Sept., 1812.

Militia General Orders.

His Honor Major General Brock finds it necessary to direct that no expense shall be incurred by any militia officer without an order from the officer commanding the district.

By order,

J. MACDONELL, Lt.-Col.,
Militia P. A. D. C.

General Van Rensselaer to Governor Tompkins.

HEADQUARTERS, LEWISTON, 17th Sept., 1812.

SIR,—I have the honor to acknowledge the receipt of your packet by Major Moore, who arrived in camp last evening. The duties of the day are too pressing to allow me the leisure I could wish to answer your letter particularly. I must therefore beg leave to refer Your Excellency to my despatches to Major General Dearborn.

I cannot, however, but express the satisfaction I feel at the approbation which my conduct thus far in the campaign has received. To perform my duty, arduous as it is, is comparatively easy, but to determine what my duty is in a wide field of action where everything is unshaped and uncertain, is often a task of no small difficulty. I am conscious to myself that I have studied it faithfully, and performed to the best of my ability. My situation is growing every hour more interesting, perhaps critical: the particulars you will find in my letter to General Dearborn. But, with my little force, I shall certainly attempt to hold my position, with full reliance on Your Excellency's assurances that every effort will be made to support me.

A retrograde movement of this army upon the back of that disaster which has befallen the one at Detroit, would stamp a stigma upon the national character which time could not wipe away. I shall therefore try to hold out against superior numbers and every disadvantage, until I shall be reinforced.

I am happy to learn that the money to pay the troops is at hand. I announced it in orders this morning. The information cheers our camp, and I hope they will soon realize their expectations, for in truth their wants are many.

(Tompkins' Papers, Vol. VIII. pp. 159-161, New York State Library.)

General Orders.

HEADQUARTERS, LEWISTON, 17th Sept., 1812.

Major General VanRensselaer revokes the sentence of death pronounced against *Reuben Schuyler* and *Thomas Moore* by the court martial, whereof Captain Leonard was president, and by general orders of the ninth instant directed to be carried into execution on the eighteenth instant, at Fort Niagara.

This act of clemency of the Major General in declaring the full and absolute pardon of those unfortunate men, it is hoped will make a lasting impression on their future conduct in life, and that they will still show by their good behavior that they are worthy of a life which they had forfeited to their country and their God.

But let it not be presumed that this first act of lenity in the Major General will be extended to others. He is under obligations of duty to his country, and with these his feelings as a man shall not interpose.

The prisoners will be released and returned to their duty.

By order of Major General VanRensselaer.

      SOL. VANRENSSELAER, Aide-de-Camp.

Major General Dearborn to Major General VanRensselaer.

    HEADQUARTERS, GREENBUSH, Sept. 17th, 1812.

DEAR SIR,—Your letter of the 8th was this day received. I have ordered two regiments from this camp and two companies of artillery for Niagara. When they arrive with the regular troops and militia from the southward, and such additional numbers of militia as I reckon upon from this State, the aggregate force will, I presume, amount to upwards of six thousand. It is intended to have a force sufficient *to enable you to act with effect, although late*. Brigadier-General Smith (Smyth) will leave this place to-morrow to take command of his brigade of regular troops when they arrive. I persuade myself that you will not, under your present circumstances, risk more than prudence will justify ; and that, of course, you will be prepared *in case you are pushed to fall back*, so as not to hazard an action on very unequal footing. If the enemy should make an attempt on you his endeavor will undoubtedly be to cut off your retreat by light parties and Indians. You will excuse my repeated cautions, but from the best information I have received, I am induced to fear an attempt will be made on your post before sufficient reinforcements will reach you. This will be conveyed by a safe hand and in confidence.

(From S. VanRensselaer's Narrative: Appendix, p. 55.)

Major General Brock to Sir George Prevost.

    FORT GEORGE, September 18th, 1812.

SIR,—I have been honored with Your Excellency's despatch dated the 7th instant. I have implicitly followed Your Excellency's instructions and abstained, under great temptation and provocation, from every act of hostility. The information received from a deserter, and which I had the honor to detail in my last, is far from correct, and where credit is to be given the facts apply solely to the regular force. The militia, being selected from the most violent democrats, are generally inclined to invade this province.

Provisions are in tolerable plenty—the only complaint arises from a want of vegetables. It is currently reported that the enemy's force is to be increased to seven thousand, and that on their arrival an attack is immediately to be made. I am convinced that the militia would not keep together in their present situation without such a prospect, nor do I think the attempt can be long deferred. Sickness prevails in some degree along the line, but principally at Black Rock.

The flank companies of the Royal Newfoundland Regiment have joined me. A sergeant and twenty-five rank and file of the Veterans arrived at the same time, whom I propose sending to Michilimackinac. The enclosed letters from Colonel Procter will inform Your Excellency of a force having been detached under Captain Muir for the reduction of Fort Wayne. I gave orders previous to my leaving Amherstburg for it, which must have induced Colonel Procter to proceed, upon receiving intelligence of the recommencement of hostilities, without waiting for further directions. I regret that this service should have been undertaken contrary to Your Excellency's wishes or intentions, but I beg leave to assure Your Excellency that the principal object in sending a British force to Fort Wayne is with the hope of preserving the lives of the garrison. By the last accounts the place was invested by a numerous body of Indians, with very little prospect of being relieved. The prisoners of war, who know perfectly the situation of the garrison, rejoiced at the measure and give us full credit for our intentions.

The Indians were likewise looking to us for assistance. They heard of the armistice with every mark of jealousy, and had we refused to joining them in the expedition it is impossible to calculate the consequences. I have already been asked to pledge my word that England would enter into no negotiation in which their interests were not consulted, and could they be brought to imagine that we should desert them the consequences must be fatal.

I have perused with every possible attention Your Excellency's instructions, "that whenever I was informed that the enemy have made an attempt to penetrate into the Lower Province, I am to concentrate all my disposable force, and immediately make such a diversion as shall indicate a disposition to operate upon his lines of communication." My force is so scattered and so immediately required for the defence of the different posts at which it was stationed, that I am at a loss to know in what manner I can possibly act so as to produce the effect expected.

I shall be obliged to Your Excellency to direct five thousand pounds to be transmitted to the Receiver-General for the civil expenditure of this Province. Army bills, I make no doubt, will answer every purpose.

This despatch is entrusted to Lt.-Colonel Nichol, Quartermaster-General of the Militia, whom I take the liberty to introduce to Your Excellency as perfectly qualified, from his local knowledge and late return, to afford every information of the state of affairs in the Western District. He is instructed to make extensive purchases of necessaries for the use of the militia, and I have to entreat Your Excellency to indulge him with the means of a speedy conveyance back to this place.

(Canadian Archives, C. 677, p. 90.)

Major General Brock to Savery Brock.

FORT GEORGE, September 18, 1812.

DEAR BROTHER,—You doubtless feel much anxiety on my account. I am really placed in a most awkward predicament. If I get through my present difficulties with tolerable success, I cannot but obtain praise. But I have already surmounted difficulties of infinitely greater magnitude than any within my view. Were the Americans of one mind the opposition I could make would be unavailing, but I am not without hope that their divisions may be the saving of this province. A river of about 500 yards broad divides the troops. My instructions oblige me to adopt defensive measures, and I have evidenced greater forbearance than was ever practised on any former occasion. It is thought that without the aid of the sword, the American people may be brought to a due sense of their own interests. I firmly believe I could at this moment sweep everything before me from Fort Niagara to Buffalo—but my success would be transient.

I have now officers in whom I can confide. When the war commenced I was really obliged to seek assistance among the militia. The 41st is an uncommonly fine regiment, but wretchedly officered. Six companies of the 49th are with me here, and the remaining four at Kingston, under Vincent. Although the regiment has been ten years in this country, drinking rum without bounds, it is still respectable and apparently ardent for an opportunity to acquire distinction. It has five captains in England and two on the staff in this country, which leaves it bare of experienced officers. The U. S. regiments of the line desert over to us frequently, as the men are tired of their service: opportunities seldom offer, otherwise I have reason to think the greater part would follow the example. The militia, being chiefly composed of enraged democrats, are more ardent and anxious to engage, but they have neither subordination nor discipline. They die very fast. You will hear of some decided action in the course of a fortnight, or in all probability we shall return to a state of tranquillity. I say decisive, because if I should be beaten the Province is inevitably gone, and should I be victorious, I do not imagine the gentry from the other side will be anxious to return to the charge.

It is certainly something singular that we should be upwards of two months in a state of warfare, and that along this widely extended frontier not a single death, either natural or by the sword, should have occurred among the troops under my command, and we have not been altogether idle; nor has a single desertion taken place.

I am quite anxious for this state of warfare to end, as I much wish to join Lord Wellington and to see you all.

(From Tupper's Life of Brock, pp. 315-17.)

Lt.-Col. John R. Fenwick to General VanRensselaer.

FORT NIAGARA, Sept. 18, 1812.

SIR,—Yesterday afternoon was sent over in a flag eleven women and nineteen children. Their situation is a distressing one. There is also a fifer of the 1st U. S. Infantry. He brings from Gen. Brock no pass or certificate. I know not in what light to view them. I beg your instructions respecting these people. I don't think it prudent to leave them here. Your order revoking the sentence upon the two unfortunate criminals was carried into effect. The scene was affecting, and I trust will be attended with beneficial consequences. No occurrence of moment has happened since I last wrote you. I beg you to order a general court martial. We have four or five deserters.

(From Bonney's Historical Gleanings, p. 235.)

General Orders.

HEADQUARTERS, LEWISTON, Sept. 18, 1812.

By virtue of a power recently vested in the Major General by His Excellency Governor Tompkins, the following troops are ordered into immediate service and will repair without delay to headquarters.

CAVALRY.

Lieut.-Colonel Boughton will detach Major Evans and three full troops of cavalry, completely equipped with good horses, arms, accoutrements, blankets, &c.

ARTILLERY.

Captain Hart, Canandaigua, Ontario County.
Captain Pierce, Genesee, do. do.
Captain Ellicott, Batavia, Genesee do.
Captain Jacks, Junius, Seneca do.
Captain Compston, Aurelius, Cayuga do.

With their cannon, small arms, equipments, and blankets complete.

RIFLEMEN.

Major Gaylord's battalion, Steuben County.
Major Granger's battalion, Ontario County.
Captain Brown's company, of Lima, Ontario County.
Captain A. Bloom's company, Genoa, Cayuga County.
Captain Allen's or Lieut. Johnson's, Genoa, Cayuga County.
Captain Ireland's company, Fayette, Seneca County.

With their rifles powder horns, blankets, and everything complete.

LIGHT INFANTRY.

Captain Hill's company, Bristol, Ontario County.
Captain McKinstry's company, Penfield, Ontario County.
Captain White's Company, Palmyra, Ontario County.
Captain Sutton's company, Ovid, Seneca County.
Captain Terry's company, Ulysses, Seneca County.
Captain John Richardson's company, styled Cayuga Rangers, Auburn, Cayuga County.
Captain Saterly's company, Sempronius, Cayuga County.
Captain Solomon Woodworth's, Cato, Cayuga County.
Captain Noble's company, Warsaw, Genesee County.
Captain Ebenezer Hillebert's company, Attica, Genesee County.

With their arms, accoutrements, and blankets complete.

These troops will be inspected by the proper officers and marched the nearest route to this place with all possible despatch.

By order of Major General VanRensselaer.

(Tompkins' Papers, Vol. VIII., pp. 177-8, New York State Library.)

Lieut. Jesse D. Elliott to Captain Chauncey.

BUFFALO, Sept. 18, 1812.

SIR,—I have with all possible despatch repaired to the headquarters of General VanRensselaer. As regards my expedition, he is entirely uninformed. He has not the most distant idea of the navigation of Lake Erie, or of any of its resources. By his advice

I have consulted with General Porter, who is perfectly acquainted with every part of the lake. He is employed by the public to build many boats, which are intended for the troops when invading Canada. He has at the general expense agreed to build me four of the description named in your letter, and have them ready in a few days. I have contracted for a sufficient quantity of plank to deck and bottom two ships of 300 tons; have examined all the situations on Lake Erie; cannot get one that will answer our purpose. Those that have shelter have not a sufficient depth of water, and those that have water cannot be defended from the enemy and the violence of the weather. In extending my view to Niagara River, I find that immediately in its mouth, receiving its water from Lake Erie, we can be handsomely situated as regards building, fitting out, and erecting barracks and magazines. I enclose you a sketch of the River Niagara, where you will observe that about three miles on our side we have an island carrying from the lake only five feet of water, and on the north side twelve feet at all times; when with a strong southerly wind, 14. One difficulty attending it is the getting our vessels through the rapids, where the water runs about four knots, and being obliged to get by a strong battery. General VanRensselaer has informed me that he would remove that difficulty by getting possession of the battery. The roads are good with the exception of about 13 miles, which are intolerable bad. Provisions are plenty. The British have a force of considerable moment: one ship of 20 guns, 10 feet water, badly manned; one brig of 14 guns, one brig of 10 guns, and two schooners of 10 guns; some other vessels unmanned, say four in all. We have only six: a brig of 90 tons, the others are schooners from 40 to 80 tons, all good vessels, and in the intended place for a navy yard. As those vessels would not be sufficiently formidable to contend with the enemy at present, General VanRensselaer has thought it advisable to direct our attention to Lake Ontario, which he says is of all importance at this moment, suspend the fitting out of small vessels on Lake Erie, go on with the barracks and magazine, and collect the timber for building. During the armistice our vessels became very much dispersed—only a few of them at Sackett's Harbor, three were chased into Genesee River, and one into Oswego. They are not very distant from this. He has satisfied me of the necessity of our attention being directed to these four vessels. His letter to me I enclose a copy of for your perusal. The carpenters have not arrived. I have by express ordered them to Genesee Falls; will set out in the morning myself. I shall get on altering these vessels until I have your further commands. Should arming these vessels meet your approbation the ordnance had better immediately come on to this place, together with the officers and men. Our movements at this place will go on in the meantime as if attended to myself. Our movements as regarding the boats will be perfectly secret. The alterations to the vessels as well as building will be immediately in sight of the enemy. The river is so narrow that the soldiers are shooting at each other across. Ordnance for this place had better come on when the snow is on the ground, and then in sleds. It will not be possible to get through in wagons. Direct your letter to me at the Genesee Falls.

(Tompkins' Papers, Vol. VIII., pp. 189-190. New York State Library.

General Orders.

HEADQUARTERS, LEWISTON, September 19th, 1812.

The Major General calls the attention of the officers to the 41st, 42d, 43d, 44th, 45th, 46th and 53d articles of war, and directs that they shall be read to the troops. If any officer or soldier has the hardihood to violate either of them, he shall be treated as those articles direct. The shameful inattention to duty in the face of a powerful enemy, by many of the officers and soldiers, will render this resort necessary, however unpleasant it may be to the Major General.

In violation of a general order of the 19th August, several of the field officers did not attend parade duty yesterday. It is hoped that such conduct in them will not occur again, for if it should the Major General will be compelled to resort to measures which will be very unpleasant to himself and them.

The guards will be augmented this night, and if any officer or soldier discloses the watchword he will be dealt with as the 53d article of the rules and articles of war directs.

The officer of the day will direct every officer and soldier to be taken up after the beating of retreat, whether he has the countersign or not, if found out of camp without permission in writing from the Major General.

Lieut.-Col. Fenwick will order a general court martial for the trial of such prisoners of the United States troops as may be brought before the court, and report the proceedings without delay to the Major General.

By order of Major General VanRensselaer.

SOL. VANRENSSELAER, Aide-de-Camp.

Major General VanRensselaer to Major General Brock.

HEADQUARTERS, LEWISTON, 20th Sept., 1812.

SIR,—It was with extreme regret and concern that I yesterday learned through Lieut.-Col. Myers that in a repetition of the practice of firing between sentinels, which I have so often peremptorily prohibited, one shot has proved fatal to a man at the Lime Kilns, on the Canada shore. Immediately on receiving information of this unfortunate event, I caused strict inquiry to be made to the end that the offender, if discovered, might be punished according to his demerit. But the result of this inquiry has not furnished me with the least evidence against any man. I cannot ascertain that a single gun has been fired at or near the place from whence the shot was supposed to have been thrown.

That these firings have been repeatedly *commenced on* both sides is not to be questioned. The fact is established by the testimony of officers whose rank and character in both armies utterly precludes all doubt. It is a circumstance which in this explanation ought not to be omitted, that there may be on both sides the river—there certainly is reason to believe there are on this side—persons not under *immediate* command in either army who occasionally approach the river, discharge their pieces at the sentries and then escape unobserved in their retreats, while the fire thus begun is returned upon an unoffending sentinel. I have caused patrols to be sent out to take such persons, but without success.

I can only repeat, sir, that I deeply regret the unfortunate occurrence which has happened; that my orders against the practice which has occasioned it have been most peremptory; my efforts to enforce them are unremitting, and every attempt to convict anyone of disobedience as yet is unavailing.

(From S. VanRensselaer's Narrative: Appendix. p. 74.)

District General Order.

FORT GEORGE, 20th September, 1812.

The Grenadier company of the 49th Regt. will hold itself in readiness to march at an hour's notice for Queenston, where it will remain under the orders of Lieutenant-Colonel Plenderleath.

No. 2.—Sixty men of the 41st Regiment, under the directions of Lieut. Bullock, will march at 5 o'clock to-morrow morning for Chippawa, and on their arrival at that post Capt. Bullock will be pleased to strengthen the detachment stationed at the head of Navy Island (under Capt. Saunders) with 20 additional men from the 41st Regiment.

No. 3.—Captain Selby's company of York militia will hold itself in immediate readiness to march for Brown's Point. The Deputy-Quartermaster-General will be pleased to signify the route and point out the quarters to be occupied by the above detachment. The commissariat will provide the necessary conveyance.

No. 4.—A board of survey to assemble at 10 o'clock to-morrow morning at the barrack master's quarters for the purpose of ascertaining the damage done to the barrack articles.

DETAIL FOR THE ABOVE SURVEY.

41st Regiment—1 Captain, 1 Q.-Master, R. Newf'l'd do. —— 1 sub. ——

1	1	—	—	1

By order.
THOMAS EVANS,
Major of Brigade.

District General Order.

FORT GEORGE, 20th Sept., 1812.

The Major General commanding most earnestly calls the attention of officers in the command of divisions and that of the officers in general to the state of the men's arms, ammunition, and appointments under their immediate superintendence, as he expects every soldier, whether of the line or militia, will be at all times in the most efficient state in this essential particular, and every way prepared to meet the enemy's attack should he venture to make it.

No. 2.—The Major General trusts that the officers in charge of the different divisions use their best exertions in forwarding the drills of the several detachments of militia placed under their orders, and that the non-commissioned officers and men selected from the line for this important duty are every way qualified to give the instruction required.

No. 3.—It is expected that officers in command of companies, both of the line and of militia, are provided with order books, and that the orders are regularly read to their men in conformity to No. 3 of the D. G. O. of the 31st July.

The Major General cannot impress too strongly on the minds of the commanders the necessity of their attention and punctuality to this part of their duty.

No. 4.—The Major General acknowledges with thanks the willing manner in which that portion of the troops stationed at Fort George have contributed by their exertions to the accomplishment of the present works established there, and directs that in future as small a number as possible may be furnished for finishing them in order that the militia last joined may have the opportunity of perfecting themselves in drill.

By order.

THOMAS EVANS.

Militia General Orders.

HEADQUARTERS, FORT GEORGE, 21 Sept., 1812.

Militia General Orders.

It having been mentioned to His Honor Major General Brock that several militiamen belonging to the flank companies of the different regiments of the Lincoln and the Second Regiment of York militia are now absent from their respective companies without leave, he has been pleased to direct that the captains or officers commanding the said companies do immediately transmit to the officers commanding the regiments or battalions to which their respective companies belong a particular return of such as are so absent, and His Honor has been further pleased to direct that officers commanding corps do use every means in their power to cause such absentees to be apprehended and sent to their respective companies, to be dealt with as the law directs, unless it shall satisfactorily appear that any such absentee is about voluntarily to return to his duty, in which case His Honor is pleased to direct that the offence may be overlooked for this time.

By order.

J. MACDONELL, Lt.-Col.,
Militia P. A. D. C.

The Secretary of War to Major General Dearborn.

WAR DEPARTMENT, Sept. 21, 1812.

(Abstract.)

The Pennsylvania Regiment has been ordered to march, agreeably to his request. Great hopes are entertained that General Harrison will recover the ground lost by General Hull, and enter Upper Canada.

District General Orders.

FORT GEORGE, 22nd Sept., 1812.

The Major General commanding returns his particular thanks to the militia for the handsome manner in which they have on all occasions volunteered their services for duties of fatigue, and is pleased to direct for the present that further services for such duties shall be dispensed with.

No. 2.—Colonel Claus will give the necessary directions for the periods of drill for the militia, and Sergeant Lyon of the 41st and Sergeant Thomas of the Royal Newfl'd will attend as instructors at the hours appointed by Col. Claus. The 41st will also furnish a second non-commissioned officer capable of instructing the men for this particular duty.

By order.

THOMAS EVANS.

Major General VanRensselaer to Governor Tompkins.

HEADQUARTERS, LEWISTON, 22nd Sept., 1812.

SIR,—Since I had the honor to address Your Excellency and Major General Dearborn on the 17th instant, nothing of very great importance has taken place. The position of the army is still the same—guarding with great vigilance (as far as our force will admit) every point accessible by the enemy. On the night of the 20th all the ships which the enemy has on Lake Ontario were anchored in the mouth of Niagara River. What was the object of this movement I know not, unless it was to avoid the violence of the most tremendous storm which we have lately had, and in which our troops have suffered much. By the great violence of the wind many tents were blown over, my own marquee, bed and all, was completely deluged.

My morning report of sick is 149.

Colonel VanRensselaer went over with a flag to Fort George to carry my answer to a communication which I had received from General Brock relative to a firing between our sentinels, by which one man on the Canadian side was killed. There was yesterday no general officer at Fort George, and the ships were all gone. As yet I have not been able to get any information respecting this movement.

Last evening Lieut. [Totten?] of the corps of engineers reported himself to me. I hear nothing of the District Paymaster, nor of a single company to reinforce the troops, whose duty is very severe.

I had ordered Lieut. Elliott of the navy, with the men engaged for the service under his command, to the mouth of the Genesee River to arm and equip such of the vessels lately blockaded there, as he might think proper for the public service. He has undoubtedly advised Captain Chauncey of this arrangement. But, since the departure of Lieut. Elliott, I have been informed that those vessels have escaped from Genesee River and gone to Oswego.

I enclose an extract from a letter I have this morning received from a gentleman who has heretofore made me several useful communications. He assures me the information may be relied on. This extract may be useful to General Dearborn.

(Tompkins' Papers, Vol. VIII., pp. 174-5, New York State Library.)

From the Buffalo Gazette, Tuesday, 22d September, 1812.

Yesterday a flag arrived from Fort Erie, bringing over Aaron Greeley, Esq., late Surveyor General of the Michigan Territory, with his family and effects, together with several other persons. They left Malden on Friday, and arrived at Fort Erie on Saturday, on board the brig *Adams*, after the remarkably short passage of 33 hours. We are authorized by Mr. Greeley to state the British officers and Indian agents do everything in their power to prevent the Indians from committing acts of cruelty. Mr. Greeley also contradicts in express terms the report that *the British either gave or offered six dollars, or any other sum, for SCALPS*, but, on the contrary, discountenanced the Indians by all possible means from acts of cruelty.

A PRIZE TO THE BRITISH.

On the 6th a boat belonging to Mr. Lovejoy of this village was freighted for Erie and went out of port in the morning, but the wind hauling unfavorable she made but little progress. In a short time a British armed boat came out from under Point Abino and gave chase. The boatmen ran ashore a few miles above 18 Mile Creek, abandoned the boat and tried to obtain assistance from the people on shore, but obtaining only 3 or 4 old muskets in bad order they could make no opposition. The British boat came up and towed away the deserted boat with all the property, which consisted of 45 barrels of salt shipped by General Porter for Erie, the remainder of the loading chiefly belonging to Mr. Lovejoy, whose loss is not less than 1000 dollars.

PLUNDERING.

On the 15th inst. a boat from the Canadian shore landed a number of soldiers near Sturgeon Point, who stopped a wagon and seized a quantity of leather, and afterwards entered the house of Mr. N. Lay (the family having previously fled to the woods) and pillaged all the wearing apparel, not excepting the small articles of women's and children's wear—all the bed furniture, sheets, pillow cases, &c., all the provisions they could carry off: all the kitchen furniture they could not take they destroyed, and afterwards took a calf tied near the house and carried off the booty to the boat. Mr. Lay's loss was not less than 300 dollars. The house of Mr. Gates was then plundered of 60 or 70 doll's. Another house was plundered of several articles, the amount of which we have not ascertained. We understand that measures will be taken to reclaim the property.

FORT NIAGARA.

We understand that Colonel Fenwick, since his arrival, has strengthened some parts of Fort Niagara very considerably, and put the ordnance in excellent commanding positions.

John Lovett to Joseph Alexander.

HEADQUARTERS, LEWISTON, 22d Sept., 1812.

DEAR ALEXANDER,—

. . . .

The enemy appear to be in a state of preparedness to give or receive an attack. Every day or two they make some movement which indicates dispositions to attack us immediately. Night before last every ship they have on Lake Ontario came into the mouth of Niagara. Then, to be sure, we thought it time to look-out for breakers. But yesterday when Col. VanRensselaer went over with a flag to Fort George there was not a ship in sight nor a general officer there; where gone we know not. Notwithstanding the most positive orders on both sides, our sentinels have kept up almost a constant warfare for a month past. On the bank of the river musket balls are about as thick as whippowills on a summer's evening. A wretch fired the other evening at Judge Barton and myself as we were sitting upon our horses on the bank. The shot came in a correct line, but fell 20 rods short in the river. Last Saturday morning one of our lads returned the compliment, and put his ball so quick thro' a lad's head on the other side that he fell dead without even winking. Over came Lieut.-Col. Myers, with whom I had the honor of an hour's conference on the bank. Both talked it largely and returned good fellows. . . .

We are promised reinforcements by companies, battalions, regiments, brigades, and I might almost say armies, but not a single man has joined us in some weeks. Besides, our men here are getting down very fast within three or four days. This morning's report of sick was 149. We have lately had the most tremendous storm of cold rains and wind that I every saw at this season of the year—it was eno' to make an ox quake. The wind was terrible; hail, lightning, thunder, and the whole army of terrors seemed pressed into requisition. Many tents blew up and over; the General's marquee was deluged, bed and all drenched.

Give Mrs. Lovett the enclosed. It contains an impression of General Brock's seal, with his most appropriate motto: "He who guards never sleeps." The campaign will wind up with some very interesting occurrences. I think I begin to see how the crisis is forming. *We shall invade Canada.*

(From Bonney's Historical Gleanings, pp. 236-7.

From the Federal Republican of Baltimore, Md., 5th October, 1812.

(Extract from a letter dated 22nd September, 1812.)

There is at Niagara about 700 United States troops; at Lewiston, 800 militia; at Black Rock, 300 militia; at Schlosser, 400 militia; at Lewiston Meadows, 40 horse and 60 infantry. The militia generally were much dissatisfied in consequence of not having received any pay, and about 20 men stacked their arms on parade and determined to return home, but were prevailed to remain by the assurance that the paymaster would be out the last of this month. Desertion on this side is frequent; two of the United States troops swam over to Fort George on the 11th inst., who were capable of giving general and correct information as to the strength and situation of the troops on this side. They were not discovered until nearly half way over, when they were fired upon, and the British sent off a boat and picked them up without injury.

Sir George Prevost to Earl Bathurst.

(No. 9.)

HEADQUARTERS, MONTREAL, 22d Sept., 1812.

MY LORD,—In my despatch No. 7, dated the 1st inst., I had the honor of transmiting to Your Lordship copies of letters from Major General Brock detailing the surrender of Fort Detroit, with copies of the capitulation, return of stores, &c., &c.

I have now the honor of reporting to Your Lordship that Brig'r-Gen'l Hull, together with the first division of prisoners, consisting of 22 officers and 343 men, part of the regular army which surrendered at Detroit, arrived at this place on the 6th inst. The remainder, amounting to about 140 men and their proportion of officers, are still in Upper Canada, and will be forwarded hither as soon as the means can be procured of sending them. The men and the greater part of the officers which have arrived have been sent to Quebec.

Brig.-Gen'l Hull being desirous of returning to the United States on his parole, for the purpose of justifying his own conduct and exposing the imbecility of that of his government in totally neglecting to support directly (or indirectly) his offensive operations, either by reinforcing his army or by making demonstrations of attack upon other points on the frontier line simultaneously with the one he was commanded to make on Amherstburg, I have therefore allowed him to proceed to Boston, for which place he set off on the 10th inst. with his aid-de-camp. I feel confident that his presence in the United States will have the effect of adding strength to the party there in opposition to the war, and that it will also tend to embarrass the American Government. The situation of several of the officers, particularly those with families, has induced me to extend to them the like indulgence. As in these instances I have conceived myself acting agreeably to the views and conciliatory disposition of His Majesty's government, I trust His Royal Highness the Prince Regent will be graciously pleased to approve of what I have done, and that the liberality thus manifested on his part will be attended with the best effects.

I am happy to be able to assure Your Lordship that the spirit and zeal which are now evinced by all classes of persons in the Province (but more particularly by the militia) to resist the attacks with which they are threatened, afford me strong hopes that the enemy will meet with disappointment should they think fit to invade the country. The volunteering of a considerable portion of the English militia of this populous town for permanent duty enables me to withdraw from hence the regulars as circumstances may require, and materially aids the public service.

(Canadian Archives, Q 118, p. 251.)

Major General Brock to Major General VanRensselaer.

HEADQUARTERS, FORT GEORGE, 23d Sept., 1812.

SIR,—I have the honor to acknowledge the receipt of your letter of the twentieth instant. I never doubted for a moment that the firing from your side of the river upon individuals was contrary to your intentions and in violation of your orders, and I beg leave to repeat that every effort shall be made on my part to prevent a recurrence of such acts of insubordination on this side.

(From S. VanRensselaer's Narrative: Appendix. p. 75.)

The Secretary of War to Major General Dearborn.

WAR DEPARTMENT, Sept. 23, 1812.

(Abstract.)

By letters received from Erastus Granger it appears that the young men of the Six Nations can no longer be restrained, and that in case of the refusal on the part of the United States to accept their services they would join the Indians under the British standard. Although the policy of the United States has been against this course, it is forced upon us by the common principle of self-defence. Mr. Granger has therefore been authorized, after every attempt to secure their neutrality has failed, to embody them. They should be engaged as far as possible against an enemy of their own description.

From the New York Evening Post, 2d June, 1813.

Letter from an Officer at Buffalo, Dated Sept. 24th, 1812.

The Indian agent at Buffalo has been instructed by the President of the United States to accept the services of the savages of the Six Nations and organize them. There will probably be within a fortnight at Buffalo between two and four hundred Indian warriors embodied and organized to the service of the United States.

(From file in the New York Society Library.)

District General Orders.

FORT GEORGE, 25th September, 1812.

D. G. Orders.

Major Merritt will please to furnish daily an orderly dragoon to be at the brigade major's office by 12 o'clock each day for the transmission of orders, &c. Heads of departments, officers in command of corps, and others having letters on the public service to forward to any part of the line betwixt this post and Fort Erie, and to Amherstburg or Detroit, will send them to brigade major's office any time before half-past eleven o'clock. Officers in command of divisions and posts stationed along the line will avail themselves of this orderly express to forward their communications to headquarters.

No. 2.—Until further orders, tattoo will beat at eight o'clock in the evening.

By order,

THOMAS EVANS, Brigade Major.

General Orders.

HEADQUARTERS, LEWISTON, 25th September, 1812.

The detachment of Lieut.-Col. Hopkins's regiment will be stationed at Tonawanta and guard the passes on the river, and will relieve the guards of Lieut.-Col. Swift's regiment now there. All the supernumerary officers of Lieut.-Col. Hopkins's regiment will be disbanded, and such only kept in service as are absolutely necessary to officer this detachment agreeable to law.

General Hall will give orders accordingly. Captain Ellicott's company of artillery will be stationed at the battery opposite Fort Erie, to which place one eighteen-pounder is ordered.

Returns of the state of the troops, their arms and accoutrements, will be made to the Major General once a week by General Hall and the commanding officer of the United States troops at Fort Niagara, and they are directed to have everything in readiness for action at a moment's warning.

By order of Major General VanRensselaer.

SOL. VANRENSSELAER, Aid-de-Camp.

From the New York Statesman, 25th September, 1812.

INDIAN AUXILIARIES.

The Indian agent at Buffalo has been instructed by the President of the United States to accept the services of the warriors of the Six Nations and to embody and organize them, and the writer of the communication in the Canandaigua paper says it is believed by all who are acquainted with the Indian character that the inhabitants of the Niagara frontier will find greater safety (in this auxiliary force of the natives of the woods) than in any other while the hostile armies remain in the neighborhood, and he adds that there will probably be within a fortnight at Buffalo between 3 and 400 Indian warriors embodied and organized in the service of the United States.

(From file in the New York Society Library.)

Major General VanRensselaer to Lieut. J. D. Elliott, U. S. N.

HEADQUARTERS, LEWISTON, Sept. 25, 1812.

SIR,—I enclose you a copy of a letter I have this day sent to Major General Hall, with my best wishes that success may crown your enterprise.

(From Correspondence in relation to the capture of the British brigs *Detroit* and *Caledonia*, p. 27.)

Major General VanRensselaer to Major General Hall.

HEADQUARTERS, LEWISTON, Sept. 25, 1812.

SIR,—I have this moment received your letter of yesterday, stating Lieut. Elliott has proposed to make an attempt to cut out one of the vessels at Erie, and has requested your assistance by men, &c., for the enterprize.

You will please to furnish Lieut. Elliott immediately with men, arms, ammunition, boats, and implements of every kind, to the uttermost of his wishes, and the means you can possibly command to render the enterprize successful.

(From Correspondence in relation to the capture of the British brigs *Detroit* and *Caledonia*, Philadelphia, 1843, p. 27.)

From the Aurora, of Philadelphia, 13th October, 1812.

MEADVILLE, Sept. 25th, 1812.

The volunteer levies under the guidance of their respective brigade orders were gathering in from the 21st to the 25th inst. They were ordered to encamp in a line with the first, taking their position as they arrived upon the left. Every day the line grew rapidly. On the 24th they were organized into regiments and battalions by the Adjutant-General. The rolls of those present amount to about 1900.

This day the election is holding. General Tannehill has been elected by four to one, brigadier-general of this detachment. The colonels are Jared Irwin, William Piper, Samuel Purviance and Jeremiah Snyder. The majors will be elected to-morrow. An express has been sent for General Tannehill. The troops await his coming. There has been grumbling and a few desertions. They were sent after but not caught.

The question of crossing the line is sometimes agitated but not determined otherwise than from the inference arising from the large majority in favor General Tannehill. One party seems to be in favor of it, the other against it. The former party holds a very large majority. Local relations and circumstances must finally settle this point.

1st Rifle Regiment—
    1st Battalion—216 rank and file.
    2d   do.   240 do. do. do.
    —— 456

2nd Rifle Regiment—
    1st Battalion—209 rank and file.
    2d   do.   209 do. do. do.
    —— 418

1st Regiment of Infantry—
    1st Battalion—285 rank and file.
    2d   do.   231 do. do. do.
    —— 516.

2d Regiment of Infantry—
    1st Battalion—240 rank and file.
    2d   do.   213 do. do. do.
    —— 453

Sir George Prevost to Major General Brock.

MONTREAL, September 25, 1812.

SIR,—It no longer appears by your letter of the 13th that you consider the enemy's operations on the Niagara frontier indicative of active operations. If the Government of America inclines to defensive measures, I can only ascribe the determination to two causes: The first is the expectation of such overtures from us as will lead to a suspension of hostilities, preparatory to negotiations for peace: the other arises from having ascertained by experience our ability in the Canadas to resist the attack of a tumultuary force.

In consequence of your having weakened the line of communication between Cornwall and Kingston, a predatory warfare is carrying on there, very prejudicial to the intercourse from hence with Upper Canada. I have ordered a company of the Glengarry to Prescott to strengthen Colonel Lethbridge, and under present circumstances you are not to expect further aid.

I agree in opinion with you that so wretched is the organization and discipline of the American army, that at this moment much might be effected against them, but as the Government at home could derive no substantial advantage from any disgrace we might inflict on them whilst the more important concerns of the country are committed in Europe, I again request that you will steadily pursue that policy which shall appear to you to promote the dwindling away of such a force by its own inefficient means.

I shall receive with much satisfaction Colonel Procter's report of having saved the garrison of Fort Wayne from the inhuman fury of the Indians. I am particularly anxious that that class of beings should be restrained and controlled as much as possible whilst there exists a pretence of implicating the national character in their cruelties.

(From Tupper's Life of Brock. pp. 317-18.)

Major General Dearborn to Major General VanRensselaer.

HEADQUARTERS, GREENBUSH, Sept. 26th, 1812.

Major General VanRensselaer:

SIR,—Your letter of the 17th inst. was not received until this morning. Although I had taken as early measures as circumstances admitted of for having your post strongly reinforced, I have been disappointed as to the time of the actual arrival of the different corps at their places of destination, and also in regard to the transportation of military stores to your camp. A strange fatality seems to have pervaded the whole arrangements. Ample reinforcements of troops and supplies of stores are on their way, but I fear their arrival will be too late to enable you to maintain your position. I had hoped from your former letter that the old fort had been abandoned and the stores removed to a place of more security. I fear it will, in the case of an attack from a superior force, be *a trap for the garrison that may be placed in it.* If this should reach you previous to the enemy's movement against you, I must take the liberty of advising to such a concentration of your force, and such arrangements for the safety of the principal military stores, boats, &c., &c., as will enable you in the last resort to risk no more than shall be absolutely necessary. I have requested the Quartermaster-General to send on a Deputy-Quartermaster, with funds and capacity for furnishing whatever may be necessary in his line. *By putting on the best face that your situation admits, the enemy may be induced to delay an attack until you will be able to meet him and carry the war into Canada. At all events, we must calculate on possessing Upper Canada before winter sets in.* Gen. Harrison will, I am assured, enter Canada by Detroit with not less than from six to seven thousand men, exclusive of the troops necessary for guarding the frontier against Indian depredations. The force at Sackett's Harbor and that vicinity is over two thousand, including an old company of regular artillery and a large company of old riflemen. I have great confidence in the exertions now in operation in the navy department on Lake Ontario. In fact we have nothing to fear and much to hope as to the ultimate success of measures now in operation with a view to Upper Canada, but much may immediately depend on what may happen at your post.

(From S. VanRensselaer's Narrative: Appendix, p. 59.)

General Orders.

HEADQUARTERS, LEWISTON, September 27th, 1812.

Complaint having been made by the troops as to the quality of the provisions issued by the commissary, Major John Beach of the town of Lewiston, a disinterested person, is appointed on the part of Major General VanRensselaer, and he together with a person to be appointed by the commissary will, without delay, inspect the quality of the provisions against which complaint has been made, and report their opinion thereupon to the Major General.

By order of Major General VanRensselaer.

SOL. VANRENSSELAER, Aid-de-Camp.

District General Orders.

FORT GEORGE, 27th September, 1812.

D. G. Orders.

The Major General having observed great deficiencies in the ammunition issued generally to the troops and the militia, he cannot too strongly impress on the minds of the officers in command of divisions the necessity of explaining to the men under their orders that, at a period like the present, a greater military offence cannot be committed than a careless negligence or wilful waste of any ammunition that may be delivered out to them for the use of the public service.

No. 2.—Whenever cartridges may be injured by wet or otherwise, the balls of such cartridges will be carefully preserved and sent in, with an account of the number, to the ordnance storekeeper, who will give a receipt for the same.

By order,
THOMAS EVANS,
Brigade-Major.

General Order.

HEADQUARTERS, LEWISTON, September 27th, 1812.

A guard of one hundred men, under the command of a major, with their tents and baggage, will be detached this day from Lieut.-Col. Bloom's regiment to protect the boats in Gill Creek. Lieut.-Col. Bloom will give orders accordingly, and will see that this detachment is encamped at that place before sunset this evening.

By order of Major General VanRensselaer.

SOL. VANRENSSELAER, Aid-de-Camp.

Major General VanRensselaer to Major General Dearborn.

HEADQUARTERS, LEWISTON, Sept. 27th, 1812.

SIR,—By Capt. Dox, who arrived in camp yesterday, I received your letter of the 17th inst., and I can assure you it is consoling to learn that I shall soon be partially relieved from that severe suspense and solicitude which have for some weeks past been inseparably connected with my situation. In the view of those important interests which I considered to be at stake, it required much deliberation to decide on the proper course to be pursued, and when that course was determined (in the manner which I have before stated to you) it required new efforts by night and day to dispose my small force to meet events in such manner as to justify the course adopted. But as yet I am satisfied of the correctness of the decision, and although I have acquired nothing I have surrendered nothing.

From the various accounts I have received we must, I think, in a few days be able to act, at least on the defensive, with better prospects.

Lieut.-Col. Boerstler has arrived, and by him I learn that three regiments will soon arrive. But I am mortified to understand, by a letter from Col. Winder, that the aggregate of the troops will be but about 900 men, and that his regiment is entirely without cloth clothing, which is indispensable for them in the field at this season.

The enemy continue their operations with great activity, fortifying their camp at Fort George in every direction. Seven of the 24-pounders taken at Detroit are there mounted, part on travelling carriages.

Notwithstanding the most positive orders on both sides, we are constantly troubled with the warfare of sentries. By their firings across the river one man on each side has fallen within the past week. It is next to impossible to keep our guards sufficiently vigilant on their posts. I presume His Excellency Governor Tompkins has shown you an extract of a letter which I lately forwarded him, relative to the strength of the enemy in the rear of Fort Erie. Captain Gibson has arrived. I presume Lieut. Elliott of the navy has apprised you of his arrangements. The vessels has escaped from Genesee River to Oswego. He is now with fifteen of his men at Buffalo. More ordnance seems indispensable for our future operations.

P. S.—As the post at Sackett's Harbor is within my command, I take the liberty of suggesting for your consideration the propriety of continuing so many troops—about sixteen hundred—there. While the enemy hold command of the lake, Sackett's Harbor is not a point from which a descent upon Canada can be made. We are not to apprehend general invasion at every point, and the village at that place is not of sufficient importance to the force which guards it. I know of no consideration which ought to claim more than a regiment of troops at that post, to man the batteries and guard the harbor. In my opinion every consideration connected with the general interest of the service dictates that part of the troops at Sackett's Harbor should be ordered immediately to this station.

(From S. VanRensselaer's Narrative: Appendix, p. 56.)

Major General Brock to Sir George Prevost.

York, Upper Canada, September 28, 1812.

Sir,—I have been honored with Your Excellency's despatch, dated the 14th instant. I shall suspend under the latitude left by Your Excellency to my discretion, the evacuation of Fort Detroit. Such a measure would most probably be followed by the total extinction of the population on that side of the river, or the Indians, aware of our weakness and inability to carry on active warfare, would only think of entering into terms with the enemy. The Indians since the Miami affair in 1793 have been extremely suspicious of our conduct, but the violent wrongs committed by the Americans on their territory have rendered it an act of policy with them to disguise their sentiments. Could they be persuaded that a peace between the belligerents would take place without admitting their claim to an extensive tract of country, fraudulently usurped from them, and opposing a frontier to the present unbounded views of the Americans, I am satisfied in my own mind that they would immediately compromise with the enemy. I cannot conceive a connexion so likely to lead to more awful consequences.

If we can maintain ourselves at Niagara and keep the communication to Montreal open, the Americans can only subdue the Indians by craft, which we ought to be prepared to see exerted to the utmost. The enmity of the Indians is now at its height, and it will require much management and large bribes to effect a change in their policy, but the moment they are convinced we either want the means to prosecute the war with spirit or are negociating a separate peace, they will begin to study in what manner they can effectually deceive us.

Should negociations for peace be opened, I cannot be too earnest with Your Excellency to represent to the King's ministers the expediency of including the Indians as allies, and not leave them exposed to the unrelenting fury of their enemies.

The enemy has evidently assumed defensive measures along the Niagara. His force, I apprehend, is not equal to attempt (with any probability of success) an expedition across the river. It is, however, currently reported that large reinforcements are on their march. Should they arrive, an attack cannot be long delayed. The approach of the rainy season will increase the sickness with which the troops are affected. Those under my command are in perfect health and spirits.

I beg leave to represent to Your Excellency the great want of bedding for the militia. I have received strong representations from Colonel Vincent on the subject. He reports that several men have retired home in consequence. He has been instructed to apply (in order to save time) direct to headquarters, where he is sure to receive such relief as circumstances will admit.

A supply for this district would likewise prove very acceptable.

I have the honor to transmit the purport of a confidential communication received in my absence by Brigade-Major Evans from Colonel VanRensselaer. As Your Excellency's instructions agree with the line of conduct he is anxious I should follow, nothing of a hostile nature shall be attempted under existing circumstances.

(Canadian Archives, C. 677, p. 94.)

Brigadier-General Alexander Smyth to Major General Van-Rensselaer.

BUFFALO, 29th September, 1812.

SIR,—I have been ordered by Major General Dearborn to take command of a brigade of the U. S. troops, and directed on my arrival in the vicinity of your quarters to report myself to you, which I now do. I intended to have reported myself personally, but the conclusions I have drawn as to the interests of the service have determined me to stop at this place for the present. From the description I have had of the river below the falls, the view of the shore below Fort Erie and the information received as to the preparations of the enemy, I am of opinion that our crossing should be effected between Fort Erie and Chippawa. It has therefore seemed to me proper to encamp the U. S. troops near Buffalo, there to prepare for offensive operations. Your instructions or better information may decide you to give me different orders, which I will await.

(From S. VanRensselaer's Narrative: Appendix, p. 67.)

District General Orders.

FORT GEORGE, 29th September, 1812.

D. G. Orders.

Until further orders the Grand Rounds will go their rounds betwixt the hours of ten and two o'clock, and the Visiting Rounds betwixt two and five o'clock in the morning.

By order.

THOS. EVANS,
Brigade-Major.

From the "Buffalo Gazette," Tuesday, September 29th, 1812.

BRITISH NAVAL MOVEMENT.

On Thursday evening last the British squadron lying at Fort Erie, consisting of the *Queen Charlotte, Adams, Hunter*, and two small vessels, suddenly hoisted sail and made up the lake under press of sail. The object or destination of the squadron are unknown.

Since the departure of the squadron, an armed vessel has been discovered lying under Point Abino.

BRITISH FORCES ON THIS LINE.

Since the conclusion of the armistice, the British forces have been constantly increased. It is almost impossible for us to conjecture the amount or quality of this force, but the *knowing ones guess* that including regulars, militia, and Indians, their forces will amount to nearly 4,000 men that could be marched to one point within 24 hours. This includes the frontier from Point Abino on Lake Erie to Little York on Lake Ontario. Though the length of the coast must be more than 150 miles, yet the British, having complete, undisturbed possession of the lakes, they move their armies with astonishing rapidity.

AFFAIRS OF OUR FRONTIERS.

On Wednesday evening last arrived in this village Captain Gibson with half a company of flying artillery, consisting of two 6-pounders and two caissons (ammunition wagons). This morning he took up his line of march for Fort Niagara, where he will join Lieut. Branch with the other half of his company in the rear of which garrison, we understand, this company is to be stationed.

On Saturday, the 14th United States Regiment of Infantry, under the command of Colonel Wm. H. Wynder, arrived and encamped in the village. They will, we understand, soon march for Lewiston. This regiment is composed of fine healthy young men, 337 in number. It is to be lamented that the number is so few and that the men have not yet received their winter clothing, as they come from the southward and are not accustomed to our climate.

On Sunday General Alexander Smyth, Inspector General of the army of the United States, and suite arrived at this place. We understand that General Smyth will take the command of the United States troops which, with the late reinforcement, will amount to more than 1,000 regular troops. This force together with the volunteers and detached militia will secure the country from invasion, to say the least. More troops are daily expected.

We are informed that Colonel Milton with the 5th United States Regiment will be in town this week. Colonel Schuyler with the 13th United States Regiment will also be on here within 10 or 12 days.

Two thousand Pennsylvania volunteers from Meadville are expected here in the course of a week.

On Thursday night last, Lewis Nyles, a centinel from Lieut.-Colonel Hopkins's regiment, posted near Field's tavern on the Niagara River, about 17 miles below this place, was shot dead on his post by some person, who, being hailed by the centinel, replied that he had not got the *countersign* but a *written pass*, which he would show him. On being permitted to approach to the point of the bayonet, he drew a pistol and shot the centinel and made his escape. The report of the pistol and the cries of the centinel, gave an immediate alarm, and it was thought the person made his escape across the river to Grand Island, as a boat was soon after heard upon the river.

We are informed that an accident occurred some time last week at the camp at Five-Mile Meadow. Some dispute arose between two of Captain Gibson's men of the flying artillery, the particulars we have not obtained, but are informed from a correct source that it terminated in the death of one of the men from a blow from the other by a piece of a broken tent pole or some similar weapon.

About 140 young warriors of the Seneca Nation from Allegany River arrived in town last week, and are encamped near the village. More are expected from different parts. Several conferences and councils have lately been held with the chiefs. They voluntarily offered to take up arms for defensive purposes. Yesterday they performed a *WAR DANCE* in the streets of this village.

From the "Repository" of Canandaigua, N. Y., 29th September, 1812.

Within the last few days the following forces have passed through this village for the Niagara frontier:—

Colonel Mead's regiment of militia from Chenango, Tioga, and Broome Counties, about 500 men.

Colonel Stranahan's regiment from Otsego, 500 militia.

Colonel Milton (from Virginia) with a regiment of United States troops, about 400.

A body of flying artillery, 140, with 4 pieces of cannon, ammunition wagons, &c.

Two companies of artillery.

Captain Ireland's rifle corps from Seneca County.

Another regiment of United States troops, the 13th, left Greenbush on the 18th instant, and may be expected along here in a few days.

Besides the above, several detachments are moving from this county, among them Captain Hart's artillery company of this town, Major Granger's battalion of riflemen, three troops of horse.

Captain Hill's company of light infantry of Bristol mustered yesterday, completely armed and equipped.

The above forces were accompanied with trains of wagons loaded with tents, camp equipage, &c. From what we can learn, there will in a short time be 8 or 10,000 men on the Niagara.

(File in the Wood Library, Canandaigua, N. Y.)

Speech by the Deputies of the Indians.

EXTRACT FROM THE SPEECH OF THE DEPUTIES OF THE ONEIDA, ONONDAGA, STOCKBRIDGE, TUSCARORA, AND SENECA INDIANS, AS FAR WEST AS TONAWANDA, IN COUNCIL AT ONONDAGA, ON THE ANCIENT COUNCIL GROUND OF THE SIX NATIONS, SEPTEMBER 29TH, 1812.

Having been told repeatedly by your agents to remain neutral, we were very much surprised and disappointed at the council held at Buffalo Creek at being invited to take up the tomahawk. We are not unfriendly to the United States, but are few in number and can do but little, but are willing to do what we can, and if you want us say so, and we will go with your people to battle. We are anxious to know your wishes as soon as possible, because we are afraid some of our young men may disperse among distant tribes and be hostile to you.

Signed by Canastota and fifteen other chiefs, and attested by Jasper Hopper, Thaddeus Patchin, and Pulaski King.

(MSS. in Third Auditor's Office, Washington, D. C.)

Jasper Hopper, Thaddeus Patchin, Pulaski King, John C. Conkey, John Adams, and Joel Phillips to Governor Tompkins.

Sept. (29?), 1812.

They recommend Ephraim Webster as a suitable man to command Indians, if the Government should think proper to call them into service.

(MSS. in the Third Auditor's Office, Washington, D. C.)

District General Order.

FORT GEORGE, 30th September, 1812.

D. G. Order.

A subaltern and 40 privates, with a due proportion of non-commissioned officers, will march this day (immediately after the men have dined) for Chippawa. On the arrival of this detachment at Chippawa, Captain Bullock will detach one subaltern, 2 sergeants, and forty rank and file of the 41st to Miller's, where they will receive their further orders from Major General Shaw. The Deputy-Quartermaster-General will be pleased to furnish the necessary conveyance for the baggage of this detachment.

By order.

THOS. EVANS, Brigade-Major.

General Orders.

HEADQUARTERS, LEWISTON, 30th Sept., 1812.

The order, whereof a copy is annexed, from the Commander-in-Chief of the United States army was received yesterday. All those interested are to govern themselves accordingly.

The Quartermaster-General will purchase twenty horses and ——— yoke of cattle for the ordnance department, with yokes, chains, &c., complete, and furnish the necessary forage for the horses and oxen. The Quartermaster-General will make a return of the number of private boats he can procure for the transportation of troops, cannon, horses and stores.

The Major General regrets that he is again compelled to remind the Quartermaster-General of the want of forage for the light artillery and dragoon horses, and directs that it shall be furnished without delay, and in future regularly.

Those light infantry companies which have already or may hereafter arrive, excepting Capt. Dox's company, will take possession of the first cantonment below Lewiston, and will be subject to the orders of Major Thomas Lee, who is directed to take charge of them until further orders. The rifle company now there will take post at the old ferry above Lewiston. Major Moseley of the rifle corps will take command of the rifle companies which are now in camp or may hereafter arrive, until further orders.

By order of Major General VanRensselaer.

SOL. VANRENSSELAER, Aid-de-Camp.

Major General VanRensselaer to Brigadier-General Smyth.

HEADQUARTERS, LEWISTON,
30th September, 1812.

SIR,—On my return this moment from Niagara, I received your letter of yesterday advising me of your arrival at Buffalo, and the encampment there of the United States troops, in consequence of the conclusions you have drawn that offensive operations against Upper Canada ought to be attempted between Fort Erie and Chippawa. Nothing could be more unpleasant to me than a difference of opinion as to the *place* of commencing those operations in which our own characters, the fate of the army, and the deepest interests of our country are concerned. But however willing I may be as a citizen soldier to surrender my opinion to a professional one, I can only make such surrender to an opinion deliberately formed upon a view of the whole ground.

It would have been highly gratifying to me could I have had a seasonable opportunity to avail myself of the opinions of the officers of the United States troops as to the time, place, and competent force for the contemplated descent. But as the season for operations was far advanced, and as the counsel I wished was not at command, it has been the task of my own judgment, guided by the best attainable information, to designate the places for our operations. This I had some time ago decided, and although on account of my small force I have been obliged to bestow much labor on measures calculated for defence in case of an attack, still have I urged as fast as possible other local preparations connected with that mode of descent on which I had determined. My judgment may have deceived me, but I shall certainly stand acquitted of a hasty decision. For many years I have had a general knowledge of the banks of Niagara River, and of the adjacent country on the Canada shore. I have now attentively explored the American side with the view of military operations, combining at the same time a great variety of circumstances and considerations intimately connected in my opinion with our object. So various are the opinions, and such the influence of personal and local interests in this vicinity, that many circumstances are to be carefully balanced before any correct conclusions can be drawn. My decision has been made with due regard to all these things, and to the important consequences connected with it. All my past measures have been calculated for one point, and I now only wait for a competent force. As the season of the year and every consideration urges me to act with promptness, I cannot hastily listen to a change of position necessarily connected with a new system of measures and the very great inconvenience of the troops. I will not say that *no considerations* shall induce me to change my plans of operation, but to this I cannot yield without very weighty reasons: conclusions drawn at least from an attentive examination of the Niagara River, and all other circumstances connected with a successful result of the campaign.

I hope soon to have the pleasure of seeing you here, and perhaps, after conference and thorough examination of the river and country, your opinion and mine as to the plans of operations may coincide. I trust we are both open to conviction, and we have but one object—the best interest of the service.

(From S. VanRensselaer's Narrative: Appendix, p. 68.)

From the National Intelligencer of Washington, D. C., 15th October, 1812.

ONONDAGA VALLEY, Sept. 30, 1812.

Colonel Stranahan passed through this village on Wednesday week (23d September) at the head of 600 fine volunteers, and was joined here with about 500 drafted militia from Cortlandt, Broome, and Chenango Counties. On Thursday Colonel Milton, from Virginia, passed here with 500 regulars. Friday two companies of artillery passed by here with four field pieces, from Baltimore and Philadelphia. On Sunday 1.000 regulars arrived here, pitched their tents and tarried till Tuesday morning, when they again commenced their march in high spirits. Tuesday morning a volunteer company of light infantry passed by here from Cherry Valley. They made a very handsome appearance. The whole number of regular troops and militia that have gone through here within a week is not far from 3,000. There were 60 men in Colonel Stranahan's regiment from Otsego County (who volunteered themselves) that were upwards of 50 years of age, and have once seen war. It is reported here that 1,500 Indians have embodied on this side of Utica and will march on the frontiers in a few days and join the American army.

LYNX.

(From file in the New York Society Library.)

INDEX.

A.
Page.

Acadians.. 60
Adams, brig of war. 287, 301
Adams, John. 303
Adams, Major. 95, 97
Albany . . 32, 33, 42, 48, 54, 67, 68, 69, 70, 71, 73, 80, 81, 83, 84, 87, 88, 90, 93, 119,
        125, 130, 141, 164, 166, 172, 177, 183, 189, 190, 210, 217, 237, 241, 246,
        247, 249, 250, 255.
Alexander, Hugh 69, 178, 182
Alexander, James. 209
Alexander, Joseph. 213, 241, 288
Allan Major. 240
Alleghany River 187, 302
Allen Captain. 280
Allen, Lieut.-Colonel Peter. 75, 80, 102, 175
Alters, David. 209
Amand, John. 208
Amelia, merchant vessel. 122
Amherst, Lord. 26
Amherstburg 20, 21, 22, 23, 28, 29, 40, 41, 43, 59, 62, 65, 94, 98, 124, 133, 146,
        149, 152, 154, 155, 158, 160, 162, 163, 174, 180, 185, 186, 188, 204,
        225, 226, 242, 249, 259, 260, 273, 277, 290, 292.
Archives, Canadian 20, 21, 25, 38, 44, 50, 51, 53, 54, 60, 62, 66, 67, 68, 73, 74,
        95, 130, 134, 138, 146, 149, 153, 154, 163, 186, 201, 202, 216,
        243, 258, 259, 278, 290, 300.
Archives, Pennsylvania. 207, 208, 210, 211, 212, 256, 269
Armstrong, Major General John 29, 34, 254
Artillery, United States Light. 267, 269, 271, 273
Assembly, House of. 39
Attica, N. Y. 280
Atwater, Judge. 266
Atwater, Major. 267
Auburn, N. Y. 280
Aurelius, N. Y. 280
Austin, Calvin. 157

B.

Baby, Hon. James. 40, 148, 162, 188, 189
Badajoz 65
Baker, Anthony. 160, 181, 226
Baker, Arthur. 127
Baker, Captain 231
Baker, Judge. 127, 151
Baldwin, Captain. 229
Baltimore 31
Baltimore, Federal Republican. 131, 289
Barclay, Consul General Thomas 60, 67, 84
Barker, Samuel A 42
Barrackman, John. 208
Barton, Benjamin. 55, 56, 71, 77, 80, 127, 173, 288
Barwis, Lieut. 29
Bascom, Mr 227
Batavia, N. Y. 48, 59, 60, 88, 89, 93, 111, 176, 280
Batavia Arsenal 71, 75
Bathurst, Earl 160, 257, 260, 289
Battersby, Lieut.-Col. F 61

B—Continued.

Baynes, Colonel E., Adjutant-General..38, 45, 60, 64, 65, 74, 99, 114, 149, 152, 157, 160, 167, 169, 172, 189, 201, 215, 226, 249, 261.
Beach, Major John 296
Beal, Colonel 147
Beard, Mr 121, 122, 219, 220
Beasley, Colonel R 212
Beaver County, Pa... 269
Bee, The, a Niagara Newspaper 213
Beebe, E 259
Bellinger, Lieut.-Colonel 125
Bemis, Mr.. 262
Bender, Lieut.. 251
Benedict, Colonel.. 142
Benton, N. Y 75
Bermuda... 129
Biddulph, Ensign 261
Black River... 47, 49, 50
Black Rock. 61, 62, 69, 71, 77, 79, 86, 87, 88, 89, 90, 94, 96, 101, 104, 117, 122, 127, 129, 134, 135, 140, 141, 150, 151, 164, 165, 166, 167, 173, 175, 176, 177, 188, 190, 192, 193, 202, 203, 205, 218, 222, 225, 227, 230, 242, 258, 266, 267, 277, 289, 303.
Blankowitz, Captain Charles... 261
Bloodgood, Senator... 42
Bloom, Captain A.. 280
Bloom, Lieut.-Col. Henry .. 75, 175, 177, 183, 191, 230, 242, 245, 246, 254, 271, 297.
Bloomfield, N. Y.. 74, 78, 79, 96
Bloomfield, Brig.-Gen.. 231
Blue, Isaac.. 208
Boerstler, Lieut.-Col. C. G.. 298
Bogert, Captain... 104
Boileau, Adjt.-Gen. N. B 207, 210, 256
Bonaparte 50, 64
Bonney, Mrs. C. V. R., Historical Gleanings. .179, 184, 199, 215, 220, 221, 231, 238, 242, 245, 253, 255, 268, 271, 279, 280.
Boston, Mass. 31, 81, 184, 290
Boston, Independent Chronicle 114
Boughton, Lieut.-Col 279
Boughton, Sergeant.. 150
Branch, Lieut 229, 301
Brickle, Abraham... 209
Brink, Aaron 151, 190
Bristol, N. Y 280
Bristol, Captain... 267
Brock, Major General Isaac ..21, 25, 26, 28, 36, 37, 38, 41, 43, 44, 45, 50, 51, 53, 56, 58, 59, 60, 61, 64, 65, 66, 74, 77, 84, 86, 92, 93, 97, 99, 100, 101, 104, 113, 114, 115, 119, 120, 122, 126, 128, 129, 130, 132, 138, 142, 143, 144, 147, 148, 149, 151, 152, 154, 157, 159, 160, 161, 162, 164, 165, 167, 170, 171, 172, 175, 179, 181, 184, 185, 186, 187, 188, 190, 200, 201, 202, 212, 213, 216, 221, 223, 225, 227, 228, 233, 236, 249, 250, 257, 258, 259, 260, 264, 265, 268, 269, 271, 273, 274, 276, 278, 279, 283, 285, 286, 289, 291, 295, 296.

B—Continued.

	Page
Brock, James	234
Brock, Savery	278
Brooks, Ensign	240
Brooks, Colonel	254
Broome County, N. Y	302
Brown, Captain	280
Brown, Doctor	218, 227, 263
Brown, Brig.-Gen. Jacob	142, 229, 248
Brownstown, Mich.	157, 166, 175, 184
Brown's Point	284
Bruyeres, Lieut.-Col. R. E.	155, 159
Bryson, Alexander	259
Buchanan, David	209
Buckhorn Island	204, 215, 216
Buffalo	24, 31, 55, 78, 80, 86, 93, 105, 116, 122, 126, 128, 136, 150, 166, 175, 176, 178, 182, 187, 191, 193, 202, 203, 204, 206, 213, 214, 215, 237, 241, 242, 244, 254, 255, 256, 262, 263, 267, 278, 280, 291, 293, 298, 300.
Buffalo Creek	62, 86, 170, 231, 232, 267
Buffalo Gazette	12, 46, 54, 60, 63, 66, 68, 134, 150, 164, 170, 190, 205, 231, 246, 267, 287, 301.
Buffalo Public Library	56, 59, 60, 63, 66, 267
Bullock, Captain	77, 91, 283, 304
Bullock, Lieutenant	204, 283
Burk, Priest	44
Burnet, Colonel	48
Burnet, Brig.-General	75, 89
Burns, Colonel	147
Bushy Park, N. Y	258
Butler County, Pa	269
Butler, Lieut.-Col	92

C.

Caldwell, Fraser, & Co	84
Caldwell, Colonel Wm	188
Caledonia, N. Y	75
Caledonia, merchant brig	283
Cambo, transport	129
Camp, Captain	220, 263
Campbell, Fort Major	132
Campbell, Judge	251
Canada, Lower	6, 34, 39
Canada, Upper	20, 21, 25, 26, 27, 34, 46, 52, 53, 60, 63, 65, 66
Canadaway	122, 170
Canadians, French	34
Canan, Moses	209
Canandaigua, N. Y	48, 70, 75, 78, 79, 80, 81, 83, 84, 87, 88, 89, 104, 105, 106, 109, 112, 141, 173, 176, 231, 256, 280, 283.
Canastota	303
Carleton Island	38, 129
Cartwright, Colonel R	25, 38
Castlereagh, Lord	53
Cattaraugus County, N. Y	93, 170
Cato, N. Y	280
Cayahoga, Ohio	122, 126, 175, 219
Cayahoga Packet	122
Cayuga	183
Cayuga Bridge	252, 266

C—Continued.

	Page.
Cayuga County, N. Y	75, 175, 246, 280
Cayuga Indians	105, 108, 109, 111, 262
Cayuga Rangers	280
Cavalry, Provincial	76
Cazenovia, N. Y	49
Chambers, Captain P. L	91, 139, 145, 149, 180, 204
Champlain, Lake	33, 34, 54, 59, 81, 119, 181, 244
Chapin, Dr. Cyrenius	122, 134, 227
Charlesbourg, P. Q	249
Charleston, S. C	31
Chasey, Ensign	203
Chauncey, Captain Isaac	237, 247, 280, 286
Chautauqua, N. Y	187
Chautauqua County, N. Y	93, 114, 170, 186, 228
Chenango County, N. Y	302
Cherry Valley, N. Y	256
Chewitt, Lieut.-Col. Wm	240
Chicago, Ill	54, 60, 267, 272
Chigkaga	253
Chipman, Dr. Daniel	218
Chippawa, Fort and Village of	19, 42, 62, 67, 77, 91, 92, 95, 127, 132, 140, 143, 161, 190, 283, 300, 304.
Chippawa River	19
Chippawa, schooner	135
Clarence, N. Y	75
Clark, Elijah	150, 151, 170, 190
Clark, Lieut. and Adjt. John	77, 85
Clark, Lieut.-Col. Thomas	76, 84, 92, 95, 138
Claus, Lieut.-Col. Wm.	58, 76, 92, 130, 131, 286
Cleveland, Ohio	31, 122, 272
Cleveland, Lieut.-Col. Erastus	69
Clinton County, N. Y	81, 83
Clinton, Mr	54
Clinton, DeWitt	84
Clinton, General D	225
Coffin, Dy.-Asst.-Comy.-Gen	144
Coffin, Mr	126
Cognawago Indians	81
Colt, Peter	78, 86, 87, 104
Coltrin, Dr. Asa	135, 246
Commencement, sloop	78, 86
Compston, Captain	280
Congress of the United States	21, 26
Conkey, John C	303
Connor, Samuel S	171
Constitution, frigate	233, 239
Contractor, schooner	90, 122, 126
Coore, Captain	34, 228
Cork	73
Cornwall	113, 121, 295
Cornplanter	167
Corp, Samuel	84
Cortlandt County, N. Y	47, 49, 217
Cotton, Major, King's Regt.	250
Cotton, Surgeon Walter	242
Couche, Dy.-Comy.-Gen. Edward	94, 143, 146, 154
Craig, Lieut.-Gen. Sir James	19, 21, 27, 41, 45, 61

C—Continued.

	Page.
Crawford County, Pa	269
Crawford, Lewis	153
Cummings, James	67, 77, 131, 143
Curzon, Mrs. Sarah	186
Cuyler, Major Wm. Howe	150, 220, 267

D.

Daley, Martin ... 185
Davis, Lieut.-Col. ... 103
Dearborn, Major General Henry ... 53, 81, 83, 119, 130, 147, 156, 159, 160, 161, 164, 167, 169, 170, 171, 172, 178, 181, 183, 184, 185, 188, 189, 190, 192, 198, 199, 201, 203, 204, 205, 206, 210, 211, 215, 216, 218, 226, 227, 229, 230, 231, 232, 235, 236, 237, 238, 243, 244, 248, 250, 252, 254, 256, 259, 260, 264, 266, 267, 269, 270, 272, 273, 275, 276, 285, 286, 287, 289, 290, 291, 292, 295, 296, 297, 298, 299, 300.
Delaware ... 144
Delaware Indians ... 105, 262
Denison, Captain ... 240
Derenzy, Captain ... 91
DeRottenburg, Major General ... 114, 121
Detroit, Mich. ... 22, 23, 28, 31, 38, 40, 44, 50, 51, 54, 61, 68, 93, 121, 122, 126, 128, 133, 147, 157, 163, 164, 166, 171, 175, 181, 186, 192, 194, 199, 200, 204, 212, 213, 216, 218, 220, 223, 224, 225, 226, 228, 231, 232, 233, 236, 243, 248, 249, 250, 259, 265.
Detroit, ship of war ... 251, 293
Dewar, Lieut. ... 29, 31
Dickson, Thomas ... 55, 56, 146, 153, 184, 192, 194
Dixon, Captain M., R. E ... 155, 180
Dobbin, Lieut.-Col. Hugh ... 75, 89, 102, 139, 175
Dodge, Brig.-General ... 205, 231, 248
Dogherty, Captain ... 188, 218
Donaldson, Captain John ... 208
Dougherty, Captain Robert ... 209
Douglas's house ... 150
Dox, Captain Abraham ... 89, 104, 130, 175, 183, 207, 304
Dragoons, 6th ... 261
Draper, Luke ... 135
Duke of Gloucester, ship of war ... 201
Dundas Militia ... 113, 121
Dyson, Captain Samuel T ... 269, 271, 273, 274

E.

Earle, Captain ... 29, 37
Earl of Moira, ship of war ... 29, 35, 36, 37, 94, 179, 185
Eastman, Lieut. John ... 207
Eighteen-Mile Creek, Lake Erie ... 287
Eighteen-Mile Creek, Lake Ontario ... 253, 266
Ellice, Colonel ... 40
Ellicott, Captain ... 280, 292
Elliott, Lieut. Jesse D ... 280, 286, 287, 293, 298
Elliott, Lieut.-Colonel Matthew ... 38, 40, 179, 181, 188, 272
Ellis, Brig.-General ... 47, 49, 69
Ellis, Major ... 261
Elmira, N. Y. ... 75
Endicott, Lieut ... 240
Erie, Pa. ... 31, 126, 287, 293

E—Continued.

Erie County, Pa 269
Erie, Lake. 19, 27, 31, 37, 53, 87, 96, 115, 129, 170, 171, 174, 187, 190, 193, 236,
    247, 268, 280, 281, 301.
Essex County, N. Y 81, 83
Essex, U. S. Frigate 161, 249
Eustis, Hon. Wm 29, 54, 68, 80, 211
Everts, Major Aranthus... 75
Evans, Major Septimus.. 190
Evans, Major Thomas .61, 92, 115, 121, 124, 125, 131, 132, 159, 185, 191, 197,
    199, 201, 214, 279, 284, 285, 286, 292, 297, 300, 304.

F.

Falkland, pseudonym for Col. R. Cartwright.. 38
Fairbanks, Joshua... 55, 56
Fanning, John.. 42
Fayette, N. Y.. 280
Federal Republican newspaper.. 85
Fenwick, Lieut.-Col. John R. .198, 200, 230, 231, 233, 235, 237, 238, 239, 241,
    245, 246, 248, 251, 252, 254, 255, 264, 265, 267,
    279, 282, 288.
Field, Lieut. James.. 261
Field's Tavern... 302
Fint, John... 209
Fish, Capt... 29
FitzGibbon, Mr... 153
Five-Mile Meadows.. 175, 302
Fleming, Lieut.-Col. George 49, 69, 125, 191, 229, 242
Fleming, Mr.. 132
Fort Dearborn.. 253, 297
Fort Erie...19, 20, 23, 24, 33, 52, 61, 69, 70, 71, 78, 86, 91, 118, 123, 127, 128, 135,
    140, 150, 165, 174, 176, 185, 190, 193, 198, 204, 223, 227, 230, 231, 232,
    251, 267, 268, 270, 273, 287, 292, 298, 300, 301.
Fort George...19, 20, 22, 23, 24, 35, 57, 62, 72, 84, 91, 93, 94, 96, 98, 103, 115, 121,
    122, 124, 125, 126, 128, 129, 131, 132, 135, 138, 140, 141, 142, 143, 144,
    147, 152, 158, 166, 167, 171, 179, 183, 184, 185, 189, 190, 191, 192, 198,
    200, 236, 237, 238, 239, 241, 242, 244, 251, 253, 254, 257, 258, 259, 260,
    265, 268, 269, 270, 271, 274, 276, 278, 283, 284, 285, 286, 288, 289, 291,
    292, 297, 298, 300, 304.
Fort Schlosser... 62
Fort Wayne.. 44, 203, 220, 250, 251, 253, 272, 277, 295
Forsyth, Richardson & Co.. 73, 74
Foster, Augustus J........................... 34, 53, 59, 64, 65, 78, 84, 88, 94, 113, 160, 226
Foster, Thomas... 209
Four-Mile Creek.. 203, 235, 238, 265
Four-Mile Point.. 76, 190
Franklin County, N. Y... 81, 83, 160
Fraser, Colonel.. 40
Freer, Captain Noah... 41, 58
Fulton, Captain... 236, 243, 260
Fuller, Major.. 35, 36

G.

Gallatin, Albert.. 273
Gansevoort, General... 81
Gansevoort, Lieut... 70, 87, 104, 267
Ganson, Major... 49, 75
Garrison Battalion, 6th... 201

G—Continued.

	Page.
Gaston, John	208
Gates, Mr.	288
Gaylord, Major	280
Genesee, N. Y.	101, 280
Genesee County, N. Y.	48, 49, 70, 71, 75, 78, 101, 102, 103, 104, 114, 280
Genesee Falls	281, 282
Genesee River	79, 80, 88, 224, 252, 260, 281, 286, 287, 298
Geneseo, N. Y.	77
Genoa, N. Y.	280
Geneva, N. Y.	75, 87, 89, 90, 105, 139
Gibson, Captain	218, 298, 301, 302
Gibson, Hugh	260
Gilkinson, Captain	29, 40
Giles, Aquila	42
Gill Creek	207
Givins, Captain James	180, 251
Glasgow, Major General George, R. A.	20
Gleaner, Ketch	160
Glegg, Major J. B.	56, 85, 138, 161, 165, 167, 171, 180, 181
Glengarry Light Infantry	61, 100, 121, 258, 260
Glengarry, County of	24, 38, 39, 46, 295
Glengarry Emigrants	100, 260
Gordon, Major	131
Gore, Lieut.-Gov	21, 27, 39, 42
Grandin, Mr.	122
Grand Island	116, 140, 150, 165, 185, 261, 302
Grand River	29, 61, 74, 94, 112, 129, 145, 162
Granger, Erastus	86, 105, 109, 111, 156, 165, 262, 264
Granger, Major	280, 303
Grant, Commodore Alexander	29, 37, 162
Grant, Lieut.-Col., 41st Regt.	21
Grant, Robert	55, 56
Gravelly Point	63, 68, 90
Gray, Captain A	35, 38, 39, 40, 228
Gray, Inspector-General Nicholas	139, 173, 193, 210, 211
Greenbush, N. Y.	33, 156, 161, 160, 198, 205, 210, 215, 230, 231, 232, 243, 250, 256, 259, 276, 295, 303.
Greeley, Aaron	287
Grimoard's book on the General Staff.	32
Guerriere, frigate	233

H.

Hale, Mr.	122
Halifax, N. S.	130, 160, 161, 228
Hall, Major General Amos	17, 48, 68, 70, 78, 79, 88, 89, 90, 93, 101, 122, 141, 150, 151, 152, 169, 178, 182, 193, 242, 266, 292, 293
Hall, Capt. Elias	203
Hall, Lieut.	29, 37
Hamburg, N. Y.	63
Hamilton, N. Y.	90
Hamilton, Captain	240
Hardison, Captain Benjamin	89, 150
Harper, Michael	208
Harrisburg, Pa.	206, 210, 211, 256, 260
Harrison, Major Gen. W. H	220, 285, 296
Hart, Captain	104, 280, 303
Hart, Mr.	84

H—Continued.

	Page.
Harvey, Major John	261
Hatt, Captain	92
Heathcote, Major	98, 167, 249
Hector, N. Y.	75
Henry, John	50
Herefordshire Militia	261
Hewit, Lieut	210
Highland Settlements	60
Hill, Captain	280, 303
Hillebert, Captain Ebenezer	280
Himrod, General	75
Hobart, Lord	19
Holcroft, Captain Wm	98, 243
Holland Land Company	108
Honeoye, N. Y.	75
Home District	212
Hoops, Major Adam	127
Hopkins, Brig.-Gen	75, 87, 89, 96, 242, 266, 267
Hopkins, Colonel	186, 292, 302
Hopper, Jasper	303
Horn, Tice	207
Hornet, Sloop of War	64
Hosmer, George	76, 150
Hotham, Captain	158
Hull, Brig.-Gen. Wm	54, 132, 133, 145, 147, 155, 159, 160, 161, 164, 166, 167, 168, 169, 170, 172, 174, 175, 176, 177, 178, 181, 184, 185, 187, 189, 190, 192, 193, 194, 197, 199, 201, 203, 205, 213, 214, 215, 216, 218, 219, 220, 221, 223, 224, 225, 226, 227, 228, 229, 230, 231, 232, 238, 239, 241, 245, 246, 249, 250, 254, 267, 268, 285, 290.
Hull, Captain	87, 233, 239
Hunter, Major General Martin	19
Hunter, General, Ship of War	29, 128, 133, 135, 154, 165, 251, 301
Hurd, General	49
Huron, Michigan	122, 126
Huron, Lake	23

I.

Ireland, Captain	280, 302
Irwin, Calender	207
Irwin, Jared	208, 294
Isle Aux Noix	250

J.

Jacks, Captain	280
Jamaica Fleet	90
Jarvis, Ensign	240
Jarvis, William	101
Jennings, Captain	202, 227, 229
Johnson, Captain	86
Johnson, Mr.	227
Johnson, Lieut	280
Johnston, Lieut	153
Jones, Mr	66
Junius, N. Y.	75, 280

K.

	Page.
Keler, General	253
Keller, Jasper	209
Kellogg, Captain	267
Kempt, General Sir James	65
Kendrick, Lieut	240
Kentucky	28, 147, 197
Kerr, Lieut	153
Kerby, James	55, 56
Keyes, Brigade-Major Julius	75, 140
King, Captain, R. A.	36
King, Major General	47, 50
King, Pulaski	303
King's House	26
King's Regiment	250
Kingston	20, 24, 25, 29, 33, 35, 36, 37, 38, 39, 40, 46, 53, 54, 57, 62, 65, 94, 95, 98, 113, 114, 115, 120, 121, 129, 134, 147, 149, 153, 156, 157, 158, 159, 160, 167, 181, 200, 201, 215, 216, 234, 236, 243, 249, 250, 278, 295.
Kleckner, Joseph	209
Knapp, General	49

L.

Lachine	167
Lady Prevost, Ship of War	185
Lafferty's	143
Lamb, Anthony	48, 178
Lamont, Mr.	153
Lane, Lieut. Charles	261
Lane, Peter	209
La Picurina	65
La Prairie	99, 114
Lay, N.	151, 287, 288
Lee, David	151, 190
Lee, Major Thomas	75, 304
Leggatt, Mr.	234
Lenox Library, N. Y.	114
Leonard, Captain	80, 85, 93, 95, 97, 102, 103, 117, 139, 141, 170, 179, 189, 192, 230, 238, 239, 255, 271.
Lethbridge, Colonel	114, 120, 149, 169, 200, 202, 205
Lewis, Quartermaster-General Morgan	51, 253
Lewiston, N. Y.	55, 59, 60, 63, 73, 80, 87, 101, 113, 116, 117, 127, 128, 134, 135, 139, 150, 167, 173, 175, 177, 182, 187, 188, 189, 191, 193, 194, 195, 197, 198, 199, 200, 202, 204, 205, 213, 216, 218, 220, 222, 226, 228, 229, 231, 232, 233, 235, 236, 237, 238, 240, 241, 242, 244, 245, 246, 252, 261, 263, 264, 267, 270, 273, 275, 279, 282, 283, 286, 288, 289, 292, 293, 296, 297, 301, 304.
Lewiston Meadows	289
Lichfield, N. Y.	255
Limerick County Militia	261
Lincoln Artillery	138
Lincoln Militia	138
Lincoln Militia, 1st	76, 77, 85, 92, 212, 285
Lincoln Militia, 2d	91, 92, 95, 212, 285
Lincoln Militia, 3d	91, 92, 142, 212, 285
Lincoln Militia, 4th	92, 212, 285
Lincoln Militia, 5th	92, 212, 285
Lincoln Militia, 6th	92, 285
Lithgow, Walter	209

L—Continued.

	Page.
Little York	126, 128
Liverpool, Lord	50, 52, 53, 58, 62, 66, 67, 68, 73, 100, 128, 153, 257
Livingston, Mr.	54
Livonia, N. Y	75
Lochry, John	209
London District	212
Long Point	29, 123, 127, 135, 144, 148, 152, 163, 165, 185
Lord Nelson, merchant ship	67, 68
Louis, Colonel, Indian Chief	166
Lovejoy, Mr.	287
Lovett, John	178, 182, 213, 220, 241, 244, 288
Lovett, Mrs	289
Lundy's Lane	143
Lyon, Sergt	286

M.

Mack, Captain	229
Mackinac, see Michilimackinac	
Mackina Indians	251
Mackinac, Straits of	128
Madison County, N. Y	47, 69
Madison, James	21, 26, 54, 254
Magher, Captain Peter	255, 256
Maguire Richard	208
Mahar, Captain	202, 203
Malden	33, 34, 155, 160, 161, 164, 165, 166, 167, 170, 174, 175, 178, 187, 190, 194, 198, 253, 270, 287.
Manchester, N. Y	90, 173, 174, 219
Mann, Lieut.-General	19
Marlow, Captain	39
Mary, merchant ship	128
Maryland	147
Massena, N. Y	69
Matteson, Captain	203
Meade, Lt.-Col. Thompson	217, 302
Meadville, Pa	206, 207, 208, 210, 211, 256, 267, 269, 294, 302
Melvin, Mr.	53
Mennonists	13, 14, 212
Mercantile Library, Phila	89, 104
Mercer County, Pa	269
Merritt, Major Thomas	85, 292
Miami	122, 126, 133, 157, 197, 253, 299
Michigan, Lake	54, 128
Michigan Territory	186, 260, 287
Michilimackinac	22, 29, 40, 41, 151, 152, 153, 163, 168, 175, 223, 251, 260, 277
Middleswarth, Ne	208
Militia, Essex	180
Militia, Kent	180
Militia, Lincoln	76, 77, 85, 91, 92, 95, 142, 180, 212, 285
Militia, Norfolk	51, 180
Militia, Oxford	180
Militia, York	See York Militia
Miller, Brig.-Gen. Daniel	217, 246
Miller, Major Frederick	86, 140, 151, 203
Miller, Thomas	209
Miller's House	304
Mills, Captain	29

M—Continued.

	Page.
Milton, Colonel	302
Mockler, Captain	180
Mohawk Indians	72, 105, 106, 108, 109
Moira, ship of war	29, 35, 36, 37, 94, 179, 185
Monroe, James	100
Montreal	33, 35, 37, 41, 50, 64, 73, 113, 114, 120, 121, 131, 141, 155, 158, 160, 167, 169, 172, 194, 205, 215, 216, 219, 225, 227, 228, 231, 232, 237, 244, 249, 257, 260, 261, 289, 295, 299.
Montreal Courier	63, 99
Moore, Judge	269
Moore, Major	275
Moore Thomas	275
Moravian Town	139, 145, 251
Morrison, Major John	75
Morse, Asa H	151
Moseley, Major Charles	69, 191, 242, 246, 304
Muir, Captain	180, 277
Muirhead, James	85, 92, 132
Mulholland, Captain	69
Mullany, Major	79, 80, 87, 89, 162, 141, 231, 215
Murray, Colonel John	250
Myers, Lieut.-Col. Christopher	143, 145, 166, 183, 184, 185, 189, 190, 191, 192, 200, 201, 202, 204, 273, 283.

Mc.

McArthur, Ensign	240
McCall, Dan	131
McClure, Brig.-Gen. George	75, 76, 80
McDonald, Colonel	214
Macdonnell, Lieut.-Colonel George	39, 40, 43, 51, 56
Macdonnell, Lieut.-Col. John	85, 86, 120, 138, 139, 142, 171, 180, 213, 228, 249, 250, 274, 285.
McDonnell, Lieut. Roland	60
McDowel, James	208
McGarry, John	209
McGee's Point	180
McGill, John	59, 162
McGinigan, Captain Robert	210
McKee, Captain Thomas	175, 179, 272
McKeon, Captain	90, 255
McKinstry, Captain	280
McMahon, Lieut.-Col.	186, 187, 229
McNair, Captain	203
Macomb, Lieut.-Col. Robert	217
McPherson, Major	62, 94, 98, 129
McTavish, Mr	84
McTavish, McGillivray & Co	73

N.

Nairn, Captain	261
Nancy, schooner	165
National Intelligencer	88, 112, 213
Navy Island	283
Nelson, Lord, merchant ship	67, 68
Newark	88, 108, 118, 126, 131, 135, 139, 151, 164, 179
New Brunswick	60
New Orleans	31

N—Continued.

Newport, R. I. 31
Newport, Ky 181
New York, City of 31, 34, 54, 60, 67, 73, 74, 84, 90, 160, 246, 247, 254
New York Evening Post 86, 87, 104, 166, 176, 291
New York Gazette 126, 132
New York Society Library 85, 87, 88, 104, 117, 166, 176, 177, 187, 291
New York State 54, 59, 108, 130, 206, 210, 225
New York State Library 187, 213, 241, 268, 275, 280, 282, 287
New York Statesman 187, 293
Niagara County, N. Y 48, 70, 71, 75, 78, 102, 103, 104, 114, 163, 194
Niagara District 212, 236
Niagara Falls 178, 182, 191, 245, 254, 261
Niagara, Fort .. 46, 47, 48, 49, 54, 61, 62, 72, 76, 78, 79, 80, 82, 87, 89, 90, 91, 92, 93, 94, 95, 97, 99, 101, 104, 114, 117, 119, 122, 125, 126, 128, 129, 130, 138, 145, 156, 159, 161, 171, 172, 175, 177, 178, 181, 182, 184, 189, 192, 197, 198, 205, 206, 210, 214, 215, 216, 224, 227, 229, 230, 231, 232, 236, 237, 238, 239, 241, 243, 244, 252, 253, 254, 259, 265, 267, 269, 270, 271, 273, 274, 275, 278, 279, 288, 289, 292, 301.
Niagara Frontier ... 29, 40, 59, 70, 75, 79, 89, 93, 96, 104, 115, 124, 128, 170, 173, 175, 176, 191, 230, 234, 248, 250, 257, 266, 276, 293, 298, 299, 302, 303.
Niagara Town 24, 67, 76
Niagara River . 19, 22, 33, 56, 68, 79, 89, 112, 116, 125, 129, 135, 150, 164, 165, 186, 187, 193, 232, 281, 286, 288, 299, 302.
Nichol, Lieut.-Col. Robert 44, 51, 57, 76, 77, 251, 278
Noble, Captain 280
Noon, Major Darby 68, 99, 247
Norfolk, Va 31
Norfolk Militia 138, 139, 180
North, William 42
North Carolina 108
North-West Company 41, 74
Nova Scotia 60, 160
Nyles, Lewis 302

O.

Oaks, Andrew 208
O'Connor, John M 89
Ogdensburg, N. Y 63, 99, 142, 166, 198, 199, 215, 224
Ohio, State of 22, 142, 181, 184, 197, 215, 225, 253
Ohio Militia 61, 147
Ohio River 221
Olmstead, Major 75
Oneida County, N. Y 42
Oneida Indians 105, 108, 109, 111, 262, 303
Oneida, ship of war 63, 67, 95, 128, 205
Onondaga Arsenal 50
Onondaga County, N. Y 47, 69
Onondaga Hollow 49
Onondaga Indians 105, 108, 262, 303
Onondaga Valley 114, 303
Ontario Arsenal 71, 101, 183
Ontario County, N. Y 63, 70, 71, 75, 78, 88, 102, 121, 266, 280
Ontario, Lake ... 19, 24, 29, 53, 59, 63, 103, 116, 118, 119, 129, 164, 179, 187, 232, 233, 236, 237, 247, 270, 281, 286, 288, 296, 301.
Ontario Repository 76, 87, 262, 263, 302
Ontario, merchant ship 68

xiii.

O - Continued.

	Page.
Ormsby, Major	166, 167
Oswagatchie	25, 39
Oswego, N. Y	17, 19, 64, 69, 90, 183, 191, 199, 224, 230, 238, 242, 252, 266, 267, 281, 287, 298
Ostrom, Judge	12
Ottawa River	33, 41, 71
Otsego, N. Y	280
Ovid, N. Y	280
Oxford	141
Oxford Militia	180

P.

Packard, Brig.-Qr.-Master	256
Palmyra, N. Y	280
Parrish, Jasper	66, 105, 111, 113, 143, 262
Patchin, Thaddeus	303
Paulding, William, Jr	69, 70, 71, 93, 126
Pelham	113, 213
Penfield, N. Y	280
Pennsylvania	125, 130, 147, 205, 206, 207, 210, 211, 212, 225, 230, 267
Pennsylvania Militia	269, 285
Perrin, James	261
Peterson, William	209
Phelps, Mr.	77
Philadelphia	31, 212, 232
Philadelphia Library	232, 262
Phillips, Joel	303
Phillips, W.	135
Pickering, Timothy	109, 110
Pictou Settlements	60
Pierce, Captain	280
Pierson, Captain	80, 88
Pinckney, Thomas	53
Pinkney, Captain	216
Piper, Wm.	200, 204
Pittsburg	122, 256, 269
Plattsburg	81, 83, 156, 198, 205, 231
Playter, Lieut.	210
Plenderleath, Major	231, 283
Point Abino	287, 301
Point Aux Pins	171, 186
Point Levi	158
Port Talbot	144, 170
Porter, Judge Augustus	68, 90, 92, 121, 126, 157, 166, 175
Porter, Hon. Peter A., MSS. of	42, 64, 68, 88, 90, 91, 95, 97, 99, 122, 126, 157
Porter, Peter B	42, 51, 63, 71, 78, 79, 87, 88, 89, 90, 95, 97, 102, 117, 121, 126, 127, 140, 184, 189, 194, 199, 203, 219, 222, 238, 254, 261, 262, 267, 281, 287
Portsmouth, N. H	31
Pothier, Toussaint	153
Prescott	29, 67, 68, 142, 228, 295
Powell Grant	153
Powell, Captain John, 1st Lincoln Artillery	138, 259
Powell, Justice William Dummer	162
Presqu' Isle	253

xiv.

P—Continued. *Page.*

Prevost, Sir George. 20, 21, 25, 26, 34, 35, 39, 43, 44, 45, 46, 50, 51, 52, 53, 56, 59, 60, 61, 62, 64, 65, 66, 67, 68, 73, 74, 93, 100, 113, 114, 115, 120, 122, 127, 128, 132, 144, 148, 149, 151, 153, 154, 157, 160, 164, 167, 169, 172, 185, 201, 203, 204, 215, 225, 227, 234, 236, 242, 249, 250, 257, 258, 260, 276, 280, 295, 299.
Prince Regent 45, 152, 257, 261, 290
Prince Regent, ship of war. 95, 179, 185
Procter, Colonel Henry. 23, 56, 62, 91, 92, 98, 115, 133, 146, 149, 154, 161, 167, 171, 179, 180, 182, 185, 203, 225, 233, 236, 242, 250, 271, 277, 295.
Prophet, The Indian. 38, 220
Providence, R. I 232
Provincial Cavalry 76
Pultneyville, N. Y 80
Purviance, Samuel. 204

Q.

Quakers 13, 14, 212
Quebec. ..4, 19, 20, 26, 29, 33, 34, 35, 39, 44, 45, 50, 51, 52, 53, 59, 60, 62, 64, 65, 66, 67, 73, 74, 95, 99, 121, 126, 128, 129, 130, 149, 154, 157, 159, 160, 168, 169, 200, 214, 221, 228, 249, 271, 290.
Queen Charlotte, ship of war 128, 213, 251, 259, 267, 301
Queenston ....55, 56, 65, 67, 68, 72, 76, 77, 84, 91, 97, 103, 126, 127, 132, 135, 139, 140, 173, 184, 193, 196, 201, 214, 219, 227, 230, 239, 244, 270, 283.
Quinte, Bay of 21

R.

Raisin, River 157, 272
Reddington, Major 49
Red Hook 29
Red Jacket 105, 109, 165, 167
Reed, General Wm 207, 210, 256, 269
Reece, Captain Daniel 157
Regiment, 8th, or Kings 99, 250
Regiment, 41st ..21, 38, 40, 46, 62, 65, 76, 91, 98, 99, 115, 127, 145, 150, 162, 163, 180, 185, 186, 234, 251, 261, 273, 278, 283, 284, 286, 301.
Regiment, 49th...38, 40, 41, 65, 74, 99, 157, 159, 160, 167, 168, 180, 201, 234, 258, 278, 283.
Regiment, 95th 46
Regiment, 98th 160
Regiment, 100th 99, 114
Regiment, 103d 99, 114
Regiment, Canadian Fencible 68, 99
Regiment, Canadian Voltigeur 99
Regiment, Glengarry Light Infantry 43, 60, 63, 99, 153
Regiment, 18th New York 75, 89, 222
Regiment, 19th New York 75, 76, 174
Regiment, 20th New York 75, 89, 222
Regiment, Royal Newfoundland 29, 46, 52, 63, 98, 157, 159, 160, 162, 167, 180, 201, 261, 277, 286.
Regiment, 1st United States Infantry 147
Regiment, 4th United States Infantry 147
Regiment, 5th United States Infantry 147, 302
Regiment, 6th United States Infantry 258
Regiment, 13th United States Infantry 302

R—Continued.

Regiment, 14th United States Infantry	301
Rhea, General	75, 89, 96
Rhode Island	232
Richardson, Captain John	280
Richardson, Mr	74
Ridge Road	214, 215, 268
Ridout, Captain	240
River Rouge	180
Roads, Jonathan	209
Roberts, Captain Charles	146, 151, 153, 168, 249
Robertson, Captain Wm	55, 85
Robinson, Commissary General W. H	154
Rodgers, Commodore	90, 158
Rolette, Lieut. Frederick	29
Rolph, Mr	242
Rome, N. Y	81, 83
Ross, Daniel	131
Rous, Mr	31
Rowley, Captain	203
Royal Artillery	98, 99, 167
Royal Artillery Drivers	99
Royal Engineers	99, 155, 180
Royal George, ship of war	29, 35, 123, 135, 201, 252, 270
Royal Veteran Battalion, 10th	62, 98, 99, 120, 159
Ryerson, Lieut.-Col	85, 86
Ryland, H. W	73, 74

S.

Sackett's Harbor	24, 29, 33, 63, 64, 67, 80, 82, 90, 112, 170, 183, 198, 205, 206, 224, 231, 248, 281, 290, 298.
Salina, merchant schooner	128
Salisbury, S. H. and H. A	55, 105
Salmon, Major	85, 86, 139
Sample, Wm	209
Sandusky	31, 68, 122, 126, 194, 272
Sandwich	44, 124, 132, 133, 144, 146, 157, 160, 164, 175, 185, 194
Saunders, Captain	283
Saunderson, Lieut	261
Saterley, Captain	280
Savannah, Ga	31
Schenectady, N. Y	198, 266
Schlosser, N. Y	97, 127, 150, 175, 289
Schuyler, Col	141, 302
Schuyler, Reuben	275
Scott, Chief Justice Thomas	57
Scott, James	209
Scotch Settlements	60
Secord, Laura	186
Secord, Lieut	85
Selby, Captain	281
Selby, Prideaux, Receiver-General	35, 59, 162
Selin's Grove, Pa	210, 211, 256
Sempronius, N. Y	280
Seneca County, N. Y	75, 175, 280, 302
Seneca Indians	105, 108, 165, 262, 302, 303
Shaw, Captain	46
Shaw, Major General Æneas	97, 124, 149, 161, 186, 212, 304

S—Continued.

Shawanese Indians 22, 23
Sheaffe, Major General Roger H..... 155, 159, 181, 185, 191, 196, 197, 198, 199, 200, 201, 204, 212, 215, 216, 226, 234, 236, 237, 239, 240, 242, 271.
Sheaffe, Nancy 184
Shekelton, Brigade-Major 167
Sherbrooke, Sir John C. 50, 130, 161
Simcoe, Lieut.-Gen. John G. 25
Simonds, Col. 81, 164
Six Nations ... 61, 66, 105, 106, 108, 109, 110, 111, 132, 145, 156, 262, 291, 293, 303
Sizer, Captain Asa B 218
Skeensborough 250
Smith, Major George 75
Smith, John 55
Smyth, Brig.-Gen. Alexander 259, 276, 300, 301
Snyder, Colonel Jeremiah 208, 294
Snyder, Governor Simon 207, 208, 210, 211, 269
Sodus, N. Y 80, 224
Solomons, Mr. 81
Somerset Militia 261
Sorel River 33
Southwest Fur Company 251
Spafford, Amos 157
Spalding, Rufus 55, 56
Spencer, John C 254
Spencer, Major W. H 127, 134
Spring Wells, Mich 180
Stanley, Captain 91
Stanley, Col. 49
Stanton, Wm 165
Stanwix, Fort 105
Steele, Commodore 29, 36, 37
Steuben County, N. Y 114, 280
Stewart, John 209
Sto, Robert 209
Stoo, J 121
Stockbridge Indians 262, 303
Stormont Militia 113, 121
Stoughton, John W 127
Stranahan, Lieut.-Col. Farrand 217, 255, 302
Sturgeon Point 86, 287
Sugar Loaf Point 161
Sutherland, Major 49
Sutton, Captain 280
Swan, Mr. 237
Swayze, Isaac 72
Swift, Lieut.-Col. Philetus. 48, 63, 68, 71, 77, 86, 90, 97, 101, 102, 117, 125, 149, 150, 151, 170, 175, 182, 188, 189, 193, 202, 214, 215, 218, 227, 229, 230, 242, 251, 292.
Symington, John 124
St. Clair River 41
St. Davids 135
St. George, Lieut.-Col. T. B. ... 23, 27, 40, 124, 132, 133, 146, 149, 154, 155, 167, 180, 181, 225, 233.
St. Johns, P. Q 26, 99, 114, 225, 250
St. Joseph's Island 20, 23, 37, 41, 71, 93, 128, 146, 163
St. Lawrence River 31, 53, 62, 63, 81, 118, 266, 270

S—Continued.

St. Mary's Falls.	37
St. Regis	125, 166
St. Regis Indians.	81

T.

Table Rock.	113
Talbot, Lieut.-Col. Thomas.	131, 138, 144, 212
Tallon, Captain	180
Tannehill, Brig.-Gen. Adamson.	201
Tawaway Indians.	157
Taylor, Mr.	90
Tecumseh.	215, 220
Ten Eyck, Jacob.	109
Terry, Captain.	280
Thames River.	139, 144
Thomas, Edward.	209
Thomas, Sergeant	286
Thompson, James.	209
Thompson, Mr.	126
Three Rivers.	61
Three River Point	252, 266
Tillotson, Brig.-Gen. John	75, 177
Tioga County, N. Y.	75, 302
Tippecanoe.	223
Todd, Isaac.	234, 249
Tompkins, Governor Daniel D.	12, 18, 19, 50, 71, 77, 78, 79, 80, 83, 84, 88, 96, 116, 117, 139, 142, 156, 166, 173, 186, 191, 193, 202, 218, 222, 225, 226, 228, 240, 241, 243, 246, 247, 255, 264, 266, 269, 275, 279, 282, 286, 298, 303.
Tompkins' Papers.	48, 49, 50, 60, 70, 71, 73, 77, 78, 79, 80, 83, 84, 85, 86, 93, 97, 101, 104, 117, 119, 126, 147, 167, 175, 178, 187, 192, 194, 203, 225, 227, 229, 240, 241, 218, 256, 275, 280, 287.
Tonewanto Creek	185, 261, 292, 303
Toronto, ship of war	36
Totten, Lieut.	286
Townsend, Mr.	93
Tracy, Mr.	218
Trenton, N. J.	117
Troughton, Lieut	201
Trout, Henry	69
Troy, N. Y.	33
Tunkers.	13, 14, 212
Tupper, John	234
Tupper's Life of Brock	26, 27, 42, 45, 46, 52, 58, 59, 60, 61, 65, 66, 74, 100, 114, 115, 121, 124, 152, 154, 161, 164, 169, 173, 204, 226, 228, 234, 236, 250, 251, 260, 273, 274, 279, 295.
Turbit, James.	209
Turkey Point	134
Tuscarora Indians.	97, 105, 108, 215, 303
Two-Mile Point.	76

U.

Ulysses, N. Y.	280
United States Gazette	262
Utica, N. Y.	42

V.

Vance, Henry 209
Vanderfelt, Jacob 209
VanRensselaer, Colonel Solomon 42, 112, 166, 177, 182, 183, 188, 189, 192,
196, 198, 199, 200, 213, 218, 219, 222, 231,
233, 235, 241, 242, 244, 246, 247, 253, 261,
262, 264, 267, 271, 273, 274, 276, 282, 286,
288, 292, 296, 297, 300, 304.
VanRensselaer's (Solomon) Narrative 143, 156, 161, 169, 171, 182, 190, 191,
196, 197, 198, 199, 204, 205, 206, 216,
219, 227, 230, 231, 233, 235, 236, 237,
239, 244, 245, 246, 249, 252, 253, 264,
283, 291, 296, 298, 300.
VanRensselaer, Major General Stephen ... 82, 125, 142, 143, 156, 161, 166, 176,
177, 178, 179, 182, 188, 189, 190, 191, 193, 201, 204, 205, 214,
215, 216, 218, 219, 221, 222, 225, 226, 228, 229, 230, 232, 233,
235, 236, 237, 238, 240, 242, 244, 245, 246, 247, 248, 251, 252,
253, 254, 255, 256, 259, 262, 264, 267, 268, 270, 273, 274, 275,
276, 279, 280, 281, 282, 283, 286, 291, 292, 293, 295, 296, 297,
300, 304.
VanVechten, Abraham 178, 213, 214, 220, 237, 244
Venango County, Pa. 269
Vermont 33, 231
Vincennes, Ind. 44, 253
Vincent, Colonel John 234, 242, 260, 288, 299
Vosburgh, Mr. 84, 88
Vosburgh, Lieut.-Col. Peter J 217

W.

Wabash River 22, 23
Wadsworth, Brig.-Gen. Wm ..70, 71, 75, 77, 88, 89, 90, 97, 101, 116, 117, 119,
127, 134, 139, 140, 141, 177, 178, 182, 183, 193,
196, 202, 203, 241, 244, 253.
Walker, Benjamin 42
Walton, Peter & Co. 67
Warren, Ohio 157
Warren County, Pa. 269
Warren, Colonel 138
Warren, Henry 112
Warren, James 209
Warren, John, Jr 69, 127
Warren, John, Sr. 69
Warsaw, N. Y 280
Washington, D. C. 30, 45, 51, 53, 59, 67, 84, 155, 160, 211, 215, 225, 226, 249
Washington County, N. Y. 81, 83
Washington, General 110, 111
Waterford, Pa. 122
Waterman, Captain 217
Watson, (a surveyor) 146
Webster, Ephraim 303
Wells, Henry, Brigade-Quartermaster 75
Wells, Captain Joseph 87, 134, 151, 202, 203
Wellington, Lord 279
Westerlo, Colonel 213
West Indies 157, 160
Westminster 146
Whaley, Major 63
Whistler, Captain J 253

W—Continued.

Whitehall, N. Y	33
Wickham, Lieut.-Col. George	191
Widrig, Major General	47, 50
William Henry, Fort	249
Wilmot, Mr	187
Willcocks, Joseph	44, 131
Wilson, Dr. Nathaniel	77
Wilson's Tavern	143
Winchester, Brig.-Gen. John	147
Winder, Colonel W. H	298, 301
Withrow, Samuel	269
Wolsy, Captain	63, 99, 247
Woodhouse	131
Wood Library, Canandaigua, N. Y	87, 263
Woodworth, Captain Solomon	280
Woolverton, Mr	121

Y.

Yates, Recorder	88
Young, Colonel	99
Youngstown, N. Y	127, 128, 175
York	20, 21, 23, 25, 29, 33, 35, 36, 37, 38, 41, 42, 43, 44, 46, 51, 53, 56, 57, 58, 60, 72, 101, 121, 145, 148, 151, 158, 161, 162, 164, 165, 182, 221, 228, 240, 244, 299, 301.
York Gazette	38
York Militia	180, 240, 285

www.ingramcontent.com/pod-product-compliance
Lightning Source LLC
Chambersburg PA
CBHW030729230426
43667CB00007B/640